GLOBAL CORRUPTION AND ETHICS MANAGEMENT

Translating Theory into Action

Edited by

CAROLE L. JURKIEWICZ

PURDUE UNIVERSITY
UNIVERSITY OF COLORADO COLORADO SPRINGS

FOREWORD BY STUART C. GILMAN AND CAROL W. LEWIS

ROWMAN & LITTLEFIELD
Lanham • Boulder • New York • London

Executive Editor: Traci Crowell
Assistant Editor: Deni Remsberg
Executive Marketing Manager: Amy Whitaker
Interior Designer: Ilze Lemesis

Credits and acknowledgments for material borrowed from other sources, and reproduced with permission, appear on the appropriate page within the text.

Published by Rowman & Littlefield
An imprint of The Rowman & Littlefield Publishing Group, Inc.
4501 Forbes Boulevard, Suite 200, Lanham, Maryland 20706
www.rowman.com

6 Tinworth Street, London SE11 5AL, United Kingdom

British Library Cataloguing in Publication Information Available

Library of Congress Cataloging-in-Publication Data Available

ISBN 978-1-5381-1739-2 (cloth : alk. paper)
ISBN 978-1-5381-1740-8 (pbk. : alk. paper)
ISBN 978-1-5381-1741-5 (electronic)

♾™ The paper used in this publication meets the minimum requirements of American National Standard for Information Sciences—Permanence of Paper for Printed Library Materials, ANSI/NISO Z39.48–1992.

For Spencer and Crosby

Contents

PART III: Best Practices in Corruption Prevention and Ethics Management

E veryone, everywhere contends with the effects of corruption on a daily basis, whether, for example, it's an individual act of duplicity or the trickle-down effect of government maladministration. The types of corruption and their impacts vary greatly across countries and regions, ranging from minor economic impacts and ideological violations to a lifetime of privation and oppression. Adopting the normative definition of corruption as the abuse of entrusted power for private gain, corruptive behaviors, even at abstracted levels, affect us personally, and the more deeply we are impacted by corruption the greater our individual experience of deceit, degradation, ignominy, and moral assault.

On a collective level, the economic, cultural, and health consequences of corruption have negative impacts across generations. To wit:

Economic Impacts:

- deteriorating infrastructures
- escalating unemployment
- rising inflation
- reduced private investment
- decreased competitiveness
- diminishing public services
- declining incomes
- lowered GDP

Cultural Impacts:

- reduced access to education
- environmental decay
- elevated ethic of distrust
- suppressed innovation
- expanding criminality
- heightened class disparities
- increased poverty
- atrophied national loyalty

Health Impacts:

- declining water and air quality
- elevated rates of infectious and stress-related diseases
- lower life expectancy
- higher infant mortality
- growing malnutrition
- rise in domestic and child abuse
- proliferation of drug abuse
- escalating incidence of mental illness

The means by which corruption is evidenced, measured, and reported has significantly altered over the past decade, along with attempts to prevent and alleviate it. A flattening of the middle class; generational demographics; urbanization; inter-sector fluidity; technology; crime; currency valuation; educational standards; laws; spiritual beliefs; and a global economy increasingly driven by capital markets rather than trade are just some of the factors catalyzing this change. In the past ten years the field has gone well beyond facilitating awareness of the problem and seeking redress through moral exhortation. We have now mapped the structural systems that fuel the intractability of corruption, identified culturally rooted best practices for its prevention and enforcement, and calculated the scale of its fiscal and societal impacts. Admonitions to reform, institute economic liberalization, and enhance accountability, while well meaning, have been found in a number of instances not only to fall short of their intended ameliorative effects but to have achieved the opposite. Such approaches have, in many cases, exacerbated the magnitude of the problem and more deeply entrenched its causes. Corruption is a dynamic, global, and elusive target that now requires an integrative perspective to effectively prevent and address it.

This book represents a new conceptualization of corruption, one that incorporates recent global research and best practices and, while honoring its historical foundations, extends beyond them to create a basis for study, action, and analysis. Scholars, students, and professionals will each find applicable and rich content, and the intersection of study and application creates a direct connection between thought and action. *Global Corruption and Ethics Management* presents a global strategy for outlining the nature of corruption, its causes, the systems and practices that facilitate it; its short- and long-term consequences, new measures for assessing and diagnosing remedies; and steps that can be taken to prevent it. Written by top experts from around the globe, each chapter is designed for utility and accessibility, with clearly articulated approaches for professional and practical application, critical knowledge indicators for student review and assessment, and a broad review of the latest cross-sector research on corruption and ethics management that provides an enduring foundation for future scholarship. The objectives are fourfold:

1. To provide professionals, scholars, and students at all levels with a broad understanding of the individual, organizational, and environmental factors causing corruption.
2. To extend the paradigm for interdisciplinary research and theory regarding corruption and ethics management.
3. To serve as an amalgam of divergent, interdisciplinary perspectives on corruption and ethics management into a cohesive whole and, in so doing, creating the seminal source for this field of inquiry.
4. To better understand the global and inter-sector nature of organizations, the mutual dependence of all populations, and how this new world order can be harnessed for instituting ethical management systems that recognize, reduce, and prevent the spread of corruption.

I wish to thank first and foremost the contributors for their breakthrough advancements in understanding corruption, and how to prevent and ameliorate its effects. Further, I'd like to recognize our editor at Rowman & Littlefield, Traci Crowell, for her vision and aplomb, and above all her integrity. I also want to thank those who provided reviews: David Schultz (Hamline University), Tony Manzanetti (University of San Francisco), Agustí Cerrillo-i-Martínez (Universitat Oberta de Catalunya), George R. Franks (Stephen F. Austin State University), and Stephen Kleinschmit (University of Illinois at Chicago). Lastly and most importantly, I want to express my appreciation for my children, who inspire me and accentuate the meaningfulness of working toward making the world a better place for all.

Carole L. Jurkiewicz
Editor

Foreword

This collection of essays is both important and timely for public administrators. The approaches are important because their breadth provides a view of the major ethics issues bureaucrats and political appointees confront daily. They are timely because of the recent confrontations between integrity laws and regulations and political interests at the executive, legislative, and even judicial branches of government. These confrontations arise at the national, state, and local levels in the United States. However, the undermining of integrity systems also threatens many other Western democracies. It is the result of what David Miliband, a former member of the British Parliament, calls a general global "recession of democracy." Grave hazards also menace ethical behavior and ethics management in authoritarian and repressive contexts and in nongovernmental agencies, as several essays in this volume make plain.

Therefore, understanding these issues is important to government senior executives as well as supervisors in carrying out their management responsibilities. Balancing carrying out the policy wishes of current political superiors with maintaining the integrity of the organization has become far more difficult. The pressures to support political agendas by distorting data, presenting selective facts, hiding issues, or lying have become far too common. Seeing the administrative universe solely through an ideological prism distorts reality and drains the "public" from public interest. Perhaps worse, it appears that many citizens do not care. Conversely, an ethics pandemic has convulsed regimes from Europe to the Middle East and North Africa, from South America to Hong Kong. Popular resistance to conspicuous corruption and demands for governmental transparency, accountability, honesty, and integrity are too often suppressed, sometimes violently.

Critics often see ethics and integrity systems as new and unnecessary add-ons to the difficult issues of governing. However, George Washington dealt with integrity issues that led to the forced resignation of the secretary of war for self-dealing. Ethics laws and regulations have become more complex because government has become more complex. Statutes on conflict of interest, misuse of public office, misuse of time and government resources as well as post-employment restrictions are common. In addition, governments create systems such as codes of conduct, financial disclosures, and ethics training to help prevent violations, and thereby guide public officials.

These laws and the tools to enforce them rest on a widely accepted foundation. More than a decade ago, the United States and more than 140 other countries ratified the UN Convention against Corruption. It obligates signatories to create ethics systems, including bodies to oversee ethics and prosecute corruption, codes of conduct, financial disclosure, post-employment restrictions, protection of whistleblowers, and the public's right to access government information. International panels supported by the UN Office on Drugs and Crime review a country's compliance with the treaty (https://www.unodc.org/unodc/en/corruption/).

In our book *The Ethics Challenge in Public Service* (Jossey-Bass, 2012, 3rd ed.), three broad principles capture the essence of governmental ethics: show impartiality in carrying out your public duties; comply with and implement the laws, such as conflict of interest; and take personal responsibility for your actions. Today a number of policy issues—including health care, the environment, immigration, and treatment of underrepresented or marginalized groups—spill over into administrative ethics and show how these straightforward principles beg for guidance, clarity, compliance, and enforcement. The conundrum faced by local police in sanctuary cities—where local elected officials have ordered the police not to cooperate with the federal government because municipal policy makers oppose

US national policy on immigrant detention—illustrates the point. Administrators' bias and harassment in response to race, ethnicity, gender, and sexual orientation expose political faults in governance systems, cause individual tragedies, and contravene principle 4 of the Code of Ethics of the American Society for Public Administration, which affirms the obligation to "treat all persons with fairness, justice, and equality and respect individual differences, rights, and freedoms." Numerous scientists, field investigators, finance officers, and policy makers in US federal, state, and local offices initially denied the toxic lead contamination in the drinking water of Flint, Michigan; others reported the catastrophe at their professional peril. This experience trumpets the salient point that professional expertise is no guarantee that administrators take their ethical responsibility seriously or know what it is.

In addition, social media; decision making using algorithms; artificial intelligence; and privacy and surveillance pose new problems in administrative ethics. These all present the challenge of separating administrative from policy issues. If administrators drift too far into the policy realm, they justifiably can be accused of taking on the role of elected officials. Ignoring administrative questions arising from these problems, administrators potentially abrogate their professional ethical responsibilities.

The chapters in this book sort these issues and present contrasting views. The concepts of ethics and corruption are explored and expanded. Ethics management grounds and shapes what ethics means in public administration. A global perspective is offered on best practices in ethics and corruption prevention. These are important contributions to the study and practice of administrative ethics.

As a whole, this selection of essays provides the reader with the essential issues of ethics and integrity in public service. Admittedly, academic interests drive the scope of topics, but practitioners ignore the questions raised at their peril. Practitioners will no doubt have to wrestle with most of the matters raised at some point in their professional lives.

For these reasons, students of public administration must take seriously the issues in this volume. Understanding the more normative, philosophical perspectives underpins effective decision making and creates the foundation for integrity in government. These same concerns also inform the rationale for ethics laws and regulations. Both theory and practice generate trust in government, which should be an essential element for every public administrator's job.

Stuart C. Gilman and Carol W. Lewis
July 2019

Contributors

Haris Alibašić is an assistant professor and the Whitman Faculty Fellow in the Public Administration program at the University of West Florida. He has written and published extensively on the topics of administrative evil, sustainability, climate resilience, economic development, climate change, and sustainable energy. He is the author of the book *Sustainability and Resilience Planning for Local Governments: The Quadruple Bottom Line Strategy* published in 2018. He brings twenty-two years of expertise and experience in the public sector, including working for the United Nations Mission and the Office of High Representative in Bosnia and Herzegovina and directing energy, sustainability, and legislative affairs policies and programs for Grand Rapids, the second-largest city in Michigan. In Grand Rapids, he promoted sustainable policies resulting in significantly reduced energy usage and cost and spurring significant renewable energy investments. In 2013, he advised the Resilient Communities of America on climate resilience and in 2014 went on to serve as cochair for the energy sector of the White House Climate Preparedness and Resilience Task Force.

Dr. Alibašić has over fourteen years of experience teaching graduate and undergraduate courses in public policy, public administration, economic development, and sustainability at Grand Valley State University, Central Michigan University, and Davenport University. As an assistant professor at UWF, he teaches doctoral and graduate level courses in public service ethics, the political economy of public administration, strategic management in administration, public budgeting and finance, and public administration. He is a partner in the Florida League of Cities Municipal Research Program. Through the Partners in Municipal Research program, the Center for Municipal Research & Innovation serves as a link between Florida's public policy researchers and municipal governments, bridging the gap between academics and public policy makers and administrators. He was a recipient of the 2012 West Michigan Environmental Action Council (WMEAC)—the C.R. Evenson Award and the 2011 Grand Valley State University's Sustainability Champion Award. In November 2016, he was awarded the Sustainable Hall of Fame Merit award from West Michigan Sustainable Business Forum. In January 2017, he received an Emerging Scholar Award at Thirteenth International Conference on Environmental, Cultural, Economic, and Social Sustainability and the On Sustainability Research Network, held in Rio, Brazil. He also received a 2017 Great Lakes-Saint Lawrence Cities Initiative (GLSLCI) Certificate of Appreciation and in 2016 a State of Michigan Special Tribute.

David Arellano-Gault is a professor at the Public Administration Department, Center for Research and Teaching in Economics, CIDE, Mexico City, since 1987. David earned his PhD in Public Administration at the University of Colorado (1998). At CIDE he has served as provost (2007–2013) and also as chair of the Public Administration Department (1998–2002 and 2013–2017). A member of the Mexican Academy of Science, he has served as co editor in the journal *Organization Studies* (2008–2013) and as editor of *Gestión y Política Pública* (1997–2010). He is also member of editorial committees in journals like *American Review of Public Administration*(ARPA), *Governance, Journal of Public Administration Research and Theory* (JPART), and *Public Integrity*, among others. His research interests are diverse, touching topics like performance evaluation, budgeting by results, transparency, and anti-corruption strategies, in general looking to emphasize the study and understanding of organizational challenges for implementing administrative reforms in the public sector.

Maria Aristigueta is the director of the Biden School of Public Policy and Administration and professor at the Charles P. Messick chair of public administration and Senior Policy Fellow at the University of Delaware. Her teaching and research interests are in creating strong institutions to strengthen democracy, particularly as it pertains to organizational behavior and performance management. Aristigueta currently serves on the National Association of Schools of Public Affairs and Administration (NASPAA) executive council, is an American Society for Public Administration past president, and a member of the National Academy for Public Administration. She has published numerous journal articles, book chapters and books, including: *Managing for Results in State Government*; coauthor of *Managing Human Behavior in Public and Nonprofit Organizations, Managing and Measuring Performance in Public and Nonprofit Organizations*, and *Organizational Behavior*; and coeditor of the *International Handbook of Practice-Based Performance Management*. Her doctorate is from the University of Southern California.

Hugo D. Asencio is an associate professor in the Department of Public Administration at California State University, Dominguez Hills. He holds a PhD in Public Administration and Public Policy from Auburn University. His research has focused on the effects of leadership on corruption, employee trust, job satisfaction, and performance in government agencies. He has also conducted research on social media utilization in nonprofit organizations, ethics training in military and police agencies, and e-government. His recent research has focused on military education programs and the impact of government policies on entrepreneurial activity in cities. Dr. Asencio's publications include *Cases on Strategic Social Media Utilization in the Nonprofit Sector* (2015) and articles in *Public Integrity, Public Administration Quarterly, International Review of Public Administration, International Journal of Public Administration*, and *Democracy and Security*, among others. He teaches graduate courses in public-sector management, leadership, ethics, and nonprofit management.

Catherine Cochrane is a doctoral researcher in the School of Social Sciences at the University of Adelaide. Her PhD thesis will present the findings of a policy analysis of standing anti-corruption commissions in Australia. Since joining the university, Catherine has worked as a research assistant, guest lecturer, and tutor. Previously, she worked in the local and national media in Australia for more than ten years. Catherine has academic qualifications in politics, policy, history, and journalism, and her research interests include corruption, accountability, and justice as well as broader public-policy issues.

Kathryn Denhardt has worked over the past twenty-five years with a broad range of government agencies, nonprofits, and community-based organizations trying to help their communities overcome tough challenges—and do so in an ethical manner. As both a consultant and university professor she has developed a deep understanding of strategies necessary to meet these challenges successfully. While working as a consultant, she led the successful creation of a public transportation system, taking an unfunded idea with plenty of opposition to a fully functioning bus and paratransit system. This involved managing the competing demands of a city commission, county commission, state department of transportation, and a local transportation advisory board. The system also involved engaging many different stakeholders and complying with complex regulations, especially those related to serving persons with disabilities. As a university professor (most recently at the University of Delaware), she has taught public-administration graduate courses in ethics, leadership, and organizational management. As a consultant she applied that knowledge to developing organizations that have the capacity to openly identify problems, seek solutions collaboratively, and continuously adhere to the ethics and values that provide a foundation for their public service mission.

J. Patrick Dobel is the John and Marguerite Corbally University Professor in Public Service Emeritus at the University of Washington and teaches at the Daniel J. Evans School of

Public Policy and Governance; he also served as adjunct professor of political science. He received his undergraduate degree from Boston College and his PhD from Princeton. After teaching political science at the University of Michigan at Dearborn for a decade he moved to the University of Washington. At Washington he served in many administrative positions as well as being involved in governance and oversight for the NCAA and intercollegiate athletics. Professor Dobel teaches strategy, leadership, and public ethics. The Evans School has three times named him "best teacher." The author of numerous articles on leadership, management, and public ethics, he has written three well-received books: *Public Integrity, Compromise and Political Action,* and most recently *Public Leadership Ethics: A Management Approach.* Among his various awards are the National Academy of Management prize for best article, the American Society of Public Administration James Webb Prize, and awards for best article and best editorial in *Public Integrity.* He often gives keynotes on ethics and leadership.

Professor Dobel has chaired numerous public committees, helped write ethics codes, and chaired the King County Washington Board of Ethics. He served on the Seattle Ethics and Election Commission and presently serves on the Port of Seattle Ethics Commission as well as the editor-at-large for the journal *Public Integrity.*

Thomas P. Dunn holds a BA (Psychology) from Western Kentucky University and MA (Sociology) and PhD (Sociology) degrees from the University of Kentucky. Having previously been awarded the rank of professor emeritus from Western Kentucky University, Dr. Dunn currently holds the academic rank of associate professor of sociology at Troy University. He has served Troy for twenty years in a number of roles, including four years as the Regional Chair of Arts and Sciences and General Studies and two years as the Interim Academic Dean of Troy's extensive Global Campus programs. Dr. Dunn is now in his fiftieth year of university-level teaching. He has published more than twenty-five articles in refereed journals and has presented in excess of sixty papers at professional meetings. His professional activities include receiving grants from the National Science Foundation to study the effects of Iceland's national television system and from the National PTA to present programs dealing with the effects of television on children to PTA groups throughout the Commonwealth of Kentucky. He has also served as a consultant to Community Leadership Programs nationwide on the use of marquee social science simulations, including Simsoc, Bafa' Bafa', and They Shoot Marbles, Don't They?

Angela M. Eikenberry is the David C. Scott Diamond Alumni Professor of Public Affairs in the School of Public Administration at the University of Nebraska at Omaha (UNO) and president of the Association for Research on Nonprofit Organizations and Voluntary Action (ARNOVA). Her research focuses on the social, economic, and political roles of philanthropy, voluntary associations, and nonprofit organizations in democratic governance. Her work has been featured on National Public Radio's *All Things Considered* and in other scholarly and popular press publications. She received a 2014–2015 Fulbright Scholar Award to conduct research on giving circles in the UK as well as the 2016 UNO Award for Distinguished Research or Creative Activity. She recently co edited a textbook on nonprofit management with Roseanne Mirabella and Billie Sandberg: *Reframing Nonprofit Management: Democracy, Inclusion, and Social Change* (2018).

Dan Feldman led significant investigations resulting in programmatic reforms and criminal convictions as executive assistant to a member of Congress, investigative counsel to a committee of the New York State Legislature, Assistant Deputy New York State Attorney General, and Special Counsel for Law and Policy to the New York State Comptroller. In between, he wrote over 140 laws as a member of the New York State Legislature for eighteen years, during twelve of which, as chair of the Assembly Committee on Correction, he investigated and corrected prison abuses and led the effort to repeal the Rockefeller drug laws. He now teaches at John Jay College of Criminal Justice as professor of public management and has written six books and many articles on American law and government, including *The Art of the Watchdog: Fighting Fraud, Waste, Abuse and Corruption in Government* (2014) with David R. Eichenthal and, most recently, *Administrative Law: The Sources and Limits of Government Agency Power* (2016). Professor Feldman majored in economics at Columbia College and earned his law degree at Harvard, where he was awarded the Williston Prize for Contract Negotiation and Drafting. He is a Fellow of the National Academy of Public Administration.

Fernando Filgueiras is director of Research and Graduate Studies at the National School of Public Administration (ENAP), Brazil, and associate professor in the Department of Political Science, Federal University of Minas Gerais (UFMG). He is a researcher at the National Institute of Science and Technology–Digital Democracy, Federal University of Bahia (UFBA), and a researcher at the Institute of Advanced Studies of the University of São Paulo (USP). He has a PhD in political science from the University Research Institute of Rio de Janeiro (IUPERJ). His work is dedicated to the study of governance in the public sector in Brazil, with a special focus on corruption in politics and public administration, accountability, and transparency and the processes of innovation and digital transformation of governments.

Barry D. Friedman has been a professor of political science at the University of North Georgia since 1992. Previously, he was a member of Valdosta State College's public-administration faculty from 1987 to 1992. He holds bachelor's degrees in engineering and political science from the University of Hartford, master's degrees in business administration and public affairs, and a PhD degree in political science from the University of Connecticut. He was the founding coordinator of North Georgia's Master of Public Administration Program from 1996 to 2016. North Georgia's alumni association presented to him its Distinguished Professor Award in 1997 and 2002. His publications include *Regulation in the Reagan-Bush Era: The Eruption of Presidential Influence* (1995).

Richard Ghere is associate professor of political science at the University of Dayton, having served there since 1984. Ghere is a core faculty member in the Master of Public Administration. He is the author of *Rhetoric in Human Rights Advocacy* (2015) and *NGO Leadership and Human Rights Advocacy* (2012) and co editor of *Ethics in Public Management* (2005) and *Ethics in Public Management*, 2nd ed. (2013).

Stuart C. Gilman is a senior partner in the Global Integrity Group working with international bodies, governments, and corporations around the world on issues of governance, integrity, and anti-corruption. He received his PhD from Miami University and completed postdoctoral work at the Center for Advanced Study in the Behavioral Sciences and the Kennedy School of Government. He has been a university professor, senior executive in the US federal government, president of a nonprofit, and head of the UN Global Programme against Corruption. As a member of the National Academy of Public Administration, he received the lifetime achievement award "for a career dedicated to advancing ethics and integrity in public administration" from the Ethics Section of the American Society for Public Administration in 2018. He can be contacted at scgilman@global-integrity.net.

Adam Graycar has held positions as professor of public policy or social policy at Griffith University, Flinders University, National University of Singapore, the Australian National University, Rutgers, the State University of New Jersey, and University of New South Wales. He has also been a visiting professor at numerous leading universities in

North America, Europe, Asia, and Australia. In 2010 he established the Transnational Research Institute on Corruption at the Australian National University. He acquired extensive policy experience over twenty-two years in the various senior level posts he has held in government in Australia, both in the Federal and the South Australian Governments. He now works extensively and globally with agencies such as the United Nations and World Bank.

Alain Hoekstra is a seasoned expert in the field of ethics and integrity management. He worked as a senior policy advisor for the Dutch Ministry of the Interior and Kingdom Relations and was one of the founders of the Dutch National Integrity Office. Currently, he works for the Dutch Whistleblowing Authority, which is an independent state agency. He is experienced in developing integrity courses and instruments and advises both public and private organizations with the implementation of integrity programs. As a PhD candidate at the RSM Erasmus University Rotterdam, he conducts research on organizational integrity. Alain published numerous articles and book chapters on this theme and is active in several international ethics and integrity networks.

Leo (L. W. J. C.) Huberts is professor of public administration at the Department of Political Science and Public Administration of the Vrije Universiteit Amsterdam. He is co director of the department's research program New Public Governance (and the research group on the Quality of Governance) and actively involved in study groups on Quality and Integrity of Governance in the International Institute of the Administrative Sciences (as co chair), the European Group of Public Administration, and the Section on Ethics and Integrity of Governance of the American Society for Public Administration.

Professor Huberts's main areas of research concern systems of governance and power and the quality, integrity, and ethics of governance. He is author or editor of more than twenty books on influence of governmental policy, power theory, and measurement; police administration and integrity; public corruption and fraud; and on integrity management, including *Integrity of Governance: What It Is, What We Know, What Is Done and Where to Go* (2014).

Carole L. Jurkiewicz, PhD, is Professor and Chair of the Department of Public Policy at Purdue University, the Ethics and Public Integrity Affiliate of the University of Colorado Colorado Springs, and principal owner of Jurkiewicz & Associates, LLC. Her work focuses on individual and organizational performance as a function of leader ethicality and cross-sector applied organizational ethics. She has authored over 160 books and articles in the areas of organizational and individual performance, ethics, and leadership, bringing to her academic career many years' experience as an executive in public, private, and nonprofit organizations. She is the former editor-in-chief of *Public Integrity*, serves on the board of a number of scholarly journals and professional associations, and has consulted with and served as an executive for a wide range of organizations in the U.S. and worldwide.

Muel Kaptein is a professor of business ethics and integrity management at the RSM Erasmus University Rotterdam. He is also equity partner at KPMG where he supports clients in auditing and improving their integrity and compliance. He cofounded KPMG Integrity in 1996, which was the first consultancy service in this field among the Big-6. Muel is author of several books, including *Ethics Management* (1998), *The Balanced Company* (2002), *The Six Principles for Managing with Integrity* (2005), *Workplace Morality* (2013), *The Servant of the People* (2018), and *Ethicisms and their Risks* (2018). He has published approximately fifty peer-reviewed articles in international journals such as

Journal of Management Studies, Journal of Organizational Behavior, Organization Studies, Journal of Management, Human Relations and *Academy of Management Review.*

John Kleinig is professor emeritus of philosophy in the Department of Criminal Justice, John Jay College of Criminal Justice and in the PhD program in philosophy, Graduate Center, City University of New York, and currently adjunct research professor in the School of Humanities and Social Sciences, Charles Sturt University (Australia). From 1987–2011 he was director of the Institute for Criminal Justice Ethics, City University of New York, and editor of the journal *Criminal Justice Ethics.* He is the author/editor of twenty-three books, most recently *Loyalty and Loyalties: The Contours of a Problematic Virtue* (2014); *The Ethics of Patriotism: A Debate* (with Simon Keller and Igor Primoratz, 2015); and *Ends and Means in Policing* (2019).

Angela Kline is an assistant professor of public administration at Bowie State University. Her research interests include performance management, strategic planning, nonprofit accountability, and social equity. She is passionate about enhancing online learning opportunities for students and is active as a peer reviewer for *Quality Matters.* Kline currently serves as the District II Representative on the National Council of the American Society for Public Administration. Before joining academia, Kline worked for several nonprofit organizations doing resource development and evaluation. She received her PhD in Urban Affairs and Public Policy from the University of Delaware's School of Public Policy and Administration and her MPA degree from Villanova University with a certificate in Nonprofit Management.

Emile Kolthoff, PhD, is professor of criminology and criminal justice at the Open University, in the Netherlands, professor of organized crime at Avans University of applied sciences in Den Bosch, and Fellow with the Research Group on Quality of Governance at VU University, Amsterdam. He started his professional career with the Dutch National Police, where he served for almost twenty years mainly in criminal investigation. His current research focuses on white-collar and state crime and organizational ethics. He is an active member of ASPA's Ethics Section and associate managing editor with the journal *Public Integrity.*

Cheon Lee is a PhD student in the School of Public Affairs and Administration at Rutgers University–Newark. His research interests include nonprofit management, citizen participation, civic engagement, and anti-corruption studies.

Carol W. Lewis is professor emerita of political science at the University of Connecticut. With her PhD from Princeton University (1975), she has authored and/or coauthored more than two dozen peer-reviewed journal articles—including a half dozen in *Public Administration Review* and three in *Public Integrity*—sat on the review committees of both journals, and authored and/or coauthored more than twenty book chapters and five books. Her professional experience also includes international and national consultancies and training. Lewis received the Award for Best Paper in Ethics and Accountability in the Public Sector from the Johnson Institute for Responsible Leadership at the University of Pittsburgh in 2006 and the inaugural lifetime achievement award "for a career dedicated to advancing ethics and integrity in public administration" from the Section on Ethics and Integrity of Governance of the American Society for Public Administration. She can be reached at cwlewis16@earthlink.net.

Leonard Lira joined San Jose State in 2017. He teaches public management, public budgeting, and organization theory at the graduate level, and international relations and

American politics at the undergraduate level. Before that he taught strategic and operational studies, leadership, and public management at the Army University's Command and General Staff College and Army Management Staff College. He also taught political science at the US Military Academy in West Point, New York. He has over twenty-seven years of public service experience with direct, organizational, and enterprise-level organizations. His research focus is on topics of organization theory, public management, and veterans' studies and policy.

Michael Macaulay is a professor of public administration at Victoria Business School, Victoria University of Wellington. He was previously the director of the Institute for Governance and Policy Studies. He is currently a visiting professor at the Universities of Sunderland (UK) and York St John (UK) and is a former visiting professor at the University of Johannesburg (South Africa). He has published extensively in the fields of integrity, ethics, and anti-corruption in leading international journals. He has worked with numerous government agencies and NGOs in New Zealand and internationally, including the New Zealand Police, the United Nations Office on Drugs and Crime (UNODC), the Council of Europe, and Transparency International. He has represented New Zealand at the Open Government Partnership (OGP) Global Summit (2015) and the inaugural Asia-Pacific Regional Summit in 2014, and he works extensively with civil society and government agencies to promote OGP initiatives throughout the country.

Jeroen Maesschalck studied public administration and philosophy at the University of Ghent (Belgium) and at the London School of Economics and Political Science. He holds a PhD in Social Sciences from the University of Leuven (Belgium). He was the founding director of the Leuven Institute of Criminology of the KU Leuven, where he still works as professor. His research and teaching focus on public administration ethics and on management and policy making in the criminal justice system. His publications include contributions in *Policing, Administration and Society, Public Administration, American Review of Public Administration, Journal of Business Ethics,* and *Public Integrity.* He has extensive experience with consulting on ethics management and training in ethical decision making, both within Belgium (local, regional, and federal government) and internationally (e.g., OECD).

Lisa Mahajan-Cusack has a PhD in Public Administration from Rutgers, the State University of New Jersey. Dr. Mahajan-Cusack's teaching interests focus on public- and private-sector management, ethics, organizational communication, citizen engagement, government transparency, and accountability. Her research focuses on the use of social media as a dominant form of communication and interaction among citizens and their government, and a global mechanism to help combat corruption and unethical behavior.

Amanda M. Main became an associate professor of management and coordinator for social entrepreneurship, social innovation, and business administration at Lynn University in Florida in August 2018. She was previously an instructional specialist in the Faculty Center for Teaching and Learning and lecturer of psychology and management at the University of Central Florida, where she received her PhD degree in industrial and organizational psychology in 2017. She is an organizational consultant working as a strategic partner with scaling organizations to design and implement leadership, team, and employee-development programs. Dr. Main's research focuses on diversity and harassment in the workplace, team dynamics, and organizational climate. The University of North Georgia alumni association recognized her with its 2018 Young Alumna Award.

Adam B. Masters lectures on corruption and organized crime at the Australian National University's Centre for Social Research and Methods. His teaching is based on his research in both fields, and he has also published on political rhetoric and the influence of organizational and professional culture on organizations, including Interpol. Before obtaining his PhD, Dr. Masters's twenty-four-year public sector career included eighteen years with the Australian Federal Police, which followed time with the Australian Taxation Office and Department of Defence.

Manfred Meine holds the academic rank of professor, as a member of the Troy University Public Administration graduate faculty, and he is the recipient of the 2011 Wallace D. Malone Distinguished Faculty Award. His college- and university-level teaching spans more than thirty years. Prior to pursuing an academic career, as a graduate of the FBI National Academy, Dr. Meine served as a Senior Special Agent for a Defense Department Criminal Investigative Organization (DCIO), where he managed various investigative units throughout the world. His professional positions include supervising personal security for two secretaries of defense, personnel management at the federal departmental level, investigative operations and training policy positions, and serving as a training consultant and training manual developer for public service organizations in New York City, New York State, and New Jersey.

Dr. Meine served as a founding member of the American Society for Public Administration, Section on Ethics and Integrity in Government (SEIGov) and has served on its executive committee. He currently serves as an editorial board member and manuscript reviewer for ASPA's *Public Integrity Journal* and served as guest editor for Public Integrity's 2017 Symposium Edition on Military Ethics. He has published extensively in the areas of criminal justice, ethics, and online education, and he serves as doctoral dissertation examiner and visiting professor for South Africa's University of Pretoria's School of Public Management and Administration (SPMA). His education includes a BS from the University of Nebraska, an MA from John Jay College, City University of New York, and a PhD in Public Administration from Golden Gate University in San Francisco. His current research interests focus on ethics in government and online education.

Roseanne Marie Mirabella is a professor in the Department of Political Science and Public Affairs at Seton Hall University. Dr. Mirabella conducts research on nonprofit management and philanthropic studies, international education for managers of NGOs, and critical perspectives on nonprofit organization management. She is past-president of the Association for Research on Nonprofit Organizations and Voluntary Action and the North Jersey Chapter of the American Society for Public Administration. As executive director of the Center for Community Research and Engagement, Dr. Mirabella has led Seton Hall's service learning and outreach initiatives for over twenty years. Together with her students and faculty colleagues, she assists local community-based organizations in planning, programming, and social-change initiatives.

Hans Nelen is a criminologist and has a law degree. Between 1986 and the beginning of 2001, he was employed as a senior researcher and research supervisor at the Research and Documentation Centre of the Ministry of Justice in the Netherlands (WODC), mainly involved in drug, fraud, organized crime, corporate crime, and police research. Between 2001 and 2006, he was a senior lecturer and senior researcher at the Institute of Criminology of the Vrije Universiteit in Amsterdam. Since January 1, 2007, he has been working as a professor of criminology at Maastricht University.

Dr. Juanita M. Rendon, CPA, CFE, is on the faculty at the Graduate School of Business and Public Policy at the Naval Postgraduate School (NPS), where she teaches auditing, accounting, finance, and fraud examination courses in the MBA and Executive

MBA programs. Prior to teaching at NPS, she worked for the U.S. Treasury Department for seventeen years. She is a certified public accountant and a certified fraud examiner. She is a member of the American Institute of Certified Public Accountants (AICPA), the Association of Certified Fraud Examiners (ACFE), and the American Accounting Association (AAA). She has published articles in the *Journal of Contract Management,* the *Managerial Auditing Journal,* and the *International Journal of Procurement Management.* She has also published book chapters in *Contract Administration: Tools, Techniques, and Best Practices* and *Cost Estimating and Contract Pricing: Tools, Techniques, and Best Practices.* In addition, she has presented at NCMA, ISM, and ASPA conferences.

Norma M. Riccucci is a Board of Governors Distinguished Professor at the School of Public Affairs and Administration at Rutgers University, Newark. She is the author of numerous publications and books including, most recently, *Policy Drift: Shared Powers and the Making of U.S. Law and Policy* (2018). Her research interests lie in the broad area of public management, with specific interests in social-equity policies and representative bureaucracy. She has received a number of national awards, including the American Political Science Association's John Gaus Award for lifetime of exemplary scholarship in the joint tradition of political science and public administration, and the American Society of Public Administration's Dwight Waldo Award for a lifelong contribution to public administration. She is a fellow of the National Academy of Public Administration (NAPA).

Jonathan Rose is an associate professor in politics and research methodology at De Montfort University, UK. His research has focused on issues of corruption and integrity, particularly within a quantitative framework. He holds a doctorate from the University of Nottingham, the dissertation of which was later published as *The Public Understanding of Political Integrity: The Case for Probity Perceptions* (2014). He is the former managing editor of the journal *Public Integrity.*

Anna Simonati, PhD, is associate professor of administrative law at Trento University, in Italy. In the field of public integrity, her areas of interest include the principles of fair administration (both at the national and at the supranational level), with a focus on the modern legal tools for participation and transparency; she is also interested in gender studies from a legal point of view.

Krishna K. Tummala is professor emeritus and was director of Graduate Program in Public Administration at K-State. He served on the governing bodies of the American Society for Public Administration (ASPA) and the National Association of Schools of Public Affairs and Administration (NASPAA) and was president of public administration honor society, Pi Alpha Alpha. Among the several awards he has received are the following: Paul H. Appleby Award for "Distinguished Service to Indian Institute of Public Administration (IIPA), and Public Administration, 2011"; Fred Riggs Award for "Lifetime Scholarly Achievement in the Field of Comparative and International Administration," SICA/ASPA, 2008; "Don Stone" award, ASPA, for "outstanding services," 2005; and a Senior Fulbright Fellowship, Summer, 1990. Besides ten books, he has published over seventy articles in refereed journals and about sixty-five op-ed pieces in popular publications. His latest book is *Politics of Preference: India, United States and South Africa* (2015). For the last few years, his academic preoccupation is with corruption, with particular reference to India.

Miguel A. Valverde Loya received his BA in public administration from El Colegio de México and his MA and PhD in government from Georgetown University. He has been a professor-researcher at the Center for Economic Research and Teaching (CIDE) in Mexico, a visiting research fellow at the Teresa Lozano Long Institute of Latin American Studies of the University of Texas at Austin, and a visiting research scholar at the Center for International Development of Harvard University. He is a member of Mexico's National Researchers System and currently teaches at Tecnológico de Monterrey, Mexico City Campus. His research interests include government reform and democratic governability.

André van Montfort holds an MSc degree in public administration, an LLM degree in Dutch law, and a PhD in sociology of law. He is an associate professor in public administration at the Vrije Universiteit Amsterdam in the Netherlands. His research activities focus on the theme "quality of governance," with special attention to the functioning of local integrity systems and legal protection procedures. André van Montfort serves as a substitute judge at a district court and as a chairman of the local appeals committee of a large Dutch municipality.

Yahong Zhang is an associate professor in the School of Public Affairs and Administration at Rutgers University–Newark and the director of the Rutgers Institute on Anti-Corruption Studies (RIACS). Her research interests include anti-corruption studies, politics-administration relationships, citizen participation, government transparency, public administration education, and quantitative research methods.

PART I

Foundations of Corruption

Causes and Types

1

The Contested Definition of Corruption

Jonathan Rose

Corruption is both a significant substantive problem for governance and an important political allegation. Accusing a political opponent of being corrupt is a common but serious charge, which calls into question both an individual's ethics and their ability to operate in the public interest. It is also a charge that demands serious consideration by citizens, officials, and markets. Nonetheless, judgments about whether an individual is corrupt or not rely inherently upon an understanding of the nature of corruption. Moreover, its definition determines the amount of corruption that it is possible to see within a country as a whole. In short, it is not possible to reach agreement on questions of who is corrupt if there is no agreement about the definition of the word "corruption." This is an issue of significant importance. An abundance of corruption definitions provides a plausible argument that any behavior is not (formally) "corrupt," even if it is nonetheless ethically problematic. Given the political and reputational impact of allegations of corruption, the definitional question is of real importance.

Disagreement about what corruption is taken to mean is, of course, not new and there has never been universal agreement about its definition. Nonetheless, while there has been some very rough homogenization of what is required for behaviors to be thought of as corrupt, not least because of the nascent interest of so-called global ethics (Lawton, Huberts, and van der Wal 2016; Rose 2016), the range of interpretations of what counts as corruption is arguably more serious now than in the past. A contested understanding of corruption is a complicating factor for the functioning of modern democracies (and perhaps even more for quasi-democracies), because it makes it more difficult for citizens to assess whether they are satisfied with the ethical performance of their leaders. Yet, arguably, the most serious concern about contested definitions of corruption relates to the very modern effort to quantitatively assess its levels in various countries and, in turn, seeking to rank them based on these numbers.

Worldwide corruption rankings began in earnest in the mid-1990s, with Transparency International's Corruption Perceptions Index (CPI), first released in 1995, and the World Bank's Worldwide Governance Indicators (WGI), which includes the Control of Corruption Index, released in 1996. In the years since these indices, in particular, were first released, they have taken on specific importance. Of special note is the use of such measures in making investment decisions. Corruption is a consideration by the sovereign credit rating agencies and, while they are not very transparent about how corruption is included, both Moody's and Fitch make use of data from the WGI in their credit ratings (Panizza 2017, 27). This serves to make it easier (or more difficult) for countries to borrow money on international markets, depending on whether they are seen as having a smaller (or larger) degree of corruption. At the same time, research has shown that countries that perform worse on the CPI generally receive less foreign portfolio investment (Jain, Kuvvet, and Pagano 2017). Nonetheless, both the CPI and the WGI Control of Corruption Index, which are in practice very similar in their ratings, are based upon a particular understanding of the nature of corruption—an understanding that ultimately is contested (see also Gilman 2018).

This chapter considers the practical consequences of decisions made about what counts as corruption and demonstrates that countries' corruption rankings can be noticeably shifted by using a slightly different, but still legitimate, conception of corruption. In turn, this implies that specific definitions of corruption, or particular applications of these definitions, can have real consequences for the economic fortunes of countries as a whole, but also for the life chances of individuals.

The Definition of Corruption

Corruption is a notoriously difficult concept to define. While many different definitions of corruption exist in both academia and third-sector bodies, these definitions are often incompatible and frequently include and exclude different actions in the scope of corruption (Rose 2018). One of the most prominent cleavages in the definitions is whether it is possible for private individuals or private businesses to be corrupt, by definition. One of the most important early academic definitions of corruption comes from J. S. Nye (1967, 419), who defined corruption as "behavior which deviates from the formal duties of a public role because of private-regarding (personal, close family, private clique) pecuniary or status gains; or violates rules against the exercise of certain types of private-regarding influence." Because this definition casts the problem exclusively in terms of violations of a duty in a *public role*, exclusively private corruption is impossible. While such an approach to corruption is obviously limited, there are some advantages. By being more specific, this definition of corruption is probably easier to operationalize into a single measure, a benefit Nye himself noted (1967). Moreover, when corruption is discussed in a lay sense, it is often (although unhelpfully not exclusively) discussed by reference to the public sector.

In academic discussions there similarly exists a definitional bias toward a focus on the public sector, although this is not always reflected in the actual wording of definitions. A large number of academic articles make use of Transparency International's definition of corruption: "the abuse of entrusted power for private gain" (Transparency International 2018). There is, of course, no reason that this definition has to focus exclusively on the public sector—a limited company that appoints a new marketing director entrusts them with power (over company resources, staff, etc.), which could be abused for private gain. And yet, Transparency International itself discusses this definition exclusively in relation to members of the public being victimized by the corruption of public officials when they attempt to access public services. Again, this has the advantage of tracking popular ideas of corruption to some degree, but it is an importantly limited approach. First, this approach is becoming increasingly outdated in the face of greater contracting out of public services, where essential state services are delivered by the private sector (Heywood 2015: 8). Second, this approach assumes that state actors have agency while those in the private sector do not. This seems to cut against empirical evidence that suggests that bribery of public officials by private companies can be a result of a complex negotiation between both the public official and the company and can be shaped by both social and organizational processes (Arellano-Gault 2018). It may be the case that most companies would choose not to pay bribes if they could avoid it, but even this is not certain. If corruption allows unscrupulous firms to bypass regulations they otherwise could not meet, or could not meet profitably, then that company may actively seek to corrupt public officials.

Nonetheless, reaching agreement about the issue of whether corruption occurs only within the public sector or across the public, nonprofit, and private sectors—if such an agreement were possible—would only be one element of de-contesting the definition of corruption. Disagreements would still exist about the nature of what counts as a private gain, about what it means to abuse power, about whether exercising power requires action or whether it can include conscious inaction and, indeed, a great many more issues. Were this contestation solely a question of academic discourse about the best way to capture a phenomenon so that it could be better studied, it would be important but not politically problematic. Unfortunately, as noted above, corruption evaluations that depend on these definitional questions are the basis of important evaluations that have direct (and potentially negative) effects for countries and their citizens.

The definitional approach taken by the WGI is interesting both because of the slant it takes and also because the WGI is one of the two major international comparative indices that track corruption. The WGI includes a distinct component, the Control of Corruption Index, which in turn is posited to capture

> perceptions of the extent to which public power is exercised for private gain, including both petty and grand forms of corruption, as well as "capture" of the state by elites and private interests. (World Bank 2018a)

The WGI goes on to list a series of concepts that are measured within Control of Corruption, including irregular payments, office abuse, accountability, trust in politicians, and a significant number of measures that purport to assess "corruption" (however defined) directly (World Bank 2018a). By virtue of originating from a variety of distinct surveys, the plethora of "corruption" measures could all plausibly have incompatible conceptual understandings of the term. This amalgamation of a wide variety of measures putatively measuring "corruption," without their necessarily sharing a consistent understanding of it, risks undermining the "conceptual clarity" of the measures, which the United Nations Development Programme (UNDP) calls "crucial" to understanding and preventing corruption (UNDP 2008, 26). Moreover, the assumption that "trust" is primarily a reflection of corruption rather than other local conditions is potentially problematic methodologically, but its inclusion is also awkward from a definitional standpoint. While trust in politicians is usually seen as a positive, and moreover may reflect that politicians are acting with integrity (Rose 2014), trust is far more complex than mere beliefs about politicians' degree of corruption.

At a more practical level, the Control of Corruption Index also has an issue in terms of how the stated definition is interpreted such that a single survey question within an individual data source can be "counted" as reflecting the specified definition. Moreover, even if the counting of a single survey question is acceptable, there still remains the possibility for contestation surrounding whether the chosen definition is indeed the most helpful (or even a correct) one. In a situation in which there is not even agreement about whether corruption only occurs in the public sector or in both the public and private sectors, the choices made here are highly debatable. Yet the validity of the choices made will have a crucial role in determining whether the final measures themselves are valid and useful (see also Andersson 2017). Nonetheless, the assignment of individual survey questions, and the extent to which these reflect specific definitional assumptions, has not been considered in detail in the literature to date. Most importantly, variable assignment could easily produce quantitatively and qualitatively different interpretations of the level of corruption in various countries and in turn could produce radically different rankings. Given the importance of these rankings, this is no small matter.

The Implications of Definitions

Hitherto it has been argued that the definition of corruption is importantly contested and that this may have practical consequences. In order to directly test this claim, this chapter analyzes data from a single data source of the WGI to evaluate both whether the assignment of questions to indicators is sensible, given the WGI's definition of corruption, and also to consider if a more expansive assignment would make a substantive difference to the scores of individual countries.

The data used here come from the 2016 Global Integrity Index data source of the WGI (World Bank 2018b). This data in turn is from the 2017 Africa Integrity Indicators collected by Global Integrity (2018). As the name implies, this dataset focuses on Africa and has data for fifty-four African countries. It features 102 questions on both the legal framework for managing integrity within a country as well as items evaluating the practical application of those legal codes. In common with most other data sources, the WGI uses a subset of the whole dataset—focusing only on the sixty-four questions probing "in practice" perceptions (World Bank 2018b). This is a conceptual choice, but one that appears sensible if the intention is to aggregate the data. Particularly in more corrupt countries, there may be a significant divergence between legal frameworks and practical application, creating an unhelpful source of variations between questions.

The data are coded on a five-point scale, which Global Integrity describes in the following way:

> Each indicator has a set of elaborate criteria that corresponds to each possible score. In general, a 100 translates into "Very Strong," a 75 into "Strong," a 50 into "Moderate," a 25 into "Weak" and a 0 into "Very Weak." (Global Integrity 2018)

Global Integrity (2018) conceptualizes its data in terms of two main categories: (1) Transparency and Accountability and (2) Social Development. The WGI instead assigns the subset of the data it uses to four of their indicators: Government Effectiveness, Rule of Law, Voice and Accountability, and Control of Corruption. The WGI's categories cut across the two used by Global Integrity, with data from both Transparency and Accountability and Social Development variables assigned to the same WGI indicator.

To generate the Control of Corruption Index component for a data source, the WGI team rescale the question responses to be on a 0–1 scale and take the average of the variables they identify as indicating corruption. This means that the overall Control of Corruption score for each data source is on a 0–1 scale. In turn, the scores arrived at from all available data sources are aggregated into an overarching Control of Corruption score for each country, on (approximately) a –2.5 to +2.5 scale. For some countries/territories this final score will include data from as many as sixteen data sources; for others it will be based on a single data source. Four variables from the Global Integrity data source are mapped to Control of Corruption in the 2016 WGI; in practice:

- Allegations of corruption against senior-level politicians and/or civil servants of any level are investigated by an independent body.
- The body/bodies that investigate/s allegations of public-sector corruption is/are effective.
- Appointments to the body/bodies that investigate/s allegations of public-sector corruption support/s the independence of the body.
- The mechanism for citizens to report police misconduct or abuse of force is effective. (World Bank 2018b)

These questions can be considered as indicators of corruption based upon the definition used by the WGI, yet they do not exhaust the questions in the dataset that plausibly relate to corruption. There is nothing inherently wrong with using a more restrictive subset of questions to measure a concept and, indeed, all questionnaires are inherently subsets of the infinite questions and variations of questions that could have been asked. Nonetheless, the way that individual questions are mapped to higher-level concepts is more problematic here. The restrictive focus in Control of Corruption noticeably reduces the scope of the indicator, which, in turn, may cause some countries to have conspicuously lower (or higher) scores than they would have had. Moreover, using only four questions to assess corruption when several more could easily meet the stated definition of corruption, let alone meeting other legitimate definitions, will, *ceteris paribus*, reduce the reliability of the final measure. This restrictive approach is also problematic if the subset of questions used provides a qualitatively different understanding of the issue than a more expansive measure would have.

In order to test the possibility that a broader reading of the definition of corruption used in the WGI can lead to substantively different results, the Control of Corruption score from the Global Integrity data source was recalculated for all fifty-four countries available. In addition to the four corruption variables already used (noted above), the following variables were added; in practice:

- The independence of the supreme audit institution is guaranteed.
- The agency/agencies mandated to organize and monitor national elections is/are protected from political interference.
- The asset disclosure process for senior officials of the three branches of government (heads of state and government, ministers, members of parliament, judges, etc.) is effective.
- Political parties regularly disclose public donations (funds that are sourced from the government) and the disclosures are easily available to the public.
- No NGOs have been shut down or harassed with unwarranted administrative burdens, investigations, or sanctions in the past year as retribution for their work.

Each of these variables also plausibly represents "corruption" according to the definition used by the WGI, even though they are presently mapped to either Voice and Accountability or Rule of Law. Adding these variables and averaging the scores in the same way as the WGI does for the existing corruption measure from this dataset produces a new index. The results, presented alongside the original score generated from only four items, are shown in table 1.1.

TABLE 1.1	The Extent of Corruption in Fifty-Four African Countries under Two Different Conceptions of Corruption		
Country	**WGI Control of Corruption Score for Global Integrity Data Source**	**Expanded Control of Corruption Score for Global Integrity Data Source**	**Score Change**
Algeria	0.188	0.125	−0.063
Angola	0.000	0.031	0.031
Benin	0.625	0.531	−0.094
Botswana	0.313	0.313	0.000
Burkina Faso	0.625	0.531	−0.094
Burundi	0.188	0.188	0.000
Cameroon	0.313	0.281	−0.031
Cape Verde	0.438	0.438	0.000
Central African Republic	0.000	0.094	0.094
Chad	0.125	0.125	0.000
Comoros	0.438	0.406	−0.031
Cote d'Ivoire	0.438	0.281	−0.156
Dem. Republic of the Congo	0.125	0.156	0.031
Djibouti	0.250	0.250	0.000
Egypt	0.375	0.344	−0.031
Equatorial Guinea	0.000	0.000	0.000

(Cont.)

TABLE 1.1	(Continued)		
Eritrea	0.063	0.031	−0.031
Ethiopia	0.563	0.469	−0.094
Gabon	0.125	0.094	−0.031
Ghana	0.688	0.531	−0.156
Guinea	0.188	0.188	0.000
Guinea-Bissau	0.188	0.219	0.031
Kenya	0.750	0.656	−0.094
Lesotho	0.438	0.313	−0.125
Liberia	0.563	0.406	−0.156
Libya	0.125	0.156	0.031
Madagascar	0.250	0.219	−0.031
Malawi	0.375	0.219	−0.156
Mali	0.375	0.375	0.000
Mauritania	0.125	0.156	0.031
Mauritius	0.625	0.625	0.000
Morocco	0.313	0.281	−0.031
Mozambique	0.250	0.125	−0.125
Namibia	0.500	0.406	−0.094
Niger	0.313	0.281	−0.031
Nigeria	0.563	0.406	−0.156
Republic of the Congo	0.313	0.219	−0.094
Rwanda	0.563	0.438	−0.125
Sao Tome and Principe	0.188	0.250	0.063
Senegal	0.375	0.281	−0.094
Seychelles	0.188	0.250	0.063
Sierra Leone	0.625	0.531	−0.094
Somalia	0.000	0.000	0.000
South Africa	0.688	0.750	0.063
South Sudan	0.125	0.094	−0.031
Sudan	0.000	0.000	0.000
Swaziland	0.313	0.156	−0.156
Tanzania	0.438	0.281	−0.156
The Gambia	0.063	0.063	0.000
Togo	0.125	0.125	0.000
Tunisia	0.438	0.438	0.000
Uganda	0.500	0.406	−0.094
Zambia	0.438	0.406	−0.031
Zimbabwe	0.438	0.313	−0.125

Source: Global Integrity 2018

Note: Scores shown on a 0–1 scale, with 0 indicating the most corruption. Figures shown to three decimal places.

As can be seen in table 1.1, the scores for most countries are different on the two different indices. The largest positive change is for the Central African Republic, whose score increased by 9.4 percent of the range of the variable. Many more countries see their scores decline, including countries like Ghana, Nigeria, and Swaziland, which see a decline of over 15 percent of the range of the variable. In the case of Swaziland, this halves its score.

Conclusion

The results presented here show two different measures leading to two different views of the scale of corruption within a wide range of African countries. That this is possible may not be surprising. Yet it is important to remember that the only fact that gave rise to the difference between the two scores is how the definition of corruption was understood. A more restrictive understanding of the definition led to the original WGI scores, while a more expansive definition led to the new scores. To some extent, neither approach is "correct." There is nothing intrinsically wrong with using tightly restricted definitions and, indeed, under some circumstances there can be advantages to this (Nye 1967). Nonetheless, when the definition is contested, and when both approaches are legitimate, it is imperative that we at least fully understand the consequences of definitional choices. The changes in scores can range from +9.4 percent to –15.6 percent of the range of the variable. This is a huge variance in a situation in which these data form an important part of how we evaluate countries, and moreover, these data have a nontrivial role in conditioning the life chances of residents of these countries.

These findings matter. As has been noted earlier, these rankings can have a more or less direct effect on the financial health of countries (Panizza 2017), which in the context of some of the world's most deprived nations can have significant substantive consequences. Yet, moreover, a needlessly restrictive view of the definition of corruption in a country can potentially have far greater consequences still. A little over a decade ago, Treisman (2007, 241) noted that comparative index measures of corruption correlate poorly with actual experiences, suggesting instead that corruption measures may be little more than self-fulfilling prophecies based on assumptions about corruption's causes. Here the self-fulfilling argument can be extended further. Corruption perceptions are likely to be informed by indices such as the WGI and the CPI, which, in turn, color the perceptions of the evaluators whose views are fed back into these same indices. Such a cycle may well explain the unreasonable stability of both the CPI and the WGI (Heywood and Rose 2014). The worst-case scenario may be the realization of the "corruption trap" driven by comparative indices that Andersson and Heywood (2009) presciently warned about: a trap caused by a perception of corruption that is very resistant to change but which, in turn, prevents the kinds of reform that could stop corruption. Such corruption traps may always be a concern, but if the initial positions on the indices in which countries found themselves could have been changed simply by using a different (similarly contestable) interpretation of a contested definition, then there seems reason to worry.

References

Andersson, S. 2017. "Beyond Unidimensional Measurement of Corruption." *Public Integrity 19*(1), 58–76.

Andersson, S., and Heywood, P. M. 2009. "The Politics of Perception: Use and Abuse of Transparency International's Approach to Measuring Corruption." *Political Studies 57*(4), 746–67.

Arellano-Gault, D. 2018. "Government Corruption: An Exogenous Factor in Companies' Victimization?" *Public Integrity* 1–20.

Gilman, S. 2018. "To Understand and to Misunderstand How Corruption Is Measured: Academic Research and the Corruption Perception Index." *Public Integrity 20* (sup1), S74–88.

Global Integrity. 2018. "Africa Integrity Indicators 2017" [Available online: https://aii.globalinteg-rity.org/scores-map?stringId=transparency_accountability&year=2017, accessed: August 9, 2018].

Heywood, P. 2015. "Introduction: Scale and Focus in the Study of Corruption," in P. Heywood (ed.) *Routledge Handbook of Political Corruption*. London: Routledge.

Heywood, P. M., and J. Rose. 2014. "'Close But No Cigar': The Measurement of Corruption." *Journal of Public Policy 34*(3), 507–29.

Jain, P. K., E. Kuvet, and M. S. Pagano. 2017. "Corruption's Impact on Foreign Portfolio Investment." *International Business Review 26*(1), 23–35.

Lawton, A., L. Huberts, and Z. van der Wal, eds. 2016. "Towards a Global Ethics: Wishful Thinking or a Strategic Necessity?" in A. Lawton, Z. van der Wal, and L. Huberts (eds.), *Ethics in Public Policy and Management: A Global Research Companion*. London: Routledge.

Nye, J. S. 1967. "Corruption and Political Development: A Cost–Benefit Analysis." *American Political Science Review 51*(2), 417–27.

Panizza, U. 2017. "The Use of Corruption Indicators in Sovereign Ratings." *Inter-American Development Bank* [Available online: https://publications.iadb.org/bitstream/handle/11319/8562/The-Use-of-Corruption-Indicators-in-Sovereign-Ratings.PDF, accessed: June 11, 2018].

Rose, J. 2014. *The Public Understanding of Political Integrity: The Case for Probity Perceptions.* Basingstoke: Palgrave Macmillan.

Rose J. 2016. "Global Ethics," in A. Farazmand (eds.), *Global Encyclopedia of Public Administration, Public Policy, and Governance*. Cham: Springer.

Rose, J. 2018. "The Meaning of Corruption: Testing the Coherence and Adequacy of Corruption Definitions." *Public Integrity 20*(3), 220–33.

Transparency International. 2018. "What Is Corruption?" [Available online: https://www.transpar-ency.org/what-is-corruption, accessed August 28, 2018].

Treisman, D. 2007. "What Have We Learned about the Causes of Corruption from Ten Years of Cross-National Empirical Research?" *Annual Review of Political Science 10*, 211–44.

United Nations Development Programme (UNDP). 2008. *A Users' Guide to Measuring Corruption.* Norway: UNDP Oslo Governance Centre.

World Bank. 2018a. "Control of Corruption" [Available online: http://info.worldbank.org/gover-nance/wgi/#doc, accessed: June 11, 2018].

World Bank. 2018b. "WGI: Download Source Data: Global Integrity Index (GII)" [Available online: http://info.worldbank.org/governance/wgi/#doc, accessed: June 11, 2018].

2

Comparative Analysis of Unethical Practices across Cultures

Reversing the Negative Social Aspects

David Arellano-Gault

Social Practices of Exchange: A Road to Unethical Actions?

Let's take a minute and consider the following situation: an elderly man by the name of Fernando is diagnosed with glaucoma. Two doctors have recommended performing an operation as soon as possible to stop the disease. A private hospital has given him a price estimate for the operation that the patient is unable to afford. Fortunately, Fernando has the option of the government health service, where he could be treated at no cost. However, this would involve a lengthy, complicated process. It could take months, perhaps over a year, according to some of his acquaintances. His illness is already advanced and waiting that amount of time would be quite risky. But the government health system is so overloaded that following the rules and procedures could be a major problem.

So Fernando is forced to do something anyone in the country where he lives (Mexico in this case, but it could be similar to several other countries) would do: look for a contact among his acquaintances, or someone who in turn has a contact, until he finds a person with decision-making power within the government health system. Why? The answer is obvious, in that society at least: so that this contact, either directly or through other contacts, their acquaintances, will speed up the bureaucratic process so that he can be treated soon.

The ending to this story is that his network of acquaintances and contacts was efficient and managed to find someone in the health system with the power to make certain decisions. The result was positive: he managed to get a doctor's appointment and be operated on within a month and a half rather than one year. Incidentally, Fernando did not have to pay anyone for this favor, at least not directly or in cash. Perhaps, at some point, he will have to give a gift to his first contact, and another one to the final contact who eventually resolved the issue. Incidentally, this is difficult to determine: these exchanges tend to be extremely discreet. The usual drill in these cases is to thank and tell your contact: "I owe you one." This short story might be useful to synthetize the customary ways people in different societies resolve some of their problems: finding parallel or informal social mechanisms to obtain what they need, even if doing so implies bending the formal rules. And, as it can be inferred from the story, the person is clear that he is bending the rules, nevertheless, assuming or rationalizing that it was the legitimate road to take, illegal, but justified, given the circumstances. This can be understood as an unyielding paradox.

In the case of Mexico and other Latin American countries, a social practice such as the one described has a popular name: *palancas*, meaning "levers." Using or having palancas is understood as a situation in which a person uses the relationships she has to obtain a favor, skirting the rules if necessary. People who use these networks of acquaintances usually regard this as a legitimate, or at least inevitable, process. It can even be socially rewarded: a person with several palancas is someone who is admired, with skills and cunning, skills that it is rational to contribute to and invest in (Arellano-Gault 2018).

The question is whether using these networks is an improper or at least an unethical act, and whether these practices encourage and sustain systemic corruption. In many of Latin American countries the answer is ambiguous; they may lead to improper or corrupt acts, but not necessarily. People judge these practices on a case-by-case basis, depending on the context. Accordingly, it is an extremely ambiguous, informal social judgment.

The purpose of this chapter is to explain the logic whereby this mechanism of acquaintances or contacts operates in different societies. Further, it examines whether this relationship perpetuates ethically dubious social practices and, therefore, is a means to understanding the systemic corruption many countries suffer—living with and, paradoxically, contributing to or reproducing through these widespread social practices. This chapter is divided into three sections. The first describes the basic elements of these practices. The second briefly presents four similar mechanisms existing in different countries—Russia, China, Brazil, and Mexico—and analyzes the ethicality of these practices. The third considers these findings in total and presents conclusions.

The Basic Elements of the Social Practice of Networks of Acquaintances

Exchanging favors beyond those among family members or friends is more common than one might think and takes place in practically all societies, with different intensities. People in every society engage in interactions with others and expect a certain type of reciprocity from that interaction (Mauss 2002). But when a system of reciprocity is *based on* this exchange of favors, the practice becomes a social norm that can be extremely stable (Pyyhtinen 2014).

The exchange of favors creates a bond between people. This bond can be quite instrumental: a favor is done in order to receive another one practically simultaneously, whereby it ceases to be a favor and becomes a commercial or pecuniary exchange. But favors usually have a less instrumental social dimension: the bond established is often more important than the favor one receives in return. In other words, people can form a link with each other through a logic of reciprocity that becomes more stable and constant over time (Douglas 2002). Exchanging favors is thus not necessarily measured by immediate reciprocity but by the expectation of the people involved that a system of continued reciprocities will be established over time.

Oddly enough, this logic of reciprocity requires a more intricate form of interaction because there is not necessarily a map or list of the favors received and granted. It requires a structure of trust, where instrumentalization of the exchange may be a counterproductive factor. The logic of reciprocity does not benefit from appearing to be a means of influence in the eyes of those involved, since that would undermine the foundation of the trust necessary to establish it as stable over time.

In certain political contexts, this network of exchanging favors can become an extremely useful social tool to solving a wide range of problems. When we speak of authoritarian political systems, rigid and overly formalized bureaucracies, it can be irrational to act in accordance with the law or follow the rules. The obstacles people face in resolving problems using formal rules can be so formidable that the rational thing to do is to look for shortcuts, or ways to bend the rules. The classical examples usually come from communist countries in Eastern Europe where getting a phone line could literally take decades. Several Latin American countries such as Mexico, Peru, or Brazil have their own stories of Kafkian bureaucracies. This can be a very complex circuit: the authorities are rigid and bureaucratic, knowing that people will look for solutions through other, non-formal means, and a vicious circle is created (Moody and Musheno 2003).

This causal chain of the social phenomenon can be viewed as follows: (1) there is a rigid authority that prevents problems from being solved in a reasonable way; (2) people turn to acquaintances who may have links with the authorities to expedite the administrative process; (3) the person(s) who can eventually help become links that unblock the bottlenecks by bending the rules; (4) the person obtains what she wanted by skirting the rules but doing so within the informal practices that are considered socially valid; and (5) the chain of favors creates extremely stable links, commitments, and informal routes that operate parallel to the formal ones.

Another important factor is the extension of the informal network that interlinks many people: the borders between formal and informal exchanges are fuzzy and linked in very different, specific ways, on a case-by-case basis. This results in ethical judgments becoming ambiguous, since the chain of relationships that proved effective in bending the rules is justified as legitimate and useful. Bending the rules, while virtually illegal, becomes rational, socially speaking and, therefore, those who adhere strictly to formal rules will be seen as abnormal and will likely fail to obtain what they need and be judged as incompetent.

Exchanging favors is usually a rich process, socially speaking. Rules of etiquette, games, symbols, and languages are specifically created for the exchange process, as will be explored in the next section. Exchanging favors requires knowledge about which words and poses convey signs regarding the position, capacity, power, and will of each person involved, and to logically create relations of reciprocity and trust that enable the exchange to take place. One *must acquire* the skill to understand and handle the customs; routines; procedures; and appropriate language in a broad range of situations. Thus, languages and practices are created with their own codes that are conveyed in practice, by word of mouth, within the family and with close friends.

These types of exchanges are context-dependent. Two people in a given society may differ with respect to their assessment of the level of legitimacy of a particular act involving the exchange of favors. Taking in consideration the story of Fernando at the start of this chapter, some people might think it is clear that Fernando deliberately trafficked with influences and therefore committed an illegal or at least an unethical act. Others might think Fernando is a victim of an unfair and inefficient health system, and that he is entitled to use whatever strategy he can to save his life. Moreover, in the social aggregate, people can agree that everyone would be better off if the formal rules worked properly, and exchanging favors were not necessary. The question is how to avoid the social trap where no one wants to be the first to pay the costs of attempting to change the situation.

These types of exchanges are paradoxical: on the one hand, the reason for their existence is seen by many as a need to do "justice" in the face of the irrationality of the formal processes imposed on them by the authorities. It is even seen by some as a need that requires skill, ability, and cunning, to the extent that these societies often produce "intermediaries" or people who provide key services to make these mechanisms and networks of acquaintances work. At the same time, these practices reproduce the conditions of inequality and privilege: the more acquaintances you have, the more resources you have to succeed in the system, placing many people with fewer networks and acquaintances at a disadvantage. In many societies, understanding this paradox is crucial in understanding the stubborn persistence of corruption.

Exchange of Favors in Russia, China, Brazil, and Mexico

Each society considers exchanges of favors differently, because their respective political systems, history, and culture have created their own rich versions, with similarities and intriguing differences. Consider: (1) *blat* in Russia; (2) *guanxi* in China; (3) *jeitinho* in Brazil; and (4) *palancas* in Mexico.

Blat can be understood as the "use of connections or contacts" (Ledeneva 1998: 12). This instrument was developed during the time of the Union of Soviet Socialist Republics (USSR). In the post-Soviet era, several of its dynamics and logics have changed, although it has not disappeared entirely. In the Soviet era, with its powerful, aggressive ideological framework, two particular characteristics were often mentioned in relation to blat. First, in a society that could not make mistakes, at least at the level of rhetoric, finding concrete, practical ways to solve problems without appearing to be subversive or anti-revolutionary was part of the discursive context of creating an instrument for exchanging favors. Thus, without directly opposing the system, people used their networks of acquaintances, in which the participants understood that everyone would need help at some point (Aliyev 2013: 106–10; Rehn and Taalas 2004, 242).

Second, this help had, however, to be carefully justified in practice, both by ordinary citizens and public officials, who necessarily participated in the logic of bending the rules. The practice of blat created suitable languages and forms for stabilizing and justifying practical processes: informal rules governing how to ask, what to ask, who to ask, and how to reciprocate. In time, an extensive list of codes was formed for very diverse circumstances: it was not the same to use blat to get a phone line or a car as it was to ask a doctor for an earlier appointment or to obtain a particular medicine more quickly.

With the fall of the USSR, blat was transformed by the dynamics of decentralization (Ledeneva 1998). For many people, however, the blat of the capitalist era is very similar to bribery: in other words, it is more complex to conceal the instrumentalization of exchanging favors, making it more difficult to justify socially.

Guanxi in China is a phenomenon that is intimately linked to the "relations of solidarity and hierarchies" existing in this ancient society. Family networks are fundamental, and the logic of reciprocity is tied to the dynamics of mutual duties and obligations, all capable of maintaining the necessary "social order" (Liang-Hung 2011). The practice of guanxi is therefore reproduced within accepted social actions because of the links it has with the family: favors must be reciprocated as an ethical obligation (Torres et al. 2015). In this respect, for most of the people in China it is somewhat easy to distinguish a corrupt practice from guanxi. For example, bribery is motivated by selfish reasons, whereas guanxi is a chain of reciprocities linked to duties, many of which involve family ties. In different circumstances, then, returning a favor is a sign of honor, expressing gratitude, and repaying a debt of honor (Yan 1994).

The reciprocity of the exchange of gifts that sustains guanxi builds its practices and symbols in conceptual constructs dependent on critical factors such as the social status, respectability, and good repute various people enjoy depending on their social or political status. The rules of etiquette in the case of guanxi are closely linked to these social and family factors (Yan 1994: 8). Its legitimacy is therefore also heavily dependent on the ability of people to "navigate" between these codes and symbols. Interestingly, the ability to use the correct languages and poses within intricate family networks and their status also confers on guanxi operators the standing of intelligent people who can be successful intermediaries so that guanxi works.

Let us now move to a very different society: Brazil. Jeitinho in Brazil consists of providing a quick fix for certain problems necessitated by the existence of rigid, unreasonable rules that fail to take "real people" into consideration (Duarte 2011; Castor 2002; Smith et al. 2012). Jeitinho begins with a vision that is assumed to be quite practical, contrary to another that can be "theoretical." Theory is beautiful and perfect, but it can never grasp the intricate, diverse reality of people who have to live in the imperfect world of practice. It is not that this mechanism ignores formal rules, simply that it must intelligently skirt them in order to find solutions to actual problems (Castor 2002). Doing jeitinho is therefore an act of intelligence and skill. There are people who are born to engage in jeitinho, their intelligence and ability being socially essential. They become *pistolao* (that is, someone who has "the right weapons" to resolve a variety of situations).

The use of jeitinho ends up being legitimized because it actually produces a certain balance and social harmony (Torres et al. 2015) when solving concrete problems through networks of people. This mechanism operates within the logic of the charm and congeniality of a person to create trust and thereby open the doors to carrying out favors (Duarte 2011).

Lastly, in Mexico, the name of the most widespread mechanism for the exchange of favors is palanca, which consists of the informal exchange of favors that occurs between people who are able to use their contacts to help others or themselves. This mechanism is highly socialized in that it seems to be the rule rather than the exception (Lomnitz 1990).

The system involves informal networks of trust and reciprocity that increase the likelihood of solving problems that are difficult to resolve within a rigid bureaucratic structure characterized by multiple procedural steps. The meaning of palancas is based on the value of "helping" others, trust, and equity (Lomnitz 1990). However, there are two sides to the coin. Since it is common practice in Mexican society, not having palancas is a symbol of stigmatization for someone who has failed and is not very effective.

Palancas in Mexico suffer from ethical ambiguity: the quantity and quality of palancas are critical to a person's success. Those who have few palancas are usually poor or unsuccessful, it is assumed. At the same time, a person who has palancas is envied and resented as someone who is a cheat or crafty. Palancas in Mexico highlights the contradiction and moral opacity of these widespread social practices.

Networks for the exchange of favors among family members or groups of friends and acquaintances are important in any society. However, in several different societies this exchange practice expands and becomes critical for obtaining social services or executing successful business transactions. It becomes a normalized practice, although it might entail bending formal rules to normalize unethical practices such as bribery or traffic with influence peddlers. In this context, exchange practices like blat or jeitinho are used to circumvent formal rules on a case-by-case, practical day-to-day basis. In other words, formal rules matter and are accepted, but it is legitimate in practice and everyday life to use networks of acquaintances to resolve the obstacles imposed on people. One of the most important effects of this contradiction is that highly ambiguous, context-dependent understandings and justifications are constructed around what is and what is not "appropriate."

These practices are, undoubtedly, one of the most important keys to understanding improper or corrupt acts in many societies. Thanks to their ambiguity, context dependence, and importance for everyday people, they manage to appear legitimate, although on a case-by-case basis they may conceal or justify corrupt acts. These acts can, at any rate, be socially justified: it was an unlawful act, but one a person was compelled to engage in due to formal, insensitive, or rigid rules or corrupt authorities. When these exchanges of favors come close to being considered improper or corrupt acts, people can be justified as victims. In many societies, people live behind a social veil that ends up justifying corruption.

This chapter presents four examples among a large list of informal practices of exchange. Ledeneva (2018) has gathered an encyclopedia of them, including practices like sociolismo, old boy network, klüngel, and zalatwianie ulatwić. Understanding and researching these practices could prove important—not only to deal with the paradoxes they create in each country, but also to understand in a more detailed and practical way how to deal with them in a globalized world.

Conclusion

This chapter began with a specific story about the use of networks of acquaintances where: (1) Fernando's health improved: if he had followed the rules, he would probably have lost his sight from glaucoma; (2) he achieved this through an effective social practice that probably created an injustice, since it harmed those who followed the formal rules and waited their turn; (3) this practice can be classified as a normal event in that society, and there were no negative consequences for the network of individuals who participated in bending the rule; and (4) whether this practice was unethical, improper, or could even have caused acts of corruption would be an ambiguous issue in many societies.

Thus, the paradox: practices such as palancas, guanxi, blat, and jeitinho are justified as effective means for people to resolve real problems in a context in which formal rules and authorities are ineffective. They are legitimate practices, socially speaking, but their overall effect on society can be overtly negative, reproducing the ineffective interactions between people and authorities, probably encouraging the normalization of corruption, and maintaining a general logic of inequality and privilege. The ambiguity and ethical confusion these societies may suffer are evident. Understanding these dynamics can be crucial to devising solutions that will enable the chains of relationships and reciprocity in different societies to be reconstructed in order to reduce the ethical ambiguity and prevent their reproduction as legitimate practices.

Changing social practices such as the ones described in this chapter will prove to be quite difficult. It will require political, legal, and economic efforts as well as ethical considerations. Practices like palancas are so stable and pervasive because people think they are using an equalizer. Given the inefficacy or perversity of the formal authorities, normal people cannot find another way. Therefore, it is fair to find alternatives, using other resources to get that to which they are entitled. However, and this has come up clearly in empirical studies of palancas in Mexico (Arellano-Gault 2018), it is quite easy to disarm the contradiction: in order to obtain justice and fair treatment, palancas create a distinction between insiders and outsiders. A distinction between those who have palancas and those who don't. In the end, Fernando got the treatment he needed, but he might begin to consider what happened to those he pushed behind on the list of treatment. Perhaps she or he got sicker? Perhaps it was a baby who badly needed to be treated? This ethical reflection is important in unmasking the paradox: palancas is not a way to produce fairness and justice, but to reproduce a system of privileges and exclusion (Holmes 2015, 7). Encouraging people in organizations, school, firms, government offices, and in the media to discuss this contradiction might prove fruitful. At some level, these practices rest at least in part on one key aspect: they are legitimate given an unfair system or situation. Deconstructing the fact that they might be at one level legitimate, but at another—more substantial—level a significant factor in the perpetuation of a system of privileges and exclusion, might offer opportunities to initiate a profound ethical change in these societies.

References

Aliyev, Huseyn. 2013. "Post-Communist Informal Networking: Blat in the South Caucasus." *Demokratizatsiya: The Journal of Post-Soviet Democratization* 21(1), 89–112.

Arellano-Gault, David. 2018. "*En México, la Vida es una Consecución de Palancas. Escapando del Monstruo Burocrático Kafkiano: Palancas y Corrupción* [In Mexico, Life Is a Sequence of Levers. Escaping from the Kafkian Bureaucratic Monster]," in Rik Peeters and Fernando Nieto, eds., La máquina de desigualdad: Una exploración de los costos y las causas de las burocracias de baja confianza. Mexico City: CIDE, forthcoming.

Castor, Belmiro. 2002. *Brazil Is Not for Amateurs. Patterns of Governances in the Land of "Jeitinho."* Philadelphia, PA: Xlibris.

Douglas, Mary. 2002. "No Free Gifts. Foreword," in Marcel Mauss, ed., *The Gift. The Form and Reason for Exchange in Archaic Societies.* London: Routledge, 9–12.

Duarte, Fernanda. 2011. "The Strategic Role of Charm, Simpatía and Jeitinho in Brazilian Society: A Qualitative Study." *Asian Journal of Latin American Studies* 24(3), 29–48.

Goffman, Erving. 1982. *Forms of Talk.* Philadelphia: University of Pennsylvania Press.

Holmes, Leslie. 2015. *Corruption. A Very Short Introduction.* Oxford: Oxford University Press.

Ledeneva, Alena. 1998. *A Russia's Economy of Favors. Blat, Networking and Informal Exchange.* Cambridge: Cambridge University Press.

Ledeneva, Alena. 2018. *The Global Encyclopaedia of Informality.* London: UCL Press.

Liang-Hung, Lin. 2011. "Cultural and Organizational Antecedents of Guanxi: The Chinese Cases." *Journal of Business Ethics 99*, 441–51. doi: 10.1007/s10551-010-0662-3.

Lomnitz, Larissa. 1990. "Redes Informales de Intercambio en Sistemas Formales: un Modelo Teórico" (Informal Exchange Networks in Formal Systems: A Theoretical Model). *Comercio Exterior 40*(3), 212–20.

Mauss, Marcel. 2002. *The Gift: The Form and Reason for Exchange in Archaic Societies.* London: Routledge.

Maynard-Moody, Steven, and Michael Mosheno. 2003. *Cops, Teachers, Counselors. Stories from the Front Lines of Public Service.* Ann Arbor: University of Michigan Press.

Pyyhtinen, Olli. 2014. *The Gift and Its Paradoxes.* Surrey, UK: Ashgate.

Rehn, Alf, and Saara Taalas. 2004. "Znakomstva I Svyazi' (Acquaintances and Connections)—Blat, the Soviet Union, and Mundane Entrepreneurship." *Entrepreneurship and Regional Development 16*(3), 235–50. doi: 10.1080/0898562042000197108.

Rose-Ackerman, Susan. 2016. *Corruption and Government: Causes, Consequences, and Reform.* New York: Cambridge University Press.

Smith, Peter, Hai Huang, Charles Harb, and Claudio Torres. 2012. "How Distinct are Indigenous Ways of Achieving Influence? A Comparative Study of Guanxi, Wasta, Jeitinho and Pulling Strings." *Journal of Cross-Cultural Psychology 1*(43), 135–50, doi: 10.1177/0022022110381430.

Tapia, Evangelina, and Genaro Zalpa. 2011. "La Corrupción a la Luz de los Dichos y Refranes" (Corruption through popular sayings). *Relaciones 32*, 21–65.

Tapia, Evangelina, Genaro Zalpa, and Jorge Reyes. 2014. "'El Que a Buen Árbol se Arrima' Intercambio de Favores y Corrupción" (Popular sayings: Exchange of favors and corruption). *Cultura y representaciones sociales 9*, 149–76.

Torres, Claudio, Alfinito Solange, Cesar De Souza, Pinto Galvao, and Bruna Yin Tse. 2015. "Brazilian Jeitinho versus Chinese Guanxi: Investigating Their Informal Influence on International Business." *Revista de Administração Mackenzie 16*(4), 77–99.

Yan, Mayfair. 1994. *Gifts, Favors & Banquets. The Art of Social Relationships in China.* Ithaca, NY: Cornell University Press.

3

Disinformation Narratives as Evidence-Free Claims

A Socio-Rhetorical Perspective

Richard K. Ghere

In his best-selling book, *Fantasyland* (2017), columnist Kurt Andersen satirically celebrates Americans' "freedom to invent and believe whatever the hell [they] like ... as a defining right in the United States ever since the Pilgrim Fathers first landed to practice their rogue beliefs" (back cover). Specifically, Andersen presents over forty American fantasy narratives prominent in American culture from the Puritan experience to present times. However, rather than dismissing these themes, some scholars of rhetoric study fantasy narratives as a means of "understanding how people explain their experiences and persuade one another using common dramatic tools" (Stoner and Perkins 2005, 201). For rhetoricians, *fantasy* serves as a technical term to support rhetorical criticism (Bormann 2001, 3) distinct from Andersen's association of fantasy with fanciful whim.

Sociologists can study fantasy narratives, as well as other forms of expression, as a means by which social relations develop, take on hierarchical structure, and impose social (dis)order in ways that satisfy or vex a human need for social stability. In this sense, communication—or (dis)information—serves as a means of mediating shared realities of social meaning, whether or not those expressions comport with analytical argumentation (Perelman and Olbrechts-Tyteca 1969, 214–18).

This chapter approaches the problem of politically and culturally significant *information* or *disinformation* from a socio-rhetorical perspective that focuses on the functionality of communication in either maintaining or upending social order and the hierarchy of (superior, inferior, or equality of) human relationships therein. This approach is anchored in the work of sociologist Hugh Daziel Duncan (1962; 1965), who traced the sociological implications of rhetorical criticism that interprets human motives and actions in terms of dramatic forms such as tragedy, melodrama, and comedy.

A socio-rhetorical perspective cannot address the totality of politically pertinent disinformation's (contestable) interpretations, various forms, or impacts on democratic governance; few frameworks could. Nonetheless, this framework offers particular insights on relationships between communicative expression, society in terms of general or specific "audiences," and perceptions of (il)legitimate authority, social order, and hierarchal ordering (Duncan 1962, 1–2). To follow are (1) brief descriptions of three types of a communicative device recognized by rhetoricians as rhetorical fantasy (restorative, exploitive, and plaintive—so designated by the author) and (2) a conclusion that assesses the utility of a socio-rhetorical framework as a macro perspective that can generate new ideas about disinformation as a form of corruption in public arenas.

Political Narratives of Disinformation:
A Socio-Rhetorical Perspective

Some rhetoricians prefer to disqualify deceptive communication as *rhetoric*, asserting that their discipline only concerns expressions of "principles we believe in" that pursue the "realization of justice." (e.g., Eubanks and Baker 1962, 158). Nonetheless, inquiry here follows a broader conception that includes potentially deceptive arguments of propaganda and of violence as matters of rhetorical study (see Perelman and Olbrechts-Tyteca 1969, 51–59). In varying degrees, each of the three types of rhetorical fantasy introduced below could potentially propagate political narratives intended to deceive either a general or specific audience. However, the first—the restorative fantasy—comprises campaigns to promote normative aspirations (perhaps of political reform or articles of faith) which, though they rely on non-factual appeals, do not necessarily intend to deceive. As construed here, *deception* not only connotes lying but other behaviors enacted to mislead, such as "playings" (joking, bluffing, etc.), "crimes," "masks," and "misrepresentations" as deceptive practices (Hopper and Bell 1984, 298). Moreover, Hopper and Bell argue that deception relates not only to the presentation of substance but also to the roles speakers assume in conveying messages (289).

The Restorative (Rhetorical) Fantasy

In *The Force of Fantasy: Restoring the American Dream* (2001), Bormann unpacks the essential elements of the fantasy theme as a discursive form that unifies groups sharing common values and critiques of the "outside world." He asserts that "[t]he technical meaning for fantasy is the creative and imaginative interpretation of events that fulfill a psychological or rhetorical need" (2001, 5). That operational definition takes on socio-logical (as well as rhetorical) significance in relating to ideas about social order determined by communication (presumably between those of comparable status—or lack thereof) in social or political hierarchies (Duncan 1962, 278–80). Bormann continues: "Rhetorical fantasies may include fanciful and fictitious scripts of imaginary characters, but they often deal with things that have actually happened to members of the [rhetorical] community or that are reported in authenticated works of history, in the news media, or in the oral history and folklore of the group" (2001, 5).

For the most part, Bormann positions prominent fantasies throughout the American experience around the central theme of "re-purification" or restoration (2)—that in turn validates the collective identity—hence, the attention to "the restorative fantasy" here. In *The Force of Fantasy*, Bormann identifies seminal fantasies that have shaped the early American experience, from Puritan preaching themes, to anti-slavery discourses, and then to Lincoln's vision for binding a fractured nation and restoring the "American promise." In his Second Inaugural Address, Lincoln relied on faith discourses to explain his vision of reunification:

> Neither party expected for the war the magnitude or the duration which it has already attained … Both read the same Bible, and pray to the same God; and each invokes [H]is aid against the other. It must seem strange that any men (sic) sure dare to ask a just God's assistance in wringing their bread for the sweat of other men's faces; but let us judge not, that we not be judged. (quoted in Bormann 2001, 226)

Again, the moral implications stand out and take on socio/rhetorical meaning. In essence, those sharing the re-purification fantasy partake in "exalted glory" in assigning themselves as "protectors" of societal values (2001, 2).

From an ethical perspective, these fantasies can serve both as *means* (a device to promote an agenda) as well as *ends*, the realization of shared visions. For example, US presidents have relied on the fantasy archetype (Bormann 2001, 7) as a way of heralding their policy initiatives. In his article analyzing George McGovern's 1972 presidential campaign, Bormann accounts for how campaign leaders attempted to create the fantasy of a "New Politics" of morality and inclusion to distinguish the candidate from the old vision that associated the Democratic Party with labor union bosses. He writes,

> The McGovern leadership group began the rhetorical effort at the convention itself. Fantasy themes began to chain through the McGovern delegations around the theme of *pragmatism*. Invoking the ultimate legitimizer of most political party visions, that is, winning an election, a move was made by the McGovern forces to create a unifying rhetoric. (1973, 146)

In a similar vein, John Patton characterizes Jimmy Carter's discourse in his 1976 presidential campaign around the theme of a "government as good as its people" on "his conception of the people as a repository of innate moral quality, competence, and potential for the future" (1977, 250). In both of these cases, the fantasy theme of restoration stands out.

Notwithstanding the "evidence-free" (Qui 2018, A14) character of campaign discourse, presidential hopefuls (such as McGovern and Carter) who rely on the fantasy archetype to project worthy aspirations appear to do so as practitioners of "honest" politics. Nonetheless, other rhetors armed with disinformation could appropriate this visioning strategy to deceive. Lyndon Johnson's first press secretary, George Reedy, recounts how that president enlisted false information (alleging that North Vietnamese torpedo boats had attacked US Navy destroyers in 1964, before the United States entered the Vietnam conflict) to fabricate a rhetorical vision to deceive Congress (and perhaps himself):

> When he presented the text [of the Gulf of Tonkin resolution] to congressional leaders the night of the retaliation, there was no doubt that he left in their minds the unmistakable impression that it would only be used in connection with the specific incident … To use it later as a blanket justification for prosecuting the war was disingenuous, to say the least … I suspect he may have meant what he said the night that he met the congressional leaders and later rearranged the facts in his own mind to the later interpretation. He was capable of such self-deception. (Reedy 1982, 164–65)

To summarize, the restorative fantasy conveys ideational "pictures," often laced with symbolic meaning, in pursuit of a community of adherents. As such, its success need not depend on factual documentation (although it may capitalize on certain facts) so much as upon whether and how the idea resonates with peoples' identities.

The Exploitative Fantasy

If Lyndon B. Johnson's Gulf of Tonkin narrative serves as a point of departure away from evidence-free but "honest" claims to a rhetoric of exploitation, the latter offers an example of the speaker devising a deceptive narrative in order to assemble an audience to exploit. According to communications scholar Michael McGee, such a speaker awakens the "dormant seeds" of common belief in a particular culture (McGee 1975; Gunn and Treat, 2005). Skeptically, McGee argues that speakers' references to "the people" are typically justifications for their political stances or ideologies in search of a critical mass of support to legitimize their fantasy (1975, 239). He explains, " 'The people,' therefore, are not objectively real in the sense that they exist as a collective entity in nature; rather, they are a fiction dreamed by an advocate and infused with an artificial, rhetorical reality" (1975, 240).

McGee points to this quote in *Mein Kampf* to describe how a charismatic leader goes about contriving such an audience:

> By "people" I mean all these hundreds of thousands who fundamentally long for the same thing without finding the words in detail to describe the outward appearances of what is

before their inner eye ... For centuries their goal is often the inner ardent wish of hundreds of thousands, till one man stands up as the proclaimer of such a general will and as the flag-bearer of an old longing [sic] he helps it to victory in the form of a new idea. (Hitler 1939, 456–57)

In essence, McGee asserts, people are bound by a widely shared *but yet to be recognized* identity until the "proclaimer" coalesces their "longing" into a collective identity (1975, 241–42). From a socio-rhetorical perspective, Hitler's exploitative ideas of divining a mass audience speak to a hierarchical re arrangement whereby people can be (and *were*) transformed into superior "self-righteous killers" of "inferiors" (Duncan 1962, 226). Duncan goes on to suggest that (according to the logic in *Mein Kampf*) the "miserable" state of German life (after World War I) stemmed from disobeying the Creator by race-mixing. Paraphrasing *Mein Kampf*'s narrative, Duncan writes that

> [t]o induce race mixture is, therefore, to sin against the will of the Eternal Creator, as well as rebel against the "iron logic of Nature." That is why alien blood must be eliminated from German blood—for the fate of Germany is really the fate of the world ... Thus in "dealing with" and "settling" the Jewish question "once and for all" and "resisting the Jew," the German simply carries out the Divine Will and obeys the laws of nature. (1962, 226–27)

Similar rhetorical techniques intended to conjure audiences through invoking a nationalist fear of ethnic and racial "mixing" are exploited by current-day political elites. For example, Geert Wilders, a current member of the Dutch parliament, is the founder and leader of the Party for Freedom, the third largest party in the Netherlands. Wilders unleashes shrill populist messages against the "elite establishment" policies of the Dutch national government and the European Union—most notably, those encouraging multiculturalism and immigration. Among other assertions, Wilder's anti-Islamic narrative blames "elites" (presumably those public officials who do *not* engage in his rhetoric) for allowing "Islamization" to take root. Hajer and Versteeg maintain that right-wing populist voices deceptively project an authentic sense of "honesty":

> A common reaction to both politicians was that they finally dared to say what so many people had thought; the suggestion was that the tolerance and calm of the previous years had been nothing but a conspiracy of silence by the leftist media and political elite. (2009, 3)

Specifically, these policy analysts comment as follows:

> What are we to make of [Wilders's] conflict-ridden rhetoric? Is it really expressing the voice of the people, as Geert Wilders claims? The problem ... is that the people [do] not exist ... Citizens are on standby, defined to mean that they are seemingly passive but can become suddenly vocal and active when their interests seem threatened. (2009, 3)

Such anti-immigrant discourses become especially potent when articulated by incumbent heads of state to further consolidate their power. Currently in Hungary, Prime Minister Viktor Orban and his far-right nationalist party, Fidesz, endeavor to reinvent a populist, ultra-national audience, largely through invective against immigrants. As one *New York Times* reporter put it, "Billboards. TV campaigns. Radio programs. The anti-immigrant government of Prime Minister Viktor Orban uses different levers to influence public opinion, particularly on the subject of the European refugee crisis" (Kingsley 2018, A19). This account details how Orban has "assaulted the hardware and software" of Hungarian democracy; the former refers to weakening public institutions and the latter to reshaping the cultural and educational spheres. Regarding education Kingsley writes, "On [p]age 155 of the latest eighth-grade history textbook, students are told that Mr. Orban thinks refugees are a threat to Hungary—and then encouraged to believe he is right. 'It can be problematic,' the book concludes, 'for different cultures to coexist' " (2018, A19).

That same article reveals Orban's conversations with Philip Zimbardo (investigator in the Stanford Prison Experiment) during the psychologist's recent visit to Budapest. Through the account of a former Fidesz official, Kingsley suggests that Orban cared little about the Stanford experiment but wanted to understand "how to energize frustrated young men who feel left behind by modern society." The story quotes Zimbardo, "I was giving him ideas about how psychology plays a central role in our lives" (2018, 19S). Other *Times* stories discuss how the prime minister wields anti-Semitic narratives, particularly those scapegoating George Soros, a Hungarian-American Jew who survived the Nazi occupation of Budapest (Novak and Santora 2018, A5; Leonhardt 2018, A27). Orban's rhetoric appears decidedly gendered in that not one woman serves as minister in his government; the speaker of the National Assembly opined that women's role is "to give birth to as many grandchildren as possible for us" (Leonhardt 2018, A27).

Stylistically, Orban creates audiences in a more nuanced and polished manner than Hitler's method as described in *Mein Kampf*, but the intended outcomes appear similar. If the exploitative fantasy involves rhetoric that creates an audience, at some point that narrative form converges with an alternative fantasy shared by an aggrieved audience in search of a speaker—as discussed next.

The Plaintive Fantasy

Seventeenth-century Puritan preachers (i.e., speakers) eventually confronted a conundrum much like that faced by current political leaders: What happens when the rhetorical promise of restoration fails to materialize? In essence, the Puritans in New England were led to believe they would embody "the light of the world" in "the city of God" if faithful to the harsh strictures laid out by their ministers (Bercovitch 1978, 4–6; Szudrowicz-Garstka 2014); Ronald Reagan drew upon this "city of God" imagery in his 1983 presidential speech. Nonetheless, the rugged New England wilderness proved no utopia; life continued to involve bitter struggle. From a sociological perspective, failed promises can lead to a sense of alienation that threatens the hierarchical status quo (Giffin 1970).

Rhetorician Harold Mixon points out that these "light of the world" and "city on a hill" narratives stemmed from the Puritan doctrine of "the fifth monarchy" that forecasted "the inauguration of the direct rule of Christ on human affairs" (1989, 1). This doctrine, he argues, reflects an apocalyptic "language of disjunctive expectation" that speaks of an instant, cataclysmic new future; clearly, rationalists who document causality on factual evidence reject this apocalyptic mindset (Mixon 1989, 2; Kreuziger 1982, 159–73). Nonetheless in his book reviews on "religion in the public square," public ethics scholar Ralph Chandler likens some policy advocates (e.g., Sierra Club members) to those whose faith is premised on apocalyptic change. He writes, "Fundamentalists and environmentalists find themselves clasped in an unintended embrace caused by a shared apocalyptic vision of the earth's dark future. While the signs are different for end-time thinkers and eco-theorists, both groups reach the same frightening conclusion" (1999, 183).

Fortunately for the American Puritans, their plaintive disappointment in an unfulfilled prophesy, presumably because they were "too sinful" to become the "light of the world," was offset by their prodigious industry and economic success. Bormann writes, "God assured that nothing happens by chance. Mysterious as it may be, when a saint or a community fell into a time of troubles, they had offended God. On the other hand, when the elect prospered in the world, their success had great significance for their fate in the spiritual realm" (2001, 44). From a socio-rhetorical viewpoint, the Puritans' industrious ethos led to a hierarchical re-ordering in their favor. European Puritans, not having experienced socio-economic advancement and thus stuck in the old-world order, had reason to complain (Bercovitch 1978, 23).

Failure to prosper socio-economically can trigger plaintive fantasies that could skew political expectations away from rational cause-effect logic. Mixon refers to Kreuziger's distinctions between "simple expectation" (future as an extension of the present) and both (1) "modified expectation" (future will be different but no telling how—candidate X will change things for the better), and (2) "disjunctive expectation" (an apocalyptic future—candidate X will turn the establishment upside down) (Mixon 1989, 2; Kreuziger 1982, 159–73).

The plaintive fantasy reflects strong emotion as well as impatience with the status quo. In this regard, sociologist Arlie Hochschild refers to such political emotionalism as an outcome of "feeling rules" ("left ones and right ones") that reflect how *people want to feel* in reacting to political issues (2016, 15–16; italics in original). She encounters this intense emotionalism in her study of disenchanted Louisianans. Specifically, she describes a common, plaintive narrative that characterizes the "politically privileged" as line cutters, presumably some of whom have pursued identity politics with success:

> In [this] story, strangers step ahead of you in line, making you anxious, making you feel distrustful, betrayed, and afraid. A president allies with the line cutters, making you feel distrusted, betrayed. A person ahead of you in line insults you as an ignorant redneck, making you feel humiliated and mad. Economically, culturally, demographically, politically, you are suddenly a stranger in your own land. (2016, 222)

Currently, the present "Yellow Vest" movement in France engages in nationwide protests to air its economic complaints against the Macron government. Spurred on by a recent gasoline tax increase, "Yellow Vest" leaders "want more, and they want it sooner than later—lower taxes, higher salaries ... and a better life" (Nossiter 2018, A12). Reporting on these protests, Adam Nossiter refers to French geographer Christopher Guilluy's studies of "the demographics of the left-behinds, the sociology of the people in revolt."

As reported recently in the *New York Times*, similar emotionalism surfaces among East German men who welcome Angela Merkel's exit as their nation's chancellor. Katrin Bennhold reports that these men account for their far-right political affiliation in terms of Merkel's failure to care about the economic and cultural marginalization of eastern men. Bennhold quotes Petra Köpping, a female serving as minister for immigration, attesting that "[w]e have a crisis of masculinity in the East and it is feeding the far right." A middle-aged man she interviewed declared, "I didn't risk my skin back then to become a third-class citizen. First there are western Germans, then there are asylum seekers, then it's us." Another, a "former factory worker, broke down in tears when he recounted how his factory had been closed down, the brand-new machines sold to a western German company." Bennhold elaborates on the linkage between economic difficulties and cultural disruption related to a reduced ratio of women to men occurring in the past decade. Referring to that shortfall of women, the integration minister states that "[m]en don't know it's there and if you show them the numbers, they're often surprised. All they know is that they have trouble finding a partner" (2018, A8).

Conclusion

This chapter introduces a socio-rhetorical macro perspective as a means of examining significant spoken or written communication in the public arena. At its essence, this framework focuses on interactions between speakers and audiences with respect to (dis)information as well as the implications of messages conveyed for maintaining or changing the social order. The discussions above relate to three particular fantasy themes (not at the exclusion of others) that have stimulated speaker–audience interaction within Western democratic societies. In each of these cases, the audience assumes a formative role in reacting and/or committing to the ideational context of communication; in one case, the plaintive fantasy, it is in fact *the audience* that projects the substance of the idea, awaiting a champion to promote it.

The socio-rhetorical lens cautions against an arbitrary presumption that deceptive disinformation inevitably victimizes the "pure and blameless" (although it could well do so). Even in the case of the exploitative fantasy, it appears that hearers find discourses of social transcendence and re-purification—such as those of Hitler, Wilders, Orban, and other political leaders—to be appealing (see Duncan 1962, 225–37; 315–25). The perspective's attention to the audience illuminates what could be characterized as "appetite" that relates to personal and collective identity and its need for validation. Whether this notion of "appetite" is appreciably different than the economist's conception of market demand appears open for debate. On one hand, to the extent that populist anti-immigrant opinion correlates with hard socio-economic factors, such as rates of unemployment and wage stagnation (Wodak 2015, 26), these conceptions appear to merge. On the other, the rhetorician's concern about identity and self-image amid profound social change seems interwoven with more nuanced character motives that are of interest both to psychologists and dramatists (see Burke 1950; 1969).

How does a socio-rhetorical perspective inform efforts to combat the corruptive effects of deceptive disinformation in the public arena? Three recommendations are worthy of consideration. First, public and civil society institutions with a normative grounding in "the rational ideal" (or the authority of fact; see Stone 2002, 305–23) cannot expect that this ideal will necessarily prevail in the current competition of ideas. Rather, in some cases the emotionalism driving one's identity and sense of appropriateness can override rational reasoning (e.g., see Haidt 2012). Second, public institutions that typically exercise fact-making authority need to call upon the assistance of aligned civil society communities to advocate the imperative of factually based truth as a guardrail that protects Western democracies. Recently a group of lawyers from within the conservative Federalist Society, calling themselves "Checks and Balances," joined together to advocate for the rule of law and the principle of truth amid the current administration's attacks on the US Department of Justice. One of the group's members, Lori S. Meyer (married to the Federalist Society's president), was quoted as being "worried about the administration's casual attitude toward the truth: "My particular concerns [relate to] all the disinformation and spin that comes out almost every day. It makes it impossible for any real dialogue to be had" (Liptak 2018).

Third, guardians of public dialogue (e.g., public administrators and social science educators) should take care *not* to discount the effect of subjectivity connected with people's day-to-day living experiences. Rather, elites such as public-service professionals, academicians, and science-focused researchers need to cultivate aptitudes for understanding subjective experience and negotiating with people in ways that affirm their identities (see Biehl et al. 2007). Specifically, these elites must put aside their presumptions of informed deliberation to recognize public discourse as "vernacular talk" that reflects any number of lived realities, selective memories, and emotions (Hauser 1999, 103–8). Put another way, there is reason to doubt that the case for evidence-grounded truth can stand alone on its merits. Rather, that case can prevail so long as its advocates in public service and professional communities can marshal rhetorical skill on its behalf.

References

Andersen, Kurt. 2017. *Fantasyland: How America Went Haywire; A 500-Year History*. New York: Random House.

Bennhold, Katrin. 2018. "One Legacy of Merkel? Angry East German Men Fueling the Far Right." *New York Times*, November 7.

Bercovitch, Sacvan. 1978. *The American Jeremiad*. Madison: University of Wisconsin Press.

Biehl, Joao, Byron Good, and Arthur Kleinman. 2007. *Subjectivity: Ethnographic Investigations*. Berkeley: University of California Press.

Bormann, Ernest G. 1973. "The Eagleton Affair: A Fantasy Theme Analysis." *Quarterly Journal of Speech 59*(2) (April), 143–59.

Bormann, Ernest G. 2001. *The Force of Fantasy: Restoring the American Dream*. Carbondale: Southern Illinois University Press.

Burke, Kenneth. 1950. *A Rhetoric of Motives*. Berkeley: University of California Press.

Burke, Kenneth. 1965. *Permanence and Change: An Anatomy of Purpose*. 2nd ed. Indianapoli, IN: Bobbs-Merrill.

Chandler, Ralph C. 1999. "Religion in the Public Square." *Public Administration Review 59*(2) (March/April), 179–86.

Duncan, Hugh Dalziel. 1962. *Communication and Social Order*. London: Oxford University Press.

Duncan, Hugh Dalziel. 1968. *Symbols in Society*. New York: Oxford University Press.

Eubanks, Ralph T., and Virgil L. Baker. 1962. "Toward an Axiology of Rhetoric." *Quarterly Journal of Speech 48*(2) (April), 157–68.

Giffin, Kim. 1970. "Social Alienation by Communication Denial." *Quarterly Journal of Speech 56*(4) (December), 347–57.

Gunn, Joshua, and Shaun Treat. 2005. "Zombie Trouble: A Propaedeutic on Idealogical Subjectification and the Unconscious." *Quarterly Journal of Speech 91* (May), 144–74.

Haidt, Jonathan. 2012. *The Righteous Mind: Why Good People Are Divided by Politics and Religion*. New York: Vintage Books.

Hajer, Maarten, and Wytske Versteeg. 2009. *Political Rhetoric in the Netherlands:Reframing Crises in the Media*. Washington, DC: Migration Policy Institute.

Hauser, Gerard. 1999. *Vernacular Voices: The Rhetoric of Publics and Public Spheres*. Columbia: University of South Carolina Press.

Hitler, Adolph. 1939. *Mein Kampf*, trans. Alvin Johnson. New York: Reynal and Hitchcock.

Hochschild, Arlie R. 2016. *Strangers in Their Own Land: Anger and Mourning on the American Right*. New York: The New Press.

Hopper, Robert, and Robert A. Bell. 1984. "Broadening the Deception Construct." *Quarterly Journal of Speech 70*(3) (August), 288–302.

Kingsley, Patrick. 2018. "How Viktor Orban Bends Hungarian Society to His Will." *New York Times*, March 27.

Kreuziger, Frederick A. 1982. *Apocalypse and Science Fiction: A Dialectic of Religious and Secular Soteriologies*. Chico, CA: Scholars Press.

Leonhardt, David. 2018. "What We Have to Fear." *New York Times*, November 5.

Liptak, Adam. 2018. "Conservative Lawyers Say Trump Has Undermined the Rule of Law." *New York Times*, November 15.

McGee, Michael C. 1975. "In Search of 'the People': A Rhetorical Alternative." *Quarterly Journal of Speech 61*(3) (October), 235–49.

Mixon, Harold. 1989. "'A City upon a Hill': John Cotton's Apocalyptic Rhetoric and the Fifth Monarchy Movement in Puritan New England." *Journal of Communication and Religion 12*(1) (March), 1–6.

Nossiter, Adam. 2018. "How the 'Yellow Vests' in France Differ from Populist Movements Elsewhere." *New York Times*, December 6.

Novak, Benjamin, and Mark Santora. 2018. "A Democratic Institution Is Forced Out of Hungary." *New York Times*, October 26.

Patton, John H. 1977. "A Government as Good as its People: Jimmy Carter and the Restoration of Transcendence to Politics." *Quarterly Journal of Speech 63*(3) (October), 249–57.

Perelman, Chaim, and Lucie Olbrechts-Tyteca. 1969. *The New Rhetoric: A Treatise on Argumentation*. Notre Dame, IN: University of Notre Dame Press.

Qui, Linda. 2018. "Evidence-Free Claims on Caravan Members." *New York Times*, October 23.

Reedy, George. 1982. *Lyndon B. Johnson: A Memoir*. New York: Andrews and McMeel.

Stone, Deborah. 2002. *Policy Paradox: The Art of Political Decision Making*. New York: W.W. Norton and Company.

Stoner, Mark, and Sally J. Perkins. 2005. *Making Sense of Messages: A Critical Apprenticeship in Rhetorical Criticism*. Boston: Houghton Mifflin.

Szudrowicz-Garstka, Malgorzata. 2014. "Searching the Origins of Political Discourse—An Intertextual Analysis of Ronald Reagan's Farewell Speech." *Styles of Communication 6*(1), 139–48.

Wodak, Ruth. 2015. *The Politics of Fear: What Right-Wing Populist Discourses Mean*. London: Sage.

4

Nonprofit/Nongovernmental Organization Sexual Corruption
A Critical Feminist Perspective

Angela M. Eikenberry and Roseanne M. Mirabella

The purpose of this chapter is to explore the implications of #metoo and #aidtoo for understanding nonprofit/nongovernmental organization (NPO/NGO) corruption. The Me Too movement started more than a decade ago as a local grassroots effort to show support for survivors of sexual violence, particularly for young women of color from low-wealth communities, but has recently gained prominence due to the viral #MeToo hashtag (Me Too 2018). After the breaking news of Oxfam workers paying for sex in Haiti, as well as other examples of abuse coming to light at organizations such as CARE International, Save the Children, and Medecins Sans Frontieres (Bacchi 2018), women in the global aid sector promoted their own version of #MeToo, using the hashtag #AidToo, to show support for victims and bring attention to sexual harassment and abuse in the humanitarian aid sector. The news was shocking to many because NPOs/NGOs—especially humanitarian NGOs—are widely expected to protect the most vulnerable in society, including refugees and women with disabilities, yet clearly fail at times as these and other cases show.

Corruption is defined as the misuse of entrusted power for private gain, including fraud and embezzlement, misuse of assets, theft, diversion of goods and services, bribery, and abusive or coercive practice (Transparency International UK 2010; Willitts-King and Harvey 2005). The literature on corruption in NPOs/NGOs most frequently focuses on financial misconduct and largely ignores sexual abuse and other gendered forms of mistreatment (Eng et al. 2016). Further, "published literature about NPO corruption with regard to international emergency relief services is extremely scarce, because of the reluctance of international and bilateral aid agencies to discuss these issues" (Willitts-King and Harvey 2005, in Eng et al. 2016, 1,335). Drawing on critical feminist theory, this chapter discusses this neglected form of corruption, highlighting the context that enables such corruption to persist.

The rest of the chapter is organized as follows: First, an overview of how vulnerable people, especially women, have been oppressed and abused by NPOs/NGOs is provided. Next, critical feminist theory is presented to try to make sense of why this is the case. Finally, implications and recommendations for what might be done to counter such corruption is discussed.

Sexual Corruption and the Oppression of Women in NPOs/NGOs

A recent Harris poll found that approximately one in two fundraising professionals have had some sort of personal exposure to sexual harassment in the workplace, either witnessing, hearing about, or experiencing sexual harassment themselves. As the report notes,

The harassment comes in many forms, most frequently as inappropriate sexual comments or unwanted touching or contact. For those who have been harassed, it is not typically a one-time occurrence (74% have had at least two experiences and 51% have had three or more). And, there seems to be some common trends: the perpetrator is nearly always male (96%), more often than not superior to them (70%), and regularly a donor (65%). (Harris Insights and Analytics 2018, 3)

The environment of humanitarian aid agencies renders women aid workers especially vulnerable to sexual abuse and assault. A survey of humanitarian aid workers conducted by Humanitarian Women's Network (2016) found 48 percent of female humanitarian workers reported being touched in an unwanted way. Further, 55 percent reported being subjected to persistent romantic or sexual advances from a male colleague. The likelihood of sexual exploitation and assault is even greater for beneficiaries who often have little power but great need, dependent on aid workers for their very survival (House of Commons 2018; Spencer 2018). A report to the UK House of Commons International Development Committee notes that sexual exploitation and abuse by aid workers and peacekeepers has been happening in the aid sector for a long time and is endemic in many developing countries. They find that this is especially the case where there is conflict and forced displacement (House of Commons 2018, 4).

The intersectionality between disability and gender creates even greater power imbalances, marginalizing women with disabilities and making them far more likely to be sexually harassed and abused, especially in cultures where being a daughter is seen as a curse and "being a disabled daughter is a fate worse than death" (Ghai 2002, 53). Women and girls living in group settings or institutions run by nonprofits or nongovernmental organizations are particularly likely to be sexually assaulted (Drew et al. 2011; Ghai 2002; Wendell 1989; Zavirsek 2002). For example, after obtaining unpublished sex crimes data from the US Justice Department, National Public Radio (NPR) (Shapiro 2018) estimated that individuals with intellectual disabilities are *seven times* more likely to be the victims of sexual assault than are individuals without disabilities.

When sexual assault does occur, women are often counseled to not come forward and report lest the media and the donor community find out about it (Costello 2018), and they would possibly be fired from their jobs (Spencer 2018). There is no better example of this than what happened to Oxfam last year when sexual assault among its staff workers and sexual exploitation among children in Haiti were exposed (Tulay-Solanke 2018). The loss of revenue from donors resulted in significant cutbacks in the organization, including the laying off of more than a hundred workers. Dyna Mazurana (2018), a research professor at Tufts University, suggests the allegations against Oxfam staff "came to light *because* Oxfam has one of the best reporting systems in the aid industry" (para. 1). She and her colleague had previously recognized Oxfam's Safeguarding Department, established to prevent and respond to acts of sexual violence, as a best practice for the field due to its quick response to reports and encouragement of reporting from the field (Mazurana and Donnelly 2017). How is it then that the NGO with perhaps the best anti-harassment policy in the industry continues to be a haven for sexual predators?

A Critical Feminist Perspective on NPO/NGO Corruption

A critical feminist perspective on NPO/NGO corruption helps to explain in part why this type of corruption persists. Critical feminist theory focuses on issues related to gender and gender identities, highlighting the gendered structures of power in organizations and social structures. There is a variety of feminist theories, but those related to critical theory include "making the politics of sexuality central to understanding oppression" (Agger 1998, 99), connecting gender politics to the workplace and public spheres, and identifying patriarchy (and capitalism) as a source of oppression. For example, Nancy Fraser advocates a critical feminism that goes beyond defining gender justice as a project aimed at "recognizing difference" and a culture or recognition, toward (or back to) a project that also focuses on political economy, class struggle, and redistribution (Fraser 2013a); she advocates for a gender emancipation that goes hand in hand with participatory democracy and social solidarity (Fraser 2013b). Critical feminist Kimberle Crenshaw (1989) also argues that gender and class oppression are inextricably bound together with race and other forms of intersectionality.

A critical feminist perspective then can help to highlight the gendered (and racial) structures of power in NPOs/NGOs and the patriarchal and capitalist political economic environment surrounding these organizations, enabling sexual corruption to persist. More than three-quarters of employees in the nonprofit sector are women (Lanfranchi and Narcy 2015; Renock 2017); yet, despite their overrepresentation in the nonprofit workforce, women are underrepresented in leadership positions (Hallock 2002; Nozowa 2010; Sampson 2008; Teasdale et al. 2011). That is, while women hold the overwhelming majority of positions in the sector, men hold the majority of leadership positions, both as executive directors and in the boardroom. Such uneven power dynamics in the sector creates structural inequalities for women employees and beneficiaries alike, putting them at greater risk of sexual harassment and abuse (Sandoval 2018). For instance, Schuller (2016) found in an examination of humanitarian aid to Haiti that NGO committees relying on local committees for the distribution of food cards were highly gendered, with fewer than a quarter of the members of these committees made up of women. Schuller found that this often led to sexual harassment and even forced sex against female refugees struggling to feed their families (114–15). Furthermore, the Sexual Assault and Humanitarian Workers Project found that chief among the factors conducive to violence against women were male domination of power, space, and decision-making in aid agencies; a macho work environment; homophobia; and a "boys will be boys" attitude (Mazurana and Donnelly 2017, 9–10).

Such corruption persists because NPOs/NGOs are often treated as neutral (or altruistic) actors when they actually exist within a larger neoliberal, patriarchal context that oppresses women, people of color, and other marginalized groups. Neoliberal ideology undergirds antigovernment sentiment, an approach to governance that favors applying market logic to ever more forms of human endeavor and the elements that accompany it: privatization, deregulation, eliminating or ignoring "the public good" in favor of individual responsibility, and using economic calculus to measure performance and accountability (Eikenberry and Mirabella 2018). Fraser (2013b) notes how women's liberation has become more and more entangled with neoliberal efforts to build a free-market society (para. 2), which explains in part why the focus on violence against women increasingly has become a behavioral, criminal, and medical phenomenon as opposed to a social justice issue (Durazo 2007, 117). Such individualized methods of intervention fail to address the social organization of violence against women (Durazo 2007). This neoliberal, individualistic frame makes it easy to discount those who sexually abuse and exploit others as a few bad apples within a barrel of well-intentioned people, when in fact, the problem is systemic (Houldey 2018)—a result of economic inequality, colonization, other forms of state violence, and patriarchal and heterosexual norms (Kivel 2007, 143).

Implications and Recommendations for Theory and Practice

A critical feminist perspective examines organizations in a larger context and calls for considering ways to reclaim a solidarity society that addresses the conditions that lead to violence against women. Fraser (2013b) suggests three "contributions" along these lines:

First, we might break the spurious link between our critique of the family wage and flexible capitalism by militating for a form of life that de-centres waged work and valorises unwaged activities, including—but not only—carework. Second, we might disrupt the passage from our critique of economism to identity politics by integrating the struggle to transform a status order premised on masculinist cultural values with the struggle for economic justice. Finally, we might sever the bogus bond between our critique of bureaucracy and free-market fundamentalism by reclaiming the mantle of participatory democracy as a means of strengthening the public powers needed to constrain capital for the sake of justice. (para. 11)

Accountability through participatory democracy is a key aspect of Fraser's argument, which goes well beyond the bureaucratic approach to accountability frequently preferred by donors (Crack 2018a). The bureaucratic accountability agenda works within a rational model of trust that may actually do more harm than good (Keating 2017, 134). Bureaucratic accountability requires measurable outputs, but activities needed to bring about larger social and cultural change are not easily quantifiable (Crack 2018a). Log frames and logic models can exacerbate the problem with planned and measurable outcomes that belie actual events on the ground (Keating 2017). These neat reporting metrics cannot expose corruption on a wider level and thereby uphold the status quo. In fact, organizations such as Oxfam that encourage reporting and transparency, and are open about abuse, are the ones that will actually suffer in this neoliberal accountability frame; the risk associated with transparency actually undermines learning (Crack 2018b).

The bureaucratic accountability approach exhibits well the downside of the "nonprofitization" of social movements, where NPO/NGO economic structure, survival, and identity take precedence over challenging and changing social structures and norms (Durazo 2007), including changing negative and incomplete beliefs about women, the disabled, and other marginalized groups (Drew et al. 2011, 1664). Nonprofitization is why organizations often focus efforts to address or minimize sexual abuse or other misconduct by adopting symbolic policies that serve as a "legitimizing symbol in a culture of professionalization and neoliberalism" (Bromley and Orchard 2016, 364). In their work on managed morality, Bromley and Orchard (2016) posit that such policies are a useful way to show the organization is doing something but having a negligible effect on reducing corruption. Organizations go to great lengths to show they are addressing corruption and assault, when in fact these initiatives do little to change the underlying power structures that perpetuate corruption; even inhibiting real solutions to corruption and violence (Rojas Durazo 2007). Addressing sexual corruption requires shifting the narrative to addressing the conditions that lead to sexual corruption: economic inequality, colonization, and other forms of state violence and patriarchal and heterosexual norms.

Bureaucratic accountability is directed toward the ruling class and its managers—toward foundations, donors, government officials, larger nonprofits and so on—toward top-down accountability. Participatory democracy requires *bottom-up* accountability. Kivel (2007) makes several suggestions for NPO/NGO leaders in thinking about bottom-up accountability:

- Be accountable to people who are on the front lines of movements for social justice; engage in critical dialogue while recognizing we are "socialized by our culture to expect answers and not to listen to those who have less social and political power" (146).
- Get involved in community-based social justice struggles.
- Connect participants to opportunities for ongoing political involvement.
- Challenge the agenda and power of those at the top of the pyramid.
- Share power with those on the front lines of the struggle.
- Support the growth and stability of cohesive communities.

For donors, Clough (2015) suggests directing substantial philanthropic funding toward advocacy organizations that specifically work to strengthen the bottom-up accountability of the state sector toward the grassroots. This is more in line with a progressive view of social-justice philanthropy that not only gives voice to those who suffer (Nickel and Eikenberry 2009, 984) but also aims to work for structural change and to redistribute social, political, and economic power. Both challenge the premises of neoliberalism, such as individual self-interest and economic calculus, as primary guides to governance (Eikenberry and Mirabella 2018).

Specifically, in the aid sector, ChangingAid (2018), a group of feminist women working in the sector, recommend that humanitarian and development agencies should, among other things:

- Acknowledge the international development and humanitarian sectors are patriarchal and therefore systemically perpetrate and excuse violence against women and girls.
- Commit to changing norms and practices to empower women—particularly women who experience multiple forms of discrimination and oppression (including oppression based on race, ethnicity, gender identity, sexual orientation, class, etc.)—change cultural norms to change and challenge gender inequality, power differentiation based on other axis of oppression, and to promote safety for all.
- Do not discriminate against or fire women (or men) who disclose sexual harassment exploitation and abuse either perpetrated against them or others—this perpetuates a climate of fear and intimidation.
- Adequately fund sexual exploitation and abuse reporting mechanisms, training, and investigations and take all reports seriously.
- Create sexual exploitation and abuse policies. Many agencies simply do not have these in place yet. But don't stop there; policies are not an end in themselves.
- Investigate sexual exploitation and abuse appropriately, report to the police in country if it is a crime, and fire the perpetrator if proven to be guilty.
- Close all loopholes in the system—including loopholes regarding taking responsibility for contractors'/subcontractors' actions.
- Assume that white men are perpetrators of gender-based violence. Gender-based violence and gender inequality are universal, and racial hierarchies are exacerbated by inequality in pay between colleagues from the global North and global South. White men in development and humanitarian contexts are in positions of great power with limited legal or organizational oversight.
- Stop deprioritizing issues relating to women and girls. There is never a greater good, and sexual exploitation and abuse and harassment are not acceptable. It is never acceptable to knowingly continue to put women and girls at risk in order to meet indicators or deliver humanitarian assistance.
- Women count when we consider do no harm.

Finally, we must provide treatment and support for sexual assault survivors who often suffer a second assault when their allegations are met with disbelief (Ullman 2010).

Conclusion

The purpose of this chapter is to explore the implications of #MeToo and #AidToo by drawing on critical feminist theory to make sense of persistent NPO/NGO sexual corruption. We showed how pervasive sexual corruption is in the NPO/NGO—and especially aid—sector, due in large part to the gendered (and racial) structures of power in NPOs/NGOs and the patriarchal and capitalist political economic environment surrounding these organizations. To address this, NPOs/NGOs must move beyond bureaucratic accountability to donors and toward bottom-up accountability to beneficiaries and workers. NPOs/NGOs must also take on the political economy and cultural issues that cause gender and racial oppression. We provided several recommendations on how to start doing this. Believe women and change the structures that oppress them.

References

Agger, Ben. 1998. *Critical Social Theories: An Introduction*. Oxford and New York: Oxford University Press.

Bacchi, Umberto. 2018. "Exclusive: More than 120 Aid Workers Sacked, Lost Jobs over Sexual Misconduct in 2017, Survey." *Reuters*, February 21. https://www.reuters.com/article/us-britain-aid-harassment-exclusive/exclusive-more-than-120-aid-workers-sacked-lost-jobs-over-sexual-misconduct-in-2017-survey-idUSKCN1G52AE.

Bromley, Patricia, and Charlene D. Orchard. 2016. "Managed Morality: The Rise of Professional Codes of Conduct in the U.S. Nonprofit Sector." *Nonprofit and Voluntary Sector Quarterly* 45(2), 351–74. doi: 10.1177/0899764015584062.

ChangingAid. 2018. "Progress Report." Sexual Harassment, Abuse and Exploitation in the Aid Sector. https://www.changingaid.org/surveyresults.html.

Clough, Emily. 2015. "Effective Altruism's Political Blind Spot." *Boston Review*, July 14. http://bostonreview.net/world/emily-clough-effective-altruism-ngos.

Costello, Amy. 2018. "Women in the Global Aid Sector Are Saying #AidToo." *GlobalPost Investigations*, March 22. https://gpinvestigations.pri.org/women-in-the-global-aid-sector-are-saying-aidtoo-e10c42957eff.

Crack, Angela. 2018a. "Donors Shouldn't Punish NGOs That Disclose Misconduct—Here's How to Help Stamp out Abuse." *The Conversation*, February 28. http://theconversation.com/donors-shouldnt-punish-ngos-that-disclose-misconduct-heres-how-to-help-stamp-out-abuse-92476.

Crack, Angela. 2018b. "The Oxfam Scandal Has Taught Us There Is No Reward for Honest Charities." *The Guardian*, March 16, sec. Voluntary Sector Network. https://www.theguardian.com/voluntary-sector-network/2018/mar/16/government-donors-reward-honest-charities-oxfam.

Crenshaw, Kimberle. 1989. "Demarginalizing the Intersection of Race and Sex: A Black Feminist Critique of Antidiscrimination Doctrine, Feminist Theory and Antiracist Politics." *University of Chicago Legal Forum*. https://chicagounbound.uchicago.edu/uclf/vol1989/iss1/8. Accessed July 4, 2019.

Donovan, Doug. 2013. "Women Remain Rare in the Ranks of Top-Earning Nonprofit CEOs." *The Chronicle of Philanthropy*, September 22. https://www.philanthropy.com/article/Women-Remain-Rare-Among/154343.

Drew, Natalie, Michelle Funk, Stephen Tang, Jagannath Lamichhane, Elena Chávez, Sylvester Katontoka, Soumitra Pathare, Oliver Lewis, Lawrence Gostin, and Benedetto Saraceno. 2011. "Human Rights Violations of People with Mental and Psychosocial Disabilities: An Unresolved Global Crisis." *The Lancet 378*(9803), 1664–75. doi: 10.1016/S0140-6736(11)61458-X.

Durazo, Ana Clarissa Rojas. 2017. "'We Were Never Meant to Survive': Fighting Violence Against Women and the Fourth World War." In *The Revolution Will Not Be Funded: Beyond the Non-Profit Industrial Complex*, edited by Incite! Women of Color Against Violence. Cambridge, MA: South End Press, 113–28. doi: 10.1215/9780822373001-010.

Eikenberry, Angela M., and Roseanne Marie Mirabella. 2018. "Extreme Philanthropy: Philanthrocapitalism, Effective Altruism, and the Discourse of Neoliberalism." *PS: Political Science & Politics* 51(1), 43–47. doi: 10.1017/S1049096517001378.

Eng, Sharon, David H. Smith, Abdulnabi H. Al-Ekry, Eleanor L. Brilliant, Gianfranco Farruggia, Lisa Faulkner, and Benny Subianto. 2016. "Crime, Misconduct, and Dysfunctions in and by Associations," in David Horton Smith, Robert A. Stebbins, and Jurgen Grotz, eds., *The Palgrave Handbook of Volunteering, Civic Participation, and Nonprofit Associations*. London: Palgrave Macmillan, 1331–59. doi: 10.1007/978-1-137-26317-9_54.

Fraser, Nancy. 2013a. *Fortunes of Feminism: From State-Managed Capitalism to Neoliberal Crisis*. London and New York: Verso. https://www.versobooks.com/books/1173-fortunes-of-feminism.

Fraser, Nancy———. 2013b. "How Feminism Became Capitalism's Handmaiden—and How to Reclaim It" *The Guardian*, October 14, sec. Opinion. https://www.theguardian.com/commentisfree/2013/oct/14/feminism-capitalist-handmaiden-neoliberal.

Ghai, Anita. 2002. "Disabled Women: An Excluded Agenda of Indian Feminism." *Hypatia 17*(3), 49–66.

Hallock, Kevin. 2002. "The Gender Pay and Employment Gaps for Top Managers in U.S. Nonprofits." Working Paper. Cornell University, School of Industrial and Labor Relations. https://digitalcommons.ilr.cornell.edu/workingpapers/93.

Harris Insights and Analytics. 2018. "Professional Harassment Survey." Prepared for The Chronicle of Philanthropy and the Association of Fundraising Professionals. https://chronicle-assets.s3.amazonaws.com/7/items/biz/pdf/ProfessionalHarassmentSurveyResultsPDF.pdf.

Houldey, Gemma. 2018. "#AidToo—What Now and What Next?" *Life in Crisis: Research and Reflections on Stress and Burnout in Aid Work* (blog), April 20. http://gemmahouldey.com/aidtoo-what-now-and-what-next/.

House of Commons. 2018. "Sexual Exploitation and Abuse in the Aid Sector." HC 840. Eighth Report of Session 2017–19. London: International Development Committee. https://publications.parliament.uk/pa/cm201719/cmselect/cmintdev/840/840.pdf.

Humanitarian Women's Network. 2016. "Full Survey Results." https://interagencystandingcommittee.org/system/files/hwn_full_survey_results_may_2016.pdf.

Keating, Vincent Charles, and Erla Thrandardottir. 2017. "NGOs, Trust, and the Accountability Agenda." *The British Journal of Politics and International Relations* 19(1), 134–51. doi: 10.1177/1369148116682655.

Kivel, Paul. 2007. "Social Service or Social Change?" In *The Revolution Will Not Be Funded: Beyond the Non-Profit Industrial Complex*, edited by Incite! Women of Color Against Violence. Cambridge, MA: South End Press, 129–49. http://sfonline.barnard.edu/navigating-neoliberalism-in-the-academy-nonprofits-and-beyond/paul-kivel-social-service-or-social-change/.

Lanfranchi, Joseph, and Mathieu Narcy. 2015. "Female Overrepresentation in Public and Nonprofit Sector Jobs: Evidence from a French National Survey." *Nonprofit and Voluntary Sector Quarterly* 44(1), 47–74. doi: 10.1177/0899764013502579.

Mazurana, Dyan. 2018. "Is Oxfam the Worst or the Best?" *World Peace Foundation* (blog), February 20. https://sites.tufts.edu/reinventingpeace/2018/02/20/is-oxfam-the-worst-or-the-best/.

Mazurana, Dyan, and Phoebe Mazurana. 2017. "STOP the Sexual Assault Against Humanitarian and Development Aid Workers." Somerville, MA: Feinstein International Center, Tufts University. http://fic.tufts.edu/publication-item/stop-sexual-assault-against-aid-workers/.

Me Too Movement. 2018. "History & Vision." https://metoomvmt.org/about/.

Nickel, Patricia Mooney, and Angela M. Eikenberry. 2009. "A Critique of the Discourse of Marketized Philanthropy." *American Behavioral Scientist* 52(7), 974–89. doi: 10.1177/0002764208327670.

Nozawa, Jennifer T. 2010. "The Glass Ceiling of Nonprofits: A Review of Gender Inequality in US Nonprofit Organization Executives." Policy In-Depth. Salt Lake City: Center for Public Policy and Administration, University of Utah. http://gardner.utah.edu/_documents/publications/nonprofit/the-glass-ceilingof-nonprofits.pdf.

Renock, Rachel. 2017. "Sexism & Nonprofits, Dismissing a Sector Run by Women." *Medium* (blog), July 19. https://medium.com/the-nonprofit-revolution/sexism-nonprofits-dismissing-a-sector-run-by-women-dc7d71790307.

Sampson, Steven. 2010. "The Anti-Corruption Industry: From Movement to Institution." *Global Crime* 11(2): 261–78. doi: 10.1080/17440571003669258.

Sampson, Susan D., and Lynda L. Moore. 2008. "Is There a Glass Ceiling for Women in Development?" *Nonprofit Management and Leadership* 18(3), 321–39. doi: 10.1002/nml.188.

Sandoval, Timothy. 2018. "Sexual Harassment Is Widespread Problem for Fundraisers, Survey Shows." *The Chronicle of Philanthropy*, April 5. https://www.philanthropy.com/interactives/fundraiser-poll.

Schuller, Mark. 2016. *Humanitarian Aftershocks in Haiti*. New Brunswick, NJ: Rutgers University Press. https://www.jstor.org/stable/j.ctt194xh2q.

Shapiro, Joseph. n.d. "The Sexual Assault Epidemic No One Talks About." NPR.Org. https://www.npr.org/2018/01/08/570224090/the-sexual-assault-epidemic-no-one-talks-about.

Spencer, Danielle. 2018. "Cowboys and Conquering Kings." Sexual Harassment, Abuse and Exploitation in the Aid Sector. ChangingAid: From the Inside Out. https://www.changingaid.org/cowboysandkings.html.

Teasdale, Simon, Stephen McKay, Jenny Phillimore, and Nina Teasdale. 2011. "Exploring Gender and Social Entrepreneurship: Women's Leadership, Employment and Participation in the Third Sector and Social Enterprises." *Voluntary Sector Review* 2(1), 57–76. doi: 10.1332/204080511X560620.

Transparency International UK. 2010. "2010 UK Bribery Act: A Briefing for NGOs." London: Transparency International UK. https://www.mango.org.uk/pool/g-ti-bribery-act-ngo-briefing-note.pdf.

Tulay-Solanke, Naomi. 2018. "The World Is Shocked That Aid Workers Are Sexual Abusers. I'm Not." *BRIGHT Magazine*, February 15. https://brightthemag.com/liberia-oxfam-aid-humanitarian-sexual-abuse-metoo-50a82d4f443e.

Ullman, Sarah E. 2010. *Talking about Sexual Assault: Society's Response to Survivors.* Washington, DC: American Psychological Association.

Wendell, Susan. 1989. "Toward a Feminist Theory of Disability." *Hypatia* 4(2), 104–24.

Willitts-King, Barnaby, and Paul Harvey. 2005. "Managing the Risks of Corruption in Humanitarian Relief Operations: A Study for the UK Department for International Development." London: Humanitarian Policy Group, Overseas Development Institute. https://www.odi.org/publications/1333-managing-risks-corruption-humanitarian-relief-operations.

Zaviršek, Darja. 2002. "Pictures and Silences: Memories of Sexual Abuse of Disabled People." *International Journal of Social Welfare 11*(4), 270–85. doi: 10.1111/1468-2397.00237.

5

Outsourcing Corruption

Adam B. Masters

What happens when public corruption is, well, no longer public? For more than thirty years the Anglo-American nations have adapted to the tenets of new public management (NPM), and most of what it entails. Alongside the classic conceptions that NPM follows the three "E"s—efficiency, effectiveness, and economy (Rhodes 1991)—have been the concept of partnerships or co-production to deliver public services and outsourcing public services entirely to the private sector or civil society. These changes demand we reconsider precisely what public corruption entails. With the advent of contracting out the delivery of public services has come subcontracting. Today, decisions on the expenditure of public resources often rests in the hands of private actors. It therefore follows that a private actor can corrupt another private actor to the detriment of the public at large: in short, corruption, along with the delivery of public services, has been outsourced. This chapter will use some case studies to illustrate outsourced corruption to frame this phenomenon in an analytically useful way.

Outsourcing

The practice of outsourcing goes under several names—contracting out, privatization, or rebalancing state–market relations. Outsourcing, when defined as contracting out, is "formally agreeing with a third party to perform tasks or activities to perform tasks or activities that used to be carried out within an organization … For policy analysis, contracting out consists of attributing to a private actor the accomplishment of an activity until then realized by the state or by another public authority" (Joana 2007, 149). We also need to differentiate contracting out from subcontracting—an important distinction for our understanding of outsourced corruption—because private-to-private corruption may occur between the original contractor and the subcontractor.

In many ways, outsourcing reversed a trend of in-sourcing, which occurred in the later part of the nineteenth and early years of the twentieth centuries. The shift toward state control occurred in multiple fields—policing oscillated between the public and private sector for generations before the *Thames River Police Act* (1800) was passed by the British Parliament and the creation of the London Metropolitan Police in 1827 (Brewer 2014, 4–5). In social welfare Kirkman Gray observed how nineteenth-century philanthropy had a sociopolitical function, yet "private corporations could not adequately deal with difficulties which result not from personal but from public causes" and further that "a State which assists [its needy citizens] cannot refrain from exercising control" (Kirkman Gray 1908, ix). In the United States, President Franklin Roosevelt's New Deal reforms of the 1930s saw the government enter the housing market through the Federal Housing Administration (Osborne and Gaebler 1992, 280–84). The involvement of states went far deeper in other fields—including government ownership and operation of everything from railroads and infrastructure to clothing manufacture, farming, and running pubs (Hood 1997, 120). While of interest to public-administration scholars and historians, the vast majority of today's citizens in the United Kingdom have no living memory of the private sector dominating policing or welfare, while American citizens have long accepted the mixture of public and private support for housing.

The growth in public-sector outsourcing commenced in the 1970s and accelerated throughout the 1980s and 1990s. Driven in the United States and the UK by the conservative governments of Reagan and Thatcher, and in Australia by the center-left governments of Hawke and Keating, outsourcing was but one of a suite of concepts associated with NPM. Today, outsourcing has become a major instrument of policy delivery for the reasons outlined by Osborne and Gaebler (1992) more than a quarter century ago—public organizations that have contracted service providers and are not required to pay on-going, sunk-costs in relation to their own human resources, which allows for greater responsiveness in organizations whose policy fields have peaks and troughs in their workload, and the removal of public monopolies creates markets and quasi-markets where competition should lead to best value for money and cost-saving innovations.

In some cases, public administration is so corrupt that outsourcing provides a solution rather than a problem. In Guatemala, the government took the innovative approach of outsourcing its anti-corruption function to an international organization—the International Commission against Impunity in Guatemala (CICIG) (Krylova 2018). The CICIG provided key state functions—policing and prosecution—because honest state officials were too vulnerable to the deadly corrupt forces within to effectively deal with the problems. The case of the CICIG is unique, with exceptional circumstances demanding an Alexandrian solution to a modern Gordian knot.

Exceptional cases aside—in the developed world we should pause to ask whether outsourcing has gone too far. The Australian government issued contracts valued at AU$48.8 billion ($38.1 billion) (Austender 2018). The single largest contract—$2.6 billion—was to CSL Behring Ltd., which had once been the government-owned and operated Commonwealth Serum Laboratories before privatization in 1992 (CSL Behring 2018; Austender 2018). Turning to the United States, where the federal government issued $510 billion worth of contracts in FY2017 (USA Spending 2018), the problem may lean more toward the prevalence of contractors replacing federal employees for political reasons (i.e., promises of "small government") to the detriment of well-delivered public policy.

Corruption and New Public Management

Outsourcing, along with public–private partnerships (PPPs) and other NPM practices are often treated as a panacea to public corruption. This is true if we operate with the common definition of corruption—the abuse of public power for private gain (Pope 2000, 1n). Even should we turn to more refined versions of corruption, those in the adjectival form, *public* corruption (Masters 2016), or *political* corruption (Heidenheimer and Johnston 2002), these continue to frame, and thus conceptually limit, corruption as the deterioration of the ideal form of public service. When in reality public services—despite now being delivered by private or civil society actors—remain as vulnerable to corruption as when these services were managed by public officials. This becomes obvious when we ask a simple question: Why would a guard in a privatized prison be any less likely to take a bribe from a prisoner than a guard in a publicly run institution? Were we to consider the situation in terms of rational actors, we can hypothesize a chain that actually makes corruption more likely: government seeks to reduce costs; they outsource the management of prisons; a competitive tender process results in the lowest bid; the outsourced management firm hires the cheapest labor (within the terms of the contract) or otherwise seeks to minimize costs (i.e., fewer staff on the floor, thus less accountability); individual prison officers thus are more financially vulnerable to attempts at corruption. This hypothesis, while untested here—but with plenty of real-world evidence to support similar scenarios (see Goldsmith, Halsey, and de Vel-Palumbo 2018; Goldsmith, Halsey, and Groves 2016)—demonstrates a need to reflect further upon *outsourced* corruption.

Outsourcing creates corruption risks. Outsourcing through simple service contracts is one thing, but when the inherent powers of the state (i.e., defense or tax collection) are outsourced, simple contracts no longer suffice (Hood 1997, 121–22). Contractual complexity has created space in which corruption can occur. For example, a storage contract requires complex additional clauses when the stored and managed items such as tax records are products and instruments of state power.

Corruption can be outsourced in several ways. Often, a private corporation wishing to secure a government contract engages a third party to offer or manage bribes to public officials. The bribes are then hidden as line items like consultant fees within the main contract (Ware et al. 2009, 2011). This is common for transnational corporations that use agents as in-country "experts" who know their way around the system. This type of outsourced bribery/corruption provides a layer of deniability between the briber and the bribe—a fall-guy so to speak.

Another type occurs when government has outsourced service delivery and the contractor then subcontracts to a third party. When the subcontractor bribes the main contractor, the costs to the public are again hidden in line items (Ware et al. 2009, 2011). In either case, the ultimate loser is the public. The following case studies reveal some of the additional complexities that have occurred.

Case 1: Outsourcing Contract Management, Outsourced Corruption

The first is the case of an individual, William Burke, an employee of a private contractor engaged by the US military (Passas 2007, 7). Burke received payments from Thomas Spellissy in exchange for favorable treatment in defense contracts. According to the indictment against Spellissy, "Burke was employed by a private contractor and assigned to the U.S. Special Operations Command Special Operations Acquisition and Logistics Center, Management Directorate. In that capacity, William E. Burke was acting for and on behalf of the U.S. and the U.S. Department of Defense" (*U.S.A. v. Spellissy*, M.D. Fla. 2005). The charges against Spellissy and his company included two counts of bribery. This underlines the premise that corruption can be fully outsourced; despite the non-involvement of any government official in the corrupt exchanges, corruption of a public good—the efficient delivery of government services—can occur.

Case 2: Note Printing Australia and Securency—Corruption Outsourced and Overseas

Aspects of the second case are still before the courts at the time of writing. It has been a protracted legal case that involved a government and a semi-privatized agency seeking to do business with foreign governments. Note Printing Australia (NPA) is a fully owned corporatized subsidiary of the Reserve Bank of Australia (RBA), which produces currency, passports, and other secure documents on behalf of the government (Parliament of Australia 2013, 5). In turn, NPA owned 50 percent of Securency International Pty Ltd, which produced a polymer substrate (i.e., plastic "paper" with in-built security features) for Australian banknotes and other secure documents—this technology is sold to other countries. Since the foreign bribery scandal broke, the government share of Securency International was bought out by Innovia Films, the private partner. Innovia has since been acquired by CCL Industries. The Australian-developed banknote technology is now used in twenty-four countries, including Australia, New Zealand, Canada, UK, Malaysia, Vietnam, and Nigeria (CCL Secure 2017a, 2017b).

According to media reports (McKenzie 2013, 2010), officials of NPA traveled to Iraq in 1998 to set up a mint in that country, thereby breaching the UN sanctions against the Hussein regime to which Australia subscribed. Other representatives allegedly paid bribes to Malaysian officials to secure note-printing contracts (McKenzie 2010, 2013). Similar practices are alleged in Nigeria (McKenzie 2010, 2013). Police first laid charges in 2011 related to "alleged bribes paid to public officials in six countries including Indonesia, Malaysia and Vietnam" and later laid charges for foreign bribery involving Nepalese officials (Parliament of Australia 2013, 10). Both NPA and Securency pleaded guilty in 2011, and in 2012, the Securency's former chief financial officer was sentenced to six months imprisonment—suspended for two years (Parliament of Australia 2013). In total, nine individuals were charged—in instances where the matter is still before the court, suppression orders prevent further details being disclosed by official sources (Commonwealth Director of Public Prosecutions 2016; Parliament of Australia 2013). To date, seven individuals have been convicted. Most recently, a former RBA and Securency Employee pleaded guilty to paying nearly AU$80,000 to a Malaysian agent (Commonwealth Director of Public Prosecutions 2018). This complex and protracted case illustrates how corruption can be outsourced by corporations and individuals to third-party agents acting as middlemen.

Case 3: Pennsylvania Judges Outsourced Services to Facilitate Corruption

Returning to the United States, two Pennsylvania county court judges were at the heart of a case of outsourced corruption. In this instance, one of the core functions of the state was corrupted through a series of deliberate actions. Justices Michael T. Conahan and Mark A. Ciavarella Jr. arranged to enrich themselves and deprive the state and its citizens of their rights to fair service (*U.S.A. v. Conahan & Ciavarella Jr.*, M.D. Pa. 2009). According to the indictment, the scheme began in 2000, when Ciavarella introduced a lawyer, who wanted to build a private juvenile detention facility, to a contractor friend. In January 2002, after land had been acquired, Conahan signed an agreement on behalf of the county to pay $1.314 million annually in rent for the new facility. Then in December the same year, Conahan removed funding from the county's public juvenile detention center; the next month, the judges received $997,600 in concealed payments from the lawyer and contractor; then, a month later, the judges began directing juveniles to the new facility (*U.S.A. v. Conahan & Ciavarella Jr.*, M.D. Pa. 2009).

Yet this was not the end of the matter. Ciavarella often ordered accused juvenile offenders to be detained, despite contrary recommendations from juvenile probation officers. Ciavarella and others acting at his direction pressured staff of another court to recommend that juveniles be detained. Furthermore, probation officers were pressured to change their recommendations from release to detention. Procedures adopted by Ciavarella in the juvenile court included a "specialty court" that potentially increased the number of juvenile offenders incarcerated in the private juvenile facilities (*U.S.A. v. Conahan & Ciavarella Jr.*, M.D. Pa. 2009). Juveniles incarcerated for minor offences—such as creating a webpage that mocked a vice-principal, trespassing, or for a minor shoplifting offense—could sometimes be remanded in custody for months before their cases were heard and then, more often than not, dismissed (Ecenbarger 2012). The success of the scheme led to a second facility being built and further corrupt payments to the judges. In total, they received over $2.6 million for their part. The pair were prosecuted, convicted, and jailed on racketeering, honest services mail fraud, money laundering, extortion, bribery, tax violations, and conspiracy charges. Conahan pleaded guilty and received a seventeen-year sentence, Ciavarella was found guilty by a jury and received twenty-eight years. Further, Pennsylvania's Supreme Court had to vacate thousands of juvenile convictions (Department of Justice 2013, 2009). In essence, these judges were instrumental in the creation of an outsourcing opportunity to create an ongoing corrupt revenue stream.

Case 4: Roads in Afghanistan—State Support for Outsourced Corruption

One of the great difficulties with corruption research is the persistent myth that corruption greases the wheels for economic development. Although the days when scholars argued the case for corruption was now gone (see Nye 1967; Huntington 1968; Leff 1964; Scott 1972), and recent literature provides strong counter-arguments (Fisman and Golden 2017), practice in the field often reverts to corruption in the name of expediency. The case of transport contracting for the US Department of Defense highlights just such a problem.

Road construction is exceedingly vulnerable to corruption. Studies by the World Bank (Messick 2011) and others (Olken 2007; Anechiarico and Jacobs 1996) demonstrate the vulnerability spanning from the bidding process to final construction. Yet the trade-offs can appear important. According to Kilcullen, road construction in Afghanistan led to increased economic activity and better security—simply put, it is hard to hide a roadside bomb in a paved road. The network also enables security forces to respond to remote regions much more rapidly. For example, the trip from Jalalabad to Asadabad once took five and a half hours, but paved roads reduced the journey to less than two hours (Kilcullen 2011). However, corruption did not end with the construction of the roads. Now that a network of supply roads is in place, corruption has shifted from road construction to road use.

In 2010, a report to Congress outlined a perverse situation involving outsourced corruption. In effect, the Pentagon was indirectly paying the Afghan warlords to enable US and allied troops in the field to receive supplies to fight the very same warlords (Tierney 2010). As Afghanistan is a landlocked country, bulk supplies must be trucked in from ports in Pakistan. The US military long ago passed the point where it could go to war without the support of private enterprise—essentially the fruition of Eisenhower's warning about the "military–industrial complex." The Pentagon therefore needs to engage host nation trucking contractors to ensure supply lines to troops in the field. These contractors then subcontract out for the provision of private security to ensure the supplies get through. The report to Congress made seven key findings:

1. **Security for the US Supply Chain Is Principally Provided by Warlords.** The principal private security subcontractors on the HNT contract are warlords, strongmen, commanders, and militia leaders who compete with the Afghan central government for power and authority. Providing "protection" services for the US supply chain empowers these warlords with money, legitimacy, and a *raison d'etre* for their private armies. Although many of these warlords nominally operate under private security companies licensed by the Afghan Ministry of Interior, they thrive in a vacuum of government authority and their interests are in fundamental conflict with US aims to build a strong Afghan government.

2. **The Highway Warlords Run a Protection Racket.** The HNT contractors and their trucking subcontractors in Afghanistan pay tens of millions of dollars annually to local warlords across Afghanistan in exchange for "protection" for HNT supply convoys to support US troops. Although the warlords do provide guards and coordinate security, the contractors have little choice but to use them in what amounts to a vast protection racket. The consequences are clear: trucking companies that pay the highway warlords for security are provided protection; trucking companies that do not pay believe they are more likely to find themselves under attack. As a result, almost everyone pays. In interviews and documents, the HNT contractors frequently referred to such payments as "extortion," "bribes," "special security," and/or "protection payments."

3. **Protection Payments for Safe Passage Are a Significant Potential Source of Funding for the Taliban.** Within the HNT contractor community, many believe that the highway warlords who provide security in turn make protection payments to insurgents to coordinate safe passage. This belief is evidenced in numerous documents, incident reports, and e-mails that refer to attempts at Taliban extortion along the road. The subcommittee staff has not uncovered any direct evidence of such payments, and a number of witnesses, including Ahmed Wali Karzai, all adamantly deny that any convoy security commanders pay insurgents. According to experts and public reporting, however, the Taliban regularly extort rents from a variety of licit and illicit industries, and it is plausible that the Taliban would try to extort protection payments from the coalition supply chain that runs through territory in which they freely operate.

4. **Unaccountable Supply Chain Security Contractors Fuel Corruption.** HNT contractors and their private security providers report widespread corruption by Afghan officials and frequent government extortion along the road. The largest private security provider for HNT trucks complained that it had to pay $1,000 to $10,000 in monthly bribes to nearly every Afghan governor, police chief, and local military unit whose territory the company passed. HNT contractors themselves reported similar corruption at a smaller scale, including significant numbers of Afghan National Police checkpoints. US military officials confirmed that they were aware of these problems.

5. **Unaccountable Supply Chain Security Contractors Undermine US Counterinsurgency Strategy.** While outsourcing principal responsibility for the supply chain in Afghanistan to local truckers and unknown security commanders has allowed the Department of Defense to devote a greater percentage of its force structure to priority operations, these logistics arrangements have significant unintended consequences for the overall counterinsurgency strategy. By fueling government corruption and funding parallel power structures, these logistics arrangements undercut efforts to establish popular confidence in a credible and sustainable Afghan government.

6. **The Department of Defense Lacks Effective Oversight of Its Supply Chain and Private Security Contractors in Afghanistan.** The Department of Defense has little to no visibility into what happens to the trucks carrying US supplies between the time they leave the gate and the time they arrive at their destination. Despite serious concerns regarding operations, no military managers have ever observed truck operations on the road or met with key security providers. The Department of Defense's regulations, promulgated in response to direction by Congress, require oversight of all private security companies working as contractors or subcontractors for the US government. These requirements include ensuring that all private security company personnel comply with US government and local country firearm laws, that all private security company equipment be tracked, and that all incidents of death, injury, or property damage be fully investigated. The Department of Defense is grossly out of compliance with applicable regulations and has no visibility into the operations of the private security companies that are subcontractors on the HNT contract.

7. **HNT Contractors Warned the Department of Defense about Protection Payments for Safe Passage to No Avail.** In meetings, interviews, e-mails, white papers, and PowerPoint presentations, many HNT prime contractors self-reported to military officials and criminal investigators that they were being forced to make "protection payments for safe passage" on the road. While military officials acknowledged receiving the warnings, these concerns were never appropriately addressed.

These problems paint a grim picture. While tackling this type of corruption in a conflict zone presents challenges, facing these challenges is critical for government credibility and the credibility of the system of outsourcing.

Modeling Outsourced Corruption

From the above case studies, three clear models of outsourced corruption can be extrapolated. The Spellissy case provides the first model, whereby *the power of the state is outsourced, and then abused by a private party entrusted with that power.* A second model sees a powerful figure—usually an oligarchic or autocrat—use *outsourcing as a form of patronage* to ensure enrichment to the powerful through kickbacks. Hood described this as contracting out in the amoral contract state (Hood 1997, 128). Conahan and Ciavarella exemplify this model, with the unusual twist that their case occurred in the United States. The third model involves *agents deliberately engaged by government to act in a corrupt manner on the state's behalf.* The trucking contracts in Afghanistan demonstrated this, particularly as the contractors warned the Pentagon of what was required on the ground to safely move supplies through hostile territory. Of course, these models are not mutually exclusive. The NPA/Securency case demonstrates how power was outsourced then abused, agents were hired to act corruptly on behalf of the state, and on the receiving end figures acting for state patrons lined their own pockets.

The risk of corruption will always be associated with outsourcing. The three models all point toward the darker side of contracting out government functions, but it should not be interpreted as a conclusion that "all outsourcing is evil." The success of CSL has created beneficial outcomes on a global scale, and Guatemala has seen great success from outsourcing anti-corruption functions. In the end, outsourcing needs to be a carefully considered strategy, with firm accountability mechanisms built into all processes. While it would be impossible to eliminate outsourced corruption, it can certainly be minimized and mitigated.

References

Anechiarico, Frank, and James B. Jacobs. 1996. *The Pursuit of Absolute Integrity: How Corruption Control Makes Government Ineffective.* Chicago, IL: University of Chicago Press.

Austender. 2018. *Contract Notices.* Canberra: Australian Government.

Brewer, Russell. 2014. *Policing the Waterfront: Networks, Partnerships and the Governance of Port Security, Clarendon Studies in Criminology.* Oxford: Oxford University Press.

CCL Secure. 2017a. "Countries around the World Using Guardian Polymer Banknotes." https://www.cclsecure.com//uploads/img/21082017%20Update%20of%20Banknote%20Map.jpg. Accessed September 24, 2018.

CCL Secure. 2017b. "History." https://cclsecure.com/history/. Accessed September 24.

Commonwealth Director of Public Prosecutions. 2016. *Annual Report 2015–16.* Canberra: Commonwealth Director of Public Prosecutions.

Commonwealth Director of Public Prosecutions. 2018. "Former RBA and Securency Employee Sentenced." Canberra: Commonwealth Director of Public Prosecutions.

CSL Behring. 2018. "Our Story." https://www.csl.com/our-company/our-story. Accessed October 6, 2018.

Department of Justice. 2013. "U.S. Court of Appeals Upholds Ciavarella's Conviction and Sentence." Washington, DC: United States Attorney's Office, Middle District of Pennsylvania.

Ecenbarger, William. 2012. *Kids for Cash: Two Judges, Thousands of Children and a $2.8 Million Kickback Scheme.* New York: The New Press.

Fisman, Ray, and Miriam A. Golden. 2017. *Corruption: What Everyone Needs to Know.* New York: Oxford University Press.

Goldsmith, Andrew, Mark Halsey, and Melissa de Vel-Palumbo. 2018. "Literature Review: Correctional Corruption," edited by Queensland Correctional Services. Adelaide: Flinders University Centre for Crime Policy and Research.

Goldsmith, Andrew, Mark Halsey, and Andrew Groves. 2016. *Tackling Correctional Corruption: An Integrity Promoting Approach,* edited by Martin Gill, Crime Prevention and Security Management. London: Springer.

Heidenheimer, Arnold J., and Michael Johnston, eds. 2002. *Political Corruption: Concepts and Contexts*. 3rd ed. New Brunswick. NJ: Transaction Publishers.

Hood, Christopher. 1997. "Which Contract State? Four Perspectives on Over-Outsourcing for Public Services." *Australian Journal of Public Administration* 56(3), 120–31.

Huntington, Samuel P. 1968. *Political Order in Changing Societies*. New Haven, CT: Yale University Press.

Joana, Jean. 2007. "Contracting Out," in Mark Bevir, ed., *Encyclopaedia of Governance*. Thousand Oaks, CA: Sage.

Kilcullen, David. 2011. *The Accidental Guerrilla: Fighting Small Wars in the Midst of a Big One*. Oxford: Oxford University Press.

Kirkman Gray, Benjamin. 1908. *Philanthropy and the State or Social Politics*, edited by Eleanor Kirkman Gray and B. L. Hutchins. Westminster: PS King & Son.

Krylova, Yulia. 2018. "Outsourcing the Fight against Corruption: Lessons from the International Commission against Impunity in Guatemala." *Global Policy* 9(1), 95–101. doi: 10.1111/1758–5899.12518.

Leff, Nathaniel H. 1964. "Economic Development through Bureaucratic Corruption." *American Behavioral Scientist* 8(2), 8–14.

Masters, Adam. 2016. "Public Corruption," in Carole Jurkiewicz, ed.,*Global Encyclopaedia of Public Administration and Public Policy*. Cham: Springer.

McKenzie, Nick. 2010. "Dirty Money." In *Four Corners*. Australia: Australian Broadcasting Corporation.

McKenzie, Nick. 2013. "Cover Up." In *Four Corners*. Australia: Australian Broadcasting Corporation.

Messick, Richard. 2011. *Curbing Fraud, Corruption and Collusion in the Roads Sector*. Washington, DC: World Bank.

Nye, Joseph S. 1967. "Corruption and Political Development: A Cost Benefit Analysis." *American Political Science Review* 61(2), 417–27.

Olken, Benjamin A. 2007. "Monitoring Corruption: Evidence from a Field Experiment in Indonesia." *Journal of Political Economy 115*(2), 200–49.

Osborne, David, and Ted Gaebler. 1992. *Reinventing Government: How the Entrepreneurial Spirit is Transforming the Public Sector*. Reading: Addison-Wesley.

Parliament of Australia. 2013. *Integrity of Overseas Commonwealth Law Enforcement Operations*. Canberra: Parliamentary Joint Committee on the Australian Commission for Law Enforcement Integrity.

Passas, Nikos. 2007. "Corruption in the Procurement Process/Outsourcing Government Functions: Issues, Case Studies, Implications." Boston: Institute for Fraud Prevention.

Pope, Jeremy. 2000. *The Transparency International Source Book*. Berlin: Transparency International.

Rhodes, R. A. W. 1991. "Introduction." *Public Administration* 69(1), 1–2.

Scott, James C. 1972. *Comparative Political Corruption*. Englewood Cliffs, NJ: Prentice Hall.

Tierney, John F. 2010. *Warlord, Inc.: Extortion and Corruption Along the U.S. Supply Chain in Afghanistan*, edited by U.S. House of Representatives. Washington, DC: Congress of the United States.

United States of America v. Thomas F. Spellissy and Strategic Defense International, Inc. (M.D. Fla. 2005).

United States of America v. Michael T. Conahan and Mark A. Ciavarella Jr. (M.D. Pa. 2009).

USA Spending. 2018. *Contracts over Time*. Washington, DC.

Ware, Glenn T., Shaun Moss, J. Edgardo Campos, and Gregory P. Noone. 2009. "Red Flags That Indicate Corruption in Public Procurement." ABS/CBN News. http://www.abs-cbnnews.com/research/02/13/09/red-flags-indicate-corruption-public-procurement. Accessed January 25, 2013.

Ware, Glenn T., Shaun Moss, J. Edgardo Campos, and Gregory P. Noone. 2011. "Corruption in Procurement," in Adam Graycar and Russell G. Smith, eds., *Handbook of Global Research and Practice in Corruption*. Cheltenham: Edward Elgar, 65–121.

6

Corruption in Mexico
New Solutions to Old Problems?
Miguel A. Valverde Loya

A Persistent Problem

Corruption in Mexico used to be related to the authoritarian regime that prevailed for decades, with clientelistic and patrimonial structures that distributed resources in order to maintain political power and headed by a powerful presidency. Corruption was perceived as a way of helping to sustain political stability and economic development, which had become a source of legitimacy for the regime. There was a disposition to benefit and assimilate political adversaries and competitors and favor regime allies through political favors, government jobs, or public-works contracts, all handed out by centralized bureaucratic arrangements under control of the president.

The absence of a civil service meant that the survival and progress of public officials' careers depended on their belonging to a political group, or *camarilla*, and its positioning within the ruling elite, and lack of job security was an important incentive for corruption. With no effective surveillance or division of powers, discretional use of information and resources was the norm. While part of the private sector benefited from close ties to public authority, with hefty contracts awarded with no contesters, another segment put up with corruption and had to consider it part of its normal operating costs. Many citizens suffered from corruption, but most dealt with it as a part of daily life or the usual functioning of authorities.

A widely used definition of corruption states that it's the use (or abuse) of public power for private gains. Public resources and information are used discretionally by individuals in positions of authority to obtain a joint benefit with counterparts in the private sector, to the detriment of third parties (competitors or citizens in general). Usually, three types are differentiated: deviating resources for one's own profit, family members, friends, or partners; the intentional distortion of norms and proceedings and their implementation to provide undue advantage; and unlawful actions of private groups to influence the legislative or public-policy process, seeking their own benefit above the general interest or welfare (World Bank 2000).

Corruption is considered a barrier for investment, both local and foreign, since its related costs increase company operations expenses and limit expectations on profits and growth. The mere perception of corruption distorts information flows, critical for investor's decisions.[1] It is also an obstacle for competitiveness, as companies apparently obtain advantages in the short term, but in the long term it reduces incentives for increasing innovation and productivity (Treisman 2007). This affects the economic development of a country, by diminishing its investment, entrepreneurship, and employment, as well as market dynamism (Mauro 1995; Bardhan 1997). The state ceases to receive means that could be used to foster productive infrastructure, and corruption also has an impact on equality, since less available resources could limit the reach of social programs or imperil education or health systems. Corruption could cause tax increases and alter expense priorities toward where there are more chances of improper or illegal benefits (Schleifer and Vishny 1993;

Liu and Mikesell 2014). Furthermore, corruption expenses are considered a sort of tax paid by citizens, since they are usually transferred to the final cost of products or services.

Corruption has also been described as a cultural phenomenon, part of the widespread beliefs and attitudes and accepted by a society. This could lead to justifying its existence, denying or diminishing its implications and gravity. Even as it is possible to identify some cultural dimensions of the problem, it is primarily related to institutional weakness, impunity and failure of the rule of law, and excessive or inadequate regulations, as well as economic incentives (De Graaf 2007). A survey found that the number of Mexicans who believe corruption is a cultural phenomenon has gone down from 45 percent in 2004 to 39 percent in 2015. Most considered it the country's major problem, ahead of unemployment or insecurity. However, 59 percent thought that it was possible to eradicate it (Moreno and León, 2015). This could signal an important change in perception, since corruption is no longer considered an endemic feature of Mexican society, or one that could take generations to change. Thus, transformation of rules and institutions, with appropriate incentives and effective enforcement, could make a difference.

Institutional Framework

The first Mexican federal constitution of 1824 created an office within the finance ministry with the task of supervising the use of public resources, and a federal law that same year created the Contaduría Mayor de Hacienda (Accountancy Office), an organism under Congress's authority and in charge of surveillance of public expenditures by the executive. Having as a reference the new constitution of 1917, later that year a law on federal public administration organization established a specialized technical agency, the Departamento de la Contraloría General de la Nación (Department of General Comptrollership), under direct command of the president (Guerrero 1985).

Since Mexico had a strong, centralized, and bureaucratized state, with historical preeminence of the executive power, it seemed reasonable to create within it a control mechanism that eventually displaced and took over functions originally granted to the legislature by the same constitution. It was considered part of the development of Mexican presidentialism and a realistic adaptation to the circumstances of the country, as well as a counterweight to the powerful finance ministry during the early stages of the regime. From the 1930s, the presidency gradually achieved control of national politics through a hegemonic political party, PNR, Partido Nacional Revolucionario (National Revolutionary Party), transformed into PRM, Partido de la Revolución Mexicana(Mexican Revolution Party), and later into PRI, Partido Revolucionario Institucional (Revolutionary Institutional Party).

The new department of controllership had a "major moral end" in charge of investigating the "use or misuse" of public resources by officials and to sanction any violations. Nevertheless, it had an essentially preventive approach (Guerrero 1985, 222; Vázquez Alfaro 1996, 136–39). In 1926, a new law increased the power of the now-named Departamento de la Contraloría de la Federación (Department of the Federal Comptrollership), with control over national accounts, spending and the public debt, a registry of public employees, and the first measures to implement a civil service. Political confrontation with the finance ministry, however, led to the department's disappearance in 1932, and the former took over most of its functions. In 1935, an office was created within the same ministry with the specific task of establishing administrative measures to identify and penalize illegal activities by government personnel.

In February 1940, a new law on public officials' and employees' responsibilities was issued (Ley de Responsabilidades de los Funcionarios y Empleados de la Federación, del Distrito y Territorios Federales y de los Altos Funcionarios del Estado), making them subject to prosecution for felonies and administrative offenses committed while in office or under employment. These felonies and offenses included attacks on democratic and republican institutions, usurpation of functions, violation of individual rights, or transgression of any law that caused severe damage to the country. Sanctions included removal from office and partial or total inability to work in the public sector, decided by a federal judge. For the first time, all public officials were obliged to present a "public disclosure of property," at the beginning and end of their appointments (Secretaría de la Contraloría General de la Federación 1988, 38–40).

By the mid-1970s, a renewal of the legal framework concerning government structure and functions, as well as a modernization strategy, were badly needed. During the presidency of José López Portillo (1976–1982) an administrative reform program was introduced. It included a law that reorganized public administration (Ley Orgánica de la Administración Pública Federal, 1976) and in 1980 a new law on public officials and employee responsibilities, which now included members of Congress and supreme court justices. The felony of "unexplained wealth" was instituted and would be severely punished, extending to spouses and descendants, with investigations on investments, both in Mexico and abroad (Pardo 2009, 145–56; Secretaría de la Contraloría General de la Federación 1988, 39–40). Despite these changes, corruption was widespread, and accusations were made against senior officials and even the president.

As an effort to improve the fight against corruption and increase confidence in governmental institutions, President Miguel de la Madrid (1982–88) created in 1982 the Ministry of General Federal Comptrollership (Secretaría de la Contraloría General de la Federación). Corruption had ceased to be merely "functional" to the regime and now seriously menaced its legitimacy. It was also now described as a heavy cost for the economy and business activity. The new ministry was to implement a "moral renovation of society" program, with the rejection and effective reaction against corrupt practices in both public and private sectors. It was justified in terms of internal control of the bureaucracy by the executive, as opposed to the constitutionally mandated external control by the existing Accountancy Office (Contaduría Mayor de Hacienda), dependent on Congress.

De la Madrid also issued a new law on public officials' responsibilities in 1982, now including mechanisms for public complaints and denouncing corruption, policies on receiving gifts, and conflicts of interest (Secretaría de la Contraloría General de la Federación 1988, 45–57). The new ministry accused, and was successful in sending to jail, the former director of PEMEX, the powerful state-owned oil company, and the chief of police in Mexico City, both high-profile affairs. Nevertheless, in most cases such action resulted only in minor administrative sanctions (Pardo 1990, 780–82). As time went by, the "moral reformation" lost momentum, becoming just one more regular governmental proceeding.

In 1989, during the government of Carlos Salinas (1988–1994), a Social Comptrollership (Contraloría Social) was created to favor public participation in the surveillance and control in the use of public resources and to have "social auditing" in place (Aguilar Villanueva 1996, quoted by Cadena 2005, 228). Complaints, observations, and denunciations were channeled through a national complaint system, and a considerable number of administrative and penal sanctions were imposed using this tool. More attention and stricter measures were applied to the disclosure of wealth and property of officials involved in critical areas, such as public works contracting and procurement.

Nevertheless, these measures were not enough to diminish corruption, in part due to the difficulties in arming a timely investigation, and the lack of capacity by authorities to integrate legal files and follow formal procedures (Cadena 2005, 228–29). At the beginning of the Salinas administration, powerful union leaders (oil workers and teachers), as well as a prominent investor, were prosecuted. But these were considered politically legitimating measures, as well as a neutralization of adversaries, more than part of the fight against corruption.

President Zedillo (1994–2000) strengthened the comptrollership ministry and provided it with the power to name and remove the comptroller of every government dependency or unit, allowing it to improve the prevention, control, and sanction of corrupt practices. The public denouncing system continued, with an increase in the number of cases indicted, although still limited. Due to anomalies during privatization operations in the previous administration, clear rules were given to assure the legality of such proceedings (Secretaría de la Contraloría y Desarrollo Administrativo 1996, 80, quoted by Cadena 2005, 250). An innovative electronic platform system to make more transparent public goods and services contracting and procurement (Compranet) was implemented, the public officials' declaration of property was available online (Declaranet), making it easier to comply with it. Important efforts were made to reduce bureaucratic procedures and red tape, trying to eliminate potential opportunities for corruption (Cadena 2005, 253, 256–57). Nevertheless, despite these measures, the problem persisted as a major challenge for the Mexican public administration

In the year 2000, the opposition won the presidential election, generating great expectations for the fight on corruption. President Vicente Fox (2000–2006) from Partido Acción Nacional (PAN, National Action Party) issued a civil-service law seeking to curb the regime's spoils system and create a merit-based professional foundation. In 2002, a transparency and public-information access law, along with the creation of a federal institute to enforce it, attempted to end the discretional use of information by public officials that fostered corruption. A new law on public officials' responsibilities included numerous felonies and misdemeanors, but they were not considered serious offenses, so officials accused of corruption could go free on bail and not go to prison.

Once again, emphasis was placed on inhibition and prevention (Pardo 2009, 398–405). On the other hand, prosecution depended on the Attorney General's Office (Procuraduría General de la República), and not the comptrollership, now called Ministry of Public Function (Secretaría de la Función Pública), which meant issues of miscommunication, miscoordination, and delays. A considerable number of investigations were initiated, but there was no adequate follow-up. Only a few sanctions were imposed, and no major public figure or "big fish" was indicted. Only minimal variations were registered in Mexico's relative position in Transparency International's perception of corruption index (Transparencia Internacional 2007).

President Felipe Calderón (2006–2012, also from PAN) reformed the constitution to increase the national reach of transparency policies and issued a national program on accountability, transparency, and the fight against corruption, although it included mostly preventive measures. For economic and political reasons, Calderón proposed the elimination of the Ministry of Public Function and the creation of a comptrollership unit in the office of the president (where it had been a few decades earlier) to concentrate efforts in the fight against corruption, but that would only impose admonitions or temporal or definitive suspensions, with prosecution still in the hands of the attorney general (Carrillo 2011, 184–87). Nevertheless, strong opposition in Congress did not allow these changes to take place, as happened with many other presidential initiatives. Once again, there were no significant advancements regarding corruption, with no improvement in the country's rank in corruption indices (Transparencia Internacional 2012), and with no major investigations undertaken or high-level officers indicted, falling short of social demands and expectations.

Corruption Data

The information on sanctions imposed on public officials in Mexico related to acts of corruption is scarce and segmented, without sufficiently uniform criteria and difficult to process. The option is to use information included in some incomplete official reports or provided by media briefings from government sources, making it difficult to follow up or compare. A notable exception is a 1988 report that includes systematic information on sanctions during the 1982–1988 presidential period, divided between those imposed by the Ministry of the Federal Comptrollership and those applied by internal comptrollerships of other dependencies, and classified by type (warning, admonition, suspension, financial penalty, dismissal, and disablement). A total of 3,793 sanctions were imposed during the period, and seventy-four officials were subject to criminal prosecution (Secretaría de la Contraloría General de la Federación 1988).

Nevertheless, typical sources are a 2001–2003 report from the Ministry of Public Function that mentions 2,360 "verification of procedures" and 76 "special operations" that resulted in 87 "administrative proceedings" against forty-seven public officials. In 2004, four thousand "improvement actions" were reported with impact on 940 "possibly irregular conducts" (Pardo 2009, 328–29). According to the Secretary of Public Function at the time, during the 2006–2012 presidential period 50,829 administrative sanctions were imposed, of which 9,528 (18.7 percent) were "harsh," involving dismissal and disablement. There were also 4,734 financial penalties, of which 608 were upon high-level officials (Reforma 2013). In May 2015, as a response to a crisis generated by media stories on conflict of interest in buying a house by President Peña Nieto's spouse, a resurgent (after being nearly eliminated) Ministry of Public Function presented a report to the Senate indicating that, between 2006 and 2014, 76,846 public officials had been penalized, and financial penalties for more than thirty-two billion pesos had been imposed (Guerrero 2015).

Lack of coordination with federal auditing authorities and the revenue service mean that only few financial assets resulting from corruption have been recovered (Milenio Datalab 2015). As corruption crimes were not considered serious offenses, accused officials can be free on bail and not go to jail. Formal prosecution can only be done by the Attorney General's Office, often in the absence of communication or coordination with the ministry. Even as an increase in the number of sanctions could be interpreted as an improvement in efficiency, it also shows how limited preventive efforts have been, and the difficulties for constructing successful cases for prosecution and public resources restitution.

Recent Developments

In 2012 the PRI won back the presidency, and the elected president, Enrique Peña Nieto, proposed the creation of a national anti-corruption commission,[2] which would continue the work of the still-existing Secretary of Public Function. Along with it, the new National Council for Public Ethics, headed by the president, would coordinate actions to strengthen ethical behavior in society. The proposal was criticized by the opposition political parties, academia, civil society, and professional organizations, which pointed out that the commission had insufficient supervision tools to effectively identify and penalize corruption. It was also dependent on the executive, who would propose its members, although they could be vetoed by the Senate. A proposal was made instead for creating an interinstitutional coordinating system, articulating efforts along with civil society. Nevertheless, no changes took place during Peña Nieto's first two years in office.

In late 2014, the disclosure of a residence acquired by the president's spouse (called in journalistic accounts the *casa blanca*, or white house) from a government contractor on very favorable terms, as well as a house bought by the finance minister from the same contractor, fostered controversy and a public opinion debate on the issues of influence-trafficking and corruption. Soon thereafter, telephone call recordings between officials and highway contractors suggesting bribery schemes were made public, and the bidding for building the Mexico-Queretaro train was canceled, after accusations of lack of transparency during the process were made.

In February 2015, Peña Nieto tried to rescue the Ministry of Public Functioning from disappearance, as a response to the crisis. He appointed a minister and gave him instructions to investigate possible misbehavior in the affair. But the minister was criticized for being close to both the president and the finance minister, a subordinate to the executive with no real autonomy. It was interpreted as a poor media strategy for damage control. The ministry concluded that no conflict of interests or wrongdoing by the president or the finance minister were to be found, since they did not have legal authority for participating directly in contract assignments, and they were not yet in office when the actual selling of the casa blanca took place. This strictly legal interpretation was not considered satisfactory for most critics.

As a result, civil society organizations sought wider and more profound anti-corruption measures.[3] Their activism and the proximity of legislative elections in mid-2015 in several Mexican states, caused the government to concede and accept important changes. The result was the creation of the National Transparency System (NTS, Sistema Nacional de Transparencia) and the National Anticorruption System (NAS, Sistema Nacional Anticorrupción), which went into effect in May 2015. The first one dealt with coordination and homologation of federal and local governments regarding transparency laws and policies, including the creation of consultant councils with citizen participation in local transparency agencies. All entities that spend public resources or exercise public authority must now comply. The NAS emerged from an intense debate that involved government officials, congress members, academics, and civil-society organizations. It contemplated the creation of a committee in charge of coordinating all authorities at all levels that prevent, investigate, and sanction corruption practices.

The Coordination Committee (Comité Coordinador)[4] included a Citizen Participation Committee, conformed with "distinguished Mexicans" who would look after society's interests. The NAS seeks an integrated strategy, making society co-responsible for confronting corruption, where private individuals and companies can also be sanctioned. In addition to the assets declaration of public officials, a declaration of interests was required for identifying and preventing any potential conflict. It creates the new Federal Tribunal of Administrative Justice, independent from the executive, able to impose penalties for serious corruption offenses, whose legal prescription increases from three to seven years, and contemplates asset confiscation. The Federal Audit Agency, dependent from Congress, was strengthened so it can supervise all public spending (including state government use of federal resources and trusteeships with public funds) as soon as it is put to use, without having a waiting time. The Minister of Public Function, internal comptrollers of autonomous public organisms and members of the new administrative justice tribunal would be proposed by the president, but ratified by the Senate. The attorney general, also approved by senators, was to become more independent, head a more professional (and less corrupt) organization, and appoint an anti-corruption prosecutor (Fiscal Anticorrupción), chief of a new specialized office within it that would be part of the National Anticorruption System's coordination committee.

To be fully operational, the NAS needed secondary legislation to be issued or reformed. By July 2016, most of the legal framework was in place, and the Coordination Committee was officially installed in April 2017. Nevertheless, by June 2018, critical components were still missing. The absence of an attorney general, named under the new rules, and along with it the anti-corruption prosecutor, meant that the Coordination Committee was incomplete, missing a fundamental piece for its functioning. Federal regulations required these appointments to be made, so recently included corruption crimes could be prosecuted. The judges for the new tribunal of administrative justice were also missing, after the selection process became stranded in the Senate.

Furthermore, a National Digital Platform (Plataforma Digital Nacional) for concentrating information and coordination efforts was not yet created. Although a new law on public officials' administrative responsibilities was passed in mid-2017, the new format for the declaration of their wealth and interests was not approved until September 2018, to go into effect on December 1, 2018, after the new government was to take office. A third of the states lacked their respective local citizen participation committees (part of local anti-corruption systems, also belonging to the NAS, and supposed to be in place by July 2017), and many of the committees that existed were questioned for their limited independence and autonomy (Morales 2017). State governments advanced slowly in the appointment of their own anti-corruption prosecutors and, in most cases, were also brought into question for their selection method (without citizen involvement) and closeness to local political figures.

Since early 2014, President Peña Nieto had proposed the transformation of the attorney general's office into a more independent institution. The proposal included the "automatic pass" of the head of the old organization into the new one, assuring the president's direct appointment during its first period, without having to go through the Senate. This was supposedly negotiated with opposition parties as part of the Pact for Mexico (Pacto por México) political arrangements.[5] Civil-society organizations criticized the measure as an attempt to cover up the administration's mischief and abuses. After the disappearance and killing of a group of students from a school for rural teachers located in Ayotzinapa in the state of Guerrero in September 2014, the leftist PRD (Democratic Revolution Party, Partido de la Revolución Democrática) strongly opposed Peña Nieto's attorney general candidate. The PAN conditioned its support on the dismissal of the automatic pass provision, pushing for more institutional autonomy and independence. In October 2016 the president appointed a new attorney general, but PAN, encouraged by recent electoral victories and the government's corruption scandals, still denied its support. Along with civil-society organizations, PAN accused the president of promoting a "Brotherhood Attorney" (fiscal carnal), too close to himself. Peña Nieto finally agreed to eliminate the automatic pass but refused to reform the constitution and provide more autonomy to the new agency. In October 2017 the attorney general resigned, and a junior officer took charge of affairs.

Civil-society organizations were actively involved in the creation of the NAS, and later in the transformation of the attorney general's office, including the anti-corruption prosecutor. Private-sector organizations also became very active, helping to provide both evidence and funding for investigating corruption, although some private companies had also been involved in several cases. The casa blanca and the Mexico-Querétaro train affairs, corruption scandals that involved several PRI governors, the disclosure of bribes to Mexican officials by the Brazilian oil company Odebrecht, and the scheme called the master swindle (*estafa maestra*, consisting of diverting public funds through fake companies and public universities), all contributed to the negative perception of the government and Peña Nieto's low approval ratings. For the 2017–2018 electoral process, corruption became the most important campaign issue for the majority of voters (29 percent, a 14 percent increase since 2015), ahead of the economy (28 percent) and insecurity related to crime (23 percent) (Parametría 2018).

In September 2017, just weeks from the beginning of the electoral process, 300 civil-society organizations delivered a proposal for constitutional reform and the creation of an independent attorney general's office to the leadership of PAN, PRD, and MC (Citizen's Movement Party, Movimiento Ciudadano), which constituted the Front for Mexico (Por México al Frente) electoral alliance. It was focused on the appointment and removal of its main officers, with a committee of "distinguished citizens" named by the Senate providing technical evaluations of the candidates. The proposal was embraced by the Front's legislative coalition, and later by its presidential candidate, Ricardo Anaya (who resigned as PAN leader). The private sector gradually but effectively showed support for Anaya's candidacy, leaving behind PRI's candidate and suspicious of MORENA's leftist alternative (National Renewal Movement Party, Movimiento de Renovación Nacional). Even as serious and independent work had been done by several civil-society organizations, and calls for support were made to all contestants, the movement became identified with the Front for Mexico's presidential candidate.

MORENA's presidential candidate, Andrés Manuel López Obrador, had opposed the proposal subscribed by civil-society organizations, including the appointment of the attorney general and other officials with the participation and input of a designated group of citizens, criticizing its legality and effectiveness. In early 2017, during the conformation of the Citizen's Participation Committee of the NAS, accusations of conflict of interest and lack of transparency were made to the selection committee (itself composed of "distinguished citizens" chosen by the Senate and supported by several academic and civil-society groups) (González de Aragón 2017; Arvizu 2017). Although clarifications were made (Morales 2017), some political actors questioned the legitimacy of the new participatory situation.

During the presidential campaign, López Obrador declared that the Mexican state could not give up or delegate such an important responsibility and that if he won he would prefer to use the former procedure of direct appointment by the executive with Senate approval. He was strongly criticized for his positioning on the matter. Nevertheless, probably given his considerable advantage in the last stages of the campaign, the constitutional reform proposal by civil society and private-sector organizations was revised and modified in June 2018, now including a "transition" attorney general (named with the old rules, prior to a fully independent one) and shortening the term in office from nine to six years.

After Lopez Obrador won the election in July, his team agreed to participate in a "dialogue table" with civil-society organizations to review the new justice procurement model and the issuing of the supporting law, including the appointments of high officials. On the other hand, an announcement was made that President Peña Nieto and López Obrador had reached an understanding, in which the latter would send a list of three candidates to the Senate for attorney general, three candidates for anti-corruption prosecutor, and three candidates for electoral felonies prosecutor, even as the new legal framework was not in place and did not entirely comply with the old procedure. The move was part of a pragmatic approach to the transition period by both sides, showing a will to collaborate, and a statement of resolution by the president-elect.

The newly elected government's dialogue team refused a constitutional reform to include direct citizen involvement in the appointments. It remained as the original 2014 proposal, the Senate presenting a list of ten candidates for attorney general to the president, who in turn will choose three finalists, from whom the senators will make the final decision. The new head of the agency will appoint other high officials, including the anti-corruption prosecutor. However, a new structure was worked out, including new human rights and internal affairs prosecutors and a technical council of citizens to provide recommendations. The attorney general gained some relative autonomy, with dismissal by the executive permitted only under specific circumstances and with senatorial approval. The MORENA legislative group in the new Senate (with a comfortable majority) introduced a law initiative containing these changes in September 2018.

Conclusion

Mexico's institutional framework against corruption has developed for many years, with important measures and policies being introduced, although most were poorly implemented, and many suffered from design flaws. The National Anticorruption System was an initiative that emerged from civil-society and private-sector organizations able to mobilize in a more democratic and pluralistic setting, responding to increased public-opinion concerns on corruption, and encouraged by their previous successes in issues like transparency and electoral observation. The objective was to create an instance of coordination, able to integrate the efforts of all federal and local agencies, with improved legislation, and citizen participation. The arrangement, however, was criticized for creating an additional (although small) bureaucratic structure, with limited enforcement capabilities of its own, and probably a distracting (even invasive) presence for government agencies' functioning.

The appointments of the anti-corruption prosecutor (member of the NAS Coordination Committee) and the attorney general as part of a legal reform, became a major concern for civil and private-sector organizations. The idea was to assure the autonomy and effectiveness of law enforcement in general, and of measures against corruption in particular. These organizations were actively involved in the politics of the process, providing policy and law-initiative proposals, making statements, and participating in discussions with government officials and lawmakers. As political actors, however, they were eventually perceived as having interests and an agenda of their own. Their activism meant running the risk of being involved in electoral politics, with its potential costs or benefits. Nevertheless, even as citizen and private-sector organizations necessarily represent only parts of society, and there are clear limitations to their involvement in public decision-making, the whole discussion process was a significant advancement. Space for citizen participation and empowerment, providing information; arguments; knowledge; and policy options was increased. Moreover, this participation contributed to society's awareness of the problem and the construction of monitoring mechanisms of government actions and policies in the fight against corruption.

Notes

[1] A national study in Mexico by the NGO México ¿Cómo vamos? calculated a net loss of one billion dollars in foreign direct investment in 2014. According to the private-sector association Consejo Coordinador Empresarial, in 2016 the cost of corruption in Mexico was 9 percent of Mexican GNP (Villafranco 2016). Since corruption is an illicit activity, difficult to measure, surveys based on perceptions are commonly used, including the annual *Corruption Perception Index* and the *Global Corruption Barometer* by Transparency International (Heinrich and Hodess 2011). Corruption cost estimates in Mexico have been questioned for their relative lack in rigor, however, they are frequently used to illustrate the seriousness of the problem.

[2] There was a tendency to suggest the creation of centralized anti-corruption agencies by international organizations during the 1990s and 2000s. Nevertheless, many of these initiatives have been criticized for the lack of clarity over their effective impact and their high cost (Recanatini 2011).

[3] Susan Rose-Ackerman has argued that public close attention to corruption, or scandals, have historically driven reformist movements on the matter (Rose-Ackerman 1999, 209–12).

[4] The Coordinator Committee includes the Federal Audit Agency (Auditoría Superior de la Federación), the Ministry of Public Function (Secretaría de la Función Pública), the Anti-corruption Prosecutor of the Attorney General (Procuraduría General de la República, which will change into the supposedly more autonomous Fiscalía General), the National Institute of Information Access and Data Protection (Instituto Nacional de Acceso a la Información y Protección de Datos Personales), the newly created Federal Tribunal of Administrative Justice (Tribunal Federal de Justicia Administrativa), and the Citizen Participation Committee.

[5] The Pact for Mexico was a coalition between Peña Nieto and opposition parties early into his presidency, ostensibly to move forward important reforms in areas such as education, telecommunications, energy, tax reform, law enforcement, fight against corruption, and electoral reform. As a result, PRI would keep the attorney general's office, PAN the anti-corruption prosecutor, and PRD the electoral felonies prosecutor (FEPADE, Fiscalía Especial para Delitos Electorales), the two latter posts dependent from the first one (Beltrán del Río 2018).

References

Aguilar Villanueva, Luis F. 1996. "Reformas y retos de la administración pública mexicana (1988–1994)." *Foro Internacional 36*(1–2) (January–June).

Arvizu, Juan. 2017. "Preocupa al Senado sistema anticorrupción. *El Universal,* July 1.

Bardhan, Pranab. 1997. "Corruption and Development: A Review of the Issues." *Journal of Economic Literature 35*(3) (September), 1320–46.

Beltrán del Río, Pascal. 2018. "Carnal o 'que sirva' resolverá poco." *Excelsior,* August 17.

Bohn, Simone R. 2012. "Corruption in Latin America: Understanding the Perception-Exposure Gap." *Journal of Politics in Latin America 4*(3), 67–95.

Cadena Inostrosa, Cecilia 2005. *Administración pública y procesos políticos en México.* Zinacantepec, Mexico: El Colegio Mexiquense.

Carrillo Castro, Alejandro. 2011. *Génesis y evolución de la Administración Pública Federal Centralizada,* book II, vol. 1. Mexico City: Instituto Nacional de Administración Pública, INAP.

De Graaf, Gjalt. 2007. "Causes of Corruption: Towards a Contextual Theory of Corruption." *Public Administration Quarterly 31*(1) (Spring), 39–86.

González de Aragón, Arturo. 2017. "Conflicto de interés en el Comité de Participación Ciudadana." *El Universal,* March 23.

Guerrero, Claudia. 2015. "Suman 32mmdp sanciones de la SFP." *Reforma,* February 28.

Guerrero, Omar. 1985. "El Departamento de Contraloría 1917–1933." *Revista de Administración Pública,* no. 57/58 (INAP, Mexico, January–June).

Heinrich, Finn and Hodess, Robin. 2011. "Measuring Corruption," in Adam Graycar and Russell Smith, eds., *Handbook of Global Research and Practice in Corruption.* Northampton, MA: Edward Elgar Publishing.

Liu, Cheol and Mikesell, John. (2014). "The Impact of Public Officials' Corruption on the Size and Allocation of U.S. State Spending." *Public Administration Review 74*(3) (May–June), 346–59.

Mauro, Paolo. (1995). "Corruption and Growth. *Quarterly Journal of Economics 110*(3) (August), 681–712.

Milenio Datalab. 2015. "Millonarias sanciones a funcionarios y sin esclarecer." *Grupo Milenio,* September 14, http://www.milenio.com/datalab/sanciones-AFP_0_591541222.html.

Morales, Alberto. 2017. "Rechazan conflicto de interés en Anticorrupción." *El Universal,* March 29.

Moreno, Alejandro, and Rodrigo León. 2015. "Encuesta Reforma: ven más corrupción." *Reforma,* February 20.

Parametría. 2018. "Identidades, candidatos, campañas y corrupción." *Carta Paramétrica,* July 19, http://www.parametria.com.mx/carta_parametrica.php?cp=5054.

Pardo, María del Carmen. 1990. "La evaluación gubernamental: prioridad política de 1982 a 1988." *Foro Internacional,* 30(4) (April–June).

Pardo, María del Carmen. 2009. *La modernización administrativa en México, 1940–2006.* Mexico City: El Colegio de México.

Recanatini, Francesca. 2011. "Anti-corruption Authorities: An Effective Tool to Curb Corruption?," in Susan Rose-Ackerman and Tina Soreide, eds., *International Handbook on the Economics of Corruption,* vol. 2. Northampton, MA: Edward Elgar Publishing.

Reforma. 2013. "Destacan resultados contra la corrupción durante el sexenio." *Reforma,* February 6.

Reséndiz, Francisco. 2015. "EPN pide a SFP a indagar si incurrió en conflicto de interés." *El Universal,* February 3.

Rose-Ackerman, Susan. 1999. *Corruption in Government: Causes, Consequences and Reform.* Cambridge: Cambridge University Press.

Schleifer, Andrei, and Vishny, Robert. 1993. "Corruption." *Quarterly Journal of Economics* 108(3) (August), 599–617.

Secretaría de la Contraloría General de la Federación. 1988. *La renovación moral de la sociedad, 1982–1988.* Mexico City: Fondo de Cultura Económica.

Secretaría de la Contraloría y Desarrollo Administrativo. 1996. "Programa de Modernización de la Administración Pública 1995–2000," in *Diario Oficial de la Federación.* Mexico City: Poder Ejecutivo Federal, May 28.

Transparencia Internacional. 2007. *Índice de percepción de la corrupción 2007,* Berlín, Secretariado Internacional, Transparencia Internacional.

Transparencia Internacional. 2012. *Índice de percepción de la corrupción 2012,* Berlín, Secretariado Internacional, Transparencia Internacional.

Treisman, Daniel. 2007. "What We Have Learned about the Causes of Corruption from Ten Years of Cross-national Empirical Research." *Annual Review of Political Science* 10(June).

Vázquez Alfaro, José Luis. 1996. *El Control de la Administración Pública en México.* Mexico City: Instituto de Investigaciones Jurídicas, UNAM.

Villafranco, Gerardo. 2016. "Corrupción cuesta 9% del PIB a México." *Forbes México* (February 2).

World Bank. 2000. *Anticorruption in Transition: A Contribution to the Policy Debate.* Washington, DC: World Bank-International Bank for Reconstruction and Development.

7

Corruption in Italy
Indigenous Impediments to Reform
Daniel L. Feldman

Anti-corruption institutions in Italy operate against a particularly challenging set of background conditions. Any assessment of their efficacy must take such conditions into account. Italy, one of the largest economies in the world, with a cultural legacy second to none, is burdened by a relatively weak national government, concomitant with strong loyalties to localities and regions and deeply rooted criminal organizations and traditions.

Analytic difficulties impede accurate assessment. If investigators expose fewer scandals, or if prosecutors convict fewer culprits, does this mean corruption has decreased? Or that those anti-corruption institutions have failed to address the problem in full measure? Conversely, if investigators expose more scandals, and prosecutors convict more culprits, has corruption increased, or are the institutions more successfully combating it? As to the latter alternative, in the face of persistent news reports of real victories against corruption, the public may simply conclude that corruption is pervasive. While, as noted below, a reputable study concludes that perceptions of corruption fairly well track experience of corruption as well as expert opinion (Charron 2016), at least in the short run, perceptions based on such press coverage could well outrun the reality to a significant degree (e.g., Perlman 2008).

This study of corruption in Italy, therefore, explains the economic burdens it imposes, cross-national and regional comparisons of the perceptions it generates, and background cultural conditions that make it harder to fight.

The Economy and the Cost of Corruption

Italy is the world's eighth-largest economy, with a gross domestic product (GDP) of $1.8 trillion, a little ahead of Brazil (Smith 2018). Based on International Monetary Fund figures, Italy's GDP per capita, adjusted for price differences, at the equivalent of $39,500 was in 2018 the 35th highest in the world, out of 191 countries. The world average was $18,089. By comparison, Qatar was the highest at $128,703; the United States was twelfth at $62,152; Sri Lanka, Bosnia and Herzegovina, and Egypt were in the middle of the pack with between $13,478 and $13,330; and Burundi and the Central African Republic were at the bottom, with $731 and $706 (List of Countries by Projected GDP per capita 2018.)

In 2016 Italian tax revenue was $842.5 billion, and government expenditures were $889.8 billion, leaving a 2.6 percent deficit; GDP per capita was $36,300 (CIA 2017) or €27,587 (European Commission for the Efficiency of Justice 2018, 12), the unemployment rate 11.4 percent, and 29.9 percent of the population was below the poverty line (CIA 2017). Italy's ratio of government debt to GDP has worsened significantly since 2008, when the two were about equal, while from 2014 onward, Italy's government debt has been about 132 percent of its GDP (Trading Economics 2018), "a fragile fiscal position" (Cimadomo and D'Agostino 2016, 5).

Estimates of the "underground" or "shadow" economy range from 13 percent of GDP, or €211 billion in 2014 (Istituto Nazionale di Statistica 2016), to 17 percent of GDP in 2017, or about €300 billion (CIA 2017), to slightly more than 20 percent in 2013 (European Commission 2014a, 4). The CIA attributes the illicit component to the construction, service, and agricultural sectors of the economy (2017).

Corruption, of course, accounts for only part of the underground economy. Much of the rest usually reflects cash transactions enabling illegal tax avoidance. Italy's low birthrate and aging population demands a high level of public expenditures. With the high level of tax evasion, those who pay honestly and properly carry a heavy and unreasonable burden (Cotta et al. 2018b, 9). As for corruption per se, the European Commission estimates its cost in Italy at €60 billion per year, about 4 percent of GDP (European Commission 2014b). The United States used the same figure, €60 billion, attributable to "corruption and organized crime," which it called "significant impediments to investment and economic growth in parts of Italy" (2016). Italy's Court of Audits dealt with a 229 percent increase in its corruption caseload from 2009 to 2010 (Zeldin 2012). By another measure, a taxpayer association reported a 71 percent increase in corruption from 2013 to 2014 (Roe 2014).

Criminal convictions for corruption have diminished throughout recent years in Italy: in 1996 there were 1,714 convictions for corruption-related crimes; in 2000 there were 1,279 convictions; in 2003 there were 654 convictions; and in 2006 there were 239 convictions (Vannucci 2009, 238). Allegations of corruption have likewise diminished, a more persuasive indicator of a decline in corruption, although allegations may have diminished for other reasons (e.g., intimidation, more effective concealment, consolidation of corruption enterprises). In 1996 there were 77 corruption allegations reported; in 2000 39; in 2003 there were 33; and in 2006 there were 35 (Vannucci 2009, 240). The public, of course, disfavors corruption, recognizing that "corruption does not only divert public wealth from legal and proper purposes, but it boosts the disproportion between the rich and poor" (Quattrocolo 2016, 2).

Perception of Corruption Rankings—World and Regional

The various statistics cited above seem contradictory, or at least unclear, as to whether corruption in Italy is on the rise or on the decline. However, Italian corruption has steadily declined in recent years, if perceptions as measured by Transparency International are accurate and meaningful.

Transparency International offers an annual ranking of 180 nations by perception levels of corruption. Their findings include a scoring system: the higher the score (based on a scale from one to one hundred), the less corrupt. Italy is one of the richest countries in the world, yet with a score of fifty, it is perceived as corrupt as poorer nations like Slovakia or Mauritius, with which it is tied at fifty-fourth. Comparatively, two politically and financially influential nations, the United States and China, are respectively ranked sixteenth with a score of 75, and seventy-ninth with a score of 40, tied with some others for those ranks (Transparency International 2018).

According to *International Budget Partnership*, Italy's transparency capability is considered above average. In 2015, a report from International Budget gave Italy a grade of 73 out of 100 in transparency: "The Government of Italy provides the public with substantial budget information" (Ricci 2015). This rating has gradually improved. In 2010, Italy received a grade of 58 and then a 60 in 2012. The global average is 45. In addition, Italy received a 79 percent for budget oversight by its legislature, which was considered adequate. Italy received a 67 percent for budget oversight by its supreme audit institution, the Court of Auditors, (Ricci 2015, 71, Annex D), which was considered adequate (Ricci 2015, 50).

FIGURE 7.1 Regions of Italy

Scholars at the University of Gothenburg, Sweden, published a cross-national comparison of "Quality of Government," factoring levels of "corruption, impartiality, and quality of public services" (Charron and Lapuente 2018, 2) using 2015 World Bank "World Governance Indicators" (12–13) and their own 2017 survey data to produce the current European Commission for the Efficiency of Justice's Quality of Governance Index (EQI) (14–15), originally created and utilized in 2010 (6). Among other thing, they found that regional differences often exceed national differences. In Italy, for example, some regions rate higher than the European average, while many rate lower (2). They also found little change over time (17), although performance declined in several regions in Italy (18), two in the north and Abruzzo in the middle (22).

Like Transparency International, the Gothenburg scholars solicited information based on perceptions, noting, however, that perceptions of corruption correlate strongly with experiences of corruption and with "expert assessments" (Charron and Lapuente 2018, 10, n. 8, citing Charron 2016, 167). They found little change in Italy's national standing between 2013 and 2017, with a rise from the twenty-fourth best to the twenty-third best overall rating (2018, 30).

However, notwithstanding its comparative standing against other countries, the Gothenburg scholars report in 2017 that virtually every region did as poorly as, or worse than, it did in 2010. Of course, as to comparisons with Transparency International's measures, based only on perceptions of corruption, the Gothenburg group also includes perceptions of "impartiality" and "quality of public services" in its assessment measurements. The five southernmost regions, Sicily, Calabria, Campagna, Basilicata, and Apulia, continued to have the worst scores of all, less than minus 1.2, the worst rating available at this point (Charron and Lapuente 2018, 15; EQI 2017), as did Lazio, while only Campagna had earned the worst possible score in 2010. Of the northern regions, all of which had had positive scores in 2010 (Charron, Dijkstra, and Lapuente 2014, xlvii), now Umbria earned zero to minus 0.5; Marche, Tuscany, Emilia-Romagna, Liguria, Lombardy, and Veneto, minus 0.5 to minus 0.9; and Valle Aosta, Piedmont, Trentino-Alba, and Venezia-Giulia, zero to minus 0.5 (Charron and Lapuente 2018, 15; EQI 2017).

Background Conditions

Relatively Weak National Government

Italians have little confidence in their national government. Its weakness, and their lack of confidence, may follow as the obverse of their strong loyalties to localities and regions. While in many countries confidence in the national government decreased after the 2008 financial crisis, it was only at about 30 percent in Italy *before* the crisis, and simply remained so thereafter (OECD 2013, 25, see figure 7.1). When measuring "trust" instead of "confidence," in 2013 only about *10 percent* gave a positive response—and fewer—about 8 percent—said they tended to trust Italian political parties (30), not a surprising response in light of the Tangentopoli scandal and the weak response to it. Close to 90 percent thought that corruption was "widespread throughout the government" (35). Perhaps this contributes to Italy's high and very problematic rate of tax evasion (Cotta, Maruhn, and Colino 2018b, 9).

Based on indicators from the World Bank, the International Monetary Fund, the United Nations, and the World Economic Forum, among other sources, *TheGlobalEconomy. com* (2018) gave Italy a score of 0.52 on government effectiveness, on a scale from 2.5 ("strong") to minus 2.5 ("weak"), based on "perceptions of the quality of public services, the quality of the civil service and the degree of its independence from political pressures, the quality of policy formation and implementation, and the credibility of the government's commitment to such policies" (2018b). Out of 193 countries, Italy ranked fifty-first, behind Qatar, the Bahamas, Poland, Uruguay, and Samoa. France, twentieth, scored 1.41; the United States, nineteenth, 1.48; the United Kingdom, sixteenth, 1.61; Germany, thirteenth, 1.74; the Netherlands, ninth, 1.84; with Singapore first, at 2.21.

Bertelsmann Stiftung provides its Sustainable Governance Indicators only for forty-one EU and OECD countries. Of those, Italy ranked twenty-seventh on policy performance, twenty-first on democracy, and twenty-fifth on governance (Bertelsmann Stiftung 2018a). The average score on policy performance was 6.17: Italy did worse, at 5.73; on democracy, 7.05: Italy did better, at 7.30; on governance, 6.31: Italy did worse, at 6.20, just behind Latvia (but ahead of Japan) (Cotta, Maruhn, and Colino 2018a, 150). In its comments on Italy's "quality of democracy," the Bertelsmann group noted that "anti-corruption efforts have been strengthened, but corruption remains a serious problem, in part due to opportunities opened by regulatory complexity" (Bertelsmann Stiftung 2018b; and see Cotta, Maruhn, and Colino 2018b, 27). The Bertelsmann study does not reference the new government sworn in on June 1, 2018, and so apparently was conducted prior. On the basis of its comments about the Renzi and Gentiloni governments preceding, it would most likely have given Italy lower scores based on the new coalition government.

The weakness, real and perceived incompetence of governmental bodies ("administrative inefficiency, clientelism, ineffective development policies, weak legality and so on," LaSpina 2014, 608), helps to lend criminal organizations their relative legitimacy and encourages corruption by others independent of criminal organizations.

Deep Roots of Corruption

Deeply rooted in the Italian tradition, certainly in much of the South, is corruption. As a knowledgeable but anonymous source explained,

> the ruling class has never managed to make the transition from a system based on wild and violent accumulation to a social order respectful of legality based on shared values. The elite in Italy has never really renounced violence. See the example of state terrorism scattered along the history of the country. (Ruggiero 2010, 102)

Just as the feudal lords of the city-states in the Renaissance came to power through violence, extracting wealth from the people they ruled, but providing governance, the leaders of criminal organizations to this day provide substantial benefits to their subject populations, often perceived as more important than whatever burdens that rule entails. As a result, those criminal organizations often enjoy considerable political support among the population in the territories they inhabit (see, e.g., Paoli 2014, 122–24, 130–31; LaSpina 2014, 607). The Camorra in the Campagna region, which includes Naples, the 'Ndràngheta in the Calabria region, the lesser-known Sacra Corona Unita in Apulia, and of course the Cosa Nostra in Sicily, could all be so characterized (see Charron, Dijkstra, and Lapuente 2014, xlvii). Organized crime and government need not be distinct entities in certain southern regions, or even elsewhere in Italy (Paoli 2014, 121, 130–31).

Further, when an organized crime organization has controlled an industry for many years, it sometimes gains certain efficiencies, enabling it to offer lower prices than its more legitimate competitors (see, e.g., Sberna 2014, 11). It may initially have used violence, threats of violence, bribery, and/or other unsavory tactics to win favorable—inexpensive—labor contracts and supplies, but over time its dominance and expertise may in fact make it more efficient in the provision of services than its honest competitors. In Rome in 2017, for example, the head of the Mafia Capitale, Rome's infamous mafia, was sent to prison on the basis of his profits from Rome's garbage-collection contracts with companies he controlled. When government officials turned to independent companies, the costs were so much higher that the city could only afford to provide certain communities with so much less frequent garbage collection that public uproar resulted (Nadeau 2018).

The foregoing does not necessarily imply that organized crime is the chief instigator of corruption in Italy today. Rather, its ethos infects a wider swath of Italian society. The well-known 2015 documentary film *Palio* explored the nature of Italy's legendary horse race in Siena, its home—in Tuscany, not the South. With far more than acceptance—pride and joy, really—the corruption that is a well-known and prominent element of the race is seen as "part of life," enabling the race as a whole to be a more truly comprehensive metaphor for life as a whole. "Bribery is not just tolerated at the Palio, it is celebrated" (Kerr 2018). The film's director called the horse race "a perfect microcosm of Italy," as it "encapsulates beauty, tradition, history, but also deception, bribery, and corruption" (Donati 2015). As far as can be determined, no one has tried to "clean up" the Palio, nor would anyone—for well over three hundred years (Kerr 2018); some say for over seven hundred years (Donati 2015). As one commentator wrote, "This sort of existential criminality, in any other country, would lead to madness among horse people and spectators. Yet in Siena, no one wishes to change a thing about the Palio" (Garner 2018).

The ethos of corruption appears to be stronger, if anything, at the higher levels of society. "Widespread corruption within the social, economic and political spheres *attracts* organised criminal groups [emphasis added], encouraging them to participate in corrupt exchange and indirectly boosting their other various illicit activities" (Ruggiero 2010, 102). Evidently, organized crime and government are recurrently intertwined entities. Still, corruption does not necessarily involve organized crime—and often, perhaps usually, does not. The statistics cited at the beginning of this chapter show the prevalence of corruption at the high level of organization of massive and massively expensive public works, compared with the relatively small percentage of individuals solicited for bribes. This suggests that a corrupt political elite invites criminal participation, organized or otherwise. Some elements of the political elite may even have modeled their behavior on that of mafiosi (95–96). Some scholars imply that Italy's failure for many years to comply with the EU's 1999 Criminal Law Convention on Corruption, thereby postponing its membership in the "Group of States Against Corruption" until it finally acquiesced in 2012, at least in part resulted from the desire of its national leadership to continue to engage in corrupt activities themselves (Sargiacomo, Ianni, D'Andreamatteo, and Servalli 2015, 92).

None of this is to say that efforts against corruption are doomed to failure, only that their effectiveness must be measured against the formidable obstacles in their way.

Regionalism

Article 5 of the Italian Constitution enshrines the principles of local "autonomy and decentralization," reflecting deeply rooted national traditions, hardly surprising in a nation unified only since the 1860s, whose proud cities—Rome, Naples, Florence, Venice, Milan, and the list goes on at length—wielded independent sovereignty and powerfully influenced the course of world history hundreds of years earlier. In Siena, for example, each local district, or "contrade," has a population, on average, of about three thousand people, and there are seventeen such districts with estimates of Siena's total population varying from about 57,000 (About the City of Siena, Undated) to about 42,000 (Population of Cities in Italy 2018). "Sienese think of themselves as belonging to their contrade first, then to Siena, and then to Italy" (Donati 2015).

Article 117 of the Constitution reserves to the regions all legislative powers not explicitly reserved to the national legislature, and Article 119 assures regions and local governments control over the tax levy revenues they impose and collect but also a share of tax revenues raised in the territory—even by the national government. Transfers of revenue from the national government to regions and localities have decreased substantially in recent decades—for the regions, down from 80 percent or so in 1985 to about 52 percent in 2000 (Buglione 2014, 325) or, according to a different source, only about 40 percent in 2000 and slightly higher in 2016 (about 44 percent) (OECD Fiscal Decentralisation Database 2018) which, while an improvement, remains a very substantial amount. Transfers to the less-developed southern regions would of course constitute a much higher percentage, as transfers to the north, in general, would constitute a much lower percentage (Giannola, Scalera, and Petraglia 2014). So the national government raises the money, and to a considerable extent the regions and localities control and spend it: "Central government has largely failed to control local and regional government spending" (Cotta et al. 2018b, 5).

Of course, throughout the second half of the twentieth century the Italian political leadership had to respond to the need for a modern national government, so regionalism as a force waxed and waned depending on the interplay of financial and political events and conditions (see, e.g., Mangiameli 2014). Nonetheless, regionalism remains "a fundamental feature of the Republican Constitution" of Italy (25), "rooted in the Italian tradition" (26).

If so many of Italy's regional and local governments have long been in thrall to criminal organizations, or to other forms of corruption, one might imagine turning to the national government for relief. However, despite the gradual decline in legitimacy suffered by organized crime, especially since the 1990s (Paoli 2014, 136–37), it would still require a vast effort by the national government to undertake to deliver social services and to do so effectively enough to win sufficient legitimacy of its own to supplant criminal political power centers. Leaving aside the considerable question of effective service delivery by the national government, this would first require a national population willing to have its regions and localities relinquish their preeminence in serving local needs. An enormous obstacle stands in the way of such an eventuality. One might analogize corruption in Italy to racism in the United States. The US Supreme Court in 1954 ordered an end to racial segregation in public schools (*Brown v. Bd. of Education*). The opposition couched its arguments in the language of "states' rights." But while in the United States by that time the principle of local control, or "states' rights," was largely a pretense in an effort to divert attention from the less socially acceptable racist ideology that truly motivated the opponents, in Italy the principle of local control commands more heartfelt adherence (see above). One might speculate that the strenuous—and for a long time, successful—opposition to racial integration in the United States, would be far exceeded by the opposition to a national takeover of the provision of social services in Italy as part of an effort to delegitimize and dislodge organized crime from its hold over certain centers of political power.

Conclusion

While efforts to combat corruption in Italy surely face serious challenges, recent years have seen a more serious and strenuous commitment to overcoming them. The rise of the National Anti-Corruption Authority, as a prime example, gives reason for hope (see, e.g., Carloni 2017; Hyeraci and Petronio 2016; Romano, M.C. 2017, 779, 799; Neri 2017, 804) as do transparency initiatives pursuant to national legislation (see Anna Simonati's chapter in this volume, "Transparency as a Tool to Combat Corruption in Italy"). The studies cited above, which rely on perceptions as a proxy for actual levels of corruption, apparently do so in recognition of the weakness of other quantitative measures. More reliable assessment of the efficacy of anti-corruption measures and institutions requires a close and nuanced analysis of the changes in attitude and behavior of both the public and of those it entrusts with that responsibility. This must be the focus of the research that lies ahead.

Acknowledgments

Most of my research for this chapter was conducted under the auspices of the Institute for the Study of Regionalism, Federalism, and Self-government of the National Research Council of Italy during the fall of 2018. I am deeply grateful for the assistance of its director, Professor Stelio Mangiameli, and its staff. I am also grateful for the fine earlier work of my research assistant, Mr. Salomon Montaguth, during the fall of 2017. Opinions expressed are those of the author only, as are any errors.

References

About the City of Siena. (Undated). Siena website. http://www.aboutsiena.com/the-city-of-Siena-Italy.html, accessed November 5, 2018.

Bertelsmann Stiftung. 2018a. "Sustainable Governance Indicators." http://www.sgi-network.org/2018/, accessed October 15, 2018.

Bertelsmann Stiftung. 2018b. "Sustainable Governance Indicators—Italy," http://www.sgi-network.org/2018/Italy, accessed October 15, 2018.

Brown v. Board of Education. 1954. 347 U.S. 483.

Buglione, E. 2014. "Regional Finance in Italy: Past and Future," in S. Mangiameli, ed., *Italian Regionalism.* Cham: Springer, 307–34.

Burea, A. 2013, June 21. "Italian Authorities and OLAF Uncover Major Fraud Involving EU Funds in Sicily—European Anti-Fraud Office—European Commission." Retrieved May 25, 2017, from https://ec.europa.eu/anti-fraud/media-corner/press-releases/italian-authorities-and-olaf-uncover-major-fraud-involving-eu-funds_en.

Carloni, E. 2017. "Fighting Corruption through Administrative Measures." *Italian Journal of Public Law 9*(2), 261–90, http://www.ijpl.eu/assets/files/pdf/2017_volume_2/IJPL_volume2_2017 .pdf.

Central Intelligence Agency (CIA). 2017. "The World Factbook: Italy." Retrieved April 26, 2017, from https://www.cia.gov/library/publications/the-world-factbook/geos/it.html.

Charron, N, 2016. "Do Corruption Measures Have a Perception Problem?" *European Political Science Review 8*(1), 147–71.

Charron, N., and V. Lapuente. 2018. *Quality of Government in EU Regions: Spatial and Temporal Patterns*, QoG Working Paper Series 2018:2, ISSN 1653–8919, University of Gothenburg: The Quality of Government Institute.

Charron, N., L. Dijkstra, and V. Lapuente. 2014. "Regional Governance Matters: Quality of Government within European Union Member States," *Regional Studies 48*(1): 68–90. doi: 10.1 080/00343404.2013.770141, Appendix and references to 2010 EQI data.

Cimadomo, J., and A. D'Agostino. 2016 "Combining Time Variation and Mixed Frequencies: An Analysis of Government Spending Multipliers in Italy." *Journal of Applied Economics 31*, 1276–90. doi: 10.1002/jae.2489.

Constitution of the Italian Republic. (Undated but current as of 2018). *Rome, Italy: The Senate.* Bookshop.

Cotta, M., R. Maruhn, and C. Colino. 2018a. "Country Profile SGI 2018 Italy," in E. Faria Lopes, T. Hellman, C. Schiller, and D. Schraad-Tischler, eds., *Policy Performance and Government Capacities in the OECD and EU*, Gütersloher, Germany: Bertelsmann Stiftung, http://www.sgi-network.org/docs/2018/basics/SGI2018_Overview.pdf, 150, accessed October 15, 2018.

Cotta, M., R. Maruhn, and C. Colino. 2018b. "Italy Report: Sustainable Governance Indicators." http://www.sgi-network.org/docs/2018/country/SGI2018_Italy.pdf, accessed October 15, 2018.

Donati, S. 2015, Nov. 27). "'Palio': An Insider View into the World's Oldest (and Most Corrupt?) Horse Race." *L'Italo-Americano*, https://italoamericano.org/story/2015-11-27/palio-movie, interviewing Cosima Spender, accessed November 5, 2018.

European Commission. 2014a, February 3. "EU Anti-Corruption Report 2014: Country Sheet Italy." Retrieved April 10, 2017, from https://ec.europa.eu/home-affairs/sites/homeaffairs/files/what-we-do/policies/organized-crime-and-human-trafficking/corruption/anti-corruption-report/docs/2014_acr_italy_factsheet_en.pdf; also Annex 12 to the EU Anti-Corruption Report, 2014, https://ec.europa.eu/homeaffairs/sites/homeaffairs/fileswhat-we-do/policies/organized-crime-and-human-trafficking/corruption/anti-corruption-report/docs/2014_acr_italy_chapter_en.pdf.

European Commission. 2014b, February 3. *European Commission, Press Release—Summaries of the National Chapters from the European Anti-Corruption Report.* Retrieved April 10, 2017, from http://europa.eu/rapid/press-release_MEMO-14-67_en.htm.

European Commission for the Efficiency of Justice. 2018. "European Judicial Systems: Efficiency and Quality of Justice." *CEPEJ Studies Number 26, Council of Europe.* https://rm.coe.int/rapport-avec-couv-18-09-2018-en/16808def9c, accessed October 26, 2018.

Garner, D. 2018, "What It's Like to Witness the Palio di Siena, Possibly the Most Lawless Horse Race on Earth." *Independent*, May 11. https://www.independent.co.uk/news/long_reads/palio-di-siena-horse-race-italy-sport-festival-medieval-contrade-tuscany-a8317956.html, accessed November 5, 2018.

Giannola, A., D. Scalera, and C. Petraglia. 2014. "Net Fiscal Flows and Interregional Redistribution in Italy: A Long-run Perspective (1951–2010)." *Munich Personal RePEc Archive*, MPRA Paper No. 57371, posted July 18, https://mpra.ub.uni-muenchen.de/57371/1/MPRA_paper_57371.pdf.

Guardia Di Finanza (GDF). 2016. *Rapporto Annuale (Annual Report): Guardia di Finanza.* Retrieved May 5, 2017, from http://www.gdf.gov.it/ente-editoriale-per-la-guardia-di-finanza/pubblicazioni/il-rapporto-annuale/anno-2016/rapporto-annuale-2016/rapporto-annuale-2016.pdf.

Hyeraci, M., and F. Petronio. 2016, April 13. "A Strengthening of Anti-corruption Legislation in Italy. https://www.ethic-intelligence.com/en/experts-corner/international-experts/124-a-strength-ening-of-anti-corruption-legislation-in-italy.html, accessed October 12, 2018.

Istituto Nazionale di Statistica. 2016, October 14. "Economy Not Observed in National Accounts." https://www.istat.it/it/archivio/191377.

Kerr, T. 2018. "Brawls, Bribery and Bedlam at the Palio, the World's Most Chaotic Race." *Racing Post*, July 17. https://www.racingpost.com/news/brawls-bribery-and-bedlam-at-the-palio-the-world-s-most-chaotic-race/338111, accessed November 5, 2018.

LaSpina, A. 2014. "The Fight Against the Italian Mafia," in Letizia Paoli, ed., *The Oxford Handbook of Organized Crime*. New York: Oxford University Press, 593–611. doi: 10.1093/oxfor dhb/9780199730445.013.025.

List of Countries by Projected GDP Per Capita. (2018). *Statistics Times*. http://statisticstimes.com/economy/countries-by-projected-gdp-capita.php, accessed November 2, 2018.

Lupkin, S., and E. Lewandowski. 2005. "Independent Private Sector Inspectors General: Privately Funded Overseers of the Public Integrity." *NY Litigator Journal 10*(1), 6–19, available at http://www.iaipsig.org/nylit-newsl-spring05-lewandowki.pdf

Mangiameli, S. 2014. "The Regions and the Reforms: Issues Resolved and Problems Pending," in S. Mangiameli, ed., *Italian Regionalism*, 1–33. Cham: Springer.

Nadeau, B. L. 2018. "Rome's Sad Decline Sums up Italy's Problems." *CNN*, March 5. https://edition.cnn.com/2018/03/02/europe/rome-decline-italy-election-intl/index.html, accessed October 12, 2018.

Neri, B. 2017. "The Controls of the Anti-Corruption National Authority on Corruption Prevention and Transparency," in Marco D'Alberti, ed., *Corruzione e pubblica amministrazione*. Translation by Google Translate. Naples: Jovene Editore, 801–19.

OECD. 2013. "Trust in Government, Policy Effectiveness and the Governance Agenda, in Government at a Glance." Paris: OECD Publishing. doi: 10.1787/gov_glance-2013-6-en, accessed October 15, 2018.

OECD Fiscal Decentralisation Database. 2018. http://www.oecd.org/tax/federalism/fiscal-decentralisation-database.htm, accessed November 5, 2018.

Paoli, L. 2014. "The Italian Mafia," in Letizia Paoli, ed., *The Oxford Handbook of Organized Crime*. New York: Oxford University Press, 121–41. doi: 10.1093/oxfordhb/9780199730445.013.025.

Perlman, S. 2008. "How Do You Measure Corruption?" *The World Bank*, East Asia and Pacific on the Rise; blog post, June 4. http://blogs.worldbank.org/eastasiapacific/how-do-you-measure-corruption, accessed October 22, 2018.

Population of Cities in Italy. 2018. *World Population Review*. http://worldpopulationreview.com/countries/italy-population/cities/, accessed November 5, 2018.

Quattrocolo, S. 2016. "The Role of Compliance Programs in Italian Counter-Corruption Policies." *Journal of Civil and Legal Sciences 5*(3): 1–6.

Ricci, C. 2015. *Open Budget Survey 2015: Italy*. Retrieved April 25, 2017, from http://www.internationalbudget.org/wp-content/uploads/OBS2015-CS-Italy-English.pdf.

Roe, A. 2014 "Massive Increase in Corruption in Italy is Killing Businesses." Italy Chronicles, August 19. Retrieved May 05, 2017, from http://italychronicles.com/corruption-italy-killing-businesses/.

Romano, F. 2017. "Support Anticorruption Measures in Albania." Presentation, October 30–November 2, available from present author.

Romano, M. C. 2017. "The Role and the Competencies of ANAC on Public Contracts," in Marco D'Alberti, ed., *Corruzione e pubblica amministrazione*. Translation by Google Translate. Naples: Jovene Editore, 769–99.

Ruggiero, V. 2010. "Who Corrupts Whom? A Criminal Eco-System Made in Italy." *Crime, Law and Social Change 54*(1), 87–105. doi: 10.1007/s10611-010-9242-9.

Sargiacomo, I., and S. D'Andreamatteo. 2015. "Accounting and the Fight against Corruption in Italian Government Procurement: A Longitudinal Critical Analysis (1992–2014)." *Critical Perspectives on Accounting 28*, 89–96.

Sberna, S. 2014. *Conceptualizing Organized Crime: A Transaction Cost Approach to Make-or-Buy Decision and Corruption*. Quality of Government Institute, European University Institute, European Commission, EU Grant Agreement #290529. http://anticorrp.eu/wp-content/uploads/2014/12/D1.1_Part4_Conceptualizing-Organized-Crime-A-transaction-cost-approach-to-make-or-buy-decisions-and-corruption.pdf, accessed October 12, 2018.

Smith, R. 2018. *The World's Biggest Economies in 2018*. World Economic Forum, April 18, https://www.weforum.org/agenda/2018/04/the-worlds-biggest-economies-in-2018/.

TheGlobalEconomy.com 2018. Website, home page. https://www.theglobaleconomy.com/ accessed October 15, 2018.

Trading Economics. 2018. *Italian Government Debt to GDP, 1988–2018*. https://tradingeconomics.com/italy/government-debt-to-gdp, accessed October 11, 2018.

Transparency International. 2018. *Corruption Perceptions Index 2017*. Retrieved September 24, 2018, from https://www.transparency.org/news/feature/corruption_perceptions_index_2017?gclid=EAIaIQobChMI3fL6493T3QIVx5TVCh2zWA7VEAAYASAAEgKjn_D_BwE#table.

Vannucci, A. 2009. "The Controversial Legacy of 'Mani Pulite': A Critical Analysis of Italian Corruption and Anti-Corruption Policies." Retrieved May 16, 2017, from http://www.gla.ac.uk/media/media_140182_en.pdf.

Zeldin, W. 2012, November 07. "Global Legal Monitor-Italy: Anti-Corruption Law Adopted." Retrieved April 14, 2017, from http://www.loc.gov/law/foreign-news/article/italy-anti-corruption-law-adopted/.

8

When Two or More Rights Make a Wrong

How Conflicts between Ethical Standards Affect Ethical Behavior

Leonard L. Lira

Most research and practice to thwart corruption and ethical violations revolves around a specific type of analysis of the action to determine whether it is corrupt or unethical. The usual definition to describe corruption in the literature comes from the anti-corruption nongovernmental organization, Transparency International (Zyglidopoulos et al. 2017), which defines it as "the abuse of entrusted power for private gain" (Transparency International 2017). This power-gain equation perspective is reductionist. It primarily views the analysis of corruption and ethical management through an economic lens that reduces the analysis to a dichotomous description of corruption as a black-and-white issue. It builds off of the foundational understanding of ethical behavior as actions that are good or evil, right or wrong (Beauchamp and Bowie 1983) or, in essence, as "what we ought and ought not do" (Kaptein 2008, 980). This perspective provides no deep analysis of the reality of the context in which the action occurs. Nowhere is the complexity of the circumstances surrounding unethical or corrupt behavior more present than in the study of the professional ethics of public servants when, while carrying out their legitimate and official duties, they encounter the dilemma of having to decide the best course of action between two competing options that place elements of their ethics in competition with one another.

Drawing from the American Society of Public Administration's code of ethics to illustrate this point further, what decision is a public servant supposed to make when the ethical value of advancing the public interest, or upholding the Constitution and the law, compete with the ethical value of demonstrating personal integrity or loyalty to family, friends, or community? To demonstrate the competing tension between these values, take for example the preservation of life, which is a universal value of all societies. It is a major part of personal integrity. It is not moral to kill or harm another human. However, during the conduct of war or the enforcement of law, public servants in the security professions (e.g., military and police professions to name two) are often confronted with situations in which they must decide between violating this fundamental social value to preserve life or carry out their professional duties and obligations to protect the Constitution and secure the peace. For military personnel, especially in the current environment in which nonstate actors are indistinguishable from the state's citizens, who receive protected status under international law, this dilemma is becoming increasingly prevalent. However, these gray-area dilemmas expand beyond the professional ethics of the military alone. In fact, they are present in the professional ethics of other multiple public-service organizations as well.

The push to view ethical violations, particularly corrupt behavior, only through the prism of an abuse of power for personal gain does not account for the complex situations in which professional public servants find that their ethical values compete. It misses the forest for the trees because it does not allow for an evaluation of this tension between competing ethical values as a potential source of unethical or corrupt behavior. This perspective further fails to analyze the potential impact this tension has on public servants and to their organizations as well as the negative consequences to the broader public interest and public good. In other words, it is a reactive analysis that does not look to the source of the behavior. It is reductionist because it does not include the larger analysis of its full impact.

To address the wider impact on the personal integrity of public servants, is it possible that what the literature describes as emotional labor, the "emotional efforts performed to fulfill perceived or explicit individual work-related expectations that serve organizational goals" (Barry, Olekalns, and Rees 2018), applies to public servants grappling with ethical dilemmas they may meet in the course of their duties? Is it further possible that the exposure of these contradictions between their personal moral identities, their professional ethical identities, and the social ethical norms contribute to moral suffering such as moral distress and injury? Especially when public service professionals encounter value-conflicting dilemmas in events that are acutely traumatic or cause public servants to question their core moral identity because the event exposes a contradiction between personal/societal/organizational concepts of morally ethical behavior? Further, does this moral suffering contribute to aggravating the negative impact of these dilemmas and lead to, or serve as an antecedent for, acts of corruption and unethical behavior?

To address these questions, this chapter reviews how these tensions affect the public-service professions of the military, law enforcement, and border security. These areas are familiar to the author, a twenty-seven-year veteran of the military, because he personally observed the conflict of these values while serving in three different combat tours. His undergraduate degree specialized in police administration and management, while his research leading to his doctorate studied police qualitatively. Lastly, during the Trump administration's implementation of the family-separation policy, he taught several minority students who had one or more family members who worked in agencies responsible for one aspect or another of border security, and who shared their feelings during class discussion on the policy.

The chapter starts with a review of the literature on ethics to lay out the framework with which to analyze ethics in those professions and in the literature concerning professional duty versus values in the public services. The purpose of this review is to highlight the gap in the literature in dealing with the conflicts between personal moral identity, organizational professional ethical identity, and societal ethical norms.

Based on this review, the chapter proposes that these value tensions may contribute to moral suffering in the form of moral distress or injury among public servants, which in turn may further contribute to observable ethical violations or corrupt behavior. The chapter sets up this proposal by discussing the prevalence of these tensions in the military, law enforcement, and border security professions. It then provides a recommended research agenda to expand the current analysis of unethical and corrupt behavior. It concludes with a discussion of what to do to manage these value-conflicting dilemmas and how they relate to the overall management of corruption and ethical behavior of public servants.

The Literature on Ethics and the Security Professions

The field of business and public ethics has long tried to identify the distinction between what we ought and what we ought not to do in situations of ethical and moral ambiguity, when competing ideals come into play. Hennessey and Gert (1985) use moral theory to parse the actions that business professionals take into either category by making the distinction between "moral rules" and "moral ideals." They find that ethical dilemmas arise from confusion between what is morally required and what is ideal to do, between the imperative and the desirable. Their main argument is that the decision one makes in situations in which personal integrity conflicts with professional organizational obligations depends on one's moral experience as expressed by one's character, personality, or personal philosophy, but also on the situational variables surrounding the context of the dilemma. Their proposition illustrates that when tension exists between professional obligations and personal obligations, two moral rights, more variables than just personal character come into play.

Another way that scholars study ethics in the public service sector is through the debate between the deontological and teleological perspectives of public service—what is the professional duty versus the professional purpose. Heckler and Ronquillo (2018) expand this understanding of ethics by incorporating external and internal sources for ethical development of public-service managers. They find that public-service professionals who have multiple sources of ethical experience to draw on can more easily deal with and solve the confusing ethical dilemmas that arise due to the conflict between the deontological and teleological perspectives.

Building from the ethical management literature, researchers use various levels of analysis to study the tensions arising from these competing ethical standards. For example, Trevinyo-Rodríguez (2007) identifies three levels of analysis to study ethical decisions through a concept of multi-level integrity that includes personal integrity, moral integrity, and organizational integrity. Personal integrity is composed of three characteristics: the integrated self, the integrity view, and the clean-hands view. These views incorporate the internal determinants of one's integrity (e.g., what one desires, what one uses to evaluate one's actions, and what commitments one has). In contrast, moral integrity encompasses the minimum moral standards of society that individuals will subscribe to and, in effect, prevents the personal integrity perspective from lapsing into moral relativism. Organizational identity on the other hand is the process in which the organization serves as the part of the social system that individuals interact most directly with and that influences their actions to achieve organizational performance.

When these three levels of analysis are in alignment, there is little ambiguity about what is the right thing to do. However, when these three sources of integrity do not align, there is risk for ethical violations, corruption, and eventually moral injury. This chapter adapts this levels-of-integrity framework into a referential framework of personal moral identity, professional organizational ethical obligations, and social ethical norms. It uses this modified framework to further analyze the ethical tensions present in professional public services.

The above non-exhaustive review offers a snapshot of the state of ethical studies as it relates to ethical dilemmas stemming from tensions between values that make up the multiple ethical standards to which public professionals subscribe. It shows the gap in the available literature regarding how to address issues of ethical dilemmas that transcend the personal, social, and organization levels of analysis and that highlights the competing pull from each direction. To further illustrate the nature of this gap as it relates to these tensions, this chapter now explores examples from the public-service professions of the military, police, and border security using the personal, societal, and organizational framework discussed above.

Tensions of Ethical Standards in the Military Profession

Faced with several recognizable and current examples of unethical behavior in the form of alleged war crimes, and by the corrupt behavior to cover up those atrocities, some scholars assume that the causes of these behaviors in military personnel stem from a flaw in character. They propose that the dilemma between professional ethics and military necessity is a false dichotomy. For example, such as in cases of the use of torture to resolve the "ticking-time-bomb" problem (Rockwood 2012). However, this is not the type of ethical dilemma that this chapter is describing, where two wrongs do not make a right. Instead, this chapter looks to the examples in war that obligate military personnel to participate in the ultimate social taboo of killing other humans in legitimate combat scenarios. In fact, these actions would not be wrong but, instead, the correct actions according to the professional duties of the military.

Nonetheless, the phenomena of soldiers suffering mental illness, such as depression, anxiety attacks, or post-traumatic syndrome indicate that military personnel experience a form of moral injury even when they have done nothing unethical (Shay 2005). This phenomena demonstrates that the ethical behavior, or the feeling of behaving in an unethical manner during war is not just dependent on character, but rather on one's sense of "goodness and humanity" (Sherman 2015), even if killing during war can be legitimately justified. When this sense is violated, it is "prima facie morally problematic" (Dill and Shue 2012, 319).

Further, by not reconciling the competing moral imperatives of the military's professional obligation to win the war with the obligation not to kill according to societal ethical norms, military personnel endure excessive risks of experiencing moral injury to their personal moral identity. This further endangers the overall mission because the ethically ambiguous environment can lead to a further breakdown in the ethical resiliency of military personnel and may contribute to other ethical violations as a result of a reduction in the capacity for decision-making (Pfaff 2016).

The tensions discussed above indicate that there is competition between the personal moral identity of the individual military professional, the societal ethical norm of the preservation of life, and the organizational professional duties instilled by the military institution. Failure to manage the tensions between these three separate ethical standards in the military profession could potentially lead to corruption, ethical misbehavior, and moral injury or undue emotional labor.

This theory may more readily lead to an explanation of antecedents to such cases as the My Lai Massacre in Vietnam, or the Muhammadiyah rape/killing and subsequent cover-up in Iraq, in which military personnel responsible for those crimes had endured intense traumatic events leading up to these crimes. Nonetheless, it is on face value a less compelling explanation of the precursors that led to such clear-cut corruption cases such as the Navy's Fat Leonard military contracting scandal. However, that is one of the main contentions of this chapter. To date, research has not explored the tensions between personal moral identity, the societal ethical norms, and the professional organizational duties in any cases that fall along the spectrum of unethical and corrupt military behavior.

Tensions of Ethical Standards in Police Profession

The similarity of ethical dilemmas faced by police and military is only recently being recognized by trauma researchers (Papazoglou and Chopko 2017). While this research makes a distinct study of moral injury in veterans (Litz et al. 2009; Maguen and Litz 2016; Nash and Litz 2013; Brock and Lettini 2012), the association of moral injury in police personnel stems from research conducted on moral distress and moral suffering in health-care professions. Moral distress, associated with the nursing profession by trauma scholars, occurs when nurses often express a moral challenge in providing care to their patients and families (Elpern, Covert, and Kleinpell 2005). This moral distress manifests as a "psychological disequilibrium," as a person is placed in a situation where a moral decision is required, but the professional is not able to make that decision due to "various hurdles: institution policy, lack of time, protocol, and so forth" (Papazoglou and Chopko 2017, 2). The literature further associates moral distress with unethical or incorrect choices that occur due to errors in judgment and decision-making, adopting the wrong course of action, or by failing to conduct the proper risk analysis for circumstances that are not accounted for in the planning process (Kälvemark et al. 2004).

Moral injury becomes more evident when police professionals make decisions and judgments that have extreme moral dilemmas associated with complex and ambiguous situations (McCarthy and Deady 2008; Papazoglou and Chopko 2017). Like the military, police are subject to situations in which they witness or participate in atrocities, gruesome crimes, and death in the line of duty (Papazoglou 2013). For example, Weiss et al. (2010) demonstrate that almost 25 percent of police sampled in a critical incident survey reported killing or seriously injuring someone in the line of duty. This participation leads to the same feelings of guilt and shame among police as among military (Komarovskaya et al. 2011). Even more noteworthy, this feeling of moral injury was more prevalent among police who strongly identified as Christian and subscribed to the religious obligation of "thou shall not kill" (Chopko et al. 2016).

There is also empirical evidence that this moral injury leads to other dysfunctional and maladaptive behavior, poor judgement, and decision-making among police such as alcohol abuse (Chopko, Palmieri, and Adams 2013). It is a small step to propose that these maladaptive behaviors might be related further to other dysfunctional behaviors such as egregious laps in ethical judgement leading to corruption. That is to say, in situations where police confront extreme tensions between their personal moral identity, societal ethical norms, and organizational professional obligations—leading to lapses in judgment of personal conduct such as alcohol abuse or domestic violence—so, too, could other malbehavior occur such as violating a citizen's rights or collaborating to cover up the violation. To date, however, no research is empirically examining this question to see if this is the case. This is despite some research indicating the there is a difference between personal identities and organizational actions. Such as, for example, research showing that while individual police overwhelmingly do not identify as racist, their organizations overwhelmingly demonstrate collective traits of institutionalized biases correlated to race (Epp, Maynard-Moody, and Haider-Markel 2014).

Tensions of Ethical Standards in the Border Security Profession

As briefly indicated earlier, tensions in the ethical standards with in the border-security professions (composed of personnel who work in any of the government or private organizations that play a part in border security and enforcement) is poignant to the author because when the United States' 2018 family separation policy was highlighted by the media as a feature of US immigration policy, he had students who shared that they had family members who worked in one or more of the agencies responsible for carrying out that policy. Some of those students indicated that not only were their parents dealing with the moral dilemma of having to enforce a policy that went against their culture, but that the same guilt transferred to other members of their family, specifically to their children who were students of the author. As such, the students displayed a hesitancy to name the exact agency their parent worked for, but they were more forthcoming about their feelings of guilt by association. Like in the military and police, the professional ethics and the subsequent tensions in the border-security profession have only just begun to be studied (Olsthoorn and Schut 2018).

To be clear, the development of the profession of border security is a new phenomenon. While the US has long had a border guard, the development of professional agencies specifically focused on the standards of border security developed with the founding of the US Customs and Border Protection and US Immigration and Customs Enforcement in 2003. While European nations have long intertwined a professional military cadre with the constabulary duties of border security—for example, the French Gendarmerie Nationale, the Spanish Guardia Civil, and the Royal Netherlands Marechaussee—the development of professional standards for a border security profession materialized in 2016 with the foundation of the Frontex, the European border and Coast Guard agency (Olsthoorn and Schut 2018). While war veterans or police, can suffer moral injury, from guilt or shame as described above, border security professionals, who also witness or are participants in events that bring into contrast societal, personal, and organizational moral ethical standards, leaving them exposed to PTSD or moral injury in the extreme (see also Frontex 2013, 49), find themselves untethered from any ethical frame of reference to guide them in the moral dilemmas they inevitably face while enacting the duties of their office.

Francisco Cantú (2018) describes a clear example of the physical and psychological effects stemming from the moral conflicts border patrol agents encounter in *The Line Becomes a River*. In his book, Cantú describes how the tensions that occur between his moral upbringing to serve his country and others, symbolized by his immigrant mother's work as a US Forest Ranger, the professional ethics of the border patrol charged with preventing unauthorized access to the United States, and the values of American societal culture of welcoming immigrants lead to a morbidly cynical and insulated culture of the patrol agents. The persistent exposure to dead bodies of immigrants lost in the desert contributes to the under-culture in the border patrol. Cantú demonstrates this when relating how agents turn on one of their own for becoming too soft and kind to immigrants and thus frame him for a crime he did not commit (2018, 187–88). The conflicting moral tensions Cantú describes lead to him enduring the psychological effects of cryptic nightmares, the physiological effects of stress-related teeth-grinding, and his eventual departure from the border patrol. While describing a situation that is neither from a police officer's nor a soldier's perspective, members of both professions could easily relate to Cantú's situation as a border patrol agent.

While the military profession and the border security profession are both susceptible to moral dilemmas and resulting moral injuries and ethical lapses, where they part ways is in the ethical viewpoint they both adopt to deal with such dilemmas. The military profession teaches its professionals the value of virtue ethics, while the latest ethical training for border security professionals is rules-based ethics. Whereas virtue ethics assume that virtues and character are interrelated, and that both are not inherent but must be developed, border security ethics may limit the discretion of border guards, thus providing some protections to them as well as to immigrants. However, the downside to this approach is that it "can impede the ability to see the moral aspect of what one is doing, while that ability is evidently an important prerequisite for moral deliberation and morally sound decision-making" (Olsthoorn and Schut 2018, 164). Essentially, if decision-making is impeded by situations out of the control of the individual border guard, then it is a short distance for persons of good character to become unmoored from any ethical standard and commit unethical, immoral, or even corrupt behavior.

It is clear from the scant discussion of this potential connection between the tension among levels of morality/integrity, moral suffering, and unethical corrupt behavior within the border security profession that more research is necessary. The next section provides recommended questions to supplement a future research agenda on the tensions that professional public servants may encounter in their work.

Toward a Research Agenda

The following questions are both ontological and epistemological in nature. From the ontological pursuit, are the personal, societal, and organizational levels of integrity/morality identifiable within public servants' frames of reference? Are there tensions between the different ethical standards of conduct at each level of analysis? If these tensions exist, does that further impede the ethical judgement and decision-making of the individual? Is this impediment worsened by the severity of the tension, or the traumatic experience of the ethical dilemma? For example, if the situation is traumatic, or completely abhorrent to the personal integrity of the individual, does that aggravate the tension and increase the potential for unethical or corrupt behavior?

While the ontological inquiry above is important to establish the relationship of the tensions or conflicts with personal moral identities, societal ethical norms, and the professional organizational duties, epistemological inquiries are equally important so as to contribute to an application of that research toward developing solutions to deal with the resulting negative consequences. Therefore, additional questions to examine could include: What type of professional training and education are required to offset these impacts? How would one measure the efficacy of this training?

Lastly, the research on ethics and corruption is very multidisciplinary, but very scant in its interdisciplinary approach. Future research efforts should look beyond the silos of internal disciplines and span academic disciplines to draw the best research from each to build upon.

Conclusion

This chapter argues that the current trajectory of research into unethical behavior, or corruption, is too simplistic. It is at once reactionary and reductionist in nature. Therefore, this chapter looks at the complexity of circumstances leading to unethical or corrupt behavior by teasing apart the impact of values-conflicting dilemmas that stem from tensions between public servants' personal moral identities, societal ethical norms, and professional organizational obligations. It proposes that when these ethical standards do not align, they pull the public servant in two or three directions. This pull may be enough to cause a cognitive dissonance between what public servants believe is in line with their sense of moral identity, what they believe are the norms that are prevalent within their society, and what their obligations are to their professional organizations.

This dissonance may be enough to diminish an individual's sense of right judgement and prove detrimental to their ethical decision-making. This may be especially so if they lack the experience or training to deal with such instances. Thus, this chapter advances this theory further by proposing that regardless of personal moral character or training to develop that ethical character, certain experiences where these tensions are acute, traumatic, or identity-shaking, may in fact contribute to an individual's inability or failure to make what would be considered by society as the right decision.

The chapter uses the security professions (military, police, and border security) within public service to illustrate tensions between separate sources of ethical obligations. It contends that not managing these tensions within these professions leaves open the possibility for future unethical or corrupt behavior. It further recommends a research agenda to explore whether there is in fact such a relationship between the tensions evident in the three ethical levels and the extreme impact this tension has on the psyche of the individual who encounters this tension and the resulting unethical or corrupt behavior. It further recommends that follow-on research be interdisciplinary to determine what can be done to mitigate this effect and reduce overall episodes of corruption or unethical behavior. In that sense, this chapter raises more questions than it answers.

References

Barry, Bruce, Mara Olekalns, and Laura Rees. 2018. "An Ethical Analysis of Emotional Labor." *Journal of Business Ethics: JBE; Dordrecht*, May, 1–18.

Beauchamp, Tom L., and Norman E. Bowie. 1983. *Ethical Theory and Business*. 2nd ed. Englewood Cliffs, NJ: Prentice-Hall.

Brock, Rita Nakashima, and Gabriella Lettini. 2012. *Soul Repair: Recovering from Moral Injury after War*. Boston: Beacon Press.

Cantú, Francisco. 2018. *The Line Becomes a River*. New York: Riverhead Books.

Chopko, Brian A., Vanessa C. Facemire, Patrick A. Palmieri, and Robert C. Schwartz. 2016. "Spirituality and Health Outcomes among Police Officers: Empirical Evidence Supporting a Paradigm Shift." *Criminal Justice Studies* 29(4), 363–77.

Chopko, Brian A., Patrick A. Palmieri, and Richard E. Adams. 2013. "Associations Between Police Stress and Alcohol Use: Implications for Practice." *Journal of Loss and Trauma* 18(5), 482–97.

Dill, Janina, and Henry Shue. 2012. "Limiting the Killing in War: Military Necessity and the St. Petersburg Assumption." *Ethics andInternational Affairs; New York* 26(3), 311–33.

Elpern, Ellen H., Barbara Covert, and Ruth Kleinpell. 2005. "Moral Distress of Staff Nurses in a Medical Intensive Care Unit" (Reprint). *American Journal of Critical Care* 14(6), 523–30.

Epp, Charles R., Steven Maynard-Moody, and Donald P. Haider-Markel. 2014. *Pulled Over: How Police Stops Define Race and Citizenship*. Chicago, IL: University of Chicago Press.

Heckler, Nuri, and John C. Ronquillo. 2018. "Effective Resolution of Ethical Dilemmas in Social Enterprise Organizations: A Moral Philosophy and Public Management Approach." *Public Integrity*, 1–15.

Hennessey, John, and Bernard Gert. 1985. "Moral Rules and Moral Ideals: A Useful Distinction in Business and Professional Practice." *Journal of Business Ethics* 4(2), 105–15.

Kälvemark, Sofia, Anna T Höglund, Mats G Hansson, Peter Westerholm, and Bengt Arnetz. 2004. "Living with Conflicts—Ethical Dilemmas and Moral Distress in the Health Care System." *Social Science & Medicine* 58(6), 1075–84.

Kaptein, Muel. 2008. "Developing a Measure of Unethical Behavior in the Workplace: A Stakeholder Perspective." *Journal of Management* 34(5), 978–1008.

Komarovskaya, Irina, Shira Maguen, Shannon E. McCaslin, Thomas J. Metzler, Anita Madan, Adam D. Brown, Isaac R. Galatzer-Levy, Clare Henn-Haase, and Charles R. Marmar. 2011. "The Impact of Killing and Injuring Others on Mental Health Symptoms among Police Officers." *Journal of Psychiatric Research* 45(10), 1332–36.

Litz, Brett T., Nathan Stein, Eileen Delaney, Leslie Lebowitz, William P. Nash, Caroline Silva, and Shira Maguen. 2009. "Moral Injury and Moral Repair in War Veterans: A Preliminary Model and Intervention Strategy." *Clinical Psychology Review* 29(8), 695–706.

Maguen, Shira, and Brett Litz. 2016. "Moral Injury in the Context of War—PTSD." Department of Veterans Affairs National Center for PTSD. https://www.ptsd.va.gov/professional/co-occurring/moral_injury_at_war.asp.

McCarthy, Joan, and Rick Deady. 2008. "Moral Distress Reconsidered." *Nursing Ethics* 15(2), 254–62.

Nash, William, and Brett Litz. 2013. "Moral Injury: A Mechanism for War-Related Psychological Trauma in Military Family Members." *Clinical Child and Family Psychology Review* 16(4), 365–75.

Olsthoorn, Peter, and Michelle Schut. 2018. "The Ethics of Border Guarding: A First Exploration and a Research Agenda for the Future." *Ethics and Education* 13(2), 157–71.

Papazoglou, Konstantinos. 2013. "Conceptualizing Police Complex Spiral Trauma and Its Applications in the Police Field." *Traumatology* 19(3), 196–209.

Papazoglou, Konstantinos, and Brian Chopko. 2017. "The Role of Moral Suffering (Moral Distress and Moral Injury) in Police Compassion Fatigue and PTSD: An Unexplored Topic." *Frontiers in Psychology* 8: 1–5. doi: 10.3389/fpsyg.2017.01999.

Pfaff, C. Anthony. 2016. "Five Myths about Military Ethics. (Myths about the Army Profession)." *Parameters* 46(3), 59–69.

Rockwood, Lawrence P. 2012. *Professional Ethics and Military Necessity: A False Dichotomy?* Washington, DC: Educational Publishing Foundation.

Shay, Jonathan. 2005. *Achilles in Vietnam: Combat Trauma and the Undoing of Character*. New York: Scribner.

Sherman, Nancy. 2015. *Afterwar: Healing the Moral Injuries of Our Soldiers*. Oxford: Oxford University Press.

Transparency International. 2017. "Transparency International—What Is Corruption?" https://www.transparency.org/what-is-corruption.

Trevinyo-Rodríguez, Rosa N. 2007. "Integrity: A Systems Theory Classification." *Journal of Management History* 13(1), 74–93.

Weiss, Daniel S., Alain Brunet, Suzanne R. Best, Thomas J. Metzler, Akiva Liberman, Nnamdi Pole, Jeffrey A. Fagan, and Charles R. Marmar. 2010. "Frequency and Severity Approaches to Indexing Exposure to Trauma: The Critical Incident History Questionnaire for Police Officers." *Journal of Traumatic Stress* 23(6), 734–43.

Zyglidopoulos, Stelios, Paul Hirsch, Pablo Martin de Holan, and Nelson Phillips. 2017. "Expanding Research on Corporate Corruption, Management, and Organizations." *Journal of Management Inquiry* 26(3), 247–53.

9

The Nonprofit Sector
Charity and Chicanery

Barry D. Friedman and Amanda M. Main

Deviance, Exploitation, and Scandals in the Nonprofit Sector

Organizational evil is a frequent phenomenon in organizations across all sectors. There are evil individuals, says Jurkiewicz (2012, ix), who are able to "create an organizational environment that is evil and at the same time sustains evil through policy, culture, and manipulations of the social environment." Smith (2017, 2) describes "the Dark Side of voluntarism," a term that refers to nonaccountability and deviance in nonprofit organizations. Grobman (2015) lists an assortment of ethics issues of which nonprofit leaders need to be mindful: accountability, conflict of interest, disclosures, acceptable amount of surplus, outside remuneration, amounts of salaries, benefits, and perquisites, and personal relationships (e.g., nepotism). The American Bar Association's Coordinating Committee on Nonprofit Governance (2005) reported that nonprofit organizations have been susceptible to scandals ranging from lack of sufficient charitable donations to substantial tax-status and compensation misuse. This evil is expensive: According to a 2008 study, approximately $40 billion every year is stolen from charities by employees (White 2010, 8). " 'Transparency,' 'accountability,' and 'conflict-of-interest' are today's buzzwords [among] . . . executives . . . in the nonprofit world, but for so many charities they . . . [are] not real action items that result in an ability to make hard decisions. . . . And the reason for that is the absence of a nonprofit ethos."

Elitism and Concentration of Authority

While one would expect that the principal beneficiaries of the charitable sector would be people in need, the sector's institutions are controlled by relatively affluent individuals who conduct the organizations' business in other than a democratic, egalitarian fashion. In his classic book *Political Parties*, Roberto Michels (1962, 365) made the memorably chilling statement, "Who says organization says oligarchy."

The elites govern these organizations and appoint each other to their boards, creating a system of interlocking directorates. Accordingly, the culture of nonprofit organizations is relatively consistent across the sector and has little to do with democracy and participation in decision-making. Rather, nonprofits continue to use corporate board models despite evidence that they are ineffective as they separate the board from the constituents and inhibit accountability (Freiwirth 2014).

The argument that organizations should freely disclose details about their operations appeals to the general public. However, actual decision makers who could implement politics of openness view the notion of equal access to information with a jaundiced eye. Organizational owners, directors, and executives harbor attitudes such as these:

- The organizations' information is the property of the organizations and their leadership. Other members of the organizations and outsiders have no claim to it, unless laws specify otherwise.
- Disclosure to other members of the organizations and outsiders has no purpose because they are not in a position to do anything productive with it.
- A policy of unrestricted disclosure would compromise the active, productive exchange of information among the leaders.

US nonprofit organizations of any size are required to record and preserve documents that reflect their governing boards' deliberations and decisions. If the Internal Revenue Service opts to inquire into the contents of a nonprofit's annual Form 990 return, and the organization cannot produce minutes of meetings, the IRS may revoke the nonprofit's income-tax exemption. However, a result of the above bulleted sentiments is that many nonprofits deem it unthinkable to make the minutes of board and committee meetings available to members, donors, and other members of the public. Attorneys Irish, Kushen, and Simon (2004) oppose any disclosure requirements for governing-body meeting records, saying that the boards' deliberations should be private. If nonprofits need to keep their discussions and decisions secret, who are the adversaries who must be kept uninformed about the decisions? Are they the same people from whom the organization asks for donations and volunteer labor? Calling for openness, Mancuso (2011) declares that sharing records with the public about the leadership's decision-making is useful in connecting the nonprofit organization with its supporters. Ahmed (2013) offers a simple suggestion: Nonprofit organizations can conveniently make all such information available on their websites.

The opinion of many organizational leaders, supported by laws, is that the owners or members of boards of directors are fully qualified to make disclosure determinations. To wit:

> The board-centered model of governance has been adopted by nonprofit and voluntary organizations throughout the United States to address a number of . . . organizational issues ranging from stakeholder management to legal supervision (LeRoux and Langer 2016, 147).

Laws and other rules that establish board members' duties of loyalty, diligence, and confidentiality tend to be explained in such a way as to assert that they may be held accountable should they use their positions for personal gain, contrary to the organizations' best interests. This approach assumes that most are acting properly, and that a devious board member might act improperly unbeknownst to the rest of the members. Thus, laws and rules demand that board members disclose to the entire board possible conflicts of interest and other threats to the organization's well-being (Hopkins and Gross 2010). A more complicated situation involves an entire board running afoul of its legitimate responsibilities. If a board member believes that the board is deficient in its service or demonstration of responsibility to such groups, his or her duties of loyalty, diligence, and confidentiality *to the board—the ultimate authority*—preclude disclosure to anyone other than the IRS and the state's attorney general. Renz (2010) emphasizes that the principal obligation of board members is to protect the board. If the board has done something improper, a dissenting member can do nothing more than resign, and even that will not release him or her from the legal duty to keep the impropriety confidential. Should the board member disclose to actual stakeholders, he or she may find himself or herself the target of a lawsuit, and the organization's cost of legal representation will be handled by the organization's treasury. This vicious circle in which the board is responsible only to itself silences board members and deprives the public of information.

Insufficiency of Reporting Requirements

Some policy makers and watchdogs complain that aspects of the 990 filing requirement spare nonprofits from demanding accountability for a number of reasons. The financial data are not necessarily reported in accordance with Generally Accepted Accounting Principles, and they have not necessarily undergone external audit. Even if they have, auditors cannot help but be influenced by the fees that charities pay them. Nonprofits can report overhead costs, staff payment, and fund-raising costs as program expenses. Ahmed (2013) states that many nonprofits falsely report the amount of fund-raising expenses on their Form 990 returns and, according to one study, 41 percent of nonprofits that reported donations acknowledge no fund-raising expenses at all.

Compounding this issue, most state governments have few laws pertaining to non-profit organizations and little enforcement activity. The website of the National Association of State Charity Officials reports on an ongoing basis when state officials do take action in response to alleged, startling charity misconduct. For example, in September and October 2018, the association reported that Michigan's attorney general imposed a notice of intended action and a cease-and-desist order against the National Emergency Medicine Association of Edgewood, Maryland, for

> over 600,000 violations of the Charitable Organizations and Solicitations Act"; Maryland's attorney general and secretary of state imposed a cease-and-desist order against Stephen D. Everhart, Lion Fundraising, *Police Journal* and *Fire Yearbook*, and Lion Fraternal Order of Police Assistance Fund LLC for collecting over $1 million in donations since 2012, in violation of the Maryland Solicitations Act; Michigan's attorney general announced a settlement with the Florida-based Food for the Poor to resolve allegations of deceptive charitable solicitations; and Minnesota's attorney general filed a lawsuit against the American Federation of Police & Concerned Citizens, Inc., of Florida for "deceptively representing that donations would primarily be used to help families of officers killed in the line of duty, when only a small percentage of funds went to such purposes (www.nasconet.org).

Exploitation

The nonprofit sector is a sprawling economic system that accounts for about 5 percent of the US gross domestic product. If the nonprofit sector is generating results contrary to society's expectations—for example, if it is bringing about a redistribution of wealth from people of modest means to people of affluent means—then the sector is depriving other institutions of resources that they might use to advance social equity.

The leadership- and management-oriented cultures and behaviors of countless non-profits often spawn the callous treatment of people in the system whose resources are modest. This includes employees who are deprived of the opportunity to participate in organizational policy making. Donors of modest donations are similarly excluded from the decision-making process and, instead of receiving informative reports about the organization's policies, are inundated with slick fund-raising messages written by shrewd professionals. This is a practice that causes donors to believe that their money is being used for a stated mission, while managers and fund-raising professionals are becoming increasingly wealthy. In a 2011 article, Pollack reported the salaries of CEOs of international charities: the International AIDS Vaccine Initiative, $489,406; Program for Appropriate Technology in Health, $406,053; the International Rescue Committee, $379,346; CARE, $379,000; World Vision, $376,799; and Human Rights Watch, $335,000. Charity Navigator (2016) found that charities whose expenses are $1 million per year pay their CEOs an average annual salary of about $90,000, while organizations whose expenses are $1 billion per year pay an average of about $750,000. Ten out of 4,587 charities paid $1 million of more to their CEOs, while 66 charities paid between $500,000 and

$1 million. Clients routinely experience impersonality and disdain as they try to receive assistance from nonprofit organizations that have supposedly been established to alleviate their misery. News reports frequently state that, when its representatives show up at a disaster scene, the American Red Cross overpromises but seems unprepared to deliver disaster-relief resources to victims. US Senator Chuck Grassley (R-Iowa), chairman of the Senate Judiciary Committee, complained that the Red Cross spent about 25 percent of the $487.6 million that it raised for earthquake relief in Haiti in 2010 on administrative fees. In November 2017, Texas governor Greg Abbott complained that the Red Cross was responding unhelpfully to many victims of Hurricane Harvey (CBS News 2017).

Remedies

The relationship between nonprofit organizations and their stakeholders is founded on trust. If a donor delivers a hundred dollars to a charity, he or she does not usually expect to receive a hundred dollars in tangible personal benefit. If the charity's mission, for example, is alleviation of hunger, the donor might expect that a number of disadvantaged individuals will be fed. Unless the donor lingers at the charity's service center to watch as hungry people receive food, the donor relies on the integrity of the charity's officials. The officials' selfishness and practice of favoritism toward other professionals will plunder the donors' good faith, and secrecy and suppression of informative data will leave donors bereft of the information that they need to make optimal decisions.

Jurkiewicz and Grossman (2012) have described the prevalence of organizational evil: Its antidote they assert, is accountability, transparency, and disclosure. These practices are facilitated by open meetings, availability of minutes, whistleblower protection, and leadership that promotes empathy for intended recipients of the charities' benevolence.

Oversight

Behn, DeVries, and Lin (2010) are among those who have offered suggestions for reform of the US nonprofit sector. They endorse the initiative of certain state governments that recommend that nonprofits conform to the Sarbanes-Oxley Act's provisions to adopt standards of accountability and responsibility. Behn and colleagues also note that the US Senate Finance Committee in 2004 proposed requiring nonprofit chief executives to sign, under penalty of perjury, declarations committing themselves to the accuracy and thoroughness of their organizations' Form 990 returns. The committee called for reforms to ensure more transparency, independent audits, and disclosure of required information on their websites. The public continues to await enactment of the necessary legislation. Grobman (2015) is among observers who have proposed that the US Congress should establish a regulatory agency, comparable to the Securities and Exchange Commission, to monitor nonprofits' financial management and disclosure. This kind of agency would arrange for disclosure of financial data generated in accordance with prescribed accounting standards in a consistent format so that prospective donors and volunteers, as well as journalists, can find and use the information.

Transparency

Capitalist theory assumes that both parties to a voluntary marketplace transaction possess complete information so that each can determine that the exchange will serve its interests. There is an imbalance of information between nonprofit organizations and their stakeholders. Access to information helps to level the playing field—that is, to ameliorate the dependence of relatively powerless people on those who possess power and information.

Culture is an essential element for transparency in a nonprofit organization. Generally, in a privately held for-profit organization, if a founding proprietor wishes to be transparent about his organization, he is able to do so without interference from others. However, a nonprofit is run by a board of directors, not the original founder. Hence, if such an individual wanted to ensure that transparency remains a priority, one method for doing so is establishing a culture for it.

It is imperative that the founder establish the culture and climate desired for the organization purposively and immediately. A constructive, ethical culture contributes to effectiveness, performance, and competitiveness. The founder sets a tone by indicating what he or she expects, supports, and rewards. If a founder wishes to have a culture and climate for transparency, he or she can develop a mission statement, a statement of core values, and a code of ethics that includes transparency and that is featured prominently with any materials regarding the organization. If the founder disavows secrecy, this will ensure that those who become active members of the administration, including the board and executive director, share the organization's values, in accordance with the attraction-selection-attrition cycle (ASA) (Schneider 1987). This cycle occurs when a founder establishes a culture and a climate conducive to his or her values. People with similar values are attracted to the organization and are thus selected. Those employees who are selected, but whose values are incompatible with the organization, leave; thus the organization becomes a function of the values of the members. Founders must truly comprehend the importance of transparency and be mindful of the actions that they take in order to ensure that their organization does not fall prey to a shroud of secrecy once a board is legally in control.

Disclosure

Given their druthers, organizations can ordinarily be expected to disclose as little information as they can get away with. An alternative maneuver that some organizations use is to flood consumers with useless information, a tactic available because of the volume of information in this era of big data (Henriques 2007; Taylor and Kelsey 2016). The preference of so many nonprofit organizations' leaders for selective disclosure provides an opportunity for progressive managers to distinguish their organizations as being generous with informative reports, such as board minutes and financial settlements.

Watchdog organizations have a key role in monitoring nonprofits' disclosures and ensuring that they meet or exceed minimum government-prescribed requirements for reporting. Expectations can include financial statements that are comprehensive in truthfully reporting overhead, fund-raising, and payroll expenses as well as reports of policy deliberations.

Educating Donors

Many people around the world have been conditioned to spontaneously respond with generosity to charitable appeals. Smith (2017, 2–3) states that "researchers, observers, and leaders in the [nonprofit] field talk and act as if the sector were indeed angelic or sanctified." This "boosterism," says Smith, "runs the risk of overlooking or deemphasizing critical flaws or dysfunctions." News media often participate in transmitting and magnifying the uncritical soliciting on behalf of charitable organizations. As long as individuals donate to charities regardless of the charities' ethical conduct or adherence to standards of transparency, nonprofit leaders will have no particular incentive to behave more responsibly. There is a need for such institutions as news organizations, watchdog organizations, and others to direct individuals to charities that are using resources effectively and efficiently and that are disclosing the information needed to evaluate the charities' commitment to the public interest.

Self-Regulation

Tschirhart and Bielefeld (2012, 28–29) report that the *Standards for Excellence: An Ethics and Accountability Code for the Nonprofit Sector*, established by the Maryland Association of Nonprofit Organizations, has gained popularity as "a model for other states' efforts to promote ethical practices and accountability." They warn that, if nonprofits do not keep "their houses clean," declining public trust "may be the [impetus] of increased government scrutiny and legislation." The ABA Coordinating Committee on Nonprofit Governance (2005) declares that all nonprofit organizations should have written conflict-of-interest policies to prevent personal use of corporate assets, use of confidential information, or abuse of privileges. The adherence to these policies should be reaffirmed annually and allow for immediate reporting of any spontaneous conflicts.

Training

Programs that train nonprofit managers must not involve mere rhapsodizing about the wonders of the nonprofit sector and the work that the sector's leaders do. There must be forthright acknowledgment about the existence of undemocratic, self-interest-oriented, secretive, and fraudulent activity, as evidenced by numerous scandals. Curricula must include intense training about selfless leadership, codes of conduct, and transparency. Agencies that accredit these programs must include in their evaluations an assessment of the programs' capacity to produce ethical leaders who are committed to organizational cultures that direct managers, other employees, and volunteers to serve the organizations' missions rather than themselves, and that fulfill the sector's obligation to the public interest.

Conclusion

Those who lead government agencies, corporations, and associations tend to be attached arrogantly to the attitude that only they should be privy to the information that they possess. Meanwhile, they reach out to the public for donations and volunteer labor, and to government officials for tax exemptions and other favorable policies. This imbalance of respect for others' intellect is emblematic of a system that exempts high-status officials of various types from scrutiny and accountability. Historically, liberal countries have had little appetite for stringent regulation of charities, in so far as there is not much of a constituency for heavy-handed control of charitable organizations. While countries such as the United States and components of the United Kingdom have imposed more elaborate reporting requirements on charities (see, e.g., Dunn 2000; Moody 2000; and Ohta 2018), few charities are singled out for audit and punishment. For its part, the public in many countries has been conditioned to be generous to charities. Pro-charity propaganda emitted by charities and the news media minimize attention to corruption and induce the public's short memory of appalling scandals.

Accordingly, the authors offer proposals that government enforcement of Section 501(c) of the Internal Revenue Code, the UK Charities Act 1993, and similar laws become more vigorous; that charities adopt cultures that value transparency and stakeholder participation in decision making; and that watchdog organizations monitor charities' disclosure of documents revealing the policy deliberations that produce the organizations' missions and outputs. The success or failure of charities must not be determined based on the manipulative effectiveness of their slick promotions. Their success should be a function of the value of their service to the public and their effective use of resources. For that to happen, donors, foundations, and government grant administrators must have access to information that will guide them toward rational decisions about their investments in the charitable sector.

References

Ahmed, Shamima. 2013. *Effective Non-profit Management:Context, Concepts, and Competencies.* Boca Raton, FL: CRC Press.

American Bar Association, Coordinating Committee on Nonprofit Governance. 2005. *Guide to Nonprofit Corporate Governance in the Wake of Sarbanes-Oxley.* Chicago: American Bar Association.

Behn, Bruce K., Delwyn D. DeVries, and Jing Lin. 2010. "The Determinants of Transparency in Nonprofit Organizations: An Exploratory Study." *Advances in Accounting 26*(1), June, 6–12.

CBS News. 2017. "Red Cross Faces Criticism Over Hurricane Harvey Relief Distribution." November 28.

Dunn, Alison. 2000. "Introduction," in Alison Dunn, ed., *The Voluntary Sector, the State and The Law.* Oxford: Hart Publishing, 1–5.

Freiwirth, Judy. 2014. "Community-Engagement Governance: Engaging Stakeholders for Community Impact," in Chris Cornforth and William A. Brown, eds., *Nonprofit Governance: Innovative Perspectives and Approaches.* Abingdon, Oxon: Routledge, 183–209.

Grobman, Gary M. 2015. *An Introduction to the Nonprofit Sector: A Practical Approach for the Twenty-First Century.* 4th ed. Harrisburg, PA: White Hat Communications.

Henriques, Adrian. 2007. *Corporate Truth: The Limits to Transparency.* Abingdon, Oxon: Earthscan.

Hopkins, Bruce R., and Virginia C. Gross. 2010. "The Legal Framework of the Nonprofit Sector in the United States," in David O. Renz et al., eds., *The Jossey-Bass Handbook of Nonprofit Leadership and Management.* 3rd ed. San Francisco: Jossey-Bass, 42–76.

Irish, Leon E., Robert Kushen, and Karla W. Simon. 2004. *Guidelines for Laws Affecting Civic Organizations.* 2nd ed. New York: Open Society Institute.

Jurkiewicz, Carole L. 2012. "Introduction," in Carole L. Jurkiewicz, ed., *The Foundations of Organizational Evil.* Armonk, NY: M. E. Sharpe, ix–x.

Jurkiewicz, Carole L., and Dave Grossman. 2012. "Evil at Work," in Carole L. Jurkiewicz, ed., *The Foundations of Organizational Evil.* Armonk, NY: M. E. Sharpe, 3–15.

LeRoux, Kelly, and Julie Langer. 2016. "What Nonprofit Executives Want and What They Get from Board Members." *Nonprofit Management & Leadership 27*(2) Winter, 147–64.

Mancuso, Anthony. 2011. *Nonprofit Meetings, Minutes and Records: How to Run Your Nonprofit Corporation So You Don't Run into Trouble.* 2nd ed. Berkeley: NOLO.

Michels, Roberto. [1911], 1962. *Political Parties: A Sociological Study of the Oligarchical Tendencies of Modern Democracies.* Eden Paul and Cedar Paul, trans. New York: Free Press.

Moody, Susan R. 2000. "Policing the Voluntary Sector: Legal Issues and Volunteer Vetting," in Alison Dunn, ed., *The Voluntary Sector, The State and the Law.* Oxford. Hart Publishing, 39–57.

Ohta, Kyoko. 2018. "Legislation and Policy for the Nonprofit Sector, Japan." *Global Encyclopedia of Public Administration, Public Policy, and Governance.* New York: Springer.

Pollack, Daniel. 2011. "Salaries of CEOs of International NGOs: Ensuring Fair Compensation while Avoiding Populist Rage." *International Social Work 54*(3) July, 599–604.

Renz, David O. 2010. "Leadership, Governance, and the Work of the Board," in Renz and Associates, ed., *The Jossey-Bass Handbook of Nonprofit Leadership and Management.* 3rd ed. San Francisco: Jossey-Bass, 125–26.

Schneider, Benjamin. 1987. "The People Make the Place." *Personnel Psychology 40*(3) (September), 437–53.

Smith, David Horton. 2017. "Misconduct and Deviance by Nonprofit Organizations." *Global Encyclopedia of Public Administration, Public Policy, and Governance.* New York: Springer.

Taylor, Roger, and Kelsey, Tim. 2016. *Transparency and the Open Society: Practical Lessons for Effective Policy.* Bristol: Policy Press.

Tschirhart, Mary, and Wolfgang Bielefeld. 2012. *Managing Nonprofit Organizations.* San Francisco: Jossey-Bass.

White, Doug. 2010. *The Nonprofit Challenge: Integrating Ethics into the Purpose and Promise of Our Nation's Charities.* New York: Palgrave Macmillan.

10

The Impact of Social Media on Trust in Local Government

Lisa Mahajan-Cusack

In recent years local governments from around the world have increasingly been adopting social media to communicate and engage with their citizens. Now that sites such as Facebook, Twitter, YouTube, and Instagram are widely used by populations globally, these can be effective tools for delivering information, facilitating the participation of citizens in the processes of government, strengthening communities, and addressing public-safety issues (Bell 2013; Burroughs 2014; Chavez, Repas, and Stefaniak 2010; Guha 2011; Heaton 2011; Nabatchi and Mergel 2010; Stephens 2011).

This chapter draws upon a range of sources to identify and discuss the main benefits to local governments of using social media, and to highlight its strengths and weaknesses. Further, the chapter identifies a number of key themes from the literature that highlight the challenges often encountered when adopting social media usage within local governments and synthesizes the evidence regarding the factors contributing to successful practice.

Purpose of Social Media Usage by Local Governments

There are several main reasons why local governments are using social media: information dissemination and for raising awareness; citizen engagement and participation; transparency and trust-building; and crisis/emergency management. These are discussed in turn below.

Information and Raising Awareness

Social media provides an instant and relatively easy way to communicate information about local government services, projects, special events, and other activities; these are the most common reasons why local governments adopt these tools. Used to communicate information about specific events or services, social media can also employed to raise public awareness about the range of government services available and how to access them, as well as information about citizens' rights and local laws (Al Aufi et al. 2017).

Citizen Engagement and Participation

When used for two-way communications by allowing users to post on and engage in discussion on the organization's social media sites, these can be very effective tools for promoting the engagement and participation of citizens in local government. Uses range from enabling citizens to report broken pavements or faulty streetlights, contribute to discussions about local issues, or interact directly with their elected local government representatives (Mundy and Umer 2013). Social media sites can also be used to support democratic processes by disseminating information about public meetings or other events (Rania 2017), or by seeking input or feedback on government policies and services (Al Aufi et al.

2017; Mundy and Umer 2013; Widyanarko 2018). Another advantage is that they can be used to target or tailor communications to specific groups, for example those in particular localities or within certain age ranges (Rania 2017), helping to ensure that everyone in the community has the opportunity to become involved.

Transparency and Trust Building

Social media is proving to be an effective means of achieving transparency of government operations, reducing corruption or its perception, and building trust in local government. As Kierkegaard (2009, 26) commented, "good government must be seen to be done." Transparency has been defined in the literature in terms of providing information about issues of importance to the public, enabling citizens to participate in political decision making and making governments accountable to the public (Graham and Avery 2013). A national online survey conducted in the United States in 2007 underscored the widespread importance of government transparency and accountability in many areas including fiscal, safety, and political (Piotrowski and Van Ryzin 2007). Achieving this involves ensuring that financial budgets, policy documents, procurement processes, strategic plans, and other key documents are made available and accessible to the public. Social media tools play an important role in enabling citizens to comment on these or to be directly involved in their development (Veal et al. 2015).

This use of social media is proving to be particularly important in helping to reverse a decline in trust in public-sector organizations in the United States and other countries in recent decades (Pew Research Centre 2015). Researchers from around the world have reported a positive impact on trust among citizens using e-government services or interacting with local governments using social media (D'Agostino et al. 2011; *Edelman Trust Barometer* 2016; Hong 2013, 346; Park and Cho 2009). One US study found this impact to be more important at the local as opposed to the state or federal levels and attributed this to positive attitudes regarding the responsiveness of local government to citizens when interacting online (Tolbert and Mossberger 2006). There is also evidence from around the world that levels of corruption in local government decrease as the usage of e-government and other online communications increase, due to the enhanced transparency and accountability of governments to their citizens (e.g., Lupu and Lazar 2015).

Crisis and Emergency Management

One of the most effective uses of social media by local governments in recent years has been crisis or emergency situations, such as floods or other natural disasters, or outbreaks of disease (Bertot, Jaeger, and Grimes 2010; Chavez et al. 2010; Al Aufi et al. 2017). Tweets or Facebook posts, for example, can be used to provide up-to-date news on developments as well as information and guidance on what to do if affected by the emergency. One of the reasons why social media has proved to be so useful in these contexts is that much of the content is often provided by citizens themselves and can be quickly shared and reposted.

For example, during the 2011 Eastern Japan tsunami, networks were formed in municipalities with mid-level disruption where there was still access to the Internet, and social media such as Facebook became one of the main forms of communication, source of information, and social support in the days immediately following the disaster (Kaigo and Tkach-Kawasaki 2015). At the same time, Del Norte County in California worked together with the local radio station and emergency management organization and used social media, especially Facebook, to respond to citizen inquiries for information, confirmations, and aid relating to the Japanese disaster (Tyshchuk and Wallace 2013).

Social Media Tools

The social media tools used most widely by local governments are Facebook and Twitter, with many also using other popular sites such as YouTube and Instagram. A 2012 survey of seventy-two cities around the world found that the three most widely used tools were Facebook (97 percent of cities), Twitter (94.5 percent), and YouTube (82 percent). The survey revealed that these tools were used mainly for the purpose of disseminating information rather than two-way communications (Kok 2012). Similarly, a survey of 463 local government officials from municipalities across the United States found that Facebook and Twitter were most commonly used, mainly to post and write about upcoming events (Graham and Avery 2013).

Critical Success Factors in Social Media Usage: Key Themes

One Tool in the Communication Box

While social media usage is essential for local governments to communicate and engage effectively with citizens, it is important to regard this as just one important component of the communication toolbox. In many countries and regions, a digital divide exists between users and non users of the Internet and social media, and groups such as the elderly and those living in rural or remote regions are often disproportionately among non users yet have high levels of demand for government services. While social media and other forms of electronic communication are becoming increasingly important in local government, it is important to use these alongside more traditional forms of communication such as local television, radio, and the print media, as well as in-person events (Hudak 2015). This is especially important when social media is being used in crisis management and communications, and there is a risk that segments of the population might be excluded from critical information conveyed using social media channels (Chavez et al. 2010). Thus, it is important to include content posted on social media in all government-to-citizen communications.

Further, social media usage in itself is unlikely to be successful as a communications and engagement tool unless the content provided is in a user-friendly, easily accessible format (Accenture 2018). Important considerations include ensuring that all electronic communications are optimized for use using a range of devices including mobile phones and making social media and other online content visually attractive and easy to read and understand.

A Strategic Approach

It is also essential that social media be fully integrated with the overall digital and citizen-engagement strategy of the local government organizations. This is supported by studies from around the world; for example, research into three city governments in Jordan, Rania (2017) stressed the important of purposeful design, while Picão's 2012 study of local councils in Northern Ireland also recommended the use of an overall social media strategy to justify and plan the use of Twitter and other tools. However, a 2015 global study of the social media usage of thirty-one cities found that many did not even include links on their main websites to their social media accounts (Mainka et al. 2015), which is likely to have had negative impacts for citizens using social media tools to interact with city governments.

A strategic approach is also essential to justify the necessary investment in resources and training to support social media tools. Studies have revealed that budgetary constraints often hinder social media use; however, effectively employed, it can result in cost savings and/or extra income generation. In an Association for Public Service Excellence 2015 survey of local authorities in the United Kingdom, for example, a high percentage of respondents reported that social media has helped create savings by eliminating more expensive forms of advertising and the use of less effective communication channels, as well as generating income through promoting council services such as pest control and the collection of bulky refuse.

Analytics and Evaluation

Analytics, measurement, and evaluation are crucial elements of a strategic approach to social media use, providing important feedback on which tools and methods are most effective, as well as important insights into the views and behaviors of the community and specific groups, which can help inform the development of policies, services, or public-relations strategies. These activities might include analysis of data from the organization's own social media sites or groups, or targeted analyses of data from social media more generally. Social media analytics can also be a valuable way of finding out about the views of those citizens who are active on sites such as Facebook or Twitter, but who are not interacting directly with local government online (Moss et al. 2015; Kavanaugh et al. 2011). In research on the Arlington, Virginia, county government in the United States, for example, Kavanaugh et al. (2012) reported that the mining, analysis, and visualization of data from multiple social media sites enabled the organization to quickly see the "big picture" in terms of community views and behaviors, and to monitor changes over time.

However, the evidence suggests that many local governments lack knowledge and expertise of how to use analytics or how to measure and evaluate their social media activity (Hansen-Flaschen and Parker 2012). While simple numbers of "likes" and "shares" are often used, local governments would benefit from the use of more sophisticated analytics as well as qualitative measures of engagement and participation.

Maximizing the Potential of Social Media Usage

Based upon global research, most local governments are not using the full potential of social media. Overwhelmingly, research has shown that these tools are predominantly used for one-way communications, with relatively small numbers of local governments using them effectively as two-way communication needed for promoting citizen engagement and empowerment.

For example, a 2015 survey of UK local authority officers found that most local government organizations included in the survey were using social media for a variety of purposes but nearly all "outward facing," such as providing information about services or responding to customer enquiries. Relatively few were using the potential of social media to involve citizens in constructive forms of engagement (APSE 2015). Similarly, in a study of social media use in three cities in Indonesia, Thailand, and the Philippines, it was found that social media is not generally being used for two-way interaction but mainly for disseminating information (Roengtam 2017). Similar findings were generated from the UAE (Darwish 2017), in a study of metropolitan and regional councils in South Australia (Heaselgrave and Simmons 2016), and in a study of social media use in the city of Karlstad, Sweden (Bellström et al. 2016).

These findings indicate that many local governments are not maximizing the potential or gaining the full benefits of social media use. This is demonstrated by the findings of a Eurobarometer survey conducted in 2012 across twenty-seven European countries, which investigated the relationship between digital interaction with government and satisfaction with the democratic process of their country. The findings revealed that the use of the

Internet and digital communications alone did not influence levels of democratic support, whereas the use of two-way social media, in which information is co-created by government and citizens, was positively associated with satisfaction with the democratic processes (Ceron and Memoli 2016).

In this respect, another important consideration is not just having a social media presence but also effectively promoting its use. Haro de Rosario et al. (2017) report that even in major European cities such as London and Madrid there are low levels of awareness of the use of Facebook by municipal and local governments. However, other studies reveal high levels of demand among citizens for more digital communication with government organizations. In the United States, for example, recent survey data reveals that a high percentage of citizens are already interacting digitally with government, with 86 percent of a national survey of a thousand citizens saying they would like to maintain or increase their level of digital interaction, with 73 percent reporting dissatisfaction with current digital services (Accenture 2018). A 2012 survey of Twitter usage among local councils in Northern Ireland, for example, revealed that while some were engaging with citizens extensively and successfully using this tool, others were not using social media at all, suggesting that underlying levels of citizen demand were not being met in some localities (Picão 2012)

Organizational Factors

Many critical success factors in the use of social media by local governments are organizational or cultural in nature. First, it is essential that adequate resources are made available to support the social media activities of the organization, including sufficient staffing and the necessary training. Once social media sites are available for public postings, these often become channels for customer-service queries, replacing at least a portion of those previously submitted by telephone or email, and these need to be channeled to and dealt with by the appropriate individuals and departments (Bellström et al. 2016). Additionally, there is a need to implement and manage social media initiatives intended to increase citizen participation and engagement in government, such as the use of these tools to seek input into policy development or the design of specific services.

Studies from around the world, including Spain, China, and Australia, as well as the United States, have also found that one of the main factors contributing to the success of social media usage in government is the existence of strong support and leadership at the executive level (Criado et al. 2017; Heaselgrave and Simmons 2016; Zhang and Xiao 2017). If this is not present, it will be difficult to achieve the cultural changes and levels of investment in social media activities, including the staff training necessary to support the strategy. A study of local government social media use in China found that top management support is the strongest predictor of success of social media uptake in government agencies, followed by perceived benefits of social media, technology competence, and citizen readiness (Zhang and Xiao 2017).

For local governments used to more traditional forms of communication, concerns about the risks of social media often hinder its use. Kaigo and Tkach-Kawasaki (2015) found that the main barrier to the use of tools such as Twitter in the Tsukuba municipal government in Japan was concern about making errors in postings or spreading inappropriate information. Similarly, in their study of councils in South Australia, Heaselgrave and Simmons (2016) found that social media usage was being inhibited by risk-averse management and councilors, as well as a lack of guidance, for example, on social media record keeping. Lack of staff training and inadequate resources for social media communications were also identified as barriers in this study. While local government leaders and officials might also be concerned about negative public feedback being posted, the benefits of transparency are likely to outweigh any risks of harm. In any case, as demonstrated in a Swedish study of Facebook content in the city of Karlstad (Bellström 2016), posts with positive feedback were just as common as negative comments.

Many of the potential barriers to successful social media use can readily be overcome, however, with adequate staff training and comprehensive social media policies and guidance for users. Indeed, studies from around the world have highlighted the importance of developing comprehensive guidance and policies for local government use (Kaigo and Tkach-Kawasaki 2015; Heaselgrave and Simmons 2016). Hrdinová et al. (2010) identified eight essential elements for a social media policy: (1) employee access; (2) account management; (3) acceptable use; (4) employee conduct; (5) content; (6) security; (7) legal issues; and (8) citizen conduct.

Local governments have often operated in silo-type structures with relatively little coordination between departments. When a social media strategy is adopted, it is important to integrate and coordinate this across departments. Various social media management structures exist, with various degrees of centralization or decentralization, but the important thing is consistency in the overall tone and content of messaging used in communications with the public and managing the risks of social media use. Often a social media manager is appointed to coordinate the overall strategy and activities.

Conclusion

As this overview has shown, local governments can benefit considerably from the use of social media for communications and citizen engagement, yet many are not utilizing this media to its full potential. Attention to the critical success factors identified here can help ensure that local governments and the communities they serve can work together more effectively in future and continue to build the levels of trust and citizen participation that are so essential for effective local governance.

References

Accenture. 2018. "Digital Government: "Good Enough" for Government is Not Good Enough." https://www.accenture.com/t20160912T095949__w__/us-en/_acnmedia/PDF-30/Accenture-Digital-Citizen-Experience-Pulse-Survey-POV.pdf.

Accenture, n.d. "Your Digital Citizens Are Ready, Willing... and Waiting." https://www.accenture.com/_acnmedia/Accenture/Conversion-Assets/DotCom/Documents/Global/PDF/Dualpub_8/Accenture-Your-Digital-Citizens-Ready-Willing-Waiting.pdf#zoom=50.

Al-Aufi, Ali, Ibrahim Al-Harthi, Yousuf AlHinai, Zahran Al-Salti, and Ali Al-Badi. 2017. "Citizens' Perceptions of Government's Participatory use of Social Media." *Transforming Government: People, Process and Policy* 11(2), 174–94.

Association for Public Service Excellence. 2015. "Membership Resources Use of Social Media in Local Government State of the Market 2015." http://apse.org.uk/apse/index.cfm/members-area/briefings/2016/16-39-social-media-in-local-government-state-of-the-market-2015/.

Bell, E. 2013. "Pummeled by Sandy, New Jersey County Delivers Emergency App to Residents." *Government Technology*, November 21. http://www.govtech.com/applications/Pummeled-by-Sandy-New-Jersey-County-Delivers-Emergency-App-to-Residents.html.

Bellström, Peter, Monika Magnusson, John Sören Pettersson, and Claes Thorén. 2016. "Facebook Usage in a Local Government." *Transforming Government: People, Process and Policy* 10(4), 548–67. doi: 10.1108/TG-12-2015-0061.

Bertot, J. C., P. T. Jaeger, and J. M. Grimes. 2012. "Promoting Transparency and Accountability through ICTs, Social Media, and Collaborative E-Government." *Transforming Government: People, Process and Policy* 6(1), 78–91.

Burroughs, A. 2014. "Mobile Apps Enable Citizen Engagement and Better Services: Innovative Apps and Portals Help Localities Transform Service Delivery." *State Tech Magazine*, April 8.

Ceron, Andrea, and Vincenzo Memoli. 2016. "Flames and Debates: Do Social Media Affect Satisfaction with Democracy?" *Social Indicators Research* 12(1), 225–40. doi: 10.1007/s11205-015-0893-x.

Chavez, Craig, Michael A. Repas, and Thomas L. Stefaniak. 2010. "A New Way to Communicate with Residents: Local Government Use of Social Media to Prepare for Emergencies." http://www.unapcict.org/ecohub/a-new-way-to-communicate-with-residents-local-government-use-of-social-media-to-prepare-for-emergencies.

Criado, J. Ignatio., Francisco Rojas-Martín, and J. Gil-Garcia. 2017. "Enacting Social Media Success in Local Public Administrations." *International Journal of Public Sector Management 30*(1), 31–47. doi: 10.1108/IJPSM-03-2016-0053.

D'Agostino, Maria J., Richard Schwester, Tony Carrizales, and James Melitski. 2011. "A Study of E-government and E-governance: An Empirical Examination of Municipal Websites." *Public Administration Quarterly 35*(1), 3–25.

Darwish, Elsayed, B. 2017. "The Effectiveness of Using Social Media in Government Communication in UAE." Zayed University Working Paper. https://www.researchgate.net/publication/228546809_A_New_Way_to_Communicate_with_Residents_Local_Government_Use_of_Social_Media_to_Prepare_for_Emergencies.

Edelman. 2016. "2016 Edelman Trust Barometer." http://www.edelman.com/insights/intellectual-property/2016-edelman-trust-barometer/.

Graham, Missy, and Elizabeth Johnson Avery. 2013. "Government Public Relations and Social Media: An Analysis of the Perceptions and Trends of Social Media Use at the Local Government Level." *Public Relations Journal 7*(4), 1–21.

Guha, A. 2011. "Somerville Leads the Way with 311 Taking Twitter and Facebook Orders." *Somerville Journal*, February 11. http://www.wickedlocal.com/somerville/news/lifestyle/x1779417907/Somerville-leads-the-way-with-311-taking-Twitter-and-Facebook-work-orders#axzz1EugFBy9F.

Hansen-Flaschen, L., and K. P. Parker. 2012. "The Rise of Social Government: An Advanced Guide and Review of Social Media's Role in Local Government Operations." Fels Institute of Government. http://www.fels.upenn.edu/sites/www.fels.upenn.edu/files/fels_promising_practices_the_rise_of_social_media_website_final.pdf.

Haro-de-Rosario, A., Saez-Martin, A., and M. Del Mar Galvez-Rodrigue. 2017. "Facebook as a Dialogic Strategic Tool for European Local Governments." *Transylvanian Review of Administrative Sciences* (50E), 73–89.

Heaselgrave, Fae, and Peter Simmons. 2016. "Culture, Competency and Policy: Why Social Media Dialogue is Limited in Australian Local Government." *Journal of Communication Management 20*(2), 133–47.

Heaton, Brian. 2011. "New App Connects Social Media Users with Municipal Services." *Government Technology*, July 19. http://www.govtech.com/e-government/New-App-Connects-Social-Media-Users-with-Municipal-Services.html.

Hong, Hyehyun. 2013. "Government Websites and Social Media's Influence on Government–Public Relationship." *Public Relations Review 39*(4), 346–56.

Hrdinová, Jana, Natalie Helbig and Catherine Stollar Peters. 2010. "Designing Social Media Policy for Government: Eight Essential Elements." Center for Technology in Government. https://www.govloop.com/community/blog/designing-social-media-policy-for-government-eight-essential-elements/.

Hudak, Kasey Clawson. 2015. "Dahntahn Discourses and Neighborhood Narratives: Communicating the City Brand of Pittsburgh, Pennsylvania." *Place Branding and Public Diplomacy 11*(1), 34–50. doi: 10.1057/pb.2014.24.

InterPARES Trust. 2016. "Social Media and Trust in Government." https://interparestrust.org/assets/public/dissemination/NA05_SocialMediaandTrustFinalReport.pdf.

Kavanaugh, Andrea L., Edward A. Fox, Steven D. Sheetz, Seungwon Yang, Lin Tzy Li, Donald J. Shoemaker, Apostol Natsev, and Lexing Xie. 2012. "Social Media Use by Government: From the Routine to the Critical." *Government Information Quarterly 29*(4), 480–91.

Kaigo, Muneo. and Leslie Tkach-Kawasaki. 2015. "Social Media for Enhancing Civil Society and Disaster Relief: Facebook Usage by Local Municipalities in Japan." *JeDEM 7*(1), 1–22.

Kierkegaard, Sylvia. 2009. "Open Access to Public Documents—More Secrecy, Less Transparency!" *Computer Law & Security Review 25*(1), 3–27.

Kok, David. 2012 "Social Media around the World." https://www.slideshare.net/socialmediadna/social-media-in-cities-around-the-world.

Köseoğlu, Özer, and Aziz Tuncer. 2016. "Designing Social Media Policy for Local Governments: Opportunities and Challenges," in Mehmet Zahid Sobaci, ed., *Social Media and Local Governments*. Cham: Springer, 23–36.

Lupu, D., and C. G. Lazar. 2015. "Influence of E-Government on the Level of Corruption in Some EU and Non-EU States." *Procedia Economics and Finance 20*, 365–371.

Mainka, Agnes., Sarah Hartmann, Wolfgang G. Stock, and Isabella Peters. 2015. "Looking for Friends and Followers: A Global Investigation of Governmental Social Media Use." *Transforming Government: People, Process and Policy 9*(2), 237–54.

Moss, Giles, Helen Kennedy, Stylianos Moshonas, and Chris Birchall. 2015. "Knowing Your Publics: The Use of Social Media Analytics in Local Government." *Information Polity 20*(4), 287–98. doi: 10.3233/IP-150376.

Mundy, Darren, and Qasim Umer. 2013. "Reflections on UK Local Government Challenges in the Use of Twitter as a Communications Channel." *International Journal on Advances in Life Sciences 5*(3/4), 15–125.

Nabatchi, T., and I. Mergel. 2010. "Participation 2.0: Using Internet and Social Media: Technologies to Promote Distributed Democracy and Create Digital Neighborhoods," in J. H. Svara and J. Denhardt, eds., *The Connected Community: Local Governments as Partners in Citizen Engagement and Community Building*, 80–87. https://icma.org/documents/connected-communities-local-governments-partner-citizen-engagement-and-community-building.

Onescu, Luminita. 2016. "E-government and Social Media as Effective Tools in Controlling Corruption in Public Administration." *Economics, Management and Financial Markets 11*(1), 66–72.

Park, Jongsoo, and Kwangrae Cho. 2009. "Declining Relational Trust between Government and Publics, and Potential Prospects of Social Media in the Government Public Relations." *Proceedings of EGPA Conference 2009: The Public Service: Service Delivery in the Information Age*. St. Julian's, Malta. http://www.egpa2009.com/documents/psg1/ParkCho.pdf.

Pew Research Center. 2014. "The Web at 25 in the U.S. Pew Research Center." http://www.pewinternet.org/files/2014/02/PIP_25th-anniversary-of-the-Web_0227141.pdf.

Pew Research Center. 2015. "15 Striking Findings from 2015." https://www.pewresearch.org/fact-tank/2015/12/22/15-striking-findings-from-2015/.

Picão, Tiago, Fiona McMahon, Valerie Purchase, and Maurice Mulvenna. 2014. "The Use of Twitter by Local Government in Northern Ireland," in *E-Business and Telecommunications. Communications in Computer and Information Science*. Heidelberg: Springer, 93–106.

Piotrowski, Suzanne J. and Greg G. Van Ryzin. 2007. "Citizen Attitudes Toward |Transparency in Local Government." *The American Review of Public Administration 37*(3), 306–23.

Rania, Q. 2017. "Using Social Hub Media to Expand Public Participation in Municipal Urban Plans." *Procedia Engineering 198*, 34–42.

Roengtam, Sataporn, Achmad Nurmandi, David N. Almarez, and Anwar Kholid. 2017. "Does Social Media Transform City Government? A Case Study of Three ASEAN Cities." *Transforming Government: People, Process and Policy 11*(3), 343–76.

Stephens, K. 2011. "Social Media and Irene, One NJ Police Chief's Experience." September 16 [Web log comment]. Retrieved from http://idisaster.wordpress.com/tag/hurricane-irene/.

Tyshchuck, Yulia, and William Wallace. 2013. "The Use of Social Media by Local Government in Response to an Extreme Event: Del Norte County, CA, Response to the 2011 Japan Tsunami." In *Proceedings of the 10th International ISCRAM Conference*, Baden-Baden, Germany, May 2013, 802–11.

Tyshchuk, Y., H. Li, H. Ji, W. A. Wallace. 2013. "Evolution of Communities on Twitter and the Role of their Leaders during Emergencies." Proceedings of ASONAM, Niagara Falls, Canada, August 25–28, 2013..

Veal, Don-Terry, William I. Sauser Jr. Maria B. Tamblyn, Lane D. Sauser, and Ronald R. Sims. 2015. "Fostering Transparency in Local Government." *Journal of Management Policy and Practice 16*(1), 11–17.

Widyanarko, P. A. 2018. "The Use of Social Media and Open Data in Promoting Civic Co-Management: Case of Jakarta." *IOP Conference Series: Earth and Environmental Science 158*, 012049.

Zhang, Hui, and Jianying Xiao. 2017. "Assimilation of Social Media in Local Government: An Examination of Key Drivers." *The Electronic Library 35*(3), 427–44.

Summary of Critical Knowledge Indicators for Part I

- Definitions of corruption vary widely. How has the push toward globalization and quantification fueled the push for a homogenized definition?

- How does the definition of corruption affect a country's politics and economy?

- Transparency International's Corruption Perceptions Index (CPI) and the World Bank's Worldwide Governance Indicators (WGI) are the two most widely accepted measures of corruption. How does their definitional variance impact a country's corruption scores, and what effects does that entail for its citizens?

- Explain how the quid pro quo relationship inherent in influence trading can lead to deterioration of government structures and how, paradoxically, it can result in greater efficiencies for citizens seeking government services.

- How does the reciprocity wheel of exchange favors become a social norm?

- Different countries have varying types of informal exchange networks, each with a different level of entrenchment in their respective societies. Explain how these systems can assist in identifying and addressing corruption.

- In what way does the study of culturally specific fantasy narratives provide the theoretical foundation for understanding the spread of disinformation?

- Provide examples of how rhetoric has the power not only to create corruptive social norms, but to hide them in the language of joking, fictional characters, fantasy landscapes, and false histories.

- How does the public's need for a collective identity create the appetite for false narratives?

- Why have reports of corruption in the NPO/NGO sector generally focused on financial violations and bypassed the arguably more egregious and common instances of sexual abuse and other gendered harms?

- How has the economic, political, and cultural marginalization of women reduced the barriers to and expanded the scope of corruptive abuses?

- While over 75 percent of NPO/NGO personnel are female, males comprise the majority of leadership positions. What role can donors and oversight bodies, amongst other entities, play in addressing this patriarchal imbalance?

- While the increasingly common practice of out-sourcing public services has created new opportunities for corruption, some governments' overall measure of corruption is actually reduced by out-sourcing. Why?

- What three factors influence the consequences of out-sourcing corruption?

- Define the key distinctions between corruption instigated by out-sourcing the power of the state vs. contracting for service delivery.

- When does corruption become a tool in legitimatizing a political regime?

- Why has Mexico's fight against corruption been historically characterized as uniquely turbulent?

- Why is corruption in Italy particularly difficult to measure?

- What sectors of Italy's economy has contributed the most to the increase in corruption over the past decade?

- At what socioeconomic level is Italy's corruption the highest, and why?

- What are the three anchors in the triad of competing values that leads to corruptive behavior?

- Identify the factors that contribute to the breakdown of ethical resiliency among military personnel.

- What elements of corruption cause an individual to suffer moral injury?

- What reasons do nonprofit executives give for circumventing the requirement for open access to information?

- Why is corruption in the nonprofit sector often considered more reprehensible than corruption in other sectors?

- Name three antidotes to corruption in the nonprofit sector.

- Describe how social media can act as a corruptive influence in local governments.

- How can social media be used to minimize corruption in local governments?

by Carole L. Jurkiewicz

PART II

Dimensions of Corruption and Ethics Management

11

The Challenges of Individual Integrity in the Fight Against Corruption

J. Patrick Dobel

This chapter tracks the ethical, political, and psychological relationships between integrity and corruption. It will examine how intimately the two connect in the realities of practicing integrity and facing personal and institutional corruption. It will discuss how the policies to promote integrity and address corruption depend heavily upon the cognitive and emotional capacity of humans to act with integrity. Finally, the chapter will explore the paradox of how a commitment to integrity can sometimes lead the human mind to accommodate and stabilize corruption in persons and institutions. It ends with an examination of the renewed importance of personal integrity and leading in a governance-based world of collaboration, augmented stakeholder influence, and partnerships.

The Entwining of Integrity and Corruption

Integrity and corruption have been deeply connected as historical concepts and ethical realities. The two concepts begin with deep-seated etymological affinities that play out in modern ethical and institutional practice.

Western Classical and Renaissance thinkers saw corruption of the person and state as linked. Plato in *The Republic* and Machiavelli in his *History of Florence* across a two-thousand-year divide make the connection between inequality in economic and political power and the decline of civic virtue quite clear. Wide governmental corruption reflects deeper social and economic forces, and inequality can destroy citizenship and weaken the state. The realities of personal and political corruption are not new and never disappear (Machiavelli 1965; Plato 1991).

The earliest written human documents from 2700BC in Mesopotamia reveal the ubiquity of institutional corruption. In the Sumerian city state of Lakash 4,700 years ago, the *Song of Praise for King Urukagina* begins, "from time immemorial ... officials acted for their own benefit." The hymn declares that state supervisors of boats steal boats, supervisors of cattle steal grain, fishery officials "steal fish and boats," and corrupt tax officials "collect and hide silver." The King is praised for his rare act of removing corrupt officials. The song concludes, "administrators no longer plunder the orchards of the poor." One of the world's oldest written documents highlights the same indictment and challenges that Plato and Machiavelli discussed and that face modern ethics and management (Uslaner 2008).

The etymological history also highlights their connections. To "corrupt" arises from the Indo-European root "rumpere" meaning to destroy, break, or fall apart. Corrupt can refer to a natural process such as aging or entropy. It often, however, takes on a normative caste where the usefulness or function degrades and decays into a less coherent array. The idea of a corrupt text, computer file, or a corrupt person suggests not just a natural decay but a normative decline from coherence or rightness. Adding "com" adds an active agency and violent intent to the breaking. Many cognates resonate with violent intention such as reave, rupture, loot/plunder, rob, or explode (*Chambers Dictionary of Etymology* 2003; Mallory 1997; *Oxford Dictionary of English Etymology* 1996; Watkins 2000).

Integrity stands as the counterpoint of corruption in the Indo-European language family. The root of integrity is "tak," which suggests something is real and whole. The roots of integrity allude to completeness, wholeness, and a sound rightness and usefulness. Integrity has from the beginning had a positive moral connotation. Other variations take on meanings of being internally consistent like a text or program or meeting standards of completeness and rightness such as structural or professional integrity (*Chambers Dictionary of Etymology* 2003; Mallory 1997; *Oxford Dictionary of English Etymology* 1996; Watkins 2000). Corrupting impacts the wholeness of integrity.

In modern usage integrity becomes the linchpin to support personal and institutional purpose and mission. Having personal integrity is a fundamental prerequisite for ethical action and for individuals in an institution to sustain a common purpose. Corruption, then, arises when an individual chooses to act against the purpose and obligations of their entrusted office to achieve personal gain or a different collective purpose. This second aspect of collective purpose can mean individuals subvert their public responsibilities to support commitments to groups such as family, clan, religion, or party (Albrecht 2011; Graycar 2013; Langseth 1997). These two concepts generate an unending ethical and institutional tension. They point to the ethical and organizational strategies to form integrity-based organizations and fight their corruption.

Integrity Model

The standard integrity model for persons and institutions proposes how individuals and institutions can develop commitment and performance in light of standards of mission and personal identity. This model depends upon a mode of human agency that constitutes the ethical and psychological architecture of integrity. This model of human self and personality enables individuals to intentionally make commitments and promises and keep them in face of challenges. It retains a deep connection to notions of classical virtue (Aristotle 1999; Cooper 1975; Macaulay and Lawton 2006; Sherman 1989).

The ability of persons to keep promises and live up to the obligations of entrusted power gives reality to integrity. Regardless of the nature of commitments, individuals need the foundational capacity to exercise self-aware discipline to intentionally make promises and cognitively guide action by them. Persons need to call upon courage, conscientiousness and tenacity to implement obligations in face of obstacles. The capacity for integrity enables individuals to commit to honor the laws, policy, obligations, authority, and accountability relations of an organization and position. This ethical capacity anchors reliable performance and accountability and is the basis to earn trust and legitimacy.

This model for ethical behavior and judgment in public service depends very heavily upon the idea of having a self. The self manifests a psychological and ethical capacity to be aware of values and character attributes that the person can call upon to direct their judgments. The self can call upon the emotional and willpower to follow through on an envisioned course of action. This self-awareness becomes the focal point for self-discipline where individuals can marshal perception, emotion, and physical action to achieve goals. The self-discipline allies with courage and will to navigate obstacles and adapt in face of conflict (Carter 1996; Huberts 2014; Korsgaard 2009; Killinger 2010).

The notion of self, integrity, and organizational commitment play out in daily decisions and cumulative purposive actions, not just in evident ethical crises (Huberts 2014; Killinger 2010; Kooistra 2014; Visser 2014). This model depends upon the reality that persons can self-consciously change themselves in ethical practice. With reflective practice and learning, people can change behavior, and behavior can react back and change neural patterns and engrave new self-narratives and understandings. Likewise, changes in belief can guide behavioral changes that create a similar neural reinforcing loop. This connects free reflection and cumulative personal development to identity and virtue (Baumeister 1991; Beilock 2010; Cialdini 2009; Damasio 1999, 2012; Klein 1998; Korsgaard 2009; Schon 1984; Solomon 2007).

Human integrity needs to be realistic and livable. For this reason, this model is grounded in modern cognitive understandings of humans deploying frames and schemata to perceive, assess, decide, and implement action in very short time frames with levels of consistency and reliability. It makes no sense to advocate a way of living that is impossible for human beings and runs up against what John Rawls called "the strain of commitment." An unattainable notion of integrity not only guarantees moral failure but will create strong incentives for individuals in organizations to create corrupt subcultures against impossible demands (Beilock 2010; Cialdini 2009; Damasio 2012; Klein 1998, 2009; LeDoux 2002; Rawls 1971).

The model assumes that individuals possess the self-awareness to align personal and institutional commitments. This self-awareness permits persons to stand back from a situation and their initial reactions for a moment and reflectively discipline their mind, emotions, and body so they can adopt standards of judgment linked to their entrusted position. It means individuals are capable of striving to act impartially and with a level of unbiased fairness. This self-awareness can be deployed to offset the limitations of cognitive heuristics that can shortcut ethical judgments. Self-awareness helps people avoid self-deception and enables them to set will and reflection above self-interest and limited information. It entails cognitive and emotional discipline to seek out diverse good information and focus upon being open and neutral in assessing decisions. This ability to minimize biases is fundamental to live up to institutional commitments (Carter 1996; Dobel 1999; Kahneman 2011; Killinger 2010; Korsgaard 2009; Kouzes 2006, 2011).

The personal-integrity model supports human capacities fundamental to high-performance integrity institutions and fighting corruption. First, humans can share integrated frames of reference. These shared frames become the basis of professional and institutional culture. An organizational culture is critical to support consistent high standards of ethical performance and to resist corruption (Burke 2011; Dutton 2010; Langseth 1997; OECD 2009; Schein 2009, 2010). Creating and sustaining a culture of integrity are fundamental to warding off corruption, for once a culture has internalized corrupt norms and mutually reinforcing peer pressure, it is very hard to root out (Miceli 2002).

Second, institutions depend upon human integrity to have reliable policy implementation and adherence to law and standards (Perrow 1972, 2014; Rawls 1971; Rohr 1988; Schein 2009). Institutions cannot function without the ability of individuals to reframe judgments in light of the demands of law and policy. A self-aware person trains his or her judgment to be guided by the dictates of law, profession, and institutional purpose. Institutions also need individuals to weigh long-term consequences more than short-term or self-interested concerns. Institutions also depend upon persons to attend to the legitimacy and stewardship of organizations (Langseth 1997; Senge 2006; Schwartz 2011; Terry 2003; Transparency International 2011).

Third, the integrity model underlies accountability. A commitment to build high integrity and performance organizations requires high levels of transparency in decision making and accountability (Langseth 1997; OECD 1998, 2009; Transparency International 2011). It depends upon individuals adhering to standards and being open to all appropriate information in face of temptations to do otherwise. People need the intellectual and emotional capacity to resist temptations to pre-bias judgment, narrow information, and hurry up decision time (Kahneman 2011; Klein 2009).

This model of self extends naturally to individual responsibility. This responsibility flows from accepting and internalizing obligations to being honest and accurate in reporting and assessing the consequences of an action. This honest receptivity needs courage to accept all information, assessment, and consequences for actions. People will always possess strong cognitive tendencies to confirm their own best intentions and disconfirm information that does not fit. They will hide information to avoid punishment. Accepting responsibility demands courage not to hide or let issues slide (Bazerman 2011; Carter 1996; Killinger 2010).

All institutional integrity strategies and corruption-fighting approaches depend upon the ability of individuals to exercise ethical integrity as persons in cooperative groups (Burke, Tomlinson, and Cooper 2011; Graycar 2013; Huberts 2014; Huberts and Hoekstra 2014; Killenberger 2010; Lipshaw 2009a; OECD, 2009). At the same time, people face the social and psychological reality that context and situation can overwhelm individual understandings and perception. Situations can overwhelm and distort ethical understandings. The situations coupled with culture can perpetuate corrupt norms and actions. Leaders and managers need to direct consistent attention to them (Ashford and Anand 2003; Burke, Tomlinson, and Cooper 2011; Graycar 2013; Janis 1982; O'Connor 2009; OECD 2009; Lipshaw 2009b).

The need to address context and culture puts a high premium upon leaders in organizations. Leaders and managers are necessary to pursue strong policy across time. They model, build culture, create processes, and develop administrative channels and controls (Dutton 2010; Lang 2008; Lipshaw 2009b). They are critical to manifesting the courage to end corrupt behaviors and manage boundaries where corruption infects organizations. True organizational control aims to integrate organizational and administrative policy within a culture. Proximate and distributed leaders at all levels need to work to promulgate, model, and enforce the integrity values and be alert to corrupt practice or subcultures (EDI 1999; Huberts and Hoekstra 2014; OECD 2009; Schwartz 2011).

The importance of leading underscores the connection between the individual integrity of the leaders and the building of the systems to sustain integrity-driven behavior. For instance, leaders regularly face the need to compromise in the pursuit of complex personal and mission goals, but compromise does not necessitate corruption or moral failure. Skilled compromise coupled with integrity illustrates to others that mission progress can be made, and purpose respected, with attention to long-term goals and political realities. Compromise and ethical progress become vital to instantiate an integrity-based but adaptable culture (Badaracco 2002; Senge 2006).

Any system's approach to integrity begins with a mission orientation. Unyielding emphasis upon fighting corruption is not enough. Anti-corruption, alone, denigrates people and provides no paths for positive action and narrative self-identity. It can lead to underground subversion unless alternative identities, rewards, and paths are forged for persons and the organization. Corruption fighting should be the corollary, but not the only focus for persons. Individuals need a self-reinforcing path that valorizes integrity, not just an approach that penalizes corruption (Bridges 2009; Kotter 1996, 2012). People should not feel beleaguered and doubted and trapped by constraints but be seen as persons of value pursuing worthy purpose and meaning (Lewis 2005; OCED 2009; Patzer 2013).

As importantly, leaders can seem to authorize corruption by their hypocrisy or indifference. Leaders can tout high values but accept the outcomes wrought by corrupt actions. Leaders can tacitly condone or simply look the other way, and their behavior makes a mockery of integrity rhetoric and encourages corrupt patterns and deep cynicism. In a classic dilemma, leaders tacitly tolerate and even reward illicit behavior that maximizes short, term career or organizational gains (Burke, Tomlinson, and Cooper 2011; Burke 2011; Bandura 1975; Patzer 2013).

Personal and organizational integrity depends on the assumption that persons can act according to standards aimed at a higher institutional good. This approach fails unless persons possess the moral capacity for self-discipline to act according to standards of entrusted office. Persons can act, even when it is difficult, and overcome internal and external temptations to favoritism or incompetence. This ethical and psychological capacity merges into organization culture, shared frames of judgment, and accountability. Organizations—public, nonprofit, and for-profit—require more than individuals. They need scaffolds of process, authority, relationships, and accountability to sustain legal and ethical outcomes. This leads to the modern approach to integrity-based organizations and fighting corruption as requiring a holistic and relentless political, leadership, and managerial approach.

The Corruption Fighting Model

The modern approach to corruption aims for an ethical culture summarized as "consistency between policies and actions as well as dimensions of the organization's ethical culture such as ethical leadership, fair treatment of employees, and open discussion of ethics" (Trevino 1999, 131–32). This goal informs the contemporary international consensus that building integrity and fighting corruption requires a holistic political and institutional approach. The United Nations, the Organisation of Economic Progress and Development (OECD), international professional organizations, and the relentless efforts of Transparency International and its allies have generated an evolving international consensus that corruption is defined as:

- the abuse of entrusted power for private gain; and
- the abuse of entrusted power for personal moral purpose or collective gain, which has extremely high costs to the welfare of citizens of countries and reinforces inequality, exclusion, and unaccountable power.

The first definition tracks the work of Transparency International and the most commonly understood meanings of corruption. The second addresses more dangerous options, where abuse of power flows from ethical justifications linked to "higher" moral commitments such as group, religious, political, or ideological loyalties. These justify a person to ignore law and organizational standards to pursue personal moral ends (Graycar and Prenzler 2013; Transparency International 2011).

Both approaches violate the legitimacy and purpose of public institutions. Both turn public institutions to purposes beyond those sanctioned by law or accountability. Both remain resolutely surreptitious and hide their long-term impact. The long-term results can be loss of revenue or legitimacy, increased cost, the displacement of merit and inclusiveness, or the creation of institutions used by one group to dominate other groups such as religious or ethnic domination of public bureaucracies.

The standard range of illegal corrupt practices covers bribery, embezzlement, theft of public property, use of property for private purposes, misappropriation of funds, destruction of property and records, lying and misreporting; these can expand to extortion and more felonious activities. Another set creates the appearance of unethical action and undermines trust in organizations. Corruption can be voluntary and collusive or induced by extortion or threat (Dobel 2018). It can become systematic or be episodic and opportunistic. Actions can be individual, but these actions can expand and corrupt organizations and culture through contagion. This expansion of corruption beyond individual decisions or opportunism extends the social cost externally to those denied service, extorted of money, forced into unwonted behavior, and excluded from deserved services (Graycar and Penzler 2013; Transparency International 2000, 2011).

The international consensus on corruption has come haltingly and been most successful among professional associations seeking to define and implement standards ranging from accounting to assessment of risk to valid data used in regulation (UNODC 2004).

The OECD and later the European Union as well as international donors have linked their funding to accepting anti-corruption policies. This has given monetary impetus to the public creation of and adherence to standards. In addition, international business sporadically attempts to address issues of bribery and access as well as giving consistent support to more technical issues such as accounting (UNODC 2013).

The standards can vary and have to account for different cultural political values. However, the major international focus has been on the integrity and autonomy of professional, efficient, and fair public service to all citizens. This has led in the public realm to a range of principles that concentrate on competence, accountability, fairness, and self-reporting. The OECD principles for managing ethics along with various United Nations proposals converge on internal coherence, consistency, and accountability for public officials, and preventing abuse of power and funds (Transparency International 2000, 2009; UNODC 2004):

- Ethical standards should be clear and public.
- Ethical standards should align with the laws and legal framework.
- Ethical guidance and support should be available for public servants.
- Processes should be available to expose wrong-doing.
- Political will should support ethical standards.
- Decisions and processes should be transparent and open to scrutiny.
- Relations with the private sector should be regulated and transparent.
- Leaders and managers as well as policies in areas such as procurement, regulation, and client service should promote ethical standards and accountability.
- Human resource systems should promote and protect ethics in public servants.
- Laws should be enforced, and violations should be prosecuted.

This approach advocates that countries create an "ethics infrastructure" and accepts variation across cultures as long as the system supports consistency accountability and clarity in the standards. This model can be expanded to influence how business should conduct itself and its relations with government (UNODC 2013). It places special emphasis upon the need for transparent accountability at the leadership level and strong cultures of integrity and compliance (Burke, Tomlinson, and Cooper 2011; Greenberg 2013).

The international consensus pushes for policies to articulate, legalize, and enforce ethical standards. This alone is a huge improvement for many regimes and provides political resources to beleaguered government agencies as well as businesses facing corrupt officials. The emphasis upon internal competence and consistency motivates the professionalization and autonomy of government agencies as well as pushes for external or internal activities that can uncover corruption and enforce standards.

Any serious attempts to develop integrity and fight corruption requires sustained political will, institutionalization, and a holistic approach. The OECD and Transparency International refer to *integrity systems* that are imbedded in each country. These systems ideally address everything from legislatures to human resources systems to enforcement patterns. Transparency International publishes periodic updates on the integrity systems of countries as well as a yearly assessment of perceptions of corruption. The holistic approach demands that leading, managing, and systems need to drive down to the daily practice at the point of task performance (Huberts and Hoekstra 2014; Kooistra 2014; Langseth 1997; OECD 2009; Schwartz 2011; Visser 2014).

These initiatives have created relative clarity and consistency about how to address and imbed integrity within institutions (OECD 2016). The ability to change organizations becomes more problematic, however, when country contexts are taken into consideration. The United Nations and OECD are painfully aware that many countries are permeated by systematic corruption either actively supported or condoned by the government. Adam Graycar and others have mapped models of the system-wide nature of corruption and suggested how the consensus can be accommodated to account for the limitations imposed by the range of government collusion. The TASP model, for instance, focuses on the "Type, Activity, Sector and Place" of the corrupt activity. This draws a more realistic picture of the range of corruption as well as the possibilities of action. It highlights the realistic need to map environments and build coalitions to address systematic or government-managed corruption. It also homes in on the question of whether the problem is a corrupt individual, corrupt organization, or corrupt culture; this focus radically changes the diagnosis and approaches (Graycar 2013; OECD 2009; UN 2004).

Political will remains the single most important long-term determinant of success. Acknowledging context means that many anti-corruption campaigns have to be approached cautiously. Governments undertake anti-corruption for many reasons. Some do so to maintain flows of international capital or aid. Others embark on campaigns to shore up legitimacy in face of public disenchantment or grass roots anger. Governments can address legitimate grievances, build up legitimacy, but also use anti-corruption as a means to eliminate opponents. These diverse and limited motives point to an underlying challenge all systematic corruption-fighting programs face—sustaining political will. This is doubly important since corrupt actors migrate underground and rise back up when campaigns move on. Even in rule-of-law and pluralistic countries, anti-corruption campaigns can ebb and flow tied to election cycles or political interest and costs.

Only sustained action by authorized agencies and support for public officials will address long-term corruption. This action needs to be supported with adequate budgets, training, and autonomy for the anti-corruption agencies. Islands of integrity can be created and sustained, especially if the country gains benefits such as trade, capital inflow, or political support. These, however, remain very fragile unless ultimately supported by strong accountability measures and transparency that push governments to build human resources and enforcement structures to uphold them.

The ebb and flow of political will everywhere leads to another dimension of corruption fighting: how to institutionalize autonomous support beyond political vicissitudes. This has led to an emphasis upon creating autonomous anti-corruption agencies or building strong quasi-independent auditing and transparency-based agencies. While these can have some costs to the relative efficiency of governments, they build standing agencies with the resources, albeit limited, and legitimacy to pursue corruption with relative autonomy from the political system. Some regimes have created institutions such as independent commissions that have both legislative and budgetary autonomy to escape the retribution from corruption privileged actors (Anechiarico 1996; OECD 1998, 2009; Pope 1999; Langseth 1997). In the same way, independent commissions or stand-alone anti-corruption agencies can have considerable success in rule-of-law countries; they have mixed and sporadic successes in other regimes where corrupt systems of patronage or party control deploy corruption as a tool of governance (Graycar 2013; Greenberg 2013; Guerber 2011).

A range of viable techniques and tools are available to frame strategic approaches to corruption. The "audit triangle" focuses upon the strategic power of auditors to not only unveil corruption but predict where the most likely slippages will occur. It focuses on the dynamic interaction among perceived pressures, perceived opportunities and risk, and the range of available rationalizations. Similarly, vulnerability assessments or ethics audits enable organizations to identify the critical leverage points to deploy leadership and resources to anticipate slippages or redress corruption (Lewis 2005; Dobel 2018; Albrecht 2011). Yet technology and commitments to methods will never suffice. ENRON had a widely recognized and honored risk-assessment office; yet the office was routinely bypassed or used to rationalize illegal and unethical actions that led to the corporation's demise. Corrupted leadership, corrupted culture, and internal pressures as well as conflicts of interest will subvert the strongest internal anti-corruption measures (Burke 2011; McLean 2013; Rapoport 2009).

Modern risk assessment has developed the sophistication to anticipate dangers from corruption, and information asymmetry and accountability loss (OECD 1998, 2009; Huberts 2014; Huberts and Hoekstra 2014). Robert Klitgaard and Susan Rose-Ackerman have refined principal-agent and economic theories into elaborate and effective maps of how to think about corruption. They can identify high-risk points and address issues involved in information asymmetry or mediating the point of contact between agencies and citizens where both opportunistic and systematic corruption results in subverted and unequal treatment of citizens (Graycar 2013; Klitgaard 1988; Rose-Ackerman 1999). The modern approach has generated an array of thoughtful and effective ways to diagnose and address corruption, but doing so remains fundamentally dependent upon sustained political will exercised by individuals and groups of integrity and courage.

The Challenge of Corruption and the Cognitive Integrity Model

The model of integrity assumed in leading and fighting corruption is strongly supported by modern cognitive psychology with its emphasis upon frames and schemata to inform the self and judgment. This commitment to integrity is embedded in how the human self constructs itself and maintains a strong capacity for self-reflection to guide judgments and action. This self-narrative depends upon the ferocious desire of the human mind for consistency and coherence in itself and the world. This can, under certain conditions, be complicit in enabling illegal or unethical official behavior.

The cognitive reality for human beings is that the *mind has a mind of its own*. This mind incessantly works to give the world coherence even when the situation often lacks coherence. The mind's approach integrates past experience with updated memory recall to scan and fit the world with probabilistic recoveries of significance and past experience (Damasio 1999, 2012; Radvansky 2006; Zimmerman 2014). Most human judgments occur quickly and silently through the efficient and robust action of cognitive frames and intuitive, efficient comprehension.

To achieve efficient and consistent judgment, human beings deploy what cognitive psychologists and neuroscientists call *mental schema* or *models* or *frames*. This chapter uses the word *frame* to describe the operational matrix that minds use to engage reality. A frame is an integrated set of mental maps, cognitions, and structured emotions where the mind shapes perception to scan and identify a situation in light of prior learned understandings. These perceptions integrate cognitive understanding with emotional significance to guide action through reliable experience and values. Frames inform the person as he or she scans the environment and identifies elements of significance. This significance becomes situational awareness and understanding. This understanding efficiently guides decisions to achieve purposes and forms the architecture of trained human intuition. The frame enables persons and leaders to comprehend and act in complex situations with practiced ease and success (Bolman 2011; Fairhust and Sarr 1996; Klein 1998).

The human mind always seeks to minimize the use of energy. The brain uses 20–25 percent of energy with 2–5 percent of body mass. Brainwork depletes glucose at incredible rates. The human brain and body strive for cognitive efficiency to function well and attend to the important stuff, and frames provide this. Operationally, the mind works on pattern recognition and cue taking from frames to make sense as fast as possible (Damasio 1999, 2012; Klein 1998; LeDoux 2002; Sapolsky 2012). Fast, efficient, and trained intuitive assessments make physiological sense for the mind.

The functioning brain and human mind prefer consistency and will actively combat perceptual, cognitive, or emotional dissonance and try to get rid of it. Dissonance deploys many approaches that help the mind and person smooth over and make sense of personal and institutional reality (Weick 1995, 2000). The waste of energy and stress due to cognitive distress will be addressed unconsciously to smooth out perception and self-understanding. This need for coherence is driven both by the necessity to accommodate limited individual perception or limitations on memory but also to expedite decision making.

The human mind prefers one consistent story where events fit comfortably with existing schema and reinforce existing knowledge and past experience. The most important frame from the ethical point of view lies in the primary self. Most humans organize their lives around a sense of self and purpose that is connected to values and character attributes. This self has many names in cognitive science such as "the ideal self," "the worthy self," "the autobiographical self." The need for some overarching coherence in identity and decisions evolves from evolutionary and psychological need for a hierarchical decision point. (Baumeister 1991; Cialdini 2009; Damasio 1999, 2012; Pinker 1999).

This meta self is the true fulcrum of personal integrity. It focuses ethical purpose, self-reflection, self-discipline, and guided action. This self provides an arbitrator to what Daniel Pinker calls the "parliament of selves" that coexist in each person and that reflect the multiple roles he or she possesses that have their internal frame logic. Different ethical or decision logics might apply to friendships, family, coworkers or hobbies, and clamor for attention and influence in a situation. People will have to adopt different frames when they move from being a functional expert to a manager. These multiple selves and roles can conflict when a person might be managing a friend at work and discover they are embezzling or harassing people and their ethical obligations as a leader and manager conflict with their obligations as a friend (Pinker 1999).

In integrity mode, the person seeks to make ethical sense and construct a narrative of all their actions that gives coherence to a complicated life of multiple roles and domains. This narrative gives the person a sense of worth, purpose, and moral worthiness. It is the heart of integrity. This fits with the brain's preference for consistency, and when people self-reflectively train and internalize professional frames, personal ethics and work decisions struggle to align and reinforce each other. They both work to maintain stability in self and action consistent with the self-narrative.

Ethical strain between corruption and integrity emerges because individuals who commit corrupt acts generally know they are committing unethical or illegal actions. This awareness initially creates psychological dissonance and pain that can drive persons and groups involved in corrupt actions to try and make consistent sense of morally conflicting actions to end stress and pain (Beilock 2010; Cialdini 2009; Festinger 1957; Sapolsky 2012).

Actions a person knows are wrong or that violate ideal self-commitments generate a wide but related range of responses in the body and mind. Persons will literally experience physiological pain where the body reacts in *disgust* and sends violent signals of distress to the brain and body. This occurs as a primordial reaction fundamental to preserving human self. *Guilt* deepens the stress and psychological and physiological pain as it connects with the sense of personal responsibility. Violating one's self and promises and doing harm intensifies the guilt and moral disgust. *Shame* can compound these reactions when it reminds a person of their failure to live up to a conception of self and honor related to their community and affiliations (Solomon 2007; Weiner 2006; Williams 2008).

The consequences of these signals are amplified over time. Persons living at this intersection experience painful and very highly stressful *cognitive dissonance*. They experience the pain of moral failure and the distance between their integrity self and their actions. This stress and moral failure play out in decreased disease immunity, declining physical resilience, and high blood pressure. It exacerbates neurotransmitter, glucocorticoid, and hormonal cascades and imbalances. The pain adversely impacts cognitive capacities such as perception and generates depression, anxiety, and loss of affective relations. It also degrades memory and sleep. The fact that these may be psychological experiences does not matter.

Neuro-cognitive studies portray psychological pain as essentially identical to physical pain. Ethical failure generates enduring stress and pain in individuals who perform immoral or illegal actions and know they are doing so (Sapolsky 2012).

These changes are aggravated by social isolation. People need to keep corrupt actions secret from their intimates and professional groups. Yet these groups are critical to maintain their self-integrity. They must lie, falsify records and reports, and keep secret their actions. The clandestine life further erodes their commitments and social relations. The demand for secrecy aggravates the stress, anxiety, and depression and infuses social relations with an awkwardness and guardedness that erodes individual's emotional, physical, and cognitive support.

The mind and body will seek to eliminate these distresses by trying to align the unethical actions with a new sense of self. The mind and person can redefine the action to narrow its consequences or redefine the rest of one's commitments to make the action consistent with oneself (Brownstein 2003; Cialdini 2009; Festinger 1957, 1964; Friedman and Fraser 1966). The self's and mind's drive to consistency in self-understanding impel them to make sense with the new commitments and actions in a way that sustains consistency (Cialdini 2009; Bandura 1975; Bazerman 2011; Festinger 1957, 1964; Tenbrunsel 2005). The very commitment to consistency and coherence demanded by a functioning mind can motivate persons to accommodate their illegal and unethical actions and stabilize corrupt practices.

The Paradox of Integrity and Corruption

The mind/brain's ferocious demand for consistency of worldview creates the paradox where a person's commitment to integrity can facilitate coming to terms with corruption. Persons and the mind need frames in order to "make sense" of the world. These frames deploy attention and decision making with efficiency and insight. The frames embody a coherent sense of self and worth, and persons must accommodate corrupt actions with their frames.

Persons deploy a wide array of psychological adaptations to protect self-narratives even when acting corruptly. These approaches are consistent with the modern focus upon how "rationalizations" can either augment the worth of what they do or minimize the psychological costs to them. Common rationalizations have been identified as: deny responsibility, deny victims, deny the harm, emphasize legality, deny injury, give social weight to values, create a utility ledger, appeal to higher loyalties, or refocus on other attributes to emphasize the good done (Gannet and Rector 2015; Rabl and Kuhlmann 2008). All attempt to minimize the moral pain evoked by unethical actions.

The word *rationalizations* is, however, too weak a word to describe what might happen. People literally change their self-understandings and social reference points. They change so much that future decisions no longer seem immoral and comport with a new self-narrative (Baumeister 1991; Gannett and Rector 2015). This revised self-understanding produces self-consistent justifications for actions that once would have been seen as problematic.

The idea of a rationalization assumes a person still understands the tension between self and the reasons they give for actions. It assumes an awareness of the pretense. The paradox of integrity and corruption is that the very drive for integrity in self and group narrative drives the reasoning deeper. Self and group identity morph under stress and change. The references of memory, perception, language, and the internal world of explanation slowly evolve into new selves reinforced by new group references and the slow transformation of the group culture to bolster the new identities. People embrace and integrate corrupt practices into the self and neutralize the psychological distance presumed by the term "rationalizations."

The mind and self deploy a number of psychological, cognitive, and emotional tactics to resolve the emotional turmoil and create new reasoning. The inner life and frames of a person change to accommodate the consequences of corruption. Over time they reinforce the neural processes to engrave new self-understandings, new memories, and new recall patterns. Persons change and imbed their new self-understandings of corrupt actions as viable and consistent with ethically positive self-narratives.

Often these changes begin with small actions, easily accommodated by frames, and evoke changes in self understandings around the edges of values and character (Friedman 1966). The actions, however, ripple out in unexpected ways, pulling other persons into collusion. A simple opportunistic action by an inspector to take a bribe involves the person who bribed or got away with it. This may spread to informal networks that alert business owners. It involves colleagues who look the other way or collude motivated by in-group loyalty. Extra money spent at home requires the silent collusion of family and friends not to ask, or else to accept thin excuses so the veneers of trust and self-image can be maintained.

A person with a strong sense of self-narrative can pursue several internal adjustments to come to terms with unethical or illegal action. The self has two ways to solve the problem that eliminates the ethical/legal tension. The first simply isolates roles and frames from each other, creating separate ethical worlds wherein each role becomes an independent frame coexisting with others in the person. The second involves a more stable solution that subordinates all obligations to higher loyalties and obligations of the self.

The first array of solutions involves loosening the role of one ideal self-narrative. Consistent with taking on roles, individuals divide the different frames of self from each other and do not permit cross-judgment. It takes energy to sustain these walls, but it creates the ability to segregate actions in one area from others at work; a person can sustain a weaker self-narrative while isolating and ultimately hiding the actions done in self-deceiving narrative. "Nothing personal" or "it's my job" compartmentalize responsibility. This denial or self-deception works well but takes immense psychological energy to keep guilt and shame at bay. It also invites anxiety and depression (Festinger 1957, 1964; Fingarette 2000; Janis and Mann 1977).

A related and more stable approach subsumes the dominant self into powerful loyalties that overshadow work obligations. Loyalty to family, religion, party, or ethnic group easily overrides institutional obligations. This commitment dominates all others and provides ethical justifications for eliminating the "unethical" dissonance by making actions serve a higher moral loyalty. Patterns of exclusion, extortion, pay to play, favoritism or preference that compromise citizen rights, efficiency, and competence does real harm, undermines legitimacy, and violates trust obligations to the persons, institutions, and society served, but they can be nullified by the priority of the higher moral loyalties (Graycar 2013; OECD 2009).

These changes to one's own self-understanding can be reinforced over time by group-think. People affiliate with new groups to overcome the initial social isolation that corruption engenders. These new affiliations create motivated blindness, groupthink and can normalize deviance for groups (Greenberg 2013; Janis 1982; Moberg 2006; Vaughan 1997). Individuals together forge a new and shared history and frame perceptions in real time to reinforce revised memories and perceptions. Memory adapts to the new sense of self (Radvansky 2006; Zimmerman 2014). Individuals reach the point where he or she no longer sees actions around them as wrong or corrupt; people rewrite history, and their recall becomes hermetically sealed to shore up the new worldview. Language, culture, social cues and new affiliations rebuild a worldview and a new self-understanding. They solidify a self who is comfortable not only with corruption but also with spreading and defending it (Ashford and Anand 2003; Moberg 2006; O'Connor 2009; Perrow 1972, 2014).

Perception and assessment change at deep and stable levels. Once moral misgivings have been quelled, the newly circumscribed ethical identity can be reinforced by the tendency of decision heuristics to reinforce preferred reasoning patterns. Confirmation bias is ever present and amply supports changes in self and cognition. Because corruption often involves changes of association, reciprocity, proximity, and anchoring heuristics reinforce the newly in-place identity and its justifications. Over-optimism about one's self pushes these decisions, and loss-aversion locks people into the new patterns of illicit gain (Heath and Heath 2013; Kahneman and Tversky 2000; Kahneman 2011). The heuristics are critical to successful professional life but can cause problems unless linked to reflection. But if trained and reflected upon, heuristics become the basis of professional managing and decision making (Cialdini 2009; Heath and Heath 2013; Klein 1998, 2009).

Finally, the depth of a person's acclimatizing to corruption is hardened by the real costs that enforce their new corrupt status. Once entrapped, it is hard to escape. Peers can bully, ostracize, or threaten persons. Job performance can become more dangerous. Personal and family exposure reinforce these threats. The risk of exposure, loss of reputation, money, and respect can be used to keep people in line. Individuals become subject to blackmail, extortion, compromised job safety, and fear or retribution. This keeps them involved even if they wish to leave.

The paradox of integrity supporting corruption lies in how people and groups will strive to keep consistent and positive self-narratives even in face of unethical and corrupt actions. These complex and interwoven patterns deploy and reinforce new cognitive frames supported by social support. They forge new self-understandings and justifications coupled with group reinforcement. These new frames justify actions and integrate them into consistent perceptual, emotional, and cognitive understandings. The mind will build emotional buffers and revised memories to sustain the new self and accounts for daily corrupt actions. This makes people capable of immense nobility, high integrity and strong culture, but makes it possible for humans to accommodate the most corrupt and ignoble behaviors (Zimbardo 2007). This reality means integrity must relentlessly guard its own self-understandings.

Conclusion: The Renewed Importance of Personal Integrity

Individuals of integrity create organizations, build culture, adhere to standards, and achieve accountability. They are essential as leaders and managers to build high integrity and performing organizations in all sectors of modern life. Their integrity plus self-awareness provides the human capacity to sustain a culture of high standards and protect processes and accountability. These same attributes support individuals in self and organizational scrutiny that fights corruption. Modern anti-corruption systems build upon this human capacity in an integrated and thoughtful way.

Paradoxically, the capacity for integrity can make people vulnerable to becoming enmeshed in self understandings that valorize and stabilize corrupt practice in persons, organizations and cultures. This reality is most important, not for discrediting integrity approaches, but for reminding policy makers that eradicating corruption is very hard. The hermetic worlds of corrupt practice are sustained not by mere rationalizations but by deep and much harder to eradicate self and group narratives.

In modern governance, individual integrity takes on renewed ethical and political importance. It remains central to building institutions and to implementing missions. But the modern world of governance and collaboration creates contested political space within which coordinated action must occur; this increases the need for leaders of personal integrity. On one hand, most modern political challenges escape existing institutional jurisdictions. Issues ranging from immigration to clean air to homelessness demand that institutions work across jurisdictions with partners. In addition, most government and nonprofit organizations are designed for single functions or domains, yet policy and management problems seldom live within one functional domain. No one resource base of funding or talent pools matches attempts to address complex problems across jurisdictions and time. Environmental, social-service, or national-security issues require cooperation across jurisdictions but also coordinating multiple organizations and contractors. Finally, very few collaborations or partnerships are successfully institutionalized; rather, they require incessant management and leadership by individuals at the intersections. This often occurs on an ad hoc basis by champions of collaboration or entrepreneurs. Most organizations collaborating together will tend to default to their preferred missions and budgets. To create and sustain a collaboration or partnership among organizations requires immense individual initiative and integrity to keep the purpose in mind, weave shared understandings, and coordinate action while keeping clarity about the moral purpose of the collaboration. This task for individuals amplifies how vital personal integrity remains (Emerson and Nabatchi 2015; Kettl 2015; Page 2010).

Concurrently, fast moving change has become a given in modern public and private organizations. The impact of globalization, the diffusion of power, the sprawl of problems and consequences along with the weakening of many governments mean modern public endeavors require cooperation across institutions and sectors. This world of governance is reinforced by multiple stakeholders demanding to influence policy making and forge accountability across the distributed power centers (Beck 2000; Bryson 2015; Scherer 2009). These combined forces create a constant undertow for organizations to gather power to themselves and incessant efforts to define a challenge in an organization's preferred frame. Collaborations emerge in multiple ways and regimes, but all require individuals working in the middle political spaces to craft a shared purpose, generate resources, and produce mutual accountability. Often, these individuals must reframe issues to gather maximum commitment and nurture shared deliberation across organizations and cultural understandings to keep people committed to adapting (Emerson and Nabatchi 2015; Kettl 2015). This also requires the capacity of individual integrity to be self-aware and stand back from the competing frames in order to see and work to develop resilient shared understandings and intentional purposes (Carter 1996; Kooistra 2014; Korsgaard 2009).

This tendency in a governance world requires individuals to emerge as leaders and act at the intersection of multiple power centers, chains of accountability, agendas, standards, and organizations. This political space has no one chain of accountability or one definition of the challenges or guarantees resource base, and the legitimacy of any endeavors can be easily lost (O'Leary and Bingham 2009b). This ethical and political space requires individual leaders to take personal responsibility and initiative to discover the common references that drive policy across jurisdictions, agencies, and sectors and to focus upon policy and management challenges. Individuals must become champions and help others change and adapt as well as connect multiple organizations and purposes; these responsibilities renew the importance of personal integrity in leaders. These multiple and growing demands place even more emphasis upon the integrity of individual leaders and managers who inhabit these intersectional spaces.

Individuals as leaders and managers need to display integrity far more extensively under modern governance conditions. First, individuals must manage changing standards or conflicts among several institutional standards. They face multiple stakeholders who seek control disguised as accountability. Stakeholders try to influence purpose, yet leaders must forge and sustain common purpose and accountability across several institutions that may have different cultures and purposes. Leaders also need to initiate changes in their organizations and manage across organizations to make collaborations work (O'Leary and Bingham 2009a).

Second, these activities require militant openness to information and relational connections. Individuals need to initiate direction across time and adapt to multiple challenges in resources, stakeholders, and new information (Huberts 2014; Patzer and Voegtlin 2013; Newton 2013). Individuals in these complex and incomplete situations make ethics salient through their modeling, decisions, reinforcement of practice as well as two-way communication and relations. Without one clear line of accountability, individuals become responsible for creating new social connections, launching and reinforcing norms, and often creating innovations and pilot programs and relations to address the changes and responsibilities.

Third, this newly empowered individual integrity places strong obligations upon the individuals to identify the ethical issues latent in conflicts or among stakeholders. Leaders can ferret out hidden ethical and equity issues that stakeholders may wish to ignore or de-emphasize. In fluid and open political environments the role of individual leaders and managers is magnified. Without being anchored to any one chain of command or accountability, individuals rely more upon their personal integrity to guide initiatives and relationships. They take on more responsibility and power by contributing to new standards, protocols, and norms of connection that get at these ethical issues. Individuals have serious potential ethical leverage at moments of change and can influence the future because of the cascade effects on path-dependent change (Moberg 2000).

Uncovering these ethical dimensions requires aggressive integrity-driven scanning of the environment and honesty to uncover and address latent ethical issues. Individuals will be the drivers to begin deliberations to create connections across groups to address them. Individuals are critical to integrating them into initiatives and engaging chaotic interactions among multiple groups (Sonenschein 2009; Weick 1995, 2000). The obligation and opportunity for ethical leverage rises when he or she discovers most groups are tempted to groupthink, cultural blindness, confirmation bias, and all the organizational and personal tendencies to narrow and intensify organizational myopia (Perrow 1972, 2014).

Even with its paradoxes, individuals of integrity rise to utmost importance in the contested political and social space between institutions and across partnerships. They are key not only to building institutions and fighting corruption but also to filling the ethical vacuums in the new spaces of governance. The shifting of goals and multiple accountability demand spotlighting the fundamental importance of individuals with integrity as well as a relentless need for transparency, since no one institutional system can achieve the goals of the integrity model.

References

Albrecht, C. C., M. L. Sanders, D. V. Holland, and C. Albrecht. 2011. "The Debilitating Effects of Fraud in Organizations," in R. J. Burke, E. C. Tomlinson, and C. L. Cooper, eds., *Crime and Corruption in Organizations: Why It Occurs and What to Do about It*. Surrey, UK: Gower Publishing, 163–86.

Anechiarico, F., and J. B. Jacobs. 1996. *The Pursuit of Absolute Integrity: How Corruption Control Makes Government Ineffective*. Chicago, IL: University of Chicago Press.

Aristotle. 1999. *Nicomachean Ethics*. 2nd ed., T. Irwin, trans. Indianapolis, IL: Hackett Publishing.

Ashford, B. E., and V. Anand. 2003. "The Normalization of Corruption in Organizations." *Research in Organizational Behavior 25*, 1–52.

Badaracco, J. L. 2002. *Leading Quietly: An Unorthodox Guide to Doing the Right Thing*. Cambridge, MA: Harvard Business School Press.

Bandura, A., B. Underwood, and M. E. Fromson. 1975. "Disinhibition of Aggression through Diffusion of Responsibility and Dehumanization of Victims." *Journal of Research in Personality 9*, 253–69.

Baumeister, R. F. 1991. *Meanings of Life*. New York: Guilford Press.

Bazerman, M. H., and A. E. Tenbrunsel. 2011. *Blind Spots: Why We Fail to Do What's Right and What to Do about It*. Princeton, NJ: Princeton University Press.

Beck, U. 2009. *What Is Globalization*. Cambridge: Cambridge University Press.

Beilock, Sian. 2010. *Choke: What the Secrets of the Brain Reveal about Getting it Right When You Have To*. New York: Simon and Schuster.

Bolman, L. G., and T. E. Deal. 2011. *Reframing Organizations: Artistry, Choice and Leadership*. New York: John Wiley and Sons.

Bridges, W. 2009. *Managing Transitions: Making the Most of Change*. New York: DeCapo Books.

Burke, R. J. 2011. "Crime and Corruption in Organizations," in R. J. Burke, E. C. Tomlinson, and C. L. Cooper, eds., *Crime and Corruption in Organizations: Why It Occurs and What to Do about It*. Surrey, UK: Gower Publishing, 3–68.

Burke, R. J., E. C. Tomlinson, and C. L. Cooper, eds. 2011. *Crime and Corruption in Organizations: Why It Occurs and What to Do about It*. Psychological and Behavioral Aspects of Risk Series. Surrey, UK: Gower Publishing.

Brownstein, A. 2003. "Biased Predecision Processing." *Psychological Bulletin 127*, 545–68.

Bryson, J., B. Crosby, and L. Bloomberg, eds. 2015. *Creating Public Value in Practice: Advancing the Common Good in a Multi-sector, Shared Power, No-One-Wholly-in-Charge World*. Boca Raton, FL: Taylor and Francis Group.

Carter, S. 1996. *Integrity*. New York: Basic Books.

Chambers Dictionary of Etymology. 2003. New York: Chambers.

Cialdini, R. B. 2009. *Influence: Science and Practice*. 5th ed. Boston: Pearson.

Cooper, J. M. 1975. *Reason and Human Good in Aristotle*. Cambridge, MA: Harvard University Press.

Cooper, T. L. 2004. "Big Questions in Administrative Ethics: A Need for Focused, Collaborative Effort." *Public Administration Review 64*(4), 395–407.

Damasio, A. 1999. *The Feeling of What Happens: Body and Emotion in the Making of Consciousness*. New York: Harcourt Brace.

Damasio, A. 2012. *Self Comes to Mind: Constructing the Conscious Brain*. New York: Vintage.

Dobel, J. P. 1999. *Public Integrity*. Baltimore, MD: Johns Hopkins University Press.

Dobel, J. P. 2018. *Public Leadership Ethics: A Management Approach*. New York: Routledge Focus.

Dutton, J. E., L. M. Morgan, and J. Bednar. 2010. "Pathways for Positive Identity Construction at Work: Four Types of Positive Identity and the Building of Social Resources." *Academy of Management Review 35*(2), 265–93.

Economic Development Institute (EDI). 1999. *Curbing Corruption: Toward a Model for Building National Integrity*. R. Stapenhurst and S. Kpundeh, eds. Washington, DC: Economic Development Institute of the World Bank.

Emerson, K., and T. Nabatchi. 2015. *Collaborative Governance Regimes*. Washington, DC: Georgetown University Press.

Fairhurst, G. T., and R. A. Sarr. 1996. *The Art of Framing: Managing the Language of Leadership*. San Francisco: Jossey-Bass Publishers.

Festinger, L. 1957. *A Theory of Cognitive Dissonance*. Stanford, CA: Stanford University Press.

Festinger, L., H. Riecken, and S. Schacter. 1964. *When Prophecy Fails*. New York: Harper and Row.

Fingarette, H. 2000. *Self-Deception: With a New Chapter*. Berkeley: University of California Press.

Friedman, J. L., and S. C. Fraser. 1966. "Compliance without Pressure: The Foot in the Door Technique." *Journal of Personality and Social Psychology 4*, 195–203.

Gannett, A., and C. Rector. 2015. "Rationalization and Political Corruption." *Public Integrity 17*(2), 165–76.

Graycar, A., and T. Prenzler. 2013. *Understanding and Preventing Corruption*. Basingstoke: Palgrave Macmillan.

Greenberg, M. 2013. *Culture, Compliance and the C-Suite: How Executives, Boards and Policymakers Can Better Safeguard against Misconduct at the Top*. Santa Monica, CA: RAND Corporation.

Guerber, A., A. Rajagoplan, and V. Anand. 2011. "The Influence of National Culture on the Rationalization of Corruption," in R. J. Burke, E. C. Tomlinson, and C. L. Cooper, eds., *Crime and Corruption in Organizations: Why It Occurs and What to Do about It*. Surrey, UK: Gower Publishing, 143–60.

Heath, C., and D. Heath. 2013. *Decisive: How to Make Better Choices in Life and Work*. New York: Crown Publishing.

Huberts, L. 2014. *The Integrity of Governance: What It Is, What We Know, What Is Done and Where to Go*. Basingstoke: Palgrave Macmillan.

Huberts, L., and A. Hoekstra, eds. 2014. *Integrity Management in the Public Sector: The Dutch Approach*. Amsterdam: Dutch National Integrity Office.

Janis, I. L., and L. Mann, 1977. *Decision Making: A Psychological Analysis of Conflict, Choice, and Commitment*. New York: Free Press.

Janis, I. L. 1982. *Groupthink: Psychological Studies of Policy Decisions and Fiascoes*. Boston: Houghton Mifflin.

Kahneman, D., and A. Tverskey. 2000. *Choices, Values and Frames*. Cambridge: Cambridge University Press.

Kahneman, D. 2011 and 2013. *Thinking, Fast and Slow*. New York: Farrar, Strauss and Giroux.

Kettl, D. F. 2015. *The Transformation of Governance: Public Administration for the Twenty-first Century*. Baltimore, MD: Johns Hopkins University Press.

Killinger, B. 2010. *Integrity: Doing the Right Thing for the Right Reason*. Montreal and Kingston: McGill-Queen's University Press.

Klein, G. A. 1998. *Sources of Power: How People Make Decisions*. Cambridge, MA. MIT Press.

Klein, G. A. 2009. *Streetlights and Shadows: Searching for the Keys to Adaptive Decision Making*. Cambridge, MA. MIT Press.

Klitgaard, R. 1988. *Controlling Corruption*. Berkeley: University of California Press.

Kotter, J. 1996, 2012. *Leading Change*. Boston: Harvard Business Review Press.

Korsgaard, C. M. 2009. *Self-Constitution: Agency, Identity, and Integrity*. Oxford: Oxford University Press.

Kooistra, J. 2014. "Integrity: Part of Day-to-Day Practice in the City of Amsterdam," in L. Huberts and A. Hoekstra, eds., *Integrity Management in the Public Sector: The Dutch Approach*. Amsterdam: Dutch National Integrity Office, 114–35.

Kouzes, J. M., and B. Z. Posner. 2006. *The Leadership Challenge*. Vol. 3. New York: John Wiley and Sons.

Kouzes, J. M., and B. Z. Posner. 2011. *Credibility: How Leaders Gain and Lose It, Why People Demand It*. Vol. 244. New York: John Wiley and Sons.

Lang, D. 2008. "A Multidimensional Conceptualization of Organizational Corruption Control." *Academy of Management Review 33*(3), 710–29.

Langseth, P., R. Stapenhurst, and J. Pope. 1997. *The Role of a National Integrity System in Fighting Corruption*. Washington, DC: Economic Development Institute of the World Bank.

LeDoux, J. 2002. *The Synaptic Brain: How Our Brains Become Who We Are*. New York: Penguin.

Lewis, C. W., and Gilman, S. C. 2005. *The Ethics Challenge in Public Service: A Problem-Solving Guide*. San Francisco: Jossey-Bass.

Lipshaw, J. 2009a. "Law as Rationalization: Getting beyond Reason to Business Ethics," in N. B. Rapoport, J. D. Van Niel, and B. G. Dharan, eds., *Enron and Other Corporate Fiascos: The Corporate Scandal Reader*, 2nd ed. New York: Thomas Reuters/Foundation Press, 929–90.

Lipshaw, J. 2009b. "Sarbanes-Oxley, Jurisprudence, Game Theory, Insurance and Kant: Towards a Moral Theory of Good Governance," in N. B. Rapoport, J. D. Van Niel, and B. G. Dharan, eds., *Enron and Other Corporate Fiascos: The Corporate Scandal Reader*, 2nd ed. New York: Thomas Reuters/Foundation Press, 709–38.

Miceli, M. P., and J. P. Near. 2002. "What Makes Whistle-Blowers Effective? Three Field Studies." *Human Relations 55*, 455–79.

Macaulay, M., and A. Lawton. 2006. "From Virtue to Competence: Changing the Principles of Public Service." *Public Administration Review 66*(5), 702–10.

Machiavell, N. 1965. "The History of Florence." In *Machiavelli: The Chief Works and Others*. Allan Gilbert, trans. Durham, NC: Duke University Press, 1025–436.

Mallory, J., and D. Q. Adams. 1997. *Encyclopedia of Indo-European Culture*. London: Adams Taylor.

McLean, B., and P. Elkind. 2013. *The Smartest Guys in the Room: The Amazing Rise and Scandalous Fall of Enron*. New York: Penguin.

Moberg, D. J. 2000. "Role Models and Moral Exemplars: How Do Employees Acquire Virtues by Observing Others?" *Business Ethics Quarterly 10*(3), 675–96.

Moberg, D. J. 2006. "Ethics Blind Spots in Organizations: How Systematic Errors in Person Perception Undermine Moral Agency." *Organization Studies 27*(3), 413–28.

Moore, D. A., D. M. Cain, G. Loewenstein, and M. H. Bazerman, eds. 2005. *Conflicts of Interest: Challenges and Solutions in Business, Law, Medicine, and Public Policy.* Cambridge: Cambridge University Press.

Newton, R. 2013. "Perception and Development of Ethical Change Leadership," in R. Tudnem and B. Burnes, eds., *Organizational Change, Leadership, and Ethics.* London: Routledge, 35–54.

OECD. 1998. "Recommendation of the Council on Improving Ethical Conduct in the Public Service Including Principles for Managing Ethics in the Public Sector." http://acts.oecd.org/Instruments/ ShowInstrumentView.aspx?InstrumentID=129&Lang=en. Accessed February 8, 2016.

OECD. 2009. "Towards a Sound Integrity Framework: Instruments, Processes, Structures and Conditions for Implementation." Paris: http://www.oecd.org/officialdocuments/publicdisplay- documentpdf/?doclanguage=en&cote=GOV/PGC/GF(2009)1. Accessed January 27, 2016.

OECD. 2016. Integrity Framework for Public Investment. Paris: OECD Public Governance Review. http://www.keepeek.com/Digital-Asset-Management/oecd/governance/integrity-frame- work-for-public-investment_9789264251762-en#page1. Accessed March 16, 2016.

O'Connor, M. A. 2009. "The Enron Board: The Perils of Groupthink," in N. B. Rapoport, J. D. Van Niel, and B. G. Dharan, eds., *Enron and Other Corporate Fiascos: The Corporate Scandal Reader,* 2nd ed. New York: Thomas Reuters/Foundation Press, 431–508.

O'Leary, R., and L. B. Bingham, eds. 2009a. *The Collaborative Public Manager: New Ideas for the Twenty-First Century.* Washington, DC: Georgetown University Press.

O'Leary, R., and L. B. Bingham. 2009b. "Surprising Findings, Paradoxes, and Thoughts On the Future of Collaborative Public Management Research," in R. O'Leary and L. B. Bingham, eds., *The Collaborative Public Manager: New Ideas for the Twenty-First Century.* Washington, DC: Georgetown University Press, 255–70.

Oxford Dictionary of English Etymology. 1960. Oxford: Oxford University Press.

Page, S. 2010. "Integrative Leadership for Collaborative Governance: Civic Engagement in Seattle." *The Leadership Quarterly* 21(2), 246–63.

Patzer, M., and Voegtlin, C. 2013. "Leadership and Organizational Change: Sketching the Field," in R. Tudnem and B. Burnes, eds., *Organizational Change, Leadership, and Ethics.* London: Routledge, 9–34.

Perrow, C. 1998. *Normal Accidents: Living with High Risk Technologies.* Princeton, NJ: Princeton University Press.

Perrow, C. 1972, 2014. *Complex Organizations: A Critical Essay.* Brattleboro, VT: Echo Point Books.

Pinker, S. 1999. *How the Mind Works.* New York: W. W. Norton.

Plato. 1991. *The Republic.* Allan Bloom, trans. New York: Basic Books.

Pope, J. 1999. *The Need and Role of an Independent Anti-Corruption Agency.* Working Paper for Transparency International. New York: Transparency International.

Rabl, T., and T. Kuhlmann. 2008. "Understanding Corruption in Organizations Development and Assessment of an Action Model." *Journal of Business Ethics* 82(2), 477–95.

Radvansky, G. 2006. *Human Memory.* New York: Pearson.

Rapoport, N. B., J. D. Van Niel, and B. G. Dharan, eds. 2009. *Enron and Other Corporate Fiascos: The Corporate Scandal Reader.* 2nd ed. New York: Thomas Reuters/Foundation Press.

Rawls, John. 1971. *A Theory of Justice.* Cambridge, MA: Harvard University Press.

Rohr, J. 1988. *Ethics for Bureaucrats: An Essay on Law and Values.* Vol. 36. Boca Raton, FL: CRC Press.

Rose-Ackerman, S. 1999. *Corruption of Government: Causes, Consequences and Reform.* Cambridge: Cambridge University Press.

Ross, L., and R. E. Nisbett. 2011. *The Person and the Situation: Perspectives of Social Psychology.* New York: Pinter & Martin Publishers.

Sapolsky, R. M. 2012. *Why Zebras Don't Get Ulcers.* New York: St. Martins.

Schein, E. H. 2009. *The Corporate Culture Survival Guide. JB Warren Bennis Series.* San Francisco: Jossey-Bass.

Schein, E. H. 2010. *Organizational Culture and Leadership.* New York: John Wiley.

Schwartz, M. S. 2011. "How to Minimize Corruption in Business Organizations: Developing and Sustaining an Ethical Corporate Culture," in R. J. Burke, E. C. Tomlinson, and C. L. Cooper, eds., *Crime and Corruption in Organizations: Why It Occurs and What to Do about It.* Surrey, UK: Gower Publishing, 273–96.

Scherer, A. G., G., Palazzo, and D. Bauman. 2009. "Globalization as a Challenge for Business Responsibilities." *Business Ethics Quarterly 19*, 327–47.

Senge, P. M. 2006. *The Fifth Discipline: The Art and Practice of the Learning Organization.* New York: Doubleday.

Sherman, N. 1989. *The Fabric of Character: Aristotle's Theory of Virtue.* Oxford: Clarendon Press.

Schon, D. 1984. *The Reflective Practitioner: How Professionals Think in Action.* New York: Basic Books.

Solomon, R. 2007. *True to Our Feelings.* Oxford: Oxford University Press.

Sonenschein, S. 2009. "Emergence of Ethical Issues during Strategic Change Implementation." *Organizational Science 20*, 223–39.

Tenbrunsel, A. E. 2005. "Bounded Ethicality and Conflicts of Interest," in D. A. Moore, D. M. Cain, G. Loewenstein, and M. H. Bazerman, eds., *Conflicts of Interest: Challenges and Solutions in Business, Law, Medicine, and Public Policy.* Cambridge: Cambridge University Press, 96–103.

Terry, L. D. 2003. *Leadership of Public Bureaucracy: The Administrator as Conservator.* New York: M. E. Sharpe.

Transparency International. undated Website https://www.transparency.org. Accessed March 16, 2016. See "Corruption by Country."

Transparency International. 2000. "TI Sourcebook 2000: Confronting Corruption: The Elements of a National Integrity System." http://archive.transparency.org/publications/sourcebook. Accessed January 27, 2016.

Transparency International. 2011. *National Integrity System: Background Rationale and Methodology.* https://www.transparency.org/files/content/nis/NIS_Background_Methodology_EN.pdf. Accessed March 2, 2016.

Trevino, L. K., G. R. Weaver, D. G. Gibson, and B. L. Toffler. 1999. "Managing Ethics and Legal Compliance: What Works and What Hurts." *California Management Review 41*(2), 131–51.

Tudnem, R., and B. Burnes, eds. 2013. *Organizational Change, Leadership, and Ethics.* London: Routledge.

UN Office on Drugs and Crime (UNODC). 2004. *United Nations Convention Against Corruption.* New York: UN Office on Drugs and Crime. https://www.unodc.org/unodc/en/treaties/CAC/. Accessed March 2, 2016.

UN Office on Drugs and Crime (UNODC). 2013. *An Anti-corruption Ethics and Compliance Program for Business: A Practical Guide.* New York: UN Office on Drugs and Crime.

Uslaner, E. M. 2008. *Corruption, Inequality and the Rule of Law.* Cambridge: Cambridge University Press.

Vaughan, D. 1997. *The Challenger Launch Decision: Risky Technology, Culture, and Deviance at NASA.* Chicago, IL: University of Chicago Press.

Visser, H. 2014. "Integrity Incorporated in Strategy and Daily Processes: The Netherlands Tax and Custom Administration," in L. Huberts and A. Hoekstra, eds., *Integrity Management in the Public Sector: The Dutch Approach.* Amsterdam: Dutch National Integrity Office, 146–58.

Watkins, C. 2000. *The American Heritage Dictionary of Indo-European Roots.* 2nd ed. Boston: Houghton Mifflin Harcourt.

Weick, K. E. 1995. *Sensemaking in Organizations.* Foundations for Organizational Science. Thousand Oaks, CA: Sage Publications.

Weick, K. E. 2000. "Emergent Change as a Universal in Organizations," in Michael Beer and Nitin Mohria, eds., *Breaking the Code of Change.* Boston: Harvard Business School Press, 223–41.

Weiner, B. 2006. *Social Motivation, Justice, and the Moral Emotions: An Attributional Approach.* New York: Psychology Press.

Williams, B. 2008. *Shame and Necessity.* Berkeley: University of California Press.

Zimbardo, P. 2007. *The Lucifer Effect: Understanding How Good People Turn Evil.* New York: Random House.

Zimmerman, K. A. 2014 "Memory Definition and Memory Formation." http://www.livescience.com/43713-memory.html. Accessed October 10, 2015.

12

Ethics Management
A Pluralistic and Dynamic Perspective
Alain Hoekstra and Muel Kaptein

Both public and private organizations play a pivotal role in combatting corruption. As organizations are responsible for managing the behavior of their employees, organizations can employ instruments to prevent their employees from being corrupted (passive corruption) and from corrupting others (active corruption), and to detect and redress the situation adequately when corruption nevertheless takes place. Because organizations also deal with other organizations and individuals, such as suppliers, customers, citizens, and capital providers, organizations can use their influence to stimulate these others not to engage in corruption (anymore). Organizations can also refuse to have any dealings with corrupt organizations and individuals.

In combatting corruption, organizations do employ many different ethics instruments. For example, research in the United States among public and private organizations with more than two hundred employees shows that 80 percent of the organizations have their own code of ethics, 69 percent have policies to investigate and take corrective action when there are allegations of misconduct, 66 percent conduct background investigations on prospective employees, 62 percent have a senior-level ethics or a compliance officer, and 61 percent have a confidential and anonymous hotline for reporting misconduct (KPMG 2013). Research among the Fortune Global 200 companies shows that 76 percent of them have a code of ethics and more than 80 percent use e-learning modules to communicate the standards of the organization and have an ethics hotline and whistleblower mechanisms and policies to investigate misconduct (KPMG 2014).

Scientific research on the effectiveness of these ethics instruments is, however, not very positive. For instance, a review by Kaptein and Schwartz (2008) of seventy-nine empirical studies on the effectiveness of organizational codes of ethics shows that 35 percent of the studies found that codes of ethics are effective, 16 percent found that codes are weakly effective, 33 percent found that codes are not effective, and 14 percent yielded mixed results. One study even found that codes of ethics could be counterproductive. A reason for these mixed results is what is called *decoupling* (cf. MacLean, Litzky, and Holderness 2015). They found that ethics instruments could not be effective when they are not implemented and embedded well in an organization; they may even be counterproductive. When employees perceive these instruments as decoupled from their day-to-day work processes, they see them as mere façade or "window dressing" and as showing a concern for ethics purely out of PR considerations. Employees will then be stimulated to commit more misconduct because there are no preventions or redress for them.

As MacLean and colleagues (2010, 2015) suggest, decoupling can be intentional, thus facilitating misconduct, but it can also be unintentional. Ethics instruments then lack effectiveness because management does not know how to implement those instruments well. The current literature on ethics management does not sufficiently inform managers about two misconceptions about managing ethics that can lead to an unintentional decoupling and thus to less-effective ethics instruments. First, many studies in this field pay attention to one ethics instrument. Warren, Gaspar, and Laufer (2014), for instance, focus on ethics training, suggesting that such a single instrument can be implemented without taking into account a broader spectrum of ethics instruments. Second, many studies suggest that once an ethics instrument is developed and implemented, this then would make it effective for a long period. For example, the study conducted by Warren and colleagues (2014) suggests that running an ethics training program just once is effective and will stay effective.

However, for ethics instruments to be more effective, a perspective on ethics management that is both pluralistic (it involves more ethics instruments) and dynamic (ethics programs follow an iterative approach) should be considered. The Deming cycle is used to ground and structure such an approach. The Deming cycle is a four-phased management model with a proven versatility to drive change and improvement in all kinds of organizations and topics (Jagusiak-Kocik 2017; Prashar 2017). Here the cycle is used to improve organizational ethics. After explaining what the Deming cycle is the chapter reflects on the programs designed for ethics management and the different types of instruments that compose them (Kaptein 2009, 2015). It is emphasized that ethics programs require a set of ethical components or instruments (implying a pluralistic instead of a monistic approach) and that ethics programs should be structured along the four phases of the Deming cycle (implying a dynamic instead of a static approach).

The Deming Cycle

The Deming Cycle, also called the Deming Wheel and Deming Circle (Taylor et al. 2014), dates back from the 1950s and was developed by William Edwards Deming, an American engineer, scholar, and management consultant. He designed the cycle as a quality-control instrument for industries and stressed the importance of constant interaction among the four steps of design, production, sales, and research. To increase the quality of products, these four steps should be rotated constantly (Moen 2009). The cycle presents a pragmatic scientific method for testing changes in complex systems (Moen and Norman 2006). The four steps, or phases or stages, mirror scientific experimental method: that is, formulate a hypothesis, collect data to test this hypothesis, analyze and interpret the results, and make inferences to iterate the hypothesis (Taylor et al. 2014).

Japanese executives reformulated these steps into the Plan-Do-Check-Act cycle, (PDCA cycle) also called the Plan-Do-Study-Act cycle (PDSA cycle) (Moen and Norman 2010). The first phase of the PDCA cycle pertains to the planning of products, including determining goals, objectives, targets, and methods to carry out the cycle (who, what, where, and when). The second phase (Do or Implementation) corresponds to the making or working on the designed product, including training and educating the workers involved in the production. The third phase involves checking the effects of and the satisfaction with the product, for instance, through monitoring and evaluation. The fourth phase (Act or React) focuses on the redesign of and changes on the product (adaptation) in case of complaints, new developments, or opportunities for further improvements (Moen and Norman 2010). This final phase also provides input for a new plan, making the process a cycle.

The Deming or PDCA cycle is related to quality improvement approaches such as the Model for Improvement; Total Quality Management; Continuous Quality Improvement; Lean Sigma; Six Sigma; Business Process Reengineering; Operational Excellence; and Business Excellence (Sokovic et al. 2010; Taylor et al. 2014). The PDCA cycle has been widely applied in different types of working environments, such as the car industry, health care, agribusiness, energy sector, and education. There has been research on the effectiveness of the PDCA cycle (Taylor 2014), and positive outcomes have been reported (e.g., Pronovost et al. 2006; Jagusiak-Kocik 2017).

In this chapter, the PDCA cycle is used to manage ethics as a dynamic (iterative) process, as opposed to a one-off, static approach. It is also used because it acknowledges that

TABLE 12.1	Perspectives on Ethics Management		
		Time frame	
		Static	*Dynamic*
Number of ethics instruments in focus	**Monistic**	Static–Monistic perspective	Dynamic–Monistic perspective
	Pluralistic	Static–Pluralistic perspective	Dynamic–Plural perspective

most situations that require change or improvement are rather complex—which managing ethics is (Kaptein 1998)—and that single-bullet interventions are most likely insufficient. Interventions need to be multi-faceted (Taylor et al. 2014), which implies that ethics management requires different ethics instruments to foster organizational ethics. In other words, ethics management requires a pluralistic and not a monistic perspective. This suggests the need for coherence among the instruments, as will be argued in the next section.

Given the distinction between static and dynamic and between monistic and plural, different perspectives on ethics management can be distinguished. Table 12.1 shows these different perspectives based on the number of ethics instruments or components that an ethics program focuses on and the program's time frame. If the ethics program focuses on just one component, it is labeled as "monistic," and "pluralistic" if more components are involved. If the ethics program's time frame is limited or restricted to one moment, it is labeled as "static," and "dynamic" if it considers an iterative perspective. This leads to four different perspectives: static–monistic; static–plural; dynamic–monistic; and dynamic–plural. The latter is our proposed approach.

Ethics Programs: A Pluralistic Perspective

An ethics program, also often referred to as compliance program or integrity program, can be described as the formal organizational control system designed to impede unethical behavior (Kaptein 2009; Weaver et al. 1999a). Besides avoiding unethical behavior (of which corruption is one), ethics programs also positively contribute to the organization's reputation, to its employees' commitment and productivity, to the decrease of its regulatory, transaction, and oversight costs, and in more general terms, to the improvement of organizational success (Dobel 2018; Foote and Ruona 2008; Peterson 2012; Weaver, Treviño, and Cochran 1999b).

Because unethical behavior is in general the result of a complex array of causes (Kish-Gephart et al. 2010), ethics programs can consist of a variety of components or instruments (Hoekstra and Heres 2016; Weber and Wasieleski 2013). Several scholarly studies have been conducted on ethical components (Ferrel et al. 1998; Foote and Ruona 2008; MacLean and Behnam 2010; Maclean et al. 2015; Reynolds and Bowie 2004), and most of the components proposed correspond closely with the US Federal Sentencing Guidelines components of an effective ethics program (Desio 2008).

Kaptein's (2009, 2015) set of nine ethics, components of an ethics program, is considered the most exhaustive to date. The first component is an ethics code, which is a distinct formal document that clarifies the desired organizational values and standards that provide guidance to employees on multiple ethical issues. The second component is a dedicated, usually in-house, ethics officer or ethics office, also called compliance office(r), ombudsperson, ethics desk, or ethics platform. The third component is ethics training and other types of information and communication about ethics that clarify the ethical policies and create ethical awareness and capability among employees. The fourth component is an ethics line, usually called an ethics hotline or helpline, with a clear procedure for reporting, sharing, and discussing ethical issues. The three other components concern the disciplinary processes within an organization. The disciplinary processes consist of policies on managerial and employee accountability for ethics violations, investigative and corrective policies dealing with allegations of ethics violations, and policies for creating incentives and rewards for employees' ethical behavior. The final two components concern the assessment of the organizational ethical culture, behavior, and performance and the ethics assessment of new recruits by means of pre-employment screenings.

Subsequently, Kaptein (2015) found that the more components are incorporated in an ethics program, the more effective those programs are. Thus, component plurality, in the sense of having an ethics program that consists of multiple instruments, is in general desirable for preventing unethical behavior and for fighting corruption. Component plurality requires component coherence. Component coherence means that the components of the ethics program fit together and reinforce each other. A unified approach sees to the complementariness of the ethical components that promotes synergy and effectiveness (Maclean and Behnam 2010; Maesschalck and Bertok 2009). This is consistent with the idea of the Deming circle that the different activities and elements in each phase of the cycle should align well. It is the combination of components that has a larger effect on the behavior of employees than the mere sum of the effects of the individual components and instruments (Brenner 1992). As such, the degree of component coherence has been highlighted as an important contributor to the effectiveness of ethics programs (Foote and Ruona 2008; Ruiz et al. 2015). Therefore, organizations should not only adopt multiple ethics instruments, but they should also take care that these instruments fit well with each other and are mutually aligned. For example, Kaptein (2015) found that the sequence by which the components are implemented determines the effectiveness of an ethics program. He found that the best sequence of adopting the components of an ethics program is (1) a code of ethics; (2) ethics training and communication; (3) accountability policies; (4) monitoring and auditing; (5) investigations and correction policies; (6) an ethics office(r); (7) ethics reporting line; and (8) incentive policies.

Ethics Programs: A Dynamic Perspective

Next to the plurality of components or content of an ethics program, it is important to acknowledge that ethics programs require a repetitive approach. This is the process part of an ethics program. Ethics programs (with their components) should not be developed and implemented only once. They should be regularly monitored, evaluated and, if necessary, adapted. This denotes the dynamic (not static) character of ethics programs. Applied to ethics management, the PDCA cycle emphasizes the need for an iterative approach, referring to the phases that the ethics program has to go through successively and continuously. At this point, the application of the PDCA cycle to ethics programs is discussed only briefly. In the next section there is a more detailed discussion in relation to the plurality of ethics instruments.

The PDCA cycle in relation to ethics management starts with the Planning phase. In this phase, the organization defines what it wants to achieve in terms of ethics management and which set of ethics instruments is needed to realize these ambitions. Next to determining the objectives and content of the ethics program and its individual components, management has to plan how to carry out the rest of the cycle. Besides deciding which organizational actors have to do what, when and where, the required organizational resources also have to be considered (Hoekstra and Kaptein 2013).

Implementation is the second phase of the PDCA cycle: the Do phase. In this phase, the ethics instruments are actually developed and introduced in the organization. However, quite often implementation proves to be a challenge (Lawton et al. 2013).

Ethics instruments have repeatedly proven to be just a paper exercise without any direct follow up (Hoekstra 2016). Demmke and Moilanen (2012) pointed out that in general ethics management does not suffer from a lack of instruments but from implementation weaknesses.

The third phase, which is the Check phase, consists of an analysis of the achieved results in terms of the progress and effects of the ethics program. Monitoring, evaluation, and reporting make it possible to establish to what extent the objectives of ethics management are actually realized, and if the specific instruments actually work. This analysis provides crucial input for the modification and improvement of the ethics program (Weber and Wasieleski 2013) and for the adjustment or replacement of specific components. As described above, monitoring is just one of the nine components of an ethics program. However, including it as phase in the cycle stresses the importance of monitoring all components, including the monitoring itself, in the sense of evaluating whether the monitoring does what it should do.

The fourth phase, which is the Act, react, or adapt phase, is based on the notion of permanent learning and improvement. As ethics programs and their instruments are often developed in times of crises and thus in great haste, they are therefore not likely to suit long-term organizational needs (Joseph 2002). Also, the context of the organization can change, and so can the ambitions within the organization. Adaptation is thus needed, and this leads to the adjustment and reformulation of the initial plan, resulting in the cycle starting again.

Framework for Ethics Programs: Towards a Pluralistic and Dynamic Perspective

Inspired by the PDCA cycle, a pluralistic and dynamic perspective of ethics management is proposed. The pluralistic character means that an ethics program is more effective when more of the ethics components are incorporated and when these components are coherent. The dynamic character means that an ethics program is more effective if it is iterative and consistently follows the four subsequent phases of the PDCA cycle. Combining these two features implies that an organization could have a coherent set of ethics instruments that are dynamically embedded (see figure 12.1). Here follows a discussion of what the combination of these two features entails in terms of the individual phases of the PDCA cycle.

The planning phase involves determining why ethics is considered an important issue for the management of the organization and what management wants to achieve in terms of ethics management. The content and process of the ethics program should be determined and aligned with the organization's ethical ambitions and objectives. To achieve these objectives, an analysis can be made of the external ethical requirements (e.g., national laws, sectorial regulations and norms) that the organizations should comply with and to what extent the organization already meets these requirements (Wulf 2012). With regard to the organization's internal need for ethics, the organization can assess the ethical dilemmas and risks that confront employees. This will inform management about the kind of ethics instruments the organization needs to develop and when these instruments should be developed. Coherence among the various ethics instruments is crucial and should be created. This requires clarity about who is responsible for coordinating and overseeing the ethics program (Driscoll and Hoffman 2000; Segon 2010). Another important aspect of this phase is determining which internal and external actors are to be involved in developing and carrying out the ethics instruments (Reynolds and Bowie 2004). Next to formulating the ambitions and objectives of management regarding the ethics program, a vision or action plan has to be developed for the required actions along the four phases of the

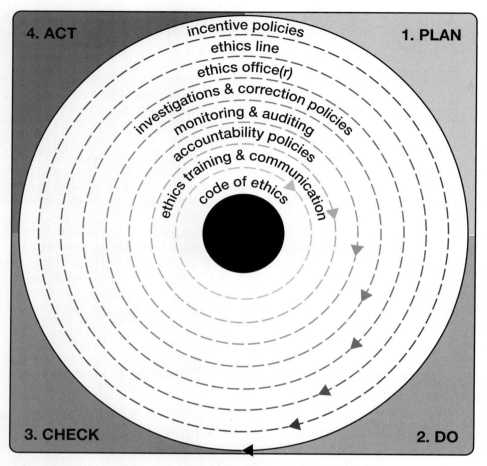

FIGURE 12.1 A Pluralistic and Dynamic Perspective on Ethics Management

cycle so that both the pluralistic and dynamic elements of ethics management are made explicit and well thought-out. An estimation of the needed resources—such as time, budget, and expertise—to realize the ambition and objectives is also necessary.

Next to a thorough and well-organized planning phase, it is of course important that the ethics program is actually implemented. This is the second phase, the Do phase, which involves developing the ethics instruments. Maybe some standard ethics instruments can be adopted (such as an ethics line similar to that offered by consultancy firms), or maybe instruments can be developed in close cooperation with organizations that belong to the same sector (Hoekstra, Talsma, and Kaptein 2016), but most likely these have to be customized or even newly developed to fulfill the organization's ethics ambitions and to mitigate the specific ethical dilemmas and risks (Brenner 1992; Pritchett et al. 2010). In this phase, coherence among the different ethics instruments can be realized by, for instance, making clear the respective functions of each of the instruments, making references between and among the ethics instruments (for example, referring to the ethics officer and ethics line in a code of ethics), or by implementing the instruments simultaneously (for example, letting the ethics officer give the ethics training to employees). It is important that management, as the key decision maker, shows its commitment and support for the real implementation of the ethics program (cf. Kaptein 2014; Weaver, Treviño, and Cochran 1999a). Management should not only emphasize the importance of the program but should also demonstrate role modeling behavior to show that they really lead the ethics program (Weaver, Treviño, and Cochran 1999a). Although the pressure to develop ethics programs might come from outside the organization, it is ultimately (top) management that has the final say on how and to what extent the organization should improve its ethics. Likewise, adequate support from lower management in applying the ethics instruments in their respective departments is part of this phase.

The Check phase sees to the monitoring of the ethics program and its constituent instruments. Monitoring, evaluation, and reporting are important to assess both the implementation process and the realization of the intended results of the ethics program and its instruments. This phase facilitates organizational learning because it clarifies the problems encountered during the implementation of the ethics program, its components, and their results. Monitoring includes checking whether the program content is honored in practice, if the instruments work in the way they were meant to, whether the ethical culture of the organization improves in the direction as planned, and if there is a decrease in the incidents of unethical behavior within the organization. Most importantly, this phase constitutes the basis for changes that can be proposed for future improvements of the ethics program. Also relevant in this phase is assessing the extent to which the different ethics instruments actually reinforce and complement each other and that, in the worst case, they do not undermine and contradict each other. Going through the cycle iteratively also creates in this phase the possibility to compare the monitoring results with previous results and to find out to what extent the ethics program has become more effective during these measurement periods.

The Act phase involves formulating to what extent the current program requires adaptation based on the evaluation report. This phase focuses on redesigning and changing the program in case of disappointing results, new developments, or new opportunities for further improvement. Updates and revisions ensure that the program connects well with all the developments within and outside the organization. New themes may arise, for instance the use of social media by individual employees and what the organizations may expect from them in this regard (see, e.g., Hoekstra and Van Dijk (2016) and Kaptein (2014)). Other themes that may require more detailed provisions in the program are, for example, the current #MeToo discussion, the ethical issues of algorithms, and the increasing organizational responsibility for corruption by others up or down the chain. There may also be new legislation that requires organizational adaptation, or new and innovative ethics instruments developed outside the organization that could be adopted (e.g., ethical dilemma apps). All these activities can lead to new inputs for the Planning phase, which makes the process circular and ensures permanent improvement of the ethics plan.

Conclusion

In this chapter, a pluralistic and dynamic perspective of ethics management is proposed. A pluralistic perspective means that organizations should not employ a single ethics instrument, but rather they should employ an ethics program that consists of a coherent set of ethics instruments. A dynamic perspective means that organizations should not define and implement those instruments just once, but that the process should be a permanent cycle of planning, doing, checking, and acting.

The pluralistic and dynamic perspective opens new and promising directions for future research into ethics management and the prevention of corruption. Instead of studying the quality and effectiveness of an ethics instrument on its own, a broader research scope involves studying the relationship between ethics instruments. Studying how coherent the different instruments are, in the sense of how much they reinforce and complement each other, leads to a better understanding of whether and when ethics programs are effective. This understanding increases further if the effectiveness and coherence of ethics instruments are not studied at one single moment in time but longitudinally, in terms of how the instruments evolve over time as an iterative process of planning, doing, checking, and acting.

In this respect, many interesting research questions arise. For instance, with regard to the pluralistic perspective: What determines which component of an ethics program an organization should adopt? What other components, outside of the nine discussed above, can organizations adopt? What makes an ethics program coherent and what does that mean for each component? And how can the coherence of an ethics program be assessed and improved? The following are possible research questions with regard to the dynamic perspective: The ideal frequency for the cycle to start again? Whether it is desirable that all instruments go through the cycle together and at the same time? Whether the process should be sequential or can it be reversed? What are the conditions for organizations to go through the cycle frequently? What is the long-term effectiveness of ethics programs? And what determines the difference between short- and long-term effectiveness?

Our proposed pluralistic and dynamic perspective of ethics management implies that managing ethics and fighting corruption necessitate taking up a coherent set of ethics instruments. It also implies taking up these instruments not just once, but frequently, going through the Deming cycle of Planning, Doing, Checking, and Acting. In this manner, ethics management can become more effective in preventing and redressing corruption.

References

Brenner, S. N. 1992. "Ethics Programs and their Dimensions." *Journal of Business Ethics 11*(5–6), 391–99.

Demmke, C., and T. Moilanen. 2012. *Effectiveness of Public Service Ethics and Good Governance in the Central Administration of the EU-27: Evaluating Reform Outcomes in the Context of the Financial Crises.* Frankfurt am Main: Peter Lang.

Desio, P. 2008. *An Overview of the Organizational Guidelines.* Washington, DC: United States Sentencing Guidelines.

Dobel, J. P. 2018. *Public Leadership Ethics: A Management Approach.* New York: Routledge.

Driscoll, D. N., and W. M. Hoffman. 2000. *Ethics Matters: How to Implement Values-Driven Management.* Waltham, MA: Bentley College Center for Business Ethics.

Ferrel, O. C., D. T. LeClair, and L. Ferrel. 1998. "The Federal Sentencing Guidelines for Organizations: A Framework for Ethical Compliance." *Journal of Business Ethics 17*(4), 353–63.

Foote, M., and W. Ruona. 2008. "Institutionalizing Ethics: A Synthesis of Frameworks and the Implications for HRD." *Human Resource Development Review 7*(3), 292–308.

Hoekstra, A. 2016. "Institutionalizing Integrity Management: Challenges and Solutions in Times of Financial Crises and Austerity Measures," in A. Lawton, Z. van der Wal, and L. W. J. C. Huberts, eds., *Ethics in Public Policy and Management: A Global Research Companion.* Oxon: Routledge, 147–64.

Hoekstra, A., and L. Heres. 2016. "Ethical Probity in Public Service." *Global Encyclopedia of Public Administration, Public Policy, and Governance.* Cham: Springer.

Hoekstra, A., and M. Kaptein. 2013. "The Institutionalization of Integrity in Local Government." *Public Integrity 15*(1), 5–27.

Hoekstra, A., and M. van Dijk. 2016. *The Marriage of Heaven and Hell: Integrity & Social Media in the Public Sector.* The Hague: BIOS Policy Paper.

Hoekstra, A., J. Talsma, and M. Kaptein. 2016. "Integrity Management as Interorganizational Activity: Exploring Integrity Partnerships that Keep the Wheel in Motion." *Public Integrity 18*(2), 167–84.

Jagusiak-Kocik, M. 2017. "PDCA Cycle as a Part of Continuous Improvement in the Production Company: Case Study." *Production Engineering Archives 14*, 19–22.

Joseph, J. 2002. "Integrating Business Ethics and Compliance Programs: A Study of Ethics Officers in Leading Organizations." *Business and Society Review 107*(3), 309–47.

Kaptein, M. 1998. *Ethics Management: Auditing and Developing the Ethical Content of Organizations.* Dordrecht: Springer.

Kaptein, M. 2009. "Ethics Programs and Ethical Culture. A Next Step in Unraveling Their Multi-Faceted Relationship." *Journal of Business Ethics 89*(2), 261–81.

Kaptein, M. 2014. *The Servant of the People: On the Power of Integrity in Politics and Government.* New York: Amazon.

Kaptein, M. 2015. "The Effectiveness of Ethics Programs: The Role of Scope, Composition and Sequence." *Journal of Business Ethics 132*(2), 415–31.

Kaptein, M., and M. S. Schwartz. 2008. "The Effectiveness of Business Codes: A Critical Examination of Existing Studies and the Development of an Integrated Research Model." *Journal of Business Ethics 77*(2), 111–27.

Kish-Gephart, J., D. Harrison, and L. Treviño. 2010. "Bad Apples, Bad Cases, and Bad Barrels: Meta-Analytic Evidence about Sources of Unethical Decisions at Work." *Journal of Applied Psychology 95*(1), 1–31.

KPMG Forensic. 2013. *Integrity Survey 2013.* New York: KPMG.

KPMG. 2014. *The Business Codes of the Fortune Global 200: What the Largest Companies in the World Say and Do.* Amsterdam: KPMG.

Lawton, A., J. Rayner, and K. Lasthuizen. 2013. *Ethics and Management in the Public Sector.* London: Routledge.

MacLean, T., B. E. Litzky, and D. K. Holderness. 2015. "When Organizations Don't Walk Their Talk: A Cross-Level Examination of How Decoupling Formal Ethics Programs Affects Organizational Members." *Journal of Business Ethics 128*(2), 351–68.

MacLean, T. L., and M. Behnam. 2010. "The Dangers of Decoupling: The Relationship between Compliance Programs, Legitimacy Perceptions, and Institutionalized Misconduct." *Academy of Management Journal 53*(6), 1499–520.

Maesschalck, J., and J. Bertok. 2009. *Towards a Sound Integrity Framework: Instruments, Processes, Structures and Conditions for Implementation.* Paris: OECD Publications.

Moen, R. D. 2009. "Foundation and History of the PDSA Cycle." Paper Presented at Asian Network for Quality Conference in Tokyo.

Moen, R. D., and C. L. Norman. 2006. "Evolution of the PDCA Cycle". http://www.uoc.cw/financesite/images/stories/NA01_Moen_Norman_fullpaper.pdf.

Moen, R. D., and C. L. Norman. 2010. "Circling Back: Clearing up the Myths about the Deming Cycle and Seeing How It Keeps Evolving." *Quality Progress 43*, 22–28.

Peterson, E. A. 2012. "Compliance and Ethics Programs: Competitive Advantage through the Law." *Journal of Management and Governance 17*(4), 1027–45.

Prashar, A. 2017. "Adopting PDCA (Plan-Do-Check-Act) Cycle for Energy Optimization in Energy-Intensive SMEs." *Journal of Cleaner Production 145*, 277–93.

Pritchett, L., M. Woolcock, and M. Andrews. 2010. *Capability Traps? The Mechanisms of Persistent Implementation Failure.* Working Paper 234. Washington DC: Center for Global Development.

Pronovost, P., D. Needham, S. Berenholtz. 2006. "An Intervention to Decrease Catheter-Related Bloodstream Infections in the ICU." *The New England Journal of Medicine 355*, 2725–32.

Reynolds, S. J., and N. E. Bowie. 2004. "A Kantian Perspective on the Characteristics of Ethics Programs." *Business Ethics Quarterly 14*(2), 275–92.

Ruiz, P., R. Martinez, J. Rodrigo, and C. Diaz. 2015. "Level of Coherence among Ethics Program Components and Its Impact on Ethical Intent." *Journal of Business Ethics 128*(4), 725–42.

Segon, M. 2010. "Managing Organisational Ethics: Professionalism, Duty and HR Practitioners." *Journal of Business Systems, Governance and Ethics 5*(4), 13–25.

Sokovic, M., D. Pavletic, and K. K. Pipan. 2010. "Quality Improvement Methodologies: PDCA Cycle, RADAR Matrix, DMAIC and DFSS." *Journal of Achievements in Materials and Manufacturing Engineering 43*(1), 477–43.

Taylor, M. J., C. McNicholas, C. Nicolay, A. Darzi, D. Bell, and J. E. Reed. 2014. "Systematic Review of the Application of the Plan-Do-Study-Act Method to Improve Quality in Healthcare." *BMJ Quality & Safety 23*(4), 290–98.

Treviño, L. K., G. R. Weaver, D. G. Gibson, and B. L. Toffler. 1999. "Managing Ethics and Legal Compliance: What Works and What Hurts?" *California Management Review 41*(2), 131–51.

Treviño, L. K., L. P. Hartman, and M. B. Brown. 2000. "Moral Person and Moral Manager: How Executives Develop a Reputation for Ethical Leadership." *California Management Review 42*(4), 128–42.

Treviño, L. K., N. A. den Nieuwenboer, G. E. Kreiner, and D. G. Bishop. 2014. "Legitimating the Legitimate: A Grounded Theory Study of Legitimacy Work among Ethics and Compliance Officers." *Organizational Behavior and Human Decision Processes* 123(2), 186–205.

Warren, D. E., J. P. Gaspar, and W. S. Laufer. 2014. "Is Formal Ethics Training Merely Cosmetic? A Study of Ethics Training and Ethical Organizational Culture." *Business Ethics Quarterly* 24(1), 85–117.

Weaver, G. R., L. K. Treviño, and P. L. Cochran. 1999a. "Corporate Ethics Programs as Control Systems: Influences of Executive Commitment and Environmental Factors." *Academy of Management Journal* 42(1), 41–57.

Weaver, G. R., L. K. Treviño, and P. L. Cochran. 1999b. "Integrated and Decoupled Corporate Social Performance: Management Values, External Pressures, and Corporate Ethics Practices." *Academy of Management Journal* 42(2), 539–52.

Weber, J. 2006. "Implementing an Organizational Ethics Program in an Academic Environment: The Challenges and Opportunities for the Duquesne University Schools of Business." *Journal of Business Ethics* 65(1), 23–42.

Weber, J., and D. M. Wasieleski. 2013. "Corporate Ethics and Compliance Programs: A Report, Analysis and Critique." *Journal of Business Ethics* 112(4), 609–26.

Wulf, K. 2012. *Ethics and Compliance Programs in Multinational Organizations.* Wiesbaden: Springer Gabler Science & Business Media.

13

The Ethical and Moral Bases of Social Equity

Norma M. Riccucci

Social equity has been a paramount concern in both practice and theory, particularly in the field of public administration. Frederickson (1971) very early on referred to it as one of the "pillars" of the field. A good deal of attention has been paid to social equity through the lens of law (e.g., in its manifestation as affirmative action) but the field has paid little attention to it from the standpoint of ethics and morality, despite the fact that its seminal concerns can be traced to such principles. This chapter examines social equity from the perspective of values or doctrines, of ethics and morality. It begins with the introduction of these values to the field and then charts the direction it has taken over the past several decades. It shows how the research construes morality in the context of justice and equity, as in the case of street-level bureaucrats who treat their clients—fairly or unfairly—based on how they judge the morality of their clients. It further shows the moral bases of social equity as manifested in the pursuit of representative bureaucracies as well as in workers' public service motivations (PSM). It concludes with the view that there is a moral vision of democracy and that democracy is grounded in the principles of equality and social equity.

Normative Beginnings

The New Public Administration (NPA) introduced a new core value to public administration: social equity. To be sure, concerns over fairness were certainly evident in the practice and even theory of public administration, but it wasn't until the NPA that the concept of social equity gained attention and momentum. And, given the NPA's perspective regarding social issues and values such as race and class inequalities, its emphasis was on ethics and morality rather than, for example, law. For the first time in its history, public administration was tasked with asking, what is "just?" "What is moral and what is right?" And, as Frederickson (2005, 32) points out, public administration was at the forefront of examining the significance of social equity to the broader society. Moreover, he found that other academic fields or disciplines or professional practices were not embracing the concept of social equity to the same extent as public administration (Frederickson 1980).

The NPA was very committed to normative theory and activism. The young scholars (all white male, ironically) who launched the NPA were responding to social turmoil at the time, and also to the behavioral movement in the field, which sought to shift epistemic traditions in the direction of positivism. Proponents of the NPA sought to bring about positive social change, and supported an active role of public administration in doing so; public employees especially at the street level were not to be neutral but to serve as change agents and advocates of clients as they sought to better their standing in society. And the ethos was morality; the right thing to do was to address the broad societal problems of poverty, homelessness and, in general, the overall inequalities that plagued the American populous.

A question that the NPA did not consider, however, was would street-level bureaucrats who possess discretionary authority make decisions that would indeed benefit disadvantaged and disenfranchised groups? Would the theory transfer to practice, and if so, would morality and ethics guide the decisions of front-line workers in government?

Social Equity and Power at the Street Level

Public administrators at the street level of bureaucracy have always wielded a good deal of discretion, which ultimately affects the outcome of the distribution of goods and services in our society. Paul Appleby (1949) in his landmark book, *Policy and Administration*, addressed how public administrators, despite the politics–administration dichotomy, were deeply involved in the development and formation of public policies particularly through their use of discretionary authority. Appleby (11) states that the exercise of administration discretion in decision making "is everywhere in government." He goes on to say that discretion is based "in some part on expert valuations; in some degree on novelty; in some part on prerogatives and other institutional valuations; in some part on dimensions and scope of the action—the weight of impact it will have or has had on citizens, and the number of citizens affected; and in some part on ideal values" (13).

Lipsky in his seminal book *Street-Level Bureaucracy: Dilemmas of the Individual in Public Services* (1980, 2010) found in his research that because front-line workers in public agencies work with massive amounts of clients, they do not have the time to engage in the "highest standards of decision making" for each individual client (2010, xi). Instead, he points out, "street-level bureaucrats manage their difficult jobs by developing routines of practice and psychologically simplifying their clientele and environment in ways that strongly influence the outcomes of their efforts. Mass producing of clients is the norm, and has important implications for the quality of treatment and services" (Lipsky 2010, xi–xii).

Lipsky also addresses the discretion wielded by street-level bureaucrats. Although they face some constraints, they have wide latitude to determine whether clients receive benefits or sanctions, and they also influence the quality of services rendered. Police officers have the power to issue speeding tickets or even arrest someone they suspect of committing a crime. Front-line case workers in welfare offices have the power to deny or grant cash assistance to clients, even though they must abide by certain rules and regulations. Although organizations continually seek to circumscribe the discretion of street-level workers, the nature of working in large bureaucracies precludes its complete elimination.

Maynard-Moody and Musheno (2003) point to not simply the power of discretion that exists at the street level of bureaucracy, but the power to dispense justice and equity. In their book *Cops, Teachers, Counselors*, Maynard-Moody and Musheno studied qualitatively, the behaviors of social service officers, police officers, and teachers in classrooms and illustrate how these front-line workers distribute justice based on "client worthiness." They write,

> street-level workers first establish citizen-clients' identities and then respond. Forming and fixing identities may involve careful evaluation, as in the case of vocational rehabilitation, or snap judgments, as with police officers patrolling a neighborhood. Once fixed, these identities shape the nature of street-level workers' responses, from bending the rules and providing extraordinary assistance to allowing only begrudging and minimal help and at times to abuse. Some of these identities—"troublemaker," "personality disorder," "nice lady"— are indelible and define, for better or worse, the ongoing relationship between workers and citizen-clients. (155)

They go on to say that client worthiness then shapes the judgments and decisions made by the street-level workers. They state,

> Their stories reveal how street-level decision making is complexly moral and contingent rather than narrowly rule-bound and static. Cops, teachers, and counselors first make normative judgments about offenders, kids, and clients and then apply, bend, or ignore rules

and procedures to support the moral reasoning. Identity-based normative judgments determine which and how rules, procedures and policies are applied. Morality trumps legality in terms of which rules, procedures, and policies are acted on; who gets what services and who is hassled or arrested; and how rules, procedures and policies are enacted. (155)

Police violence against blacks in our society, which is once again escalating, is indicative of the use of discretion by police officers. A number of studies consistently show patterns of racial profiling, for example, in that blacks and Latinos are more likely to be targeted by police than whites (Brunson 2007; Harris 2002; Gelman, Andrew, Fagan, and Kiss 2007). There are no legal or moral justifications for racial profiling. It is humiliating to an individual, and it alienates and stigmatizes entire communities because it targets people based on physical characteristics. It singles people out because they look different and then feeds into the fears of the general citizenry. But, aside from moral and legal grounds, research shows that racial profiling simply does not work. That is to say, practices such as racial profiling and stop-and-frisk do not lead to a decline in city wide crime (see, e.g., Harcourt and Ludwig 2006; Rosenfeld and Fornango 2014; Rosenfeld, Terry, and Chauhan 2014). A prominent sociologist at New York University, David Greenberg (2014, 154), conducted the most comprehensive analysis of the relationship between the New York City Police Department's practice of racial profiling and crime levels to date, and he found "no evidence that misdemeanor arrests reduced levels of homicide, robbery, or aggravated assaults."

In their study of police stops in *Pulled Over: How Police Stops Define Race and Citizenship*, Epp, Maynard-Moody, and Haider-Markel point to racial bias in judgments of morality. They state,

> it is well established that racial minorities are more likely than whites to be stopped by the police. But, disparities in who is stopped are only the most obvious indicator of how police stops both reflect and define racial division in the United States. In stops, racial minorities are questioned, handcuffed, and searched at dramatically higher rates than whites are; they are much more likely than whites to perceive the stop as unfair; and they distrust the police in general at much higher rates than do whites (2014, 3).

Epp, Maynard-Moody, and Haider-Markel go on to say,

> The nonconscious and automatic nature of intergroup bias has important implications for the understanding of prejudice: individuals who express little overt prejudice—and indeed may consider racial prejudice morally wrong—may still respond on a gut level to racially biased stereotypes ... The automatic activation of implicit negative stereotypes—especially those conjuring images of black criminality and violence—may have profound and enduring effects on social judgment and people's lives. Stereotypes can have literally life-or-death consequences. (43–44)

In a more recent study, Epp, Maynard-Moody, and Haider-Markel (2017) find racial profiling by police in investigatory vehicle stops, where officers disproportionately stop blacks who are driving or walking to question and search them. Not only are they innocent, but the experience of such investigatory stops erodes their trust in police and it also leads to psychological harm. Their research found that blacks' "common experience of investigatory stops contributes to their perception that they are not regarded by the police as full and equal members of society ... Investigatory stops ... are significantly more likely to foster the perception that the police are "out to get people like me" (174). They also point out that many of the high-profile shootings of blacks in recent years occurred during these stops.

Such stops include what are known as "stop-and-frisk" practices. Here police detain and question pedestrians and search them if they believe a crime is being or about to be committed. Often, these encounters can escalate into aggressive actions by police officers, including deadly violence by police. As noted earlier, police often become violent particularly when citizens are engaging in constitutionally protected free speech, as the US Justice Department has found in their reports examining police violence against blacks. The stop-and-frisk practices of New York City gained national attention because of their pervasive use and propensity to target blacks and Latinos, which has perpetuated inequalities and unjust, immoral treatment of these groups.

In sum, street-level bureaucrats possess a good deal of discretion which can negatively impact some groups more than others. In the area of law enforcement where justice and equity are dispensed, we are witnessing a resurgence of police violence against blacks, resulting in the deaths of a number of young black men, including Michael Brown, Eric Garner, Tamir Rice, Walter Scott, Alton Sterling, Philando Castile, and Terence Crutcher. While the US Justice Department under the direction of former Attorney Generals Eric Holder and Loretta Lynch had sought to limit police violence against blacks in cities across the country, since 2017 when Mr. Trump took office, the Justice Department under his attorney general, Jeff Sessions, has been unwilling to interfere with local police matters. Indeed, President Trump publically stated that police officers do not need to be "too nice" to suspects being transported in police cars. He went so far as to say that police need not protect the heads of suspected persons when they put them in police cars (Rosenthal 2017).

Social Equity and Representative Bureaucracy

Some of the pioneers of public administration envisioned political, moral, and democratic considerations for making bureaucracies representative of the people they serve. It was Mosher (1968) who argued that bureaucrats should push for the needs and interests of their social counterparts in the general population; this manifesto squarely falls within the normative traditions of the New Public Administration and its commitment to the pursuit of social equity. Moreover, Mosher envisioned administrative morality as ensuring that not just special and majority, but that *all* interests in society are addressed and fulfilled. One mechanism for doing so according to Mosher was ensuring the representativeness of bureaucracies. In this sense administrative morality would bridge the gap between democracy and bureaucracy.

Sandra Groeneveld and Steven Van de Walle (2010) argue that it is imperative that representative bureaucracy be built in part on a moral foundation to ensure the fair distribution of goods, services, and even power throughout society. Indeed, early political philosophical treatments of social equity focused on distributive justice. One of the most critical treatises here is John Rawls' *A Theory of Justice* (1971). A basic premise of this thesis is that justice ensures that everyone is afforded the same rights under the law. Rawls' difference principle suggests that to the extent society distributes more power or resources to some persons, it must ensure that material circumstances for the disadvantaged will be improved. That is, income and wealth must be distributed in a manner that over time, works in the best interests of the least advantaged in society. Another feature of Rawlsian justice is the existence of fair equality of opportunity to fill government positions (also see Guy and McCandless 2012; Wooldridge and Gooden 2009). To be sure, this would include bureaucratic posts, and to the extent bureaucracies are representative, they can be instruments of distributive justice.

There has been a good deal of empirical work on representative bureaucracy from the perspectives of passive, active, and symbolic representation. Briefly, passive representation refers to the degree to which the demographics of public organizations reflect the demographics of the general population (Meier 1993; Selden 1997). Studies on passive representation have consistently found that, although women and people of color may be well represented in bureaucracies in the aggregate at various levels, they are generally underrepresented in the higher, policy-making positions (Smith and Monaghan 2013).

Ken Meier greatly advanced the theory of representative bureaucracy. He was one of the first scholars to empirically examine the link between passive and active representation, finding that minority bureaucrats will pursue policies or actions that benefit minorities in the citizenry (see Meier, Wrinkle, and Polinard 1999). And, a study by Keiser, Wilkins, Meier, and Holland (2002) was the first to find a linkage between passive and active representation for women. More recent research on representative bureaucracy examines the symbolic effects of passive representation in that the social origins of bureaucrats can induce certain attitudes or behaviors on the part of citizens or clients without the bureaucrat taking any action (Theobald and Haider-Markel 2009). Research by Gade and Wilkins (2013), for example, found that veterans who know or believe that their counselors in the Department of Veterans Affairs are veterans report greater satisfaction with services. As they point out, "passive representation can . . . translate into symbolic representation, where representation may change the attitudes and behaviors of the represented client without any action taken by the bureaucrat" (Gade and Wilkins 2013, 267).

Although the research here does not explicitly state that there is a moral imperative to representative bureaucracies, it is certainly implied. For example, when studies show that women police officers are better able to address the epidemic of domestic violence, the implication is that police departments across the country need women police officers (Meier and Nicholson-Crotty 2006; Riccucci, Van Ryzin, and Lavena 2014). Similarly, when representative bureaucracy studies indicate the benefits to society of having black police officers, the value of increased representation of blacks in police departments is apparent (Nicholson-Crotty, Nicholson-Crotty, and Fernandez 2017; Riccucci, Van Ryzin, and Jackson forthcoming).

Also important, studies have shown that representative bureaucracy results not in redistributive but rather in *distributive* equity. For example, Meier, Wrinkle, and Polinard (1999) examined whether representative bureaucracies produced minority gains at the expense of non-minorities. Relying on a pooled time-series analysis of 350 school districts over a period of six years, they found that both minority and non-minority students perform better in the presence of a representative bureaucracy (also see Krislov 1974). More recent studies have also found such a spillover effect (see Riccucci, Van Ryzin, and Li 2016).

Morality Social Equity and Public Service Motivation (PSM)

There is a vast literature on public service motivation, which points to reasons why individuals choose to work for the public good (Perry 1996; Brewer, Selden, and Facer 2000; DeHart-Davis, Marlowe, and Pandey 2006; Pandey and Stazyk 2008). As Perry and Wise (1990, 367) point out,

> Calls for a recommitment of Americans to values associated with government service, among them personal sacrifice and duty to the public interest, raise practical questions about the power of these values to stimulate and direct human behavior. At their core, calls for a renewal of public service motivation assume the importance of such motivations for an effective and efficient public service.

They go on to note that public service embodies a sense of public morality—doing what is right and just. And that a motivation for public service is loyalty to "doing good," which is a particular "moral position" (Perry and Wise 1990; Staats 1988; Frederickson and Hart 1985). Indeed, one of the measurement items for Perry's (1996, 10) PSM scale is: "I believe everyone has a moral commitment to civic affairs no matter how busy they are."

Some of the research shows that morally committed persons are drawn to public service because they desire to perform important public services for others; that they possess "moral and ethical values concerning helping others, especially those in distress" (Perry, Brudney, Coursey, and Littlepage 2008, 447). The research on PSM consistently indicates that it hinges on a sense of morality and justice. For example, in one study, individuals were interviewed about their commitment to doing good work for others. One interviewee linked this to her fundamental understanding of morality, stating,

> I think it's the basic ... social awareness, having to leave the world a better place than they found it. And I think the best way to do that is not by giving money necessarily, although that's nice, but most of the people didn't actually make the money that they give. But I think that it's really putting yourself out there, and doing the work, and getting into the trenches. ... I think it's a moral issue" (Perry, Brudney, Coursey, and Littlepage 2008, 453).

Research on PSM also points to motivations to pursue social equity. For example, Kim and Vandenabeele (2010, 703) point out that "normative orientations [of PSM] are based on social values and norms of what is proper and appropriate ... [and are] closely connected with enhancing social equity, fostering loyalty to duty and to the government as a whole, and serving the public interest" (also see Christensen, Sassler, and Moon 2014). They go on to say that the values-based motives of PSM include social equity, social responsibility, fairness, and social justice. Similarly, and in addition to PSM, research on public service ethos and values also point to the importance of moral integrity, awareness, and social equity (Denhardt and Denhardt 2000; Heywood 2012). Indeed, the standards of public service require equity and transparency, which ultimately promote democratic accountability (Norris 2003).

Conclusions

The field of public administration continues to focus on the importance of social equity and social justice and developing public policies to promote equity and justice. Promoting diversity in government workforces and achieving representative bureaucracies continue to receive a good deal of attention in the field. Moreover, there is a moral and ethical motivation on the part of public servants to promote social equity and justice. Moral clarity in effect steers the behaviors and conduct of public servants to ensure equitable outcomes for the citizenry; that is, to promote social justice and strive to eliminate inequalities and inequities in our society.

But the moral imperative to fulfill the need and desire for social equity also satisfies efforts to promote the moral foundations of our democracy. Growing disparities in income, wealth, and access to opportunity preclude progress toward the realization of American ideals of democracy. Democratic ideals of equality, freedom, and justice have always been viewed as morally good. And, social inequities have always violated American's core ideals, values and beliefs. The preeminent philosopher Émile Marie Boutroux, who wrote extensively on the moral vision of democracy, asserted almost a century ago that democracy is grounded in the principle of equality and that morality is self-government: "Rule over oneself. Democracy ... means the people's rule over itself; the government of the people by the people. Consequently, is not democracy the express application of the moral idea to politics? Democratic government and government based on morality would appear to be one and the same thing" (Boutroux 1921, 166).

References

Appleby, Paul H. 1949. *Policy and Administration*. Birmingham: University of Alabama Press.
Boutroux, Emile. 1921. "Morality and Democracy." *North American Review* 214(789), 166–76.
Brewer, Gene A., and Sally Coleman Selden. 1998. "Whistle Blowers in the Federal Civil Service: New Evidence of the Public Service Ethic." *Journal of Public Administration Research and Theory* 8(3), 413–40.

Brunson, Rod K. 2007. "'Police Don't Like Black People: African-American Young Men's Accumulated Police Experiences." *Criminology & Public Policy* 6(1), 71–102.

Christensen, Robert K., Elizabeth Sassler and Kukkyoung Moon. 2014 "Organizational Equity, Justice, and Individual Public Service Motives." *Academy of Management Annual Meeting Proceedings* 1(1), 1.

DeHart-Davis, Leisha, Justin Marlowe, and Sanjay K. Pandey. 2006. "Gender Dimensions of Public Service Motivation." *Public Administration Review* 66(6), 873–87.

Denhardt, Robert B., and Janet Vinzant Denhardt. 2000. "The New Public Service: Serving Rather than Steering." *Public Administration Review* 60(6), 549–59.

Epp Charles R., Steven Maynard-Moody, and Donald Haider-Markel. 2014. *Pulled Over: How Police Stops Define Race and Citizenship.* Chicago, IL: University of Chicago Press.

Epp Charles R., Steven Maynard-Moody, and Donald Haider-Markel. 2017. "Beyond Profiling: The Institutional Sources of Racial Disparities in Policing." *Public Administration Review* 77(2), 168–78.

Frederickson, H. George. 1971. "Toward a New Public Administration," in Frank Marini, ed., *Toward a New Public Administration: The Minnowbrook Perspective.* Scranton, PA: Chandler, 309–31.

Frederickson, H. George. 1980. *New Public Administration.* Tuscaloosa: University of Alabama Press.

Frederickson, H. George. 2005. "The State of Social Equity in American Public Administration." *National Civic Review* (Winter), 31–38.

Frederickson, H. George, and David K. Hart. 1985. "The Public Service and the Patriotism of Benevolence." *Public Administration Review* 45(5), 547–53.

Gade, Daniel M., and Vicky M. Wilkins. 2013. "Where Did You Serve? Veteran Identity, Representative Bureaucracy, and Vocational Rehabilitation." *Journal of Public Administration Research and Theory* 23(2), 267–88.

Gelman, Andrew, Jeffrey A. Fagan, and Alex Kiss. 2007. "An Analysis of the New York City Police Department's 'Stop-and-Frisk' Policy in the Context of Claims of Racial Bias." *Journal of the American Statistical Association* 102(479), 813–23.

Greenberg, David F. 2014. "Studying New York City's Crime Decline: Methodological Issues." *Justice Quarterly* 31(1), 154–88.

Groeneveld, Sandra, and Steven Van de Walle. 2010. "A Contingency Approach to Representative Bureaucracy: Power, Equal Opportunities and Diversity." *International Review of Administrative Sciences* 76(2), 239–58.

Guy, Mary E., and Sean A. McCandless. 2012. "Social Equity: Its Legacy, Its Promise." *Public Administration Review* 72(S1), S5–S13.

Harcourt, Bernard E., and Jens Ludwig. 2006. "Broken Windows: New Evidence from New York City and a Five-City Social Experiment." *University of Chicago Law Review* 73(1), 271–320.

Harris, David A. 2002. *Profiles in Injustice: Why Racial Profiling Cannot Work.* New York: The New Press.

Heywood, Paul M. 2012. "Integrity Management and the Public Service Ethos in the UK: Patchwork Quilt or Threadbare Blanket?" *International Review of Administrative Sciences* 78(3), 474–93.

Keiser, Lael R., Vicky M. Wilkins, Kenneth J. Meier, and Catherine Holland. 2002. "Lipstick and Logarithms: Gender, Institutional Context, and Representative Bureaucracy." *American Political Science Review* 96(3), 553–64.

Kim, Sangmook, and Wouter Vandenabeele. 2010. "A Strategy for Building Public Service Motivation Research Internationally." *Public Administration Review* 70(5), 701–9.

Krislov, Samuel. 1974. *Representative Bureaucracy.* Englewood Cliffs, NJ: Prentice Hall.

Lipsky, Michael. 1980. *Street Level Bureaucracy: Dilemmas of the Individual in Public Services.* New York: Russell Sage Foundation.

Lipsky, Michael. 2010. *Street Level Bureaucracy: Dilemmas of the Individual in Public Services.* Russell Sage Foundation 30th Anniversary Expanded Edition. New York: Russell Sage Foundation.

Maynard-Moody, Steven Musheno, and Michael Musheno. 2003. *Cops, Teachers, Counselors: Stories from the Front Lines of Public Service.* Ann Arbor: University of Michigan Press.

Meier, Kenneth J. 1993b. "Representative Bureaucracy: A Theoretical and Empirical Exposition." *Research in Public Administration* 2(1), 1–35.

Meier, Kenneth J., and Jill Nicholson-Crotty. 2006. "Gender, Representative Bureaucracy, and Law Enforcement: The Case of Sexual Assault." *Public Administration Review* 66(6), 850–60.

Meier, Kenneth J., Robert D. Wrinkle, and J. L. Polinard. 1999. "Representative Bureaucracy and Distributional Equity: Addressing the Hard Question." *Journal of Politics* 61(4), 1025–39.

Mosher, Frederick. 1968. *Democracy and the Public Service*. New York: Oxford University Press.

Nicholson-Crotty, Sean, Jill Nicholson-Crotty, and Sergio Fernandez. 2017. "Will More Black Cops Matter? Officer Race and Police-Involved Homicides of Black Citizens." *Public Administration Review* 77(2), 206–16.

Norris, Pippa. 2003. "Is There Still A Public Service Ethos? Work Values, Experience, and Job Satisfaction Among Government Workers," in John D. Donahue and Joseph S. Nye, Jr., eds., *For the People: Public Service in the 21ˢᵗ Century*. Washington, DC: Brookings Institution, 72–89.

Pandey, Sanjay K., and Edmund C. Stazyk. 2008. "Antecedents and Correlates of Public Service Motivation," in James L. Perry and Annie Hondeghem, eds., *Motivation in Public Management: The Call of Public Service*. Oxford: Oxford University Press, 101–17.

Perry, James L. 1996. "Measuring Public Service Motivation: An Assessment of Construct Reliability and Validity." *Journal of Public Administration Research and Theory* 6(1), 5–22.

Perry, James L., and Lois Recascino Wise. 1990. "The Motivational Bases of Public Service." *Public Administration Review* 50(3): 367–73.

Perry, James L., Jeffrey L. Brudney, David Coursey, and Laura Littlepage. 2008. "What Drives Morally Committed Citizens? A Study of the Antecedents of Public Service Motivation." *Public Administration Review* 68(3): 445–58.

Riccucci, Norma M., Gregg G. Van Ryzin, and Karima Jackson. "Representative Bureaucracy, Race and Policing: A Survey Experiment." *Journal of Public Administration Research and Theory*, online first, doi: 10.1093/jopart/muy023.

Riccucci, N. M., G. G. Van Ryzin, and C. F. Lavena. 2014. "Representative Bureaucracy in Policing: Does It Increase Perceived Legitimacy?" *Journal of Public Administration Research and Theory* 24(3), 537–51.

Riccucci, Norma M., Gregg G. Van Ryzin, and Huafang Li. 2016. "Representative Bureaucracy and the Willingness to Coproduce: An Experimental Study." *Public Administration Review* 76(1), 121–30.

Rosenfeld, Richard, and Robert Fornango. 2014. "The Impact of Police Stops on Precinct Robbery and Burglary Rates in New York City, 2003–2010." *Justice Quarterly* 31(1), 96–122.

Rosenfeld, Richard, Karen Terry, and Preeti Chauhan. 2014. "New York's Crime Drop Puzzle: Introduction to the Special Issue." *Justice Quarterly* 31(1), 1–4.

Rosenthal, Brian M. 2017. "Police Criticize Trump for Urging Officers Not to Be 'Too Nice' With Suspects." *New York Times*, July 29. https://www.nytimes.com/2017/07/29/nyregion/trump-police-too-nice.html, accessed September 20, 2018.

Selden, Sally Coleman. 1997a. *The Promise of Representative Bureaucracy: Diversity and Responsiveness in a Government Agency*. Armonk, NY: M. E. Sharpe.

Smith, Amy, and Karen R. Monaghan. 2013. "Some Ceilings Have More Cracks: Representative Bureaucracy in Federal Agencies." *American Review of Public Administration* 43(1), 50–71.

Staats, Elmer B. 1988. "Public Service and the Public Interest." *Public Administration Review* 48(2), 601–5.

Theobald, Nick A., and Donald P. Haider-Markel. 2009. "Race, Bureaucracy, and Symbolic Representation: Interactions between Citizens and Police." *Journal of Public Administration Research and Theory* 19(2), 409–26.

Wooldridge, Blue, and Susan Gooden. 2009. "The Epic of Social Equity: Evolution, Essence and Emergence." *Administrative Theory and Praxis* 31(2), 222–34.

14

Moving from Trust to Trustworthiness in the Public Services

Michael Macaulay

The importance of trust to mutual cooperation in any activity is so obvious as to almost appear banal. Yet the world is experiencing a remarkable burst of research on trust from a wide array of disciplines, from neuroscience to organizational behavior, towards the shared goal of creating greater levels of trust in organizations (see, e.g., Zak 2017). Trust is the "social adhesive" (Atkinson and Butcher 2003, 84) that unites us all. Despite these great moves forward, however, we simultaneously seem to be inhabiting a time of increasing uncertainty around trust: socially, politically, economically, and organizationally. Surveys such as the *Edelman Trust Barometer* suggest that the world is undergoing a "global implosion of trust" across four key institutional pillars: government, media, business, and nongovernmental organizations (NGOs). Globally, trust in these areas is down both *individually* (for example, governments are now distrusted in 75 percent of countries) and *collectively*, with the barometer reporting that 85 percent of respondents no longer have full belief in the system. There is deep concern that this will lead to further erosion of social values, which will only serve to further increase distrust.

This chapter sets out to investigate these perspectives and to offer a pathway forward. It will argue that one possible problem is due to us collectively chasing rainbows and trying to build what is ultimately outside of our control. It will suggest that we cannot, ultimately, govern trust in the way we would like but instead we can profitably build on our own trustworthiness, both as individuals and as organizations. Building on evidence from psychology, organizational behavior, and public ethics, the chapter will put forward an applied model for trustworthiness. It has been stated many times that public ethics is a branch of applied philosophy (Rohr 2005; Macaulay 2009) that is undermined if it remains at the level of theory. The model of trustworthiness presented here, therefore, elucidates practical steps. Although the chapter will discuss values and abstract concepts, the intention is to do so in as open and accessible a fashion as possible. The model is grounded in the belief that building trustworthiness is relatively easy to do, but too often discussions coalesce around abstractions: what trust is rather than how, practically, it is developed. To counter this, the proposed model is developed as an applied framework and, in bringing together different disciplinary approaches, it is hoped that some advances in this area might be made

What Do We Mean by Trust?

Trust is a value that mediates relationships; this is most obvious at the interpersonal levels but applies equally at organizational and institutional levels. The 2018 *Edelman Trust Barometer*, for example, titles its report *The Battle for Truth* and explicates how levels of institutional trust are affecting the public perception of, among other things, the effectiveness and honesty of governments, the media, business, and other key institutional pillars.[1] There is substantial evidence to show that high levels of trust have very positive mediating effects in organizations. The links between high trust and high job satisfaction are well known (e.g., Perry and Mankin 2007) and more recent research shows that trust combats the negative effects of cynicism in the workplace (Archimi et al. 2018). Siddiki and colleagues (2017) demonstrate positive correlations between high levels of trust and high levels of commitment to diversity, while others have found that it helps form strong attachments to identity (Ghosh et al. 2018). Some researchers have even posited that trust is a key determinant in combatting bureaucratic dehumanization (i.e., Väyrnen and Lilla-Salmela 2018).

Partly as a result of such a weight of evidence, it may be taken for granted that trust is something that we must always aspire to, that it is an inherent good. But this view would be misleading. Because trust is a relational value it is dynamic and is open to reinterpretation and reassessment.

Just because X trusts Y one week, it does not mean that X will do so indefinitely. Nor should X, necessarily, without good reason. Kramer and Tyler (1996), for example, suggest that trusting first is wrong 77 percent of the time. A trusted brand can soon be adversely affected by a big enough scandal. Trust, therefore, needs to be earned and re-earned almost constantly. It is not an end point. Indeed, if trust degrades into blind faith, many ethical problems may result (Jennings 2004). There are sound reasons for people being distrustful, or at least exhibiting a healthy skepticism, depending on context.

From Trust to Trustworthiness

The quicksilver nature of trust relationships is perhaps one reason why it is notable by its absence in many codes of conduct around the world. The UK's *principles of public life*, for example, does not mention trust in any of its definitions of other values.[2] Other codes promote trust as an aspirational value. The American Society for Public Administration's code of ethics, for example, simply states that as a matter of personal integrity, ASPA members should "adhere to the highest standards of conduct to inspire public confidence and trust in public service."[3] In its extensive work on trust, the Organisation for Economic Co-operation and Development (OECD) lists a number of reasons why trust is important, including public policy success, and also some of the areas where it needs to be further developed. It suggests that public bodies create stronger value alignment, especially with integrity and transparency, and develop public trust, and that this is especially important for trust in local services (OECD 2017). In terms of definition, however, the OECD simply stresses its complexity rather than anything more concrete (see textbox 14.1).

This complexity is frequently reflected in academic literature by breaking trust down into constituent components or values. Güçer and Demírdağ (2018: 13), for example, suggest that trust comprises benevolence, reliability, competence, honesty, and openness. Psychological literature makes further distinctions. McAllister (1995) distinguishes between *cognitive* and *affective* trust. Cognitive trust is based on rational decisions we can make about a person (or organization) and their ability to demonstrate responsibility, dependability, and

Textbox 14.1 OECD and Trust[4]

Trust is important for the success of a wide range of public policies that depend on behavioral responses from the public.

Trust is necessary to increase the confidence of investors and consumers.

Trust is essential for key economic activities, most notably finance.

Trust in institutions is important for the success of many government policies, programs, and regulations that depend on cooperation and compliance of citizens.

good judgment. Affective trust is built through perceptions of care and concern for welfare for others, and arguably creates the most lasting damage when trust breaks down.

Thomson and Brandenburg's (2018) study of public trust and perceptions of political promise keeping uses data from the United Kingdom to show that voters use different thought processes depending on their trust perspectives. They find that voters who claim to *mistrust* politicians do so from the cognitive perspective; they use empirical evidence to foster their opinions and see themselves as well-read, politically knowledgeable, and vigilant. Those who *distrust* politicians, however, do so through heuristics rather than empiricism, and indeed empirical evidence has very little sway on these voters' beliefs or voting intentions. To approach trust from one or the other side of this spectrum is, therefore, not going to be able to produce a full picture.

The further power of affective trust can be felt by most people reading this chapter: there are probably many readers who have at some stage been betrayed by a friend, family member, or a colleague, which has almost certainly had an extremely negative impact on their well-being. Breaches of trust can cause serious psychological and emotional pain, and this can spill over into physical symptoms of anxiety and stress. Frequently these consequences are compounded by victims blaming themselves, and a serious breach of personal trust usually makes a person question their own beliefs and behavior: *Why didn't I know what was happening? How could I not see the signs?* Most common of all: *Why did I trust this person at all?*

These problems apply equally to organizations and even society. A lack of trust corrodes social relationships and belief not only in politicians but the political *system* as a whole. We see the consequences of this all over the world at this very moment: the echo chambers of social media; the twenty-four-hour attack on news and media; the rise of authoritarianism, even within democracies, as a response to distrust in politics.

McAllister's delineation is important for a number of reasons. First, he and others (e.g, Maharani and Riantoputra 2018) show there is a link between the two. High levels of cognitive trust can increase affective trust because reliable behavior becomes attributed to sound motivations and intent. Second, the two forms of trust work together to provide a suitable context-dependent approach to decision-making: "We choose whom we will trust in which respects and under what circumstances, and we base the choice on what we take to be good reasons, constituting elements of trustworthiness" (McAllister 1995, 25).

Finally, the distinction between cognitive and affective trust shows a pathway between what we can and cannot control. As stated previously, trust itself is a dynamic, mediating value the fluctuations of which may not always be within our grasp. *Trustworthiness*, however, is something that we can develop as individuals and organizations. These are all points that have been raised in the past, both in theory and practice. Hardin (2002) for example, suggested that when we speak of trust we frequently mean trustworthiness. The Australian Public Service values, for example, include that the APS is trustworthy,[5] and this is also one of the four key values of the New Zealand public service, where it is broken down into several constituent components, including honesty, working to the best of a person's ability, and avoiding conflicts of interest.[6]

The Building Blocks of Organizational Trustworthiness

Taking McAllister's distinction as a starting point, we can see that cognitive and affective trust can be translated into three groups of trustworthy behaviors, revolving around *credibility*, *reliability*, and *intimacy*.

Credibility can, of course, take many forms, from natural authority to technical expertise, but is essential in assuring people that the person (or group) responsible for an action is the most appropriate to enact it. It is the degree of credibility that appears to be causing numerous issues in the world today: as the Edelman Trust barometer shows, globally, people's trust in the reliability and honesty of news sources is continuing to decline. Global political leaders are beset by attacks on their credibility, fueled at least in part by their own attacks on the credibility of their opponents.

To use a high-profile example occurring at the time of this publication, the nomination of Brett Kavanagh to the Supreme Court in the United States has tested the relationship between credibility and trust to its limits. The Senate Judiciary Committee heard sworn testimony from Dr. Christine Blasey Ford regarding an alleged sexual assault on her by Kavanagh when the two were at high school. Her testimony, and Kavanagh's own defense, highlight a huge number of credibility issues: the credibility of memory, especially after many years and a great deal of trauma; the credibility of expertise, especially Dr. Ford who, as an expert in the field, gave impressive scientific explanations for the neuroscientific workings of memory. Credibility of character was called into question, especially through myriad references and commendations for Kavanagh from his female friends. Away from purely personal elements, the credibility of due process has been under fire, as well as the Senate Judiciary Committee itself. And, perhaps inevitably, the systemic credibility of the media, of digital media, and of political parties and party leaders have all been called into doubt.

To develop trustworthiness, then, we need to be able to demonstrate credibility across a range of areas: knowledge, skills, character, capability, competency, and, of course, authority and legitimacy.

Reliability is, as we have already seen, critical to the development of trustworthiness. It is not enough to do something once, but it needs to be done consistently and reliably again and again. Its opposite, erratic behavior, is frequently recognized as a key to poor leadership. Reliability is a key aspect of political interpretation: Does an agency live up to its values and react in consistent ways? Do governments enact manifesto promises? Does that new washing powder really clean your clothes whiter-than-white?

Recent evidence from New Zealand illustrate the links between reliability and trustworthiness. In 2016 the Institute for Governance and Policy Studies (IGPS) published its inaugural public-trust survey,[7] which showed that trust in politicians and government was much lower than usually acknowledged in New Zealand: only 9 percent of respondents had either "complete trust" or "lots of trust" in government Ministers, and that shrank to 8 percent for members of Parliament. Only the media scored lower: 8 percent for TV/print media and a measly 5 percent for online and digital media.

The second IGPS Public Trust survey, however, published in June 2018,[8] detailed a substantial increase in trust in both MPs and government ministers, which both stand at a net total of 62 percent trust (both up from a net total of 46 percent in 2016). How do we explain these changes? Partly, it may be down to the classic "honeymoon effect." A newly elected government frequently has a fillip in public trust, and this is usually more pronounced when a new party leads that government. This is a pattern that is seen in democratic countries around the world.

Similarly, new governments score highly on the *reliability* scale simply because they are new. There has not been enough time to test reliability and consistency of performance either against the day-to-day cut and thrust of government life, or even against manifesto pledges. Not for nothing is being seen as a politically reliable "safe pair of hands" sometimes more curse than blessing: reliability becomes a more important determinant as time passes and can damage many careers as a result. Crucially, though, a person's or organization's ability to behave in a consistent manner is within their locus of control and is therefore an element that can be translated into a building block of trustworthiness.

The New Zealand evidence also points to the relationship between intimacy and trustworthiness. Intimacy in this case means awareness and knowledge of, and relates to, the fact that trust usually needs to be earned. It is very difficult to have trust in an organization that we know nothing about, or of a manager who is new to us. Intimacy relates to the affective and emotional aspects of trust. Familiarity (or perceived familiarity) grants an emotional connection that engenders a trusting relationship. This correlation exists equally with institutions as it does with individuals. To give just one example, New Zealand evidence shows that trust in the NZ public service has steadily risen over the last decade and is, at the time of this writing, at 45 percent. When the same question is asked of people who have had personal experience of the public sector the levels of trust are shown to be much higher, at 79 percent (see below).[9] This pattern is reflected in the IGPS public-trust surveys: respondents scored trust of their own politicians and councils much more highly than they did of local government or MPs generally. It also exists in the private sector, and is demonstrated by Jensen (2016) as the key factor in trust relationships that lead to the marketing of new technologies. The relationship between intimacy and trustworthiness is very clear: in general, we trust who and what we know.

There is a wealth of evidence, therefore, to show that credibility, reliability, and intimacy are three elements in building and maintaining positive trust relationships. Before turning to a more detailed model of organizational trustworthiness, though, it is useful to identify some of the negative aspects of trust building.

The Downsides of Trustworthiness

Despite the obvious importance of trust and trustworthiness, there are a number of potential downsides. Intimacy can also create echo chambers, and a distrust of evidence that is contrary to our own established views. No matter how effective our efforts may be in developing trustworthiness, the affective side of trust can be so strong that it can neither create nor sever a preexisting bond. We continue to trust people who let us down simply because we like them so much, for example, and this will be clear to the readers who have undergone personal heartbreak, familial breakdown, or professional betrayal.

In addition, trustworthiness is bound up with elements of risk. The more trustworthy we are perceived to be, the bigger the disconnect if that breaks down in any way. Theorists as far back as Machiavelli, writing in 1515, noted a very similar point. The political leader who is loved sets up expectations that will almost always ultimately be thwarted. We have seen leaders around the world have drastic falls in public trust, and partly this can be attributed to the fact that people felt they knew the person in question. When a let-down occurs the sense of loss is more tangible and acute.

The final concern is that people can create trust even though they might be completely untrustworthy. Some people can, and do, distill trust-building down into a technique to advance their own interests. Many people reading this chapter will, alas, have been made victims of these techniques. It is not correct to assume that trust is an inherently positive value, nor that it is necessarily something to which we should always aspire.

To use a deeply unpleasant example, Ted Bundy was such a prolific murderer that the term "serial killer" had to be invented to cover his range of crimes: the term did not exist before his arrest. A few hours before his execution in 1989, he finally confessed to over thirty murders, although it is unlikely that we will ever know the exact tally. How was he so effective? There are no easy answers, but one notable point was in his approach to victims. Bundy frequently made himself appear vulnerable. One trick that he used on several occasions was to wear a fake plaster-cast on his arm while carrying a pile of books (many of his victims were abducted from universities and colleges). He would drop the books, ask for help, and then assault his victims as they tried to assist him.

All of the above may seem slightly grim, but these downsides point the way toward the final building block of trustworthiness: authenticity. Authenticity of intent is what McAllister was driving at with the relationship between cognitive and affective pathways to trust. As public servants and political leaders, however, there also needs be an authenticity around desired outcomes and processes.

Authenticity may perhaps seem at face value to be too subjective to be helpful here, but there is evidence to show a range of different ways in which this can be translated into practice. Guthrie and Taylor's (2017) work on the effectiveness of whistleblowing bounties in the United States, for example, shows people involved in exposing misconduct look to the authenticity of the offer available. High dollar-value rewards only increase the intent to action if people feel that there is authenticity to their safety and protection from retaliation. On a very different note, Guo and colleagues (2018) argue that timeliness is a significant element of rebuilding trust relationships: the swifter the response the more likely it is to be successful.

Fundamentally, authenticity requires self-reflection. As Carter (1996) and many others have shown, reflection is frequently associated with integrity. The ethical leadership literature is full of examples of those who have been open to the views of others, even where such views have been critical, before making judgment (see, for example, Balch and Armstrong, 2010). Organizations that are closed off and non-reflective are more likely to degrade towards toxic cultures (Macaulay 2011).

Towards a Model of Organizational Trustworthiness

It is not enough to posit a model of trustworthiness that simply recasts other values, or abstract concepts, in an attempt to highlight generic messages. We must always be aware of falling into Pollitt and Hupé's (2012) trap of creating "magic concepts" whose meaning lies in the interpretations of the reader. Such arguments can often be found in the trust literature (see Hardin's 2002 discussion, for example, on anticipated moral commitment; see figure 14.1). The following model, therefore, is built on the evidence presented in this chapter and demonstrates tangible suggestions for practitioners and applied theorists.

In order to develop trustworthiness, we need to start at the end and establish what outcomes we are trying to achieve and why. In so doing there will be a range of questions

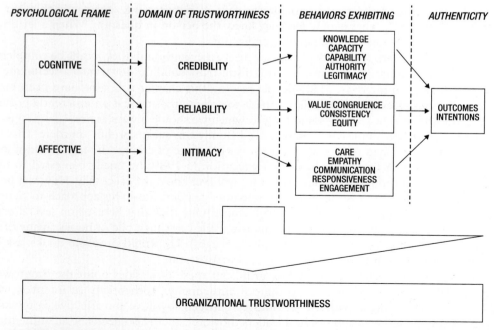

FIGURE 14.1 Practitioner Model of Organizational Trustworthiness

that need to be asked (who will be affected by what we are trying to achieve, with what impacts, etc.) but it is crucial so that behaviors and messages can be geared towards these outcomes in an authentic manner. Even if things go awry, the perception of authenticity acts as a bulwark. Developing trustworthiness for purely instrumental purposes is inevitably self-defeating as well as being, in the view of the author, unethical.

Leaders of organizations must also take into account both the cognitive and affective domains of trust and build behaviors around the key domains of credibility, reliability, and intimacy that emerge from both heuristic and reasoned thinking. Here we can identify key behaviors with which to develop each of these domains. A credible organization has the capacity and capability to deliver the goals that it sets for itself, based on knowledge and expertise that are acknowledged and recognized as pertinent to the task. Organizational intimacy can be developed by many specific behaviors: information sharing, stakeholder engagement, and explicit care and compassion. Reliability is perhaps most easily demonstrated through congruence between actions and organizational values, but it is also reliant on notions of fairness and timeliness.

Conclusion

Building trust is one of the most practical, and natural, things that we do as human beings. We would not have managed to cooperate in the societies we find ourselves in without trusting one another. Yet, often, work on trust can be quite abstract, occasionally even abstruse, and even through terminology can be focused on things outside of our control. We can never fully legislate for the levels of trust, but we can create an authentic trustworthiness, as individuals and as organizations.

We do this through very practical steps that have their root in evidence. We do not need purely abstract philosophy. The building blocks of trust apply to both individuals and organizations alike. Second, that trust is dynamic and is therefore something that needs to be revisited, readjusted, and recalibrated at various points. Third, that a key mechanism to enable this is *reflection* on both an individual and institutional level. Leaders who reflect will be more open and, frequently, more ethical in their approach. Institutions that enable reflection have cultures that are accessible and supportive. Those that do not reflect are in danger of becoming hermetically sealed and turning toxic.

Acknowledgments

I would like to sincerely thank all master's students in our class on public integrity for the excellent discussions on trust we had in 2018 and for their work, which has inspired some of the ideas contained in this chapter. In particular, I would like to thank Simon Laube for his insights on cognitive and affective trust.

Notes

[1] https://www.edelman.com/trust-barometer.
[2] https://www.gov.uk/government/publications/the-7-principles-of-public-life/the-7-principles-of-public-life--2.
[3] https://www.aspanet.org/ASPA/Code-of-Ethics/Code-of-Ethics.aspx.
[4] http://www.oecd.org/gov/trust-in-government.htm.
[5] https://www.apsc.gov.au/aps-values-1.
[6] The full definition of the NZ public service view on trustworthiness can be found here: http://www.ssc.govt.nz/node/2072.
[7] https://www.victoria.ac.nz/sog/pdf/IGPS-Who-Do-We-Trust-Survey-March2016.pdf.
[8] https://www.victoria.ac.nz/__data/assets/pdf_file/0007/1616380/IGPS-Trust-Presentation-June2018.pdf#download%20the%20Public%20Trust%20PDF.
[9] http://www.ssc.govt.nz/sites/all/files/2016-kiwis-count-ar.pdf.

References

Archimi, Carolina Serrano, Emmanuelle Reynaud, Hina Mahboob Yasin, and Zeeshan Ahmed Bhatti. 2018. "How Perceived Corporate Social Responsibility Affects Employee Cynicism: The Mediating Role of Organizational Trust," *Journal of Business Ethics* 151(4), 907–21.

Atkinson, Sally, and David Butcher. 2003. "Trust in Managerial Relationships." *Journal of Managerial Psychology* 18(4), 282–304.

Balch, D. R., and R. W. Armstrong. 2010. "Ethical Marginality: The Icarus Syndrome and Banality of Wrongdoing," *Journal of Business Ethics* 92(2), 291–303.

Carter, S. 1996. *Integrity*. New York: Harper Perennial.

Ghosh, K. 2018. "How and When Do Employees Identify with Their Organization? Perceived CSR, First-party (In)justice, and Organizational (Mis)trust at Workplace." *Personnel Review* 47(5), 1157–75.

Güçer E., and Ş. A. Demírdağ. 2018. "Organizational Trust and Job Satisfaction: A Study on Hotels." *Business Management Dynamics* 7(9), 12–28.

Guo, Rui, Wei Zhang, Tao Wang, Caroline Bingxin Li, and Lan Tao. 2018. "Timely or Considered? Brand Trust Repair Strategies and Mechanism after Greenwashing in China—From a Legitimacy Perspective." *Industrial Marketing Management* 72(July), 127–37.

Guthrie, C. P., and E. Z. Taylor. 2017. "Whistleblowing on Fraud for Pay: Can I Trust You?" *Journal of Forensic Accounting Research* 2(1), A1–A19.

Hardin, R. 2002. *Trust and Trustworthiness*. New York: Russell Sage Foundation.

Jennings, M. 2004. "Preventing Organizational Ethical Collapse." *Journal of Government Financial Management* 53(1), 12–19.

Keszey, Tamara. 2018. "Trust, Perception, and Managerial Use of Market Information." *International Business Review* 27(6), 1161–71.

Kramer, R. M., and T. R. Tyler, eds. 1996. *Trust in Organizations*. Thousand Oaks, CA: Sage.

Macaulay, M. 2009. "Adapted Morality: The Challenge of Evolutionary Psychology for Administrative Ethics." *Public Integrity* 11(1), 35–44.

Macaulay, M. 2011. *Corruption in the UK Vol 2: Survey of Key Sectors*. London: Transparency International UK.

Maharani, P., and C. D. Riantoputra . 2017. "The Relationship between Behavioral Integrity and Leader Effectiveness Mediated by Cognitive Trust and Affective Trust," in A. Ariyanto et al., eds. *Diversity in Unity: Perspectives from Psychology and Behavioral Sciences*. London: Routledge, 521–28.

McAllister, D. J. 1995. "Affect- and Cognition-Based Trust as Foundations for Interpersonal Cooperation in Organizations." *Academy of Management Journal* 38(1), 24–59.

OECD. 2017. *Trust and Public Policy: How Better Governance Can Help Rebuild Public Trust*. Paris: OECD Public Governance Reviews, OECD Publishing.

Perry, R. W., and L. D. Mankin. 2007. "Organizational Trust, Trust in the Chief Executive and Work Satisfaction." *Public Personnel Management* 36(2), 165–79.

Pollitt, C., and P. Hupé. 2011. "Talking about Government: The Role of Magic Concepts," *Public Management Review* 13(5), 641–58.

Rohr, J. 1989. *Ethics for Bureaucrats*. New York: Marcel Dekker.

Thomson, R., and H. Brandenburg. 2018. "Trust and Citizens' Evaluations of Promise Keeping by Governing Parties." *Political Studies* 67(1), 249–66.

Väyrynen, Tuure, and Sari Laari-Salmela. 2018. "Men, Mammals, or Machines? Dehumanization Embedded in Organizational Practices." *Journal of Business Ethics* 147(1), 95–113.

Zak, Paul, J. 2017. "The Neuroscience of Trust: Management Behaviors that Foster Employee Engagement." *Harvard Business Review* 95(1), 84–91.

15

Corruption in Criminal Justice

John Kleinig

Background

In ancient thought, corruption was often identified with a *departure from some pristine condition*, always a change for the worse. It signaled deterioration or decay. This is a sense of the term we still recognize when we speak of corrupt texts or data files. Or, to use an example taken from recent controversies, there has been "a corruption of the process by which facts are credibly gathered and reliably used to shape one's beliefs about reality" (McIntyre 2018, 1). The normative overtones of such corruption tend to be moralized when we speak—as we more often do—of *motivational corruption*. Although the most commonly intended reference for motivational corruption is to those who use public office for private gain, a broader scope can encompass institutions as well as role occupants, and private individuals and office holders as well as public ones. Within the domain of criminal justice an even broader understanding has taken root, corruption motivated by a *noble cause*. Although moralized understandings of corruption have a negative valence, such corruption is sometimes considered only one factor in a larger moral equation and, in that context, it is sometimes (even if controversially) deemed justifiable. Some have argued for the value of corruption in stimulating a moribund economy, noble cause corruption has had its advocates, and in a different context the corruption of youth with which Socrates was charged may be seen as a valuable pushback against problematic societal norms. As with many social concepts, the contours of corruption are often contested (Gallie 1956; but cf. Swanton 1985 with Väyrynen 2014).

The so-called (because it is really a patchwork of institutional arrangements: see Kleinig 2017) criminal justice *system*—comprising, at its core, policing, judicial processes, and penal institutions—has long been a site for corrupt individuals, organizations/units, and practices. By its very nature, the system has beneficiaries and casualties, and participants have reasons to corrupt it or players within it. Police officers may be tempted by money or services, while the objects of their enforcement activities may wish to avoid the costs associated with their alleged breaches. Those who come before the courts for adjudication may wish to tamper with witnesses or illicitly tip the process in their favor. Prisoners may wish to obtain special privileges in austere conditions and prison officers may seek sexual or other favors.

We may distinguish between corruption *within* the criminal justice system and corruption *of* the criminal justice system. Corruption *of* the criminal justice system, which is the most general form of corruption, occurs when the criminal justice system itself is manipulated in a way that no longer serves the purposes of criminal justice. This most often occurs in nondemocratic societies, in which the major institutions, including the criminal justice system, are made to serve the interests of the regime or demagogue in power. Police become agents of social pacification, not of social peace keeping; "telephone justice" and similar interventions in the judicial processes are rampant; and prisons become psychiatric facilities, warehousing and otherwise mistreating political dissidents. The Nazi years with their camps, the USSR and its gulags, China with its reeducation facilities, and

North Korea's detention facilities are different expressions of the corruption *of* the criminal justice system. Some have argued that even the United States has bordered on such a system—reflecting the disparate treatment of African Americans by the criminal justice system (Reiman and Leighton 2016). To the extent that it is so, we may think of a spectrum of systems, some more or less corrupted than others—and no doubt, some more easily restored than others. Corruption *within* the criminal justice system presumes that the criminal justice system functions tolerably to penalize those and only those who ought to be societally punished. Even so, such a criminal justice system may be corrupted by various features and happenings.

But before we continue, a definitional consideration: It has been common among those who discuss police corruption to distinguish *corruption* (taking bribes) from *misconduct* (use of excessive force), on the one side, and *incompetence* (botched investigation), on the other. However, in his report on police corruption (Commission Report 1994), Judge Milton Mollen argued that these were somewhat academic distinctions—that where there is corruption there will also be misconduct and incompetence. In a way he was right. Even if conceptually distinct, the failures tend to be causally interrelated, and attempts to eradicate one should also target the others.

Corruption *within* the criminal justice system tends to corrupt the system itself, and corruption of the latter can be more potent than corruption in business, banking, education, and government, for it is through the criminal justice system that corruption within these other areas may be discouraged, contained, and counteracted. Although most societies have a variety of accountability mechanisms—the news media, the education system, public and private watchdogs, and normative traditions such as religious institutions and cultural mores—the criminal justice system is society's accountability mechanism of last and probably best resort, and the all-too-present tendencies of people to behave corruptly depend ultimately upon there being an enforceable system of societal accountability. If the criminal justice system is corrupt, especially at its judicial apex, a functional social order is placed at risk.

Whatever the shortfalls of social-contract theory as a theory of governmental authority, it offers a liberal and democratic response to a deep concern about human inclinations: We cannot rely exclusively on innate or learned human goodness to dispel our flawed tendencies but need reliable institutions of adjudication and enforcement to preserve us from the insecurities, hazards, and even chaos of the state of nature. We have, therefore, a special reason to be concerned about corruption within the criminal justice system.

Although this chapter focuses on the central criminal justice tasks of policing, adjudication, and punishment, and the corruption that may occur within them, it should be kept in mind that some of that corruption may precede and succeed the operations of the institutions devoted to such tasks. Some criminal laws may themselves be the product of corrupted political processes, and their enforcement may either perpetuate that corruption or, given its partisanship, encourage bribery or other corruptions. Laws may be introduced to criminalize the behavior of those who exercise their free speech, associational, or religious rights. They can also be administered in an arbitrary and corrupt manner in advance of eventually being found unconstitutional. In the early days of the war on terrorism the author was on a panel in which a defender of the US government's anti-terrorist policies (including extraordinary rendition) praised the constitutional traditions of the United States because—*in time*—improper uses of authority would be revealed for what they were. However, he also took satisfaction in the knowledge that by the time they were shown to be unconstitutional, these policies/practices would have served their strategic purpose! Other laws, such as the suppression of voting rights, either through unreasonable registration requirements or after sentences have been served, perpetuate a form of voter suppression that tends to be, and is usually intended to be, strongly partisan in its effects. These are cases of corruption that have links to the criminal justice system.

Corruption in Policing

Police corruption, which, like other forms of criminal justice corruption, can be individual, collective, or institutional, can also take many forms. Most generally, it can involve the use of policing as a political tool—in the distinction I made earlier between social pacification and social peace keeping. But, even in democratic societies, troubling corruption may occur. Some of the more common forms are reflected in police codes of ethics, which generally outlaw various forms of favoritism or partiality (such as racial, gender, and status-based) and forbid the acceptance of gratuities and bribes. Not that there is something inherently problematic wrong with gratuities; in the context of policing, however, gratuities may create, or be seen to reflect, partial treatment. The enforcement and order-maintenance roles of police need to be administered in ways that are not and do not appear discriminatory or unfair. First-line police officers have considerable discretion in how they exercise their powers, and their powers are such that misuses can have devastating consequences for citizens. Even something as minor as a gratuitous arrest can have continuing employment repercussions.

Police powers can constitute an inherent source of temptation. Whether for personal reasons (greed, or as responses to disrespect) or to allay institutional pressures (quotas; achieving closure), police may engage in shakedowns, acts of framing, flaking, verballing, and retaliation. Add to that two further considerations: (1) street police are not usually among the better-paid in society and their work can often confront them with considerable temptations to augment their salaries, and (2) they work in an environment in which other police are unlikely to testify against them (the "blue wall of silence"). If there is a culture in which corruption is tolerated, it may be very difficult to avoid its entanglements. That culture may be perpetuated by the deliberate exposure of inexperienced officers to compromising situations. Once compromised, officers may be unwilling to protest or blow the whistle (Kleinig 2001).

Because operational policing is highly pragmatic—focused on solving or resolving social crises or problems, often under considerable public and/or political pressure—police are expected to show their professionalism through results. This can foster an "ends justifies the means" mentality in which various ethical and other normative constraints are circumvented. What has come to be known as "noble cause corruption" in policing (Kleinig 2002; Miller 2017, ch. 4) sometimes trades on the very difficult moral compromises that may sometimes confront police—rare cases in which they may have to "dirty their hands" in order to resolve a situation (Delattre 1989, ch. 11)—and sustains moral corner-cutting that appears to satisfy the need for socially desirable results. Such moral corner-cutting may result in the conviction of those who should be convicted, but sometimes the moral corner-cutting also removes safeguards against wrongful convictions, and (whether or not it is discovered) justice is not served. The "New York Central Park Jogger" case, in which five black youths were jailed for assault and rape for several years before the true perpetrator was discovered, is one dramatic example in which corner-cutting "pragmatism," supposedly for a noble cause, went badly astray (Burns 2011). In Australia, a similarly dramatic case involved the murder conviction, following investigative efforts that were compromised by prejudice and corruptive protection, of a parent of a young child who, it was later shown, had been taken and killed by a dingo (Chamberlain 2012). Even if moral corner-cutting sometimes gets the right "result," it often does so at considerable cost to the liberal democratic values that police are intended to serve. The easy pragmatism of noble-cause corruption fails to do justice to the genuinely hard choices that police sometimes have to make.

The foregoing is not intended to suggest that police corruption is (always) systemic or confined to uniformed or lower-level or operational officers, although there are more than enough cases in which several police officers have combined to constitute a corrupt clique (see, e.g., Commission Report 1994). Any hierarchical organization—and police organizations are typically hierarchical—presents temptations for corruption for personal gain or advancement and, at the highest level of such organizations, there are usually reputational expectations that can foster cover-ups, deflections of responsibility, backstabbing, and other practices that undermine the collective purposes of the institution and organization of policing (see, e.g., Murano 1984).

Corruption in the Courts

Judicial corruption may or may not be linked to police corruption. Prosecutors and police tend to have a synergistic relationship, and prosecutors who have an interest in winning cases may advise police on what they "need to do" in order to maximize the likelihood of a case being successful. Whether or not a case goes to trial—although most times it does not, plea bargaining accounting for most convictions (National Association of Criminal Defense Lawyers 2018)—it may be in the interests of a prosecutor to exaggerate the available evidence or, in a more complex case, to magnify the evidentiary issues in order to justify not proceeding with a case. There are few mechanisms to hold prosecutorial discretion accountable (Gershman 2002; Marshall Project 2014–2019).

In an adversarial tradition such as is found in the United States, there is a temptation for the competing parties to do what has to be done, within the rules, to win or resolve their cases satisfactorily. On the surface such zealousness appears to be exactly right: each party is encouraged to put forward its strongest case prior to adjudication. But the reality is sometimes otherwise, as one or both of the parties seek to "game" the system: factfinding becomes psychodrama. Even in the standard cases, in which plea-bargaining is the path to resolution, the alternatives may be structured coercively that smacks of equally undesirable alternatives: plead guilty to A or risk the much heavier sentence that you would face if also charged with B and C at trial. An innocent party or one guilty of a lesser offense may be "persuaded" to opt for A (Lippke 2011).

The judicial or adjudicative process within criminal justice is populated by a variety of participants, each having distinctive functions within the process. Within adversarial traditions, prosecutors are opposed by defense lawyers, and the merits of particular criminal charges are argued before judges or juries. Each is corruptible in various ways. Prosecutorial discretion may be corrupted by political, racial, and morally partisan considerations, or by the personal desire for resume enhancement, leading to what James Comey characterized as "chickenshit lawyering" (see Eisinger 2017). The task of a prosecutor is not (primarily) to win cases but to obtain convictions through substantively and procedurally fair means. Cross-examining defense lawyers may also act corruptly by exploiting the emotional or cognitive weaknesses of witnesses or cleverly suborning perjury. In extreme cases, they may engage in jury tampering.

In the United States, a country in which judges are mostly elected, local politics may favor voting for a judge on grounds that have limited connection with competence or fairness. Traditional codes of judicial ethics—which emphasize values such as independence, impartiality, integrity, propriety, equality, competence, and diligence (United Nations 2002)—identify qualities that are critical to fair adjudication and that may be corrupted by those whose individual or partisan interests are threatened by the legitimate processes of criminal justice. In theory, a hierarchy of courts enabling appeals in the event of dissatisfaction with lower-court decisions constitutes a significant protection against judicial corruption. And judges in higher courts may be granted long-term tenure to shield them from political and other pressures. But it has become clear in recent years that no level of the US judiciary has managed to secure itself against the influence of partisan politics. The fabled "checks and balances" of liberal democratic society have been skewed by partisan interests at the point of selection, if not elsewhere.

Because of the desire to secure judges against external pressures, subsequent to their appointment (especially at the higher levels) there may be few resources for holding them accountable should decisions be questionable. The situation is very serious in so-called developing countries, in which the judiciary is not secured, and in which mechanisms for countering criminal justice corruption are often underdeveloped (Buscaglia 2001; Transparency International 2019). Nevertheless, other democratic countries may have better protections against partisan judicial appointments than in the United States, as well as other controls on the perpetuation of judicial influence (such as fixed retirement ages).

Even though jury trials now constitute a small proportion of adjudicative decisions, juries can also be corrupted by factors that compromise fair decision-making. Despite the rules that govern the *voir dire* process, racial and other discriminatory factors still make it through, and jury deliberations may also be tainted by powerful personalities and other factors (Kleinig and Levine 2006). Moreover, in a technologically adept world, it has become increasingly difficult to keep jury members from accessing external data and opinions, in theory tainting the carefully circumscribed trial process.

Corruption in Corrections

Corruption can of course occur at the nexus of the judicial and correctional spheres of criminal justice, in sentencing decisions (which may be influenced by racial or status factors), and also in some of the so-called downward departures that are granted as a result of "cooperation" between defendants and prosecutors (Schwartz 2004).

Within the prison system itself, various types of corruption occur. At one end of the spectrum, well-connected prisoners may secure favorable treatment for themselves, whereas at the other end, conditions of austerity may be alleviated by giving sexual or other favors. Sometimes the corruption may be relatively benign (smuggling personal items); on other occasions the corruption may aid criminal activities within (e.g., weapons) or beyond the prison walls (e.g., cell phones). Then there are the cover-ups that mask such transactions (see Heyward 2015; Ball 2018). The burgeoning of private prisons has generated further opportunities for corruption, whether by way of political lobbying or corruption of accountability (American Bar Association 2012).

Combatting Corruption

Corruption within criminal justice can be either/both individual or institutional (and in between). How it is tackled will depend on the kind of corruption involved and the resources available to tackle it. In some developing countries, corruption within the criminal justice system is of a piece with larger governmental and societal corruption and must be tackled as part of a wider societal project (Buscaglia 2001).

Ideally, criminal justice institutions should be structured and populated so that an anti-corruptive culture is encouraged, rewarded, and sustained. Ultimately, a culture that does not tolerate corruption will provide the only reliable prophylactic against corruptive practices. Of course, no human institution will be entirely free from corruptive temptations or even practices. But a spirit of professionalism, in which those who occupy criminal justice roles take professional pride in the work they do, and find institutional support, would go a considerable way toward countering the corruption that is so often present. Professional pride arises out of a commitment to the legitimate ends of one's professional work, whether that is policing, prosecution, judicial decision-making, or prison oversight. Careful selection processes, training that focuses on professional responsibility as well as skills, wages, conditions, and expectations that are conducive to competence and integrity, and exemplary leadership, along with fair and transparent institutional processes, would do much to encourage the development and maintenance of a culture that is unconducive to corrupting influences.

In the real world of criminal justice, these are to varying degrees unrealistic expectations. Many governmental agencies are not willing to make the financial commitments that would support such professionalism, and many criminal-justice institutions are wasteful of what they have. Additional anti-corruptive measures have come to be adopted (integrity testing, internal affairs surveillance, encouragement of whistle blowers, disciplinary systems, paperwork). Yet if professional ideals are forgotten or foreclosed by such measures, the battle against corruption will lead to an unending attempt to counteract corrupt conflagrations in the accumulating undergrowth. Every measure taken will have its limitations and, soon after an accountability strategy is introduced, ways will be sought to circumvent its intent. The recent introduction of police body cameras provides an instructive example (White 2014). No doubt if police training encouraged more professional police–citizen encounters, greater use of de-escalation techniques, and more honest reporting of incidents, there would be fewer problems on the street. Body cameras are intended to enhance accountability by making such encounters more transparent. Early indications were that excessive force and complaints thereof were considerably diminished (Carroll 2013; Barak et al. 2014). But as their use has burgeoned, critical incidents have increasingly avoided the scrutiny cameras were intended to provide (e.g., *Washington Post* 2018). Stories of forgetting to turn on the camera and of dislodgment and malfunction have multiplied; lack of audio has sometimes been exploited; police departments have become increasingly unwilling to release tapes in a timely fashion; and, as with every device, ways to diminish the usefulness of their data have been devised. The unintended as well as intended effects of accountability measures need far more attention than they have been given. As it has been discovered from incidents with taser use, and is now being discovered with body cameras, police departments have too often been the "victims" of lobbyists whose deepest interests, despite their claims, have been profiting from the latest, greatest technology (Goodyear 2018).

It is difficult both to design institutions and then to nurture their cultures so that they are immunized against all of the failings of the state of nature, especially given that the state of nature was as precarious as it was because of the same tendencies and flaws that characterize those who establish and enter into our institutions of civil society. Yet we have no alternative to human imagination. Its flaws and excesses, nevertheless, should warn us of the important even if not absolute liberal value of transparency in public institutions.

References

American Bar Association. 2012. "Prisons for Profit: Incarceration for Sale," *Human Rights Magazine 38*(March 6), available at: https://www.americanbar.org/publications/human_rights_magazine_home/human_rights_vol38_2011/human_rights_summer11/prisons_for_profit_incarceration_for_sale.html/.

Ariel, Barak, William A. Farrar, and Alex Sutherland. 2014. "The Effect of Police Body-Worn Cameras on Use of Force and Citizens' Complaints Against the Police: A Randomized Controlled Trial." *Journal of Quantitative Criminology 31*(3), 509–35, available at: https://link.springer.com/article/10.1007/s10940-01.-9236-3.

Ball, Sam. 2018. "Tales from Inside Rikers, the Notorious NYC Jail Set to Close," *France* 24(March 3), available at: https://www.france24.com/en/20180226-tales-inside-rikers-island-notorious-new-york-jail-prison-close.

Burns, Sarah. 2011. *The Central Park Five: A Chronicle of a City Wilding*. New York: Knopf.

Buscaglia, Edgardo. 2001. *Judicial Corruption in Developing Countries: Its Causes and Economic Consequences*. Vienna: UNODCCP, available at: http://www.unodc.org/pdf/crime/gpacpublications/cicp14.pdf.

Carroll, Rory. 2013. "California Police Use of Body Cameras Cuts Violence and Complaints." *The Guardian*, November 4, available at: http://www.theguardian.com/world/2013/nov/04/california-police-body-cameras-cuts-violence-complaints-rialto.

Chamberlain, Michael. 2012. *Heart of Stone: My Quest for Justice for Azaria*. Sydney: New Holland.

Delattre, Edwin J. 1989. *Character and Cops: Ethics in Policing*. Washington, DC: American Enterprise Institute, ch. 11.

Eisinger, Jesse. 2017. *The Chickenshit Club: Why the Justice Department Fails to Prosecute Executives*. New York: Simon & Schuster.

Gallie, W. B. 1956. "Essentially Contested Concepts." *Proceedings of the Aristotelian Society 56*(1), 167–98.

Gershman, Bennett L. 2002. *Prosecutorial Misconduct*. 2ⁿᵈ ed. with annual updates. Toronto: Thomson Reuters.

Goodyear, Dana. 2018. "Shock to the System." *New Yorker*, August 27, 36–43, available at: https://www.newyorker.com/magazine/2018/08/27/can-the-manufacturer-of-tasers-provide-the-answer-to-police.

Heyward, Gary L. 2015. *Corruption Officer: From Jail Guard to Perpetrator Inside Rikers Island*. New York: Simon & Schuster/Atria Books.

Kleinig, John. 2001. "The Blue Wall of Silence: An Ethical Analysis." *International Journal of Applied Philosophy 15*(1), 1–23.

Kleinig, John. 2002. "Rethinking Noble Cause Corruption." *International Journal of Police Science and Management 4*(4), 287–314.

Kleinig, John. 2017. "Introduction." In *Routledge Handbook of Criminal Justice Ethics*. Jonathan Jacobs and Jonathan Jackson, eds. London: Routledge, 1–14.

Kleinig, John, and James P. Levine, eds. 2006. *Jury Ethics: Juror Conduct and Jury Dynamics*. Boulder: Paradigm Publishers.

Lippke, Richard L. 2011. *The Ethics of Plea Bargaining*. Oxford: Oxford University Press.

Marshall Project, The. 2014–2019. "Prosecutorial Misconduct," available at: https://www.themarshallproject.org/records/1-prosecutorial-misconduct

McIntyre, Lee. 2018. *Post-Truth*. Cambridge, MA: MIT Press.

Miller, Seumas. 2017. *Institutional Corruption*. Cambridge: Cambridge University Press.

Murano, Vincent, with William Hoffer. 1990. *Cop Hunter: The True Story of a Cop Who Spends His Career Keeping Other Cops Honest*. New York: Simon & Schuster.

National Association of Criminal Defense Lawyers. 2018. "The Trial Penalty: The Sixth Amendment Right to Trial on the Verge of Extinction and How To Save It." Available at: https://www.nacdl.org/trialpenaltyreport/.

New York City Report on Alleged Police Corruption. 1994. *Commission to Investigate Allegations of Police Corruption and the Anti-Corruption Procedures of the Police Department*. Chair: Milton Mollen. New York City.

Reiman, Jeffrey and Paul Leighton. 2017. *The Rich Get Richer and the Poor Get Prison: Ideology, Class, and Criminal Justice*. 11ᵗʰ ed. New York: Routledge.

Schwartz, Adina. 2004. "A Market in Liberty: Corruption, Cooperation, and the Federal Criminal Justice System," in William C. Heffernan and John Kleinig, eds., *Private and Public Corruption*. Lanham, MD: Rowman & Littlefield: 173–223.

Swanton, Christine. 1985. "On the 'Essential Contestedness' of Political Concepts." *Ethics 95*(4), 811–27.

Transparency International. 2019. Available at: http://ww1.transparency.org/.

United Nations. 2002. "(Bangalore) Principles of Judicial Conduct." Available at: https://www.unodc.org/pdf/crime/corruption/judicial_group/Bangalore_principles.pdf.

Väyrynen, Pekka. 2014. "Essential Contestability and Evaluation." *Australasian Journal of Philosophy 92*(3), 471–88.

Washington Post. 2018. "Watch this Police Captain Answer Questions about His Force's Chronic Failure to Use Body Cameras," video available at: https://www.washingtonpost.com/video/editorial/opinion/watch-this-police-captain-answer-questions-about-his-forces-chronic-failure-to-use-body-cameras/2018/06/28/f44aeef2-7af2-11e8-ac4e-421ef7165923_video.html?utm_term=.d238d9e7984c&wpisrc=nl_popns&wpmm=1.

White, Michael D. 2014. *Police Officer Body-Worn Cameras: Assessing the Evidence*. Washington, DC: Office of Community Oriented Policing Services.

16

Ethical Decision Making

Angela Kline and Maria P. Aristigueta

Introduction

Ethics is a system of moral standards for guiding behavior. When applied to decision making, it helps guide individuals when faced with important and challenging dilemmas. These dilemmas are intensified by considering the global context of competing values. Public administrators are to uphold the standards and values of the stakeholders in their society. An individual's values may conflict with that of the polis, and the predominant standards of the polis may conflict with other republics. Because the endeavor of determining what ought to be done may be rife with disputes, it is wise to ground the study of ethical decision making in frameworks to help guide the process.

Foundations of Ethics

An important layer is virtue ethics, which focuses on the internal factors of the individual. A commonly used definition of virtue ethics are the forces that are shaped by an individual's character attributes, experiences, opinions, and education, among many others.

In the basic meaning, ontology is the study of what is or what exists. Originated by Aristotle in *Metaphysics*, ontology is the study of what is being or not being (Aristotle 350 AD). Raadschelders (2011) contrasts ontology as the nature of reality whereas epistemology is what we know. He expands the list of Aristotelian ontological and epistemological questions to ask about the nature of reality, justifiable knowledge, the varying definitions of knowledge, and the sources of knowledge. Stout and Love (2013) expand on these definitions of ontology as the source of knowledge that informs an individual's worldview. Deontology is the study of duty or obligation. Deontological ethics place expectations on public administrators to adhere to laws with obligation and consistency (Stout and Love 2013).

Frameworks

It is wise to use a framework for thinking through potential actions and future consequences when faced with decisions. The usability and practicality of a decision-making tool are of utmost importance when selecting a framework. It is important to note that the late 1990s witnessed the creation of international and regional efforts to standardize ethics frameworks for public administration. To review ethical frameworks, table 16.1 is broadly categorized by approaches in virtues, principles, and consequences (Svara 2015).

Bridge Frameworks

Finally, an additional category of ethical frameworks serves to bridge components of the previous sections on virtues, principles, and consequences.

TABLE 16.1	Ethical Frameworks	
Virtue-based Frameworks	**Principle-based Frameworks**	**Consequence-based Frameworks**
Virtue-based Frameworks assert an intuitive understanding of good or bad, right or wrong; virtues include trustworthiness, respect, responsibility, fairness, caring, citizenship, rationality, prudence, respect for laws, self-discipline, civility, and independence (Svara 2015).	**A Principle-Based** approach seeks ethical guidance from an external source. This source could be a professional oath, conduct guidelines, or a code of ethics. This approach assumes a deontological philosophy to ethical decision making as there is a duty or obligation to an external force.	**The Consequences-Based Frameworks** emphasize the result of the decision. Broadly included in this category are the philosophies of teleology and utilitarianism.
The Stout and Love Ontological Ideal-Type Model maintains that conflicts are best mediated through weighing decisions that are considered good and right within a larger consideration of the governance process. This model recognizes the challenges that can arise around language and making and understanding the meaning of words.	The **ASPA Code of Ethics** exists to help public administrators put professional standards into practice and encourage assessment of their own knowledge and behavior (American Society for Public Administration, Ethics and Implementation Committee 2015). The American Society for Public Administration is an important organization and seeks to advance the professionalism of public service.	**The Comprehensive Accountability Framework (CAF)** identifies six accountability categories: bureaucratic, legal, professional, political, social, and moral/ethical. This approach enables users to focus on the accountability factors of a decision, including the goals, consequences, and evaluative criteria (Christie 2018).
Petrick Quinn Integrity Capacity Model emphasizes the importance of developing integrity at the individual and institutional level to enhance the ability to make an ethical decision (Petrick and Quinn 2000). The Petrick Quinn Integrity Capacity Model outlines three components: moral awareness, moral deliberation, and moral character. Moral awareness is being perceptive and sensitive to ethical issues that will impact other individuals. Moral deliberation is a process by which the participants weigh the causal factors and moral options to make a sound decision. Moral character is an individual's or institution's ability to act ethically.		The **Issue-Contingent Model** focuses on Moral Intensity, which emphasizes one's moral imperative dependent upon the context. In the conception of moral intensity, Jones emphasizes the result of the decision with understanding the magnitude of consequences, probability of effect, temporal immediacy, and concentration of effect. (Jones 1991).

Specifically, the Low Road and High Road Ethical Decision-Making Model is a classic framework that has been adapted by modern scholars (Stazyk and Davis 2015). Rohr's original Low Road and High Road Ethical Decision-Making Model proposed that the low road emphasizes the importance of following formal rules, whereas the high road focuses on social equity as the guiding force (Rohr 1989). As Stazyk and Davis expanded this framework: the low road follows established rules and principle-based reasoning, and the high road observes one's personal integrity through reflection and discretion (Stazyk and Davis 2015). In order to maintain integrity in the public and nonprofit sectors, decision makers maintain formal and informal elements to reinforce ethical behavior. The formal components include regulatory functions, codes of ethics, and sanctions. On the informal side are social norms and psychological contracts that guide individuals through ethical decision making on a daily basis.

Emerging Global Standards

As early as 1970, international stakeholders, including the United Nations, became interested in developing international ethical standards. And, as the world grew more interconnected, organizations engaged in developing global frameworks. These global frameworks were geared to fight corruption and promote integrity and transparency in public administration. Most noteworthy was the Organization for Economic Cooperation and Development (OECD) regional initiative referred to as an ethics infrastructure consisting of eight elements to control, guide, and manage. The exact manifestation and balance of these elements were left to individual countries to create based on their culturally specific requirements (Cooper and Yoder 2012). The elements included in the OECD frameworks included political commitment, effective legal framework, efficient accountability mechanisms, supportive public service conditions, coordinating ethics bodies, and public involvement and scrutiny (Organization for Economic Cooperation and Development 2017).

More recently, ethics received attention from the OECD Secretary General Angel Furria calling for global standards (see http://www.oecd.org/corruption/oecdsgurri-awelcomesg7movetoestablishsetofethicalprinciplesonglobalbusiness.htm). As of 2009, the OECD had developed the following global standards:

- The OECD Anti-Bribery Convention requiring governments to establish bribery of foreign public officials as a criminal offense.
- The OECD Guidelines for Multinational Enterprises, first agreed by governments in 1975 set out standards for business behavior in areas such as employment, industrial relations, environment, competition, and taxation.
- The OECD Principles of Corporate Governance set out broad rules to guide business conduct.
- The OECD has developed international standards for transparency and cooperation on taxation to counter tax abuse, particularly in tax havens and countries with strict bank secrecy.
- The Financial Action Task Force engages a worldwide network to adhere to its recommendations to combat money laundering and the financing of terrorism.

In 2017, OECD published the recommendations of the Council on Public Integrity. The recommendations made are intended to shift the focus from ad hoc integrity policies to a more comprehensive, risk-based global approach focusing on context and behavior. It aims to cultivate a culture of integrity across the whole society (Organization for Economic Cooperation and Development 2017). The OECD's recommendations are in support of the literature addressing the effective incorporation of ethical frameworks. Specifically, modern scholars have embraced the concept of "sensemaking" in relation to ethical behavior. Sensemaking incorporates the context as the individual processes an event through social construction and develops plausible meaning to rationalize the individual's behavior (Maitlis and Sonenshein 2010). The concept of sensemaking reinforces the OECD's guidelines as it requires participating countries to develop their own processes for addressing each standard. This enables the participating countries to operationalize each standard based on the context and culturally relevant information.

The OECD's revised global standards align with recent research addressing cross-cultural ethics. For example, in a study of a moral decision-making competence training program of the Swiss Armed Forces, researchers found that participants maintained positive long-term effects six months following the training (Seiler, Fischer, and Voegtli 2011). The significant finding from this study was that the participants increased their overall moral awareness as a result of the training. This approach mirrors the OECD's emphasis on context and behavior. Furthermore, in research of comparative codes of ethics, scholars assert that a centralized code of ethics could stifle the possibility of a thoughtful and considered ethical standard (Helin and Sandstrom 2008).

Addressing the issue of utilization of data collection in the era of Big Data, Jurkiewicz calls for a global code of ethics for the use of Big Data (Jurkiewicz 2018). Due to the potential harm to individuals and communities, the need for such a code is imminent. It appears that progress is being made on global ethical standards. The European Union has been a leader in establishing data standards; the European General Data Protection Regulation (GDPR) was enacted in 2018 created rules for data collection, storage, and usage (Pardes 2018). While the GDPR is not a code of ethics, it does establish laws that protect the data and privacy rights of citizens. The GDPR outlines a process for citizens to make an inquiry to a company regarding their personal data and how to file a formal complaint if their personal data has been leaked (Pardes 2018). However, questions remain in the global application as it pertains to specific areas like Big Data. For example, who is responsible for developing the global code of ethics on the collection and use of Big Data? How will this global code of ethics remain nimble to adapt with the rapid pace of change in the application of Big Data?

Formal Elements: Regulatory Functions

To maintain public trust and fiduciary obligations, nonprofits and the public-sector agencies have conflict-of-interest policies, including requirements that employees and board members disclose all financial interest in companies that may engage in transactions with the organization. At a minimum, these policies also require transparency about the existence of potential conflicts and the process by which these conflicts will be addressed.

Unfortunately, sometimes nonprofits and public-sector organizations hesitate to enforce restrictions because they rely on insiders to provide donations or goods and services at discounted special rates (Rhode and Packel 2009). Ethical challenges may arise at all levels and in all types of organizations—for-profit, nonprofit, and government—and involve a complex relationship between individual character and cultural influences. Unethical behavior in an organization can have negative effects on employee retention and lead to harmful health behaviors, including diminished psychological and physiological well-being (Giacalone, Promislo, and Jurkiewicz 2018). Rhode and Packel wrote that a policy governing conflicts of interest is perhaps the most important policy to adopt (2009). The Council of Nonprofits recommends a written policy and advises that these include the following two directives: (1) a requirement that those with a conflict (or who think they may have a conflict) disclose the conflict/potential conflict, and (2) prohibit interested board members from voting on any matter in which there is a conflict or potential conflict (National Council of Nonprofits 2018). More specifically the DC Bar ProBono Center recommends that policy specify what constitutes a conflict of interest by identifying the individuals within the organization covered by the conflict-of-interest policy, thereby providing a means for the individuals to disclose information that may help identify conflicts of interest and outline the procedures to be followed in managing conflicts of interest (DC Bar ProBono Center 2015).

Informal Functions: Informal Violations

Informal violations come from a variety of sources. Two that have been well documented and will be discussed here are the psychological contract and perceived injustice. Informal functions are significant because they can result in changes in ethical behavior. The informal functions of an institution have a "trickle-down" effect that sets the tone for employees' ethical behaviors (Cropanzano and Stein 2009).

Psychological contract is a concept developed by Rousseau in 1989. Psychological contracts are individual beliefs in a reciprocal obligation between two individuals or employee and the employer (Rousseau 1989). It solidified Argyris's earlier work by focusing on unwritten expectations in the work relationship (Argyris 1960). This unwritten contract represents the mutual beliefs, perceptions, and informal obligations based on trust, respect, and compassion between an employee and an employer. A breach in the psychological contract occurs when there is an incompatibility on what is expected versus what is delivered from either the employee or employer.

Likewise, *perceived injustice* is caused by violation of agreed-upon social norms. Cropanzano and Stein point out that employees may be less likely to abide by ethical rules if they perceive the institution as unfair. This perception of injustice can be deviations from moral standards or from psychological contracts. Perceived injustice can result in employees treating others less morally, based on the institution's sense of fairness (Cropanzano and Stein 2009)

One of the universal norms held in work contexts is the need for employees' rewards to be reflective of the employee's contribution. If equity is perceived as insufficient, then this violation of an equity-norm is likely to provoke perceived injustice (Shapiro and Sherf 2015). Let us take for example the negotiating of salaries in a nonprofit organization where men may negotiate much more aggressively and successfully than their female counterparts. The nonprofit executive pays what is negotiated without concerns for pay equity among employees. If salaries become public, it may lead to perceived injustice. Unmanaged injustice may escalate into conflict.

Cognitive Bias

An individual's cognitive bias can have a profound impact on their behavior. Whether conscious or unconscious, an individual's biases can influence the decisions that they make. Recognizing one's biases is an important step to ensuring that sound decisions can be made without showing prejudice against groups of people (Schwartz 2016).

Implicit bias or unconscious bias is defined as prejudice or judgment in favor of or against a thing, individual, or group as compared to another in a way that is typically considered unfair. Explicit or conscious bias means that individuals are aware of their biases, so they are able to monitor or control it. The goal of monitoring one's explicit bias is to limit the effect it has on personal behavior (Stone and Moskowitz 2011).

Unconscious bias occurs automatically as the brain makes quick judgments based on past experiences, stereotypes, and personal background (Cialdini 2009; Kahneman 2011). In contrast, deliberate prejudice is defined as conscious bias (or explicit bias). In both cases, certain people benefit, and other people are penalized. Although each individual has biases, unconscious bias is often exhibited toward minority groups based on factors such as class, gender, race, ethnicity, sexual orientation, religious beliefs, disabilities, and other diverse traits.

Cognitive biases in decision making and the incentive systems they create can negatively skew behavior. In order to make ethical decisions, one must understand what is influencing the behavior. Bazerman and Tensbrusel identify five such influences:

(1) *Goals that are ill-conceived* may lead to unethical behavior. This is particularly the case when achieving the goal is held as more important than the consequences. See the case below.

(2) *Motivated blindness* occurs when people may perceive that it is in their best interest to remain ignorant. Public administrators need to be mindful of the conflicts of interest not readily visible and work to remove them from the organization, including existing incentive systems.

(3) *Indirect blindness* also occurs in organizations, but this time the manager delegates the unethical behavior to others, not necessarily consciously. Managers must take responsibility for an assignment's ethical implications and be alert to the indirect blindness that may obscure unethical behavior.

(4) Research suggests that individuals are likely to *accept increasingly major infractions as long as each violation is only incrementally more serious* than the preceding one.

(5) *Rewarding unethical decisions* because they have good outcomes is a recipe for disaster over the long run (Bazerman and Tenbrunsel 2011).

In order to act on personal values, administrators need skills with which to approach their decisions. When faced with many activities and counter-pressures, the public manager needs to be able to think through the problems at hand. This requires not only the use of decision tools but also the use of what Newell referred to as *moral imagination* (Newell 2012). Moral imagination requires that administrators ask the right questions to act ethically.

For example, in their study of school administrators, Begley and Johansson discovered that the relevance of principles or ethics to a given situation seemed to be prompted by circumstances (Begley and Johansson 2008). These included situations where an ethical posture is socially appropriate (e.g., the importance of freedom of choice), situations where consensus is difficult to achieve (e.g., an issue involving gun control), or a situation when high stakes and urgency require decisive action (e.g., student safety). Furthermore, it is important to consider when an ethical principle may be used to undermine human rights. Some culturally based ethics may be invoked to justify unacceptable behavior or acts. Scholars warn against this tendency and encourage vigilance against inappropriately using culturally based ethics (Begley 2006).

Teaching Cases

Because an important aspect of ethical decision making is considering the context of a situation, the following cases provide an opportunity to practice thinking through situations to make a sound decision. The concepts from this chapter are applied in case studies from real and hypothetical public and nonprofit management. Read the following scenarios and answer the questions. It may be helpful to discuss your answers with others to learn different perspectives on the cases.

1. As director of a nonprofit program, you have received donations to provide healthy snacks for the after-school program. Your program is intended for elementary school children and services an urban community where most of the students fall within the Department of Health and Human Services' poverty guidelines. The children who attend your program have multiple needs, and good nutrition is among them. The

businesses in your area have been fundraising to provide funds for school supplies for these children. One of the teachers would like to use the money to purchase new play equipment instead, and her husband has started his own business manufacturing playground equipment. She assures you that the program would receive the highest quality equipment at the lowest price.

    a. What potential ethical dilemmas do you foresee?
    b. As director, what flexibility, if any, should you have for the use of these funds?
    c. What are available alternatives?
    d. What documents may assist in providing answers?

2. In 2008, *Business Week* editor Peter Coy wrote, "Add President Clinton to the long list of people who deserve a share of the blame for the housing bubble and bust. A recently re-exposed document shows that his administration went to ridiculous lengths to increase the national homeownership rate. It prompted paper thin down payments and pushed for ways to get lenders to give mortgage loans to first time buyers with shaky financing and incomes. It's clear now that the erosion of lending standards pushed prices up by increasing demand, and later led to waves of default by people who never should have bought a home in the first place" (Bazerman and Tenbrunsel 2011).

    a. What triggered this behavior?
    b. Was this a potential case of ill-conceived goals? Why?
    c. What were the consequences?

3. Fox reports, "A 'heartbroken' blogger claims she was denied access to the Louvre gallery in Paris because her dress was too revealing. Newsha Syeah, from Australia, says a security guard on the door turned her away after making "disgusted and horrible gestures" before telling her to cover up The same article also states that "the Louvre website states that it is forbidden for visitors to wear swimsuits or be naked, barefoot or bare-chested" (Richardson 2018).

    a. This incident happened in Paris, and the guest is from Australia. Do you think that cultural differences may be at play here?
    b. Should a museum have a dress code?
    c. Should dress codes be part of global ethical standards?

References

American Society for Public Administration, Ethics and Implementation Committee. 2015. "Implementing the ASPA Code of Ethics: Workbook and Assessment Guide." Retrieved from American Society for Public Administration website: https://www.aspanet.org/ASPADocs/Resources/Ethics_Assessment_Guide.pdf.

Argyis, Chris. 1960. *Understanding Organizational Behavior.* Homewood, IL: Dorsey Press.

Aristotle. 350 AD. *Metaphysics.* Retrieved from Documenta Catholica Omnia website: http://www.documentacatholicaomnia.eu/03d/-384_-322,_Aristoteles,_13_Metaphysics,_EN.pdf. Accessed July 9, 2019.

Bazerman, Max, and Ann Tenbrunsel. 2011. "Ethical Breakdowns." *Harvard Business Review* (April 1). Retrieved from https://hbr.org/2011/04/ethical-breakdowns.

Begley, Paul T. 2006. "Self-Knowledge, Capacity and Sensitivity." *Journal of Educational Administration.* doi: 10.1108/09578230610704792.

Begley, Paul T., and Olof Johansson. 2008. "The Values of School Administration: Preferences, Ethics, and Conflicts." *Journal of School Leadership* 18(4), 421–44.

Christie, Natasha V. 2018. "A Comprehensive Accountability Framework for Public Administrators." *Public Integrity* 20(1), 80–92. doi: 10.1080/10999922.2016.1257349.

Cialdini, Robert. 2009. *Influence: The Psychology of Persuasion.* New York: HarperCollins.

Cooper, Terry L., and Diane E. Yoder. 2012. "Public Management Ethics Standards in a Transnational World." *Public Integrity* 4(4), 333–52. doi: 10.1080/15580989.2002. 11770926.

Cropanzano, Russell, and Jordan H. Stein. 2009. "Organizational Justice and Behavioral Ethics: Promises and Prospects." *Business Ethics Quarterly* 19(2), 193–233. doi: 10.5840/beq200919211.

DC Bar ProBono Center. 2015. "Conflict of Interest Policies: Disclosure, Monitoring, and Enforcement." *DC Bar ProBono Center.* https://www.probonopartner.org/wp-content/uploads/2016/08/dc-bar-alert-conflict-of-interest-disclosure-10-15.pdf. Accessed July 9, 2019.

Promislo, Mark D., Robert A. Giacalone, and Carole L. Jurkiewicz. 2018. "Ethical Impact Theory: How Unethical Behavior at Work Affects Individual Well-Being," in Ai Farazmand, ed., *Global Encyclopedia of Public Administration.* New York: Springer, 1–5.

Helin, Sven, and Johan Sandstrom. 2008. "Codes, Ethics and Cross-Cultural Differences: Stories from the Implementation of a Corporate Code of Ethics in a MNC Subsidiary." *Journal of Business Ethics* 82(2), 281–91. doi: 10.1007/s10551-008-9887-9.

Jones, Thomas M. 1991. "Ethical Decision Making by Individuals in Organizations: An Issue-Contingent Model." *Academy of Management Review* 16(2), 366–95. doi: 10.2307/258867.

Jurkiewicz, Carole L. 2018. "Big Data, Big Concerns: Ethics in the Digital Age." *Public Integrity* 20(sup1), 46–59. doi: 10.1080/10999922.2018.1448218.

Kahneman, Daniel. 2011. *Thinking Fast and Slow.* New York: Farrar, Straus and Giroux.

Maitlis, Sally, and Scott Sonenshein. 2010. "Sensemaking in Crisis and Change: Inspiration and Insights from Weick (1988)." *Journal of Management Studies* 47(3), 551–80. doi: 10.1111/j.1467-6486.2010.00908.x.

National Council of Nonprofits. 2018. *Conflict of Interest.* https://www.councinprofits.org/tools-resources/conflicts-of-interest. Accessed July 19, 2018.

Newell, Terry. 2012. "Values-Based Leadership for a Democratic Society ," in Terry Newell, Grant Reeher, and Peter Ronayne, eds., *The Trusted Leader: Building the Relationships That Make Government Work.* 2nd ed. Washington, DC: CQ Press, 21–52. doi: 10.4135/9781506335667.

Organization for Economic Cooperation and Development. 2017. *Public Integrity: A Strategy Against Corruption.* Paris: OECD. http://www.oecd.org/gov/ethics/OECD-Recommendation-Public-Integrity.pdf.

Pardes, Arielle. 2018. "What is GDPR and Why Should You Care?" *Wired,* May 24. https://www.wired.com/story/how-gdpr-affects-you/. Accessed July 9, 2019.

Petrick, Joseph A., and John F. Quinn. 2000. "The Integrity Capacity Construct and Moral Progress in Business." *Journal of Business Ethics* 23(1), 3–18. doi: 10.1023/A:1006214726062.

Raadschelders, Jos C. N. 2011. "The Future of the Study of Public Administration: Embedding Research Object and Methodology in Epistemology and Ontology." *Public Administration Review* 71(6), 916–24. doi: 10.1111/j.1540-6210.2011.02433.x.

Rhode, Deborah L., and Amanda K. Packel. 2009. "Ethics and Nonprofits." Retrieved from *Stanford Social Innovation Review:* https://ssir.org/articles/entry/ethics_and_nonprofits. Accessed July 9, 2019.

Richardson, Hayley. 2018. "Instagram Influencer Reportedly Booted from the Louvre for Revealing Outfit." Fox News. November 9. https://www.foxnews.com/travel/instagram-influencer-reportedly-turned-away-from-the-louvre-for-revealing-outfit. Accessed July 9, 2019.

Rohr, John. 1989. *Ethics for Bureaucrats: An Essay on Law and Values.* 2nd ed. New York: Routledge.

Rousseau, Denise M. 1989. "Psychological and Implied Contracts in Organizations." *Employee Responsibilities and Rights Journal* 2(2),121–39. doi: 10.1007/BF01384942.

Schwartz, Mark S. 2016. "Ethical Decision-Making Theory: An Integrated Approach." *Journal of Business Ethics* 139(4), 755–76. doi: 10.1007/s10551-015-2886-8.

Seiler, Stefan, Andreas Fischer, and Sibylle A. Voegtli. 2011. "Developing Moral Decision-Making Competence: A Quasi-Experimental Intervention Study in the Swiss Armed Forces." *Ethics & Behavior* 21(6), 452–70. doi: 10.1080/10508422.2011.622177.

Shapiro, Debra L., and Elad N. Sherf. 2015. "The Role of Conflict in Managing Injustice," in Russell Cropanzano and Maureen L. Ambrose, eds., *Oxford Handbook of Justice in the Workplace.* New York: Oxford University Press, 443–60. Retrieved from https://www.oxfordhandbooks.com/view/10.1093/oxfordhb/9780199981410.001.0001/oxfordhb-9780199981410-e-21.

Stazyk, Edmund C., and Randall S. Davis. 2015. "Taking the 'High Road': Does Public Service Motivation Alter Ethical Decision-Making Processes?." *Public Administration* 93(3), 627–45. doi: 10.1111/padm.12158.

Stone, Jeff, and Gordon B. Moskowitz. 2011. "Non-Conscious Bias in Medical Decision Making: What Can be Done to Reduce It?" *Medical Education* 45(8), 768–76. doi: 10.1111/j.1365-2923.2011.04026.x.

Stout, Margaret, and Jeannine Love. 2013. "Ethical Choice Making." *Public Administration Quarterly 37*(2), 280–96.

Svara, James. 2015. *The Ethics Primer for Public Administrators in Government and Nonprofit Organizations.* 2nd ed. Burlington, MA: Jones & Bartlett Learning.

17

The Ethinomics of Corruption

Carole L. Jurkiewicz

Is corruption the inevitable result of any behavioral cost-benefit analysis? This chapter examines the ethinomics of corruption; rather than a focus only on financial outcomes, the scope of study here is on the ethical welfare resultant from corrupt behavior at both the micro and macro levels. It is predicated on rational choice theory and assesses the value of ethical behavior in organizations for individuals, and for societies as a whole, as a cost-benefit analysis. Beyond doing good in pursuit of intangible benefits, this area of study seeks to quantify the value of ethicality as an area of growing interest in ethics scholarship.

Ethinomics is a relatively new area of study that focuses on the cost of ethical and unethical behavior for individuals, organizations, and societies (Jurkiewicz and Morozov 2012). It assumes that the decision to be ethical or corrupt is a rational choice rooted in personal assessments of costs versus benefits. Rational choice theory is a specific term implying prudence and logic in making choices toward the end of providing the optimal level of utility and satisfaction in pursuit of self-interest, yet in ordinary usage it implies a value judgment inclusive of intelligence, impartiality, judiciousness, sensibility, and reliability. Thus, a caveat that while this chapter affirms that individuals make the choice to be ethical or engage in corrupt activities in seeking to maximize their advantages and minimize their losses, the quality of the judgments made generally fail the standard of perfect utility; in other words, they are often irrational and lacking in self-control (Thaler 2015).

A number of emotional, value-laden, psychological, and physiological elements impede that ideal, as will be discussed here. Administrative decisions, although ostensibly about costs, efficiency, quality, or performance, are each laden at the core with moral judgments rooted in individual ethics; to quote Piaget (1932/1965, 404), "morality is the logic of action." Ethical choices include those of omission and commission, and their effects may be short and/or long-term. Micro-ethinomics addresses the cost–benefit comparison for an individual and those in their immediate sphere of influence. Macro-ethinomics focuses more widely on the ethical impact of decisions on organizations and societies as a whole. The study of ethinomics has further been adapted by legal scholars to address questions of the ethical impacts of legal decisions in establishing precedents and influencing societal shifts (Jurkiewicz 2016).

Defining corruption is a popular sport among many (cf. Rose 2018), and generally centers on issues of cultural relativism and style of government. Rather than continue that debate here, the most common definition will be adopted: "the abuse of entrusted power for private gain" (Transparency International 2017). Corrupt behaviors range from installing individuals to positions of power via illicit use of big data (Jurkiewicz 2018) and bribery to more equivocal forms such as quid pro quo and conflicts of interest; it is asserted here that such behaviors would be classified as unethical. As an individual making the "rational" choice of whether to engage in corruption or not, what are the key considerations in conducting the cost-benefit analysis? There are a few methods by which to analyze this choice, and the first to be considered is Kohlberg's moral development model (Kohlberg 1976, 1981), the most widely sanctioned rubric for understanding ethical decision making (Jurkiewicz 2012).

Cost-Benefit Analysis: Advantage Corruption

To vastly oversimplify an intricate model, Kohlberg asserts there are six stages of ethical decision making, ranging from a simplistic choice to avoid punishment (Stage 1); to increasingly complex levels of following only those rules that confer immediate gain (Stage 2); acting to fulfill the expectations of authority (Stage 3); fulfilling one's social duties (Stage 4); abiding by the social contract, and in consideration of individual rights (Stages 5a and 5b); and, finally, deciding on the basis of principles, or categorical imperatives (Stage 6). Avoiding corruptive choices then, at a minimum, would mean eschewing private gain for the greater good, in accord with one's social duties (Stage 4). Ideally it would extend to making the right decision, even though it may not be popular (Stages 5a/5b), and acting upon considered principles, such as justice, human rights, and respect for the dignity of all (Stage 6). However, most adults generally score at Stage 3 and rarely exceed Stage 4 (Muzumara 2018), which translates into behavioral norms that abide by the letter rather than the spirit of law, and laws rather than ethics, or at most behavior is motivated by the need to fit in and go along with the majority group; less than 2 percent of the population employs principle-based decision making (Jurkiewicz 2012).

In summary, Kohlberg's model suggests that most individuals compute the cost–benefit ratio of ethical vs. corruptive conduct based upon what laws prohibit, rather than on what ethical standards require of them. A clear example is the current president of the United States, as of this writing, who pressures his attorneys to aggressively interpret statutes to provide the legal latitude for his preferred methods of operation (Wendel 2017). Laws and ethics are not synonymous; laws can be contradictory, shift from jurisdiction to jurisdiction, and often declare unethical conduct to be lawful (e.g., slavery, gender and racial discrimination, denial of individual rights). Laws "can never fully obviate the need for certain human virtues" (Nadon 2017). The likelihood that individuals will be charged or prosecuted for corrupt activities is quite small (Cartier-Bresson 1997). Thus, ethinomics in this analysis is more likely to result in corruptive rather than ethical behavior.

Further toward the need of most people to fit in with the majority are studies from a variety of disciplines. From a sociopolitical perspective, obedience to authority can distort judgment and lead to prioritizing feelings of acceptance over ethical regard (Russell 2018). Milgram's classic study on obedience to authority (1974) revealed the psychological dominance of the need to obey over even the most basic of ethical considerations. Political and organizational studies provide substantial evidence that unethicality becomes normative, as such behavior usually goes unchecked and becomes another means of obeying authority and fitting in with the majority (cf. Gorsira, Steg, Denkers, and Huisman 2018; Jurkiewicz 2012b; Gino, Aval, and Ariely 2009); this is especially so for bureaucratic organizational structures (Jurkiewicz and Giacalone 2017). Many individuals report that their own ethical framework often conflicts with the unethical demands of their workplace (Jurkiewicz and Thompson 2000). Adherence to the *omertá* of corrupt systems is enforced through attacks on anyone, as well as their family members, who seeks justice outside the organization (e.g., Trump's attacks on Michael Cohen and his family [Shabad 2019; Earle 2018]), or who become whistleblowers (Chassang and Miquel 2018; ECI 2018).

A sampling of additional studies, as space limitations allow, magnify the evidence for net gain realized through corruption over ethics. Rose-Ackerman (1999) notably demonstrated that unethical and corruptive acts do result in short-term advantages for the perpetrator, financially, professionally, and often-times personally. Ethical multiplicity, wherein individuals may maintain varying ethical and corruptive fronts, enables unethical sleights of hand to be shielded by acts of apparent good (Jurkiewicz 2002a). Corruption becomes easier over time: each corruptive act precipitates the ability to morally disengage, enabling increasingly unethical subsequent behaviors down a proverbial slippery slope (Engelmann and Fehr 2016; Welsh, Ordóñez, Snyder, and Christian 2015; Shu and Gino 2012). Corruptive acts also result in higher levels of self-satisfaction and a boost to one's general positive affect among most individuals (Ruedy, Moore, Gino, and Schweitzer 2013), especially if the actor can configure the corrupt behavior as benefitting others, in the image of Robin Hood (deBock, Vermeir, and Kenhove 2013; Gino, Ayal, and Ariely 2009). Lastly, in this sample, corruptive behavior unleashes creativity in the perpetrator, said to do so because s/he feels freed from standard rules (Gino and Wiltermuth 2014).

Given the abundant body of research documenting the benefits of corruption, and further that most individuals are cognitively predisposed to make ethical decisions based upon the need to obey authority and fit in with the majority, why not acknowledge that corrupt behavior is the norm, as both Hobbes ([1656]2013) and Rousseau ([1762]2018) would implicitly agree in this context, and train individuals to be more corrupt and better at it? The number of individuals advocating such learning programs is by no means small.

Cost-Benefit Analysis: Advantage Ethics

On the other side of the ethical scale are the negative consequences of corrupt behaviors.

Collectively, corruptive behavior causes societal harm and lessens the credibility of public organizations in conducting business, such as tax collection, citizen/government interactions, and judicial oversight (Cordis 2009), and reduces trust in government (Jurkiewicz and Vogel 2015). Further, it can cause environmental damage (Cole 2007), increase costs, and depress economic development (Dearmon and Grier 2011). And just as individuals seek to fit in with the majority, so do jurisdictions, leading to corruptive contagion of adjoining areas (Becker, Eggar, and Seidel 2009; Attila 2008; Goel and Nelson 2007).

Discriminatory policies (Landrine and Klonoff 1996); decreased protection of abused women and children (Schnurr, Friedman, and Bernardy 2002); increased bullying (Krieger 1999); increased crime and professional neglect (Promislo, Giacalone, and Jurkiewicz 2012); and sexual harassment (Fitzgerald, Swan, and Magley 1997), all are resultant from corruption in the public sector and undermine the intent of progressive public policies (Reed, Curtis, and Lovrich, Jr. 2018). Declines in human rights and increases in organized crime and terrorist activities are also concomitant with corruption (Annan 2004). Individual declines in citizen well-being, including anxiety, cardiovascular problems, mental health issues, sleep disorders, and increases in alcohol, tobacco, and drug abuse have all been associated with the corruptive behaviors of administrators (Deckop, Jurkiewicz, and Giacalone 2008). In addition, corruption contributes to increased morbidity (Jackson, Kubzansky, and Wright 2006), not only to those directly disadvantaged but the targets' families and friends as well (Giacalone, Jurkiewicz, and Promislo 2016). Each of these add to, both directly and indirectly, the social and economic costs to individuals, organizations, and societies.

That corruption is bad is a truism, and the negative impacts of corruption are archetypal, consuming time, energy, resources, and a collective conscience. Yet when considered as a cost–benefit analysis, knowing that less than 2 percent of the population operate on principle-based ethical models, as well as the benefits accrued to individuals who behave in a corrupt manner, rational choice theory or bounded rational choice theory both suggest corruption will not only continue, but continue to increase. It's not possible to enact enough laws or punishments to prevent it; if anyone is intent on engaging in unethical behavior, they will find a way.

Corruption in the Balance

Recent work in moral psychology (Dungan, Waytz, and Young 2014) applies corruptive behavior in echoing a framework introduced two decades ago (Jurkiewicz and Brown 2000), suggesting individuals choose from a roster of competing ethical frameworks, often rationalizing their choices by claims of altruism but which actually are in pursuit of

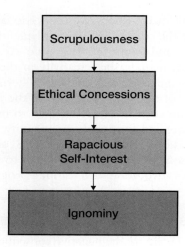

Scrupulousness – Acting to achieve the greatest good for all; operating from principles and considerations of social justice in seeking to uphold rights, integrity, and equity; eschewing personal gain for long-term societal benefit; example: Mahatma Gandhi

Ethical Concessions – Occasionally compromising the greater good by making decisions that satisfice personal advantage to the detriment of the many; periodically displaying deceptive and solipsistic; example: Winston Churchill

Rapacious Self-Interest – Aggressively avaricious, considers decisions as opportunities to maximize self-advantage. Motivated to consider the self/others benefit of all decisions. Concerned about one's reputation, yet moderates it through calculated risk assessments in maximizing personal gain with some restraint with regard to the perceived likelihood of having one's true motivations revealed; example: Richard Nixon

Ignominy – Motivated almost entirely by self-gain, makes decisions based upon self-advantage regardless of the intended purpose of the policy or program. Engages with the intent to conceal one's self-serving behavior and frame it in terms of a greater good or altruistic motive; example: Idi Amin

FIGURE 17.1 The Corruption Continuum

maximizing individual gain. Extending this avenue of inquiry, it is asserted here that a single continuum of ethical/corrupt is no longer viable, and that there may be greater utility in reframing the problem as one of competing interests. Figure 17.1 illustrates the dimensionality of corruption along a continuum.

Behavior here ranges from scrupulousness and descends incrementally to full ignominy. Putting a face on each from the public domain might include Gandhi as Scrupulousness; Churchill as Ethical Concessions; Nixon as Rapacious Self-Interest; and Idi Amin as Ignominy. The progression from one to another is a matter of ethical regression and is largely inevitable as an evolutionary tactic for professional survival. Given that individuals usually act to maximize their personal gain and, by default, base decisions on obedience to authority and on fitting in with their reference group, applying what is known about corruptive restraint to minimize this may be a reasonable approach. The continuum does work in the other direction as well, wherein one can literally step up and demonstrate an ethical progression, but this is rare without effective intervention practices. Being ethical, for most, is a learned behavior that takes both practice and discipline; corruption and increasingly corrupt behavior appears the effortless choice. What works in weighting the calculation more in favor of ethical as opposed to corruptive behavior, toward one end of the continuum than the other? The following four categories have proven the most influential in this regard (Jurkiewicz and Giacalone 2017).

Ethics Education

The principal components of effective ethics education, as detailed by Jurkiewicz (2012), are applied moral philosophy, the ability to identify ethical issues as distinct, logical reasoning, awareness of one's intuitive ethical framework, and an instructor who models the highest levels of ethical reasoning. This approach has significant and empowering long-term positive effects in reducing corruptive behaviors (Jurkiewicz 2002b).

Ethics Audits

Aspects of organizational governance measured in an ethics audit comprise three dimensions: cultural values, organizational governance, and legal compliance (Jurkiewicz and Vogel 2015). Organizational governance entails a systematic review of the organization's missions, goals, and values, followed by the collection and analysis of relevant data. Notwithstanding the need for it to be officially sanctioned by top management and oversight boards, ethics auditors operate independently of them.

Ethical Codes

The existence of an organizational code does not, de facto, make individuals less corrupt; they are in fact generally developed and implemented in reactive ways that actually decrease ethical behavior. Effective ethical codes have three key elements: they emerge from an egalitarian consideration of aspirational values, such as that which emerges from a nominal group technique; they are dynamic and are integrated into strategic planning; and they include clear consequences for transgressions—consequences that are consistently and equitably enforced (Jurkiewicz 2012; Kaptein 2011).

Ethical Leadership

Both ethical and corruptive influence are top-down processes, attributable to those at the top of a hierarchy (Williams and Jurkiewicz 1993). Leadership characteristics that reduce corruptive behaviors include flexibility, trust, respect, accountability, justness, emotional maturity, and benignancy (Jurkiewicz and Giacalone 2016).

Conclusion

Choosing to behave ethically or corruptly usually involves an instinctive cost–benefit analysis that seeks to maximize personal advancement and minimize negative consequences. The key motivators for most individuals in making decisions of ethical import are to avoid punishment, align with authority, and fit in with the majority; such orientations often lead to corruptive activities framed as involuntary capitulation to external or pseudo-altruistic forces. Attempts to address corruption are customarily focused on reactive law-making. Yet without the four modulators that weight ethicality more heavily than corruption, such behavior can be contagious both within and between organizational units. Exempt from knowledge of the ethical consequences of corruptive behavior, any cost–benefit analysis would be unavoidably incomplete. Stanching corruptive behavior thus requires intentional action by the organization, including selecting capable leaders, effectively educating employees, establishing dynamic behavioral codes and enforcing them, and conducting ethics audits. Corruption can never be completely eliminated, as humans are evolutionarily programmed toward self-interest, but such behaviors can be tempered by informed and consistent administrative oversight.

References

Annan, K. 2004. "Foreword." United Nations Convention against Corruption. Vienna: United Nations Office on Drugs and Crime. https://www.unodc.org/documents/brussels/UN_Convention_Against_Corruption.pdf.

Attila, G. 2008. "Is Corruption Contagious? An Econometric Analysis." Department of International Economics. http://ssrn.com/abstract=1275804.

Becker, S. O., P. H. Eggar, and T. Seidel. 2009. "Common Political Culture: Evidence on Regional Corruption Contagion." *European Journal of Political Economy 25*(3), 300–10.

Cartier-Bresson, J. 1997. "Corruption Networks, Transaction Security and Illegal Social Exchange." *Political Studies 45*(3), 463–76.

Chassang, S., and G. P. Miquel. 2018. "Crime, Intimidation, and Whistleblowing: A Theory of Inference from Unverifiable Reports." *Review of Economic Studies.* doi: 10.1093/restud/rdy075.

Chris, R. 2018. "Friendly Governance: Assessing Sociopolitical Factors in Allegations of Corruption." *Public Integrity.* doi: 10.1080/10999922.2018.1446630.

Cole, M. A. 2007. "Corruption, Income, and the Environment: An Empirical Analysis." *Ecological Economics 62*(3–4), 637–47.

Cordis, A. S. 2009. "Judicial Checks on Corruption in the United States." *Economics of Governance 10*(4), 375–401.

De Bock, T., I. Vermeir, and P. Van Kenhove. 2013. "'What's the Harm in Being Unethical? These Strangers are Rich Anyway!' Exploring Underlying Factors of Double Standards." *Journal of Business Ethics 112*(2), 225–40.

Dearmon, J., and R. Grier. 2011. "Trust and the Accumulation of Physical and Human Capital." *European Journal of Political Economy 27*(3), 507–19.

Dungan, J., A. Waytz, and L. Young. 2014. "Corruption in the Context of Moral Trade-offs." *Journal of Interdisciplinary Economics 26*(1 and 2), 97–118.

Earle, G. 2018. "Trump Launches Fresh Attack on Fixer Michael Cohen Saying His Wife and Father-in-Law Were Facing Jail until He Flipped and Claims Payoff Deal with National Enquirer Was NOT a Crime." *Daily Mail UK.* 13 December. Accessed at https://www.dailymail.co.uk/news/article-6493411/Trump-attacks-Cohens-family-claims-payoff-deal-National-Enquirer-NOT-crime.html. Accessed August 7, 2019.

Engelmann, J. B., and E. Fehr. 2016. "The Slippery Slope of Dishonesty." *Nature Neuroscience 19*(12), 1543–44. Accessed August 7, 2019.

Ethics and Compliance Initiative (ECI). 2018. *Global Business Ethics Survey.* Accessed https://www.ethics.org/download-the-2018-global-business-ethics-survey/. Accessed August 7, 2019.

Fitzgerald, L. F., S. Swan, and V. J. Magley. 1997. "But Was It Really Sexual Harassment? Legal, Behavioral, and Psychological Definitions of the Workplace Victimization of Women," in W. O'Donohue, ed., *Sexual Harassment: Theory, Research and Treatment.* Boston: Allyn & Bacon.

Giacalone, R. A., C. L. Jurkiewicz, and J. Deckop. 2008. "On Ethics and Social Responsibility: The Impact of Materialism, Postmaterialism, and Hope." *Human Relations 61*, 483–514.

Giacalone, R. A., C. L. Jurkiewicz, and M. D. Promislo, 2016. "Ethics and Well-Being: The Paradoxical Implications of Individual Differences in Ethical Orientation." *Journal of Business Ethics 137*(3), 491–506.

Gino, F., S. Ayal, and D. Ariely. 2013. "Self-Serving Altruism? The Lure of Unethical Actions that Benefit Others." *Journal of Economic Behavior & Organization 93*(September), 285–92. doi: 0.1016/j.jebo.2013.04.005.

Gino, F., S. Ayal, and D. Ariely. 2009. "Contagion and Differentiation in Unethical Behavior: The Effect of One Bad Apple on the Barrel." *Psychological Science 20*(3), 393–98.

Gino, F., and S. S. Wiltermuth. 2014. "Evil Genius? How Dishonesty Can Lead to Greater Creativity." *Psychological Science 25*(4), 973–81. doi: 10.1177/0956797614520714.

Goel, R. K., and M. A. Nelson. 2007. "Are Corrupt Acts Contagious? Evidence from the United States." *Journal of Policy Modeling 29*, 839–50.

Gorsira, M., L. Steg, A. Denkers, and W. Huisman. 2018. "Corruption in Organizations: Ethical Climate and Individual Motives." *Administrative Sciences 8*(4).

Hobbes, T. 1656/2013. *Leviathan by Thomas Hobbes.* New York: Cambridge University Press.

Jackson, B., L. D. Kubzansky, and R. J. Wright. 2006. "Linking Perceived Unfairness to Physical Health: The Perceived Unfairness Model." *Review of General Psychology 10*(1), 21–40.

Jurkiewicz, C. L. 2016. "Ethinomics," in D. Bearfield and M. Dubnick, eds., *Encyclopedia of Public Administration and Public Policy.* 3rd ed., 1332–34. New York: Taylor & Francis.

Jurkiewicz, C. L. 2012a. "Advancing Ethical Competency through Pedagogy," in T. L Cooper and D. C. Menzel, eds. *Achieving Ethical Competence for Public Service Leadership.* Armonk, NY: M. E. Sharpe. Accessed August 7, 2019.

Jurkiewicz, C. L. 2012b. *The Foundations of Organizational Evil.* Armonk, NY: M. E. Sharpe.

Jurkiewicz, C. L. 2002a. "The Phantom Code of Ethics and Public Sector Reform." *Journal of Public Affairs and Issues 6*(3), 1–19.

Jurkiewicz, C. L. 2002b. "The Influence of Pedagogical Style on Students' Level of Ethical Reasoning." *Journal of Public Affairs Education 8*(4), 263–74.

Jurkiewicz, C. L., and R. G. Brown. 2000. "The P/E Ratio that Really Counts." *Journal of Power and Ethics 1*(3), 172–95.

Jurkiewicz, C. L., and R. A. Giacalone. 2017. "You Can Lead a Man to Oughta, But You Can't Make Him Think: The Disparity between Knowing What Is Right and Doing It," in C. L. Jurkiewicz and R. A. Giacalone, eds., *Radical Thoughts on Ethical Leadership.* Greenwich, CT: Information Age Publishing.

Jurkiewicz, C. L., and Giacalone, R. A. 2016. "Organizational Determinants of Ethical Dysfunctionality." *Journal of Business Ethics 136*(1), 1–12.

Jurkiewicz, C. L., and Thompson, C. R. 2000. "Conflicts of Interest: Organizational vs. Individual Ethics in Healthcare Administration." *Journal of Health and Human Services Administration, 23*(1), 100–23.

Jurkiewicz, C. L., and Vogel, G. M. 2015. "The Ethics Audit: Measuring the Effectiveness of Ethics Education across the Sectors." *Journal of Management Systems 25*(2), 1041–2808.

Kaptein, M. 2011. "Understanding Unethical Behavior by Unraveling Ethical Culture." *Human Relations 64*(6), 843–69.

Kohlberg, L. 1981. *Philosophy of Moral Development.* New York: Harper & Row.

Kohlberg, L. 1976. "Moral Stages and Moralization: The Cognitive-Developmental Approach," in T. Lickona, ed., *Moral Development and Behavior.* New York: Holt, Rinehart & Winston.

Landrine, H., and E. A. Klonoff, 1996. "The Schedule of Racist Events: A Measure of Racial Discrimination and a Study of its Negative Physical and Mental Health Consequences." *Journal of Black Psychology 22*(2), 144–68.

Milgram, S. 1974. *Obedience to Authority: An Experimental View.* New York: Harper & Row.

Muzumara, P. M. 2018. *Ethics, Morals and Values in Education.* Pittsburgh: Dorrance Publishing.

Nadon, C. 2017. "Self-Restraint in the Executive." *The Weekly Standard,* 17 March. Accessed at https://www.weeklystandard.com/christopher-nadon/self-restraint-in-the-executive.

Piaget, J. 1932/1965. *The Moral Judgment of the Child.* M. Gabain, trans. New York: Free Press.

Promislo, M. D., R. A. Giacalone, and C. L. Jurkiewicz. 2012. "Ethical Impact Theory (EIT): Unethical Work Behavior and Well-Being," in R. A. Giacalone and M. Promislo, eds., *The Handbook of Unethical Behavior and Well-being.* Armonk, NY: M. E. Sharpe.

Rose, J. 2018 "The Meaning of Corruption: Testing the Coherence and Adequacy of Corruption Definitions." *Public Integrity 20*(3), 220–33.

Rose-Ackerman, S. 1999. *Corruption and Government: Causes, Consequences, and Reform.* New York: Cambridge University Press.

Rousseau, J. 1762/1997. *Rousseau: The Social Contract and Other Later Political Writings.* New York: Cambridge University Press.

Ruedy, N. E., C. Moore, F. Gino, and M. E. Schweitzer. 2013. "The Cheater's High: The Unexpected Affective Benefits of Unethical Behavior." *Journal of Personality and Social Psychology 105*(4), 531–48.

Russell, C. 2018. "Friendly Governance: Assessing Sociopolitical Factors in Allegations of Corruption." *Public Integrity 21*(2), 195–213. doi: 10.1080/10999922.2018.1446630.

Ryan, R., C. Curtis, and N. P. Lovrich Jr. 2018. "Does Democracy Entail an Obligation to Make Rational Policy Decisions? The Muddling through vs. Bounded Rationality Debate through a Lockean and Madisonian Lens." *Public Integrity.* doi: 10.1080/10999922.2018.1518557.

Schnurr, P. P., M. J. Friedman, and N. C. Bernardy. 2002. "Research on Posttraumatic Stress Disorder: Epidemiology, Pathophysiology, and Assessment." *Journal of Clinical Psychology 58*(8), 877–89.

Shabad, R. 2019. "Michael Cohen Says Trump's 'Threats against His Family' Will Delay His Testimony before the House." *NBC News.* 23 January. Accessed at https://www.nbcnews.com/politics/congress/michael-cohen-says-trump-s-threats-against-his-family-will-n961816.

Shu, L. L., and F. Gino. 2012. "Sweeping Dishonesty under the Rug: How Unethical Actions Lead to Forgetting of Moral Rules." *Journal of Personality and Social Psychology 102*(6), 1164–77.

Thaler, R. H. 2015. *Misbehaving: The Making of Behavioral Economics.* London: Allen Lane.

Transparency International 2017. *What Is Corruption?* Retrieved from https://www.transparency.org/what-iscorruption.

Welsh, D. T., L. D. Ordóñez, D. G. Snyder, and M. S. Christian. 2015. "The Slippery Slope: How Small Ethical Transgressions Pave the Way for Larger Future Transgressions." *Journal of Applied Psychology 100*(1): 114–27. doi: 10.1037/a0036950.

Wendel, W. 2017. "Government Lawyers in the Trump Administration." *Hastings Law Journal 69*(275). Accessed at http://www.hastingslawjournal.org/wp-content/uploads/Wendel-69.1.pdf. Accessed August 7, 2019.

Williams, A. R., and Jurkiewicz, C. L. 1993. "In God We Trust ... All Others Pay Cash: Trust, Vulnerability, and Deceit in Professional Organizations." *Business & Professional Ethics Journal 12*(2), 67–96.

18

Facing the Dark Side
On the Unintended, Unanticipated, and Unwelcome Consequences of Ethics Management

Jeroen Maesschalck

The idea that the ethics or integrity of public administrators can, at least partly, be managed has a long history in public administration, going back to seminal work of Max Weber, Woodrow Wilson, and others. Yet, the framing of "ethics management" as a separate domain in public administration is a more recent phenomenon. Indeed, more and more research confirms that ethics management interventions (e.g., ethics codes, ethics training, whistle-blowing arrangements) can help to reduce unethical behavior and to improve the quality of the ethical decision making of administrators. Yet, as with all management interventions, there is also a potential "dark side" to these interventions. With dark side, we refer to "bad surprises" (6 2010, 53): consequences of ethics management interventions that are unintended, unanticipated, and unwelcome (Margretts, 6, and Hood 2010). This chapter addresses these bad surprises, particularly focusing on the "perverse consequences" (Hirschman 1991): those consequences that are the exact opposite of what the intervention originally intended. As this chapter intends to show, some well-meant ethics management interventions might indeed increase unethical behavior and weaken the quality of staff members' ethical decision making.

The chapter is organized around five roads to the dark side of ethics management, which can also be seen as five lines of critique of ethics management. The chapter argues that each of these lines of critique are, at least to some extent, justified. Thus, the chapter is not about unfounded excuses used by managers and others to avoid taking necessary ethics management measures; those have been addressed elsewhere (e.g., Maesschalck and Bertok 2009, 18–20). The first two roads to the dark side of ethics management are (1) not taking ethics management seriously enough, and (2) applying flawed ethics management. These have received ample attention in the existing ethics management literature. In fact, most of the that literature can be read as a discussion of ways in which to avoid those two roads. The other three roads to the dark side have received much less attention in the ethics management literature: (3) taking ethics management too seriously, (4) taking ethics too seriously, and (5) ignoring the power dimension of ethics management. Particularly these three latter critiques offer an invitation to all of us involved in the "ethics industry" to take a critical look in the mirror. As is argued in this chapter, an understanding of these roads will strengthen the self-reflection one can expect from ethics researchers and what henceforth is described as "ethics practitioners" (e.g., ethics officer, ethics consultant, manager supervising the introduction of ethics management). The chapter concludes with the argument that this kind of sensitivity to unintended, unanticipated, and unwelcome consequences of ethics management and, hence, to its dark side will help to improve and thus strengthen rather than to weaken ethics management.

Not Taking Ethics and Ethics Management Seriously

The first road to the dark side occurs when managers do take some ethics management initiatives but without taking them seriously. There are at least two manifestations of this road, that is, two ways in which doing ethics management without taking it seriously can bring about unintended, unanticipated, and unwelcome consequences.

First, probably the best-known version of this road is ethics management as a window-dressing, public-relations exercise. This occurs, for example, when a new ethics code is announced in attractive external communications, but no serious efforts are taken to discuss it internally. Another instance is the situation in which an ethics officer is appointed in the organization, not with a mandate to actually change something, but only with a kind of ritualized "devil's-advocate" role. She is allowed to do a little performance now and then to point at some ethics issues, after which it is all back to work and nothing really changed. Such interventions can be very damaging, because they strengthen cynicism about ethics and ethics management. Those in the organization who are serious about ethics and were hoping for real support in dealing with ethical dilemmas or were hoping that unethical behavior by colleagues would finally be addressed, feel even more alone than before. Managers who think that ethics management as window dressing is harmless and good marketing, should think again.

A second manifestation occurs when ethics measures are introduced purely to satisfy bureaucratic requirements, to tick the boxes of a checklist. An example of this is a superficial "ethics workshop" required by the auditor that does not really address anything of relevance to daily practice. Another example is a whistle-blowing system required by the law that nobody knows about and nobody dares to use. Such interventions only serve to increase cynicism.

For well-meaning managers, it should be easy to avoid the first manifestation. The second manifestation is somewhat more challenging to avoid. Regulators, auditors, or clients can sometimes require particular interventions that managers honestly think to be useless. In many cases, with some creativity those interventions can be turned into something useful and appropriate for the context of the organization. In those cases where this is not possible, it will probably be best to invest only the minimum of means to satisfy the requirements and use the means available for interventions that are more useful.

Applying Flawed Ethics Management

Practical experience and scholarly research both have generated an impressive body of knowledge on the many instruments of ethics management and their effectiveness (e.g., Huberts 2014, 167–97; Treviño and Weaver 2003; Waples, Antes, Murphy, Connelly, and Mumford 2009). This knowledge offers useful insights that, regrettably, are still often overlooked in practice. This results in flawed ethics management interventions, which generate unintended, unanticipated, and unwelcome consequences. This second road to the dark side of ethics management can be observed at at least two levels of analysis.

Sometimes the flaws occur at the level of specific instruments of ethics management. Two such flaws deserve some discussion here. First, a very common flaw is to shape and/or implement instruments of ethics management only half-heartedly. An illustration of this is a half-hearted attempt to establish a whistleblowing policy. For such a policy to be effective, it needs not only reporting channels, but also proper protection for those using those channels and ethical as well as competent investigators to receive and handle what has been reported. It is not difficult to see how damaging a system is that establishes reporting channels but does not ensure sufficient whistleblower protection nor investigation capacity. This might lead to disastrous consequences, not only for the unprotected whistleblower, but also for those who might be wrongfully accused, as well as for the overall trust within the organization. Second, another common flaw is to introduce an instrument of ethics management without ensuring that the conditions for it to be successful are properly met. An illustration of this is the introduction of deliberative ethics training (which requires participants to openly debate their doubts and mistakes) in a learning group where there is insufficient psychological safety (Edmondson 1999; Sims 2004). In such a context, the training could become very damaging. The trainees' fear of the consequences of being honest might turn the training into a hypocritical pretense where only socially desirable answers are given (e.g., "we never accept any gifts from citizens, not even of the smallest value"). Participants would leave this training feeling more lonely in facing ethical dilemmas, more cynical about the effectiveness of ethics training, and more convinced that hypocrisy is the right strategy in their organization.

Sometimes the flaws do not occur at the level of individual instruments of ethics management, but at level of the overall approach. Arguably one of the most widely shared recommendations in the "what works" literature on ethics management is that different approaches should be combined. The most classic distinction of approaches is between the rules-based (or compliance-based) and values-based approaches (Cooper 2006; Paine 1994). The former approach emphasizes extensive formal controls that reduce individual administrators' discretion: detailed rules, extensive procedures to monitor the observance of these rules, and strict and powerful enforcement for those who break the rules. The values-based approach, instead, allows for significant discretion and offers support for staff members to use that discretion in an ethically competent way: ethics training that emphasizes moral imagination, coaching, frequent deliberation about ethical dilemmas, aspirational codes of ethics (rather than detailed codes of conduct), and so forth (e.g., Cooper 2006; Maesschalck 2004; Paine 1994).

Each of these approaches has its own dark side. When an organization allows the rules-based approach to develop unabatedly, it will weaken moral competence (and particularly moral imagination) of its staff, undermine employee morale, stimulate soulless rule-fetishism and rigidity, generate increasingly complex layers of rules and exceptions, and so forth. Of course, the values-based approach has its own dark side as well. An organization with only the values-based approach would exhibit indecisiveness because of endless discussions, risk to treat citizens unequally because of the power left to individual administrators, be exposed to the risk of individual administrators abusing their discretion to their individual advantage, and so forth. There has been some debate over the value of this twofold distinction (e.g., Maesschalck 2004), but most authors agree that each of the separate approaches will generate its own excesses if the approach is allowed to grow unabatedly. Ensuring a sufficient degree of each of the approaches allows them to compensate for each other's weaknesses and blind spots. Thus, the rule-fetishism and rigidity of the rules-based approach will be alleviated by the discretion and strengthened moral imagination that follow from the values-based approach. Likewise, cunning administrators' abuse of a naïve form of the values-based approach can be prevented by having at least a minimum of the rules, monitoring, and enforcement that are typical for the rules-based approach. Thus, the recommendation to ensure some kind of context-sensitive balance between the two approaches offers a way to block the road to the dark sides of the values-based and rules-based approaches.

In theory, this second road to the dark side of ethics management should be easy for ethics practitioners to avoid. The growing literature on what works in ethics management provides useful advice on how to avoid flaws of specific ethics management instruments. It also offers many useful illustrations of how different approaches to ethics management can be combined so as to allow them to compensate for each other's deficiencies. In practice, however, it turns out to be difficult to actually apply all this advice. This partly has to do with limited time, expertise, or budget to design and implement ethics management properly. While these limitations are understandable, ethics practitioners should be aware that quick-and-dirty solutions are usually not the best way to cope with these limitations. In fact, as shown in the discussion of the previous road, they might make matters much worse. Another reason for the fact that flawed design and implementation of ethics management is not uncommon has to do with the "what works" literature on ethics management itself. This literature sometimes suggests a degree of certainty that is unwarranted by research, and its recommendations sometimes overlook the importance of context sensitivity. In this respect, a lot of work is still to be done by researchers (Huberts 2014).

Taking Ethics Management Too Seriously

Perhaps somewhat counterintuitively, taking ethics management too seriously can also generate unintended, unanticipated, and unwelcome consequences. This third road towards the dark side particularly concerns the institutionalization of ethics management. More and more organizations install a full-time or part-time ethics officer, an ethics network, or even an ethics bureau. Combined with a growing group of external consultants (including, of course, academics) this now constitutes an "ethics industry" (e.g., Huberts 2014, 9). These developments have a number of advantages. Appointing an ethics officer ensures attention for ethics even when attention is waning after initial enthusiasm, allows for better coordination of the different ethics management instruments, and permits the accumulation of expertise (Maesschalck 2010). Yet, it also creates a number of risks, particularly because of compartmentalization. As a separate field with its own professionals, ethics management tends to develop its own jargon, its own models, and its own instruments, tempting ethics practitioners to succumb to tunnel vision. This might lead to the development of instruments that are not coordinated with instruments from other adjacent fields (e.g., personnel management, quality management, health and safety) and that also have the risk of becoming aloof from the daily working life of those they are supposed to help and support.

Within organizations, these risks can be to a large extent reduced by technical and structural interventions. These could be coordination mechanisms (e.g., regular meetings, rotating staff) between the ethics office and other departments as well as arrangements to bring the ethics officers closer to the street-level administrators (e.g., the ethics officer could coordinate an "ethics network" of staff spread across the organization). While useful, these technical interventions will not be enough. This third road to the dark side of ethics also calls for a sensitivity to the risks of biases. These biases could be the result of material, reputational, and other interests. Indeed, advocates' enthusiasm for the ethics training they offer might simply be the consequence of the money and reputation it offers them. Biases could also be of a more cognitive and often more unobtrusive nature. To someone whose job focuses on ethics management, most problems will start looking like ethical problems that need an answer from ethics management. Without a self-reflective attitude, these biases could combine to bring about an unquestioning conviction that there never is enough ethics management (Bovens 2006). This paragraph showed that this is a road to the dark side that can and should be avoided.

Taking Ethics Too Seriously

Implementing ethics management self-evidently implies taking ethics seriously. Indeed, many ethics management approaches aim to raise ethical awareness and sensitivity among administrators. While this emphasis on ethics is in many cases desirable, it could also produce unintended, unanticipated, and unwelcome consequences and thus open a fourth road to the dark side. However, before addressing that road, it is important to clarify what should not be considered the effect of taking ethics too seriously: that is, rigidity and paralysis.

Some might argue that the emphasis on ethics leads to a fear of making mistakes and thus to rigidity and paralysis. The emphasis on ethics, the argument goes, contrasts with the realities of modern public administration, which require flexibility, some pragmatism in dealing with rules and laws, and a certain degree of risk taking. The fallacy in this reasoning is to think that rigidity and paralysis are the consequence of taking ethics too seriously, while in fact they are the consequence of taking the rules-based approach of ethics management too seriously and ignoring the values-based approach. When, alternatively, ethics is taken seriously in a values-based fashion, this is anything but rigidity- and paralysis-inducing. In fact, the values-based approach explicitly allows for rule breaking and risk taking, albeit on the condition that decisions to do so are taken carefully, with consequences, values, and other ethical considerations in mind. The values-based approach aims at avoiding rigidity and paralysis by stimulating moral imagination, flexibility, and creativity. Thus, when one observes rigidity and paralysis as a consequence of paying attention to ethics, the answer is not to pay less attention to ethics, but to introduce ethics management that compensates for the excesses of the rules-based approached with a better developed values-based approach.

Having established that rigidity and paralysis are not the effect of paying too much attention to ethics, we can now turn to the problematic phenomenon that can follow when ethics is taken too seriously: *integritism* (Huberts 2014, 62–65). It has two manifestations with almost opposite effects.

The first manifestation occurs when (almost) all norms and values acquire an ethical connotation. With some flexibility, one can indeed stretch the meaning of ethics to such an extent that it covers a very broad range of behaviours such as laziness, having bad taste in clothing, inefficient time management, not listening to constituencies, and so forth. While all these behaviours show deviance from norms or values, it is questionable whether those norms or values are all to be considered ethical. Indeed, if all issues are translated into ethical terms, if all values and norms are considered ethical, then ethics loses its distinctive character. Saying that something is ethical then becomes an almost hollow statement. This manifestation of integritism thus results in a trivialization of ethics: if everything is (un)ethical, then nothing is (un)ethical.

The second manifestation of integritism occurs when ethics is really taken seriously and becomes pervasive in the organization. Issues, problems, and debates are all very quickly framed as ethical in nature. This results in the opposite of the trivialization of ethics. It sets in motion various unintended, but potentially very damaging, dynamics. One of these dynamics has famously been described at societal level by the political theorist Chantal Mouffe in her critique of what she observes as the contemporary replacement of political discourse by moral discourse (e.g., Mouffe 2002). A similar dynamic could also occur at the organizational level. When differences in opinion are phrased in ethical terms, there is a risk that they turn into an ethical reproach not only of the other opinion but also of those defending that opinion. Hence, our colleagues with a different view on what the main goal of our organization should be are not simply colleagues with a different view. They are *unethical* colleagues, to be contrasted with us as *ethical* colleagues. This in turn could set in motion mechanisms of exclusion of those who are seen as unethical. As such, the efforts of proponents of ethics management to increase ethical awareness might inadvertently increase the risks of scapegoating and bullying.

Some might argue that, in many cases, these risks are irrelevant. Many ethics practitioners are still working hard to raise ethical awareness and do not have the luxury of wondering about the effects of too much ethical awareness. Overlooking this risk is a mistake, however. Both risks are very real and ethics practitioners should be aware of them and look for ways to avoid them. They should cultivate a degree of self-restraint (not everything is ethical) and a sensitivity for the risks of framing issues and discussions in ethical terms.

Ignoring the Power Dimension of Ethics Management

Ethics management interventions often have an impact on the distribution of power in an organization. Some of these effects are intended and welcome; others are not. Those who ignore the power dimension of ethics management risk traveling this fifth road to the dark side of ethics management. The work of the French philosopher Michel Foucault, among others, has inspired analyses of ethics management as a way to discipline staff members, ensuring "a subjugation of morality to power" (Crane, Knights, and Starkey 2008, 302). "The disciplinary power of the ordering, categorization and ritualization of daily activities … rewards conformity and penalizes resistance in order to impose and enforce norms of behavior" (Crane et al. 2008, 302). Ethics management then becomes a tool for (self-)surveillance of employees. This is most obvious with ethics management that emphasizes the rules-based approach. It reduces discretion and establishes an extensive system for monitoring and control. A good values-based approach should help to avoid this. By increasing discretion, emphasizing moral responsibility, and stimulating moral imagination, it should actually empower staff members. However, even the values-based approach can be used to increase the power of the powerful rather than empower those in the lower levels of the hierarchy. Helin, Jensen, Sandström, and Clegg (2011), for example, report on a case study of an ethics code that was intended to create a common values base and encourage dialogue, but that was used in practice to recalibrate power relations in the organization. More generally, Stansbury and Barry (2007) argue that not only rules-based but also values-based interventions can lead to indoctrination, that is, the "learned unwillingness to consider the relative limitations of a system of thought, based on the authority of the teacher of that system" (248).

While the more academic versions of this critical approach might be less useful for ethics practitioners in daily life, it does represent an important perspective. Self-reflective ethics practitioners should be sensitive to the impact their interventions have on power relations. This refers to the often very obvious power implications of their rules-based interventions, but also to the more subtle indoctrinating implications of their values-based interventions. While some of those implications might be intended and welcome, others are not.

Conclusion

This chapter addressed the dark side of ethics management: its unintended, unanticipated and unwelcome consequences. In a discussion of the five roads to this dark side, it presented many painful examples of such "bad surprises." More generally, all these problematic consequences can also undermine the legitimacy of ethics management itself, because they might generate a feeling of futility and fatalism about the very possibility of ethics management making a difference. Hence, anyone believing in the importance of ethics and the effectiveness of ethics management should, perhaps somewhat paradoxically, take this dark side seriously.

How can this be done? The answer certainly is not to simply do away with ethics management or to do "less" ethics management. This would go against all the research that showed the beneficial effects of ethics management. Instead, this chapter argued for a self-reflective attitude of ethics practitioners. Such an attitude implies not only an awareness of each of these five roads, but also the development of an expertise in ways to avoid these roads. The discussion above already suggested some ways to do so for each of the five roads. First, ethics practitioners should be aware of the damaging consequences of ethics management as mere window-dressing or ticking audit boxes. Second, ethics practitioners should rely on research and expertise so as to apply ethics management instruments in a correct and context-sensitive way, and they should look for the right balance between the rules-based and values-based approaches. Ethics researchers should help them by offering more nuanced and context-sensitive advice on "what works." Third, ethics practitioners should use coordination and other mechanisms to avoid compartmentalization of ethics management. They should also be aware of the biases that might lead them to see ethics management as the solution to virtually any problem. Fourth, ethics managers should develop a sense of self-restraint and be mindful of the two risks of taking ethics too seriously: trivializing ethics by considering everything as ethics, and initiating exclusion mechanisms and other destructive dynamics. Fifth, ethics practitioners should be sensitive to the impact of their interventions on power relations. All these are examples of the self-reflective attitude one can expect from ethics practitioners. In fact, at risk of offering an illustration of the fourth road to the dark side, one could argue that this self-reflective attitude is not only their practical, but also their ethical responsibility.

While this chapter was mainly addressed at ethics practitioners, its observations are also very relevant for researchers. Obviously, researchers are not immune to the biases and dynamics that are described in this chapter, particularly when they are ethics management enthusiasts. The self-reflective attitude described above is at least as important for researchers as it is for ethics practitioners. Moreover, the examples in this chapter could inspire a broader and more systematic research agenda on the dark side of ethics management. How do these roads to the dark side look in practice? Do the dynamics and mechanisms described above actually occur? What are the conditions that can propel or block these dynamics? Such an agenda could address ethics management within organizations, as was done in this chapter, but it is not difficult to find examples of at least some of these dynamics at the level of the public sector as a whole or of the broader system in a national or international context. Those also deserve further research.

References

6, P. 2010. "When Forethought and Outturn Part: Types of Unanticipated and Unintended Consequences," in H. Margetts, P. 6, and C. Hood, eds., *Paradoxes of Modernization. Unintended Consequences of Public Policy Reform.* Oxford: Oxford University Press, 44–60.

Bovens, M. 2006. "Het ongelijk van Ien Dales; over de onbedoelde negatieve effecten van het integriteitsbeleid." *Bestuurskunde 15*(1), 64–74.

Cooper, T. L. 2006. *The Responsible Administrator: An Approach to Ethics for the Administrative Role.* 5th ed. San Francisco: Jossey-Bass.

Crane, A., D. Knights, and K. Starkey. 2008. "The Conditions of Our Freedom: Foucault, Organization, and Ethics." *Business Ethics Quarterly 18*(3), 299–320. doi: 10.5840/beq200818324.

Edmondson, A. 1999. "Psychological Safety and Learning Behavior in Work Teams." *Administrative Science Quarterly 44*(2), 350–83. doi: 10.2307/2666999.

Helin, S., T. Jensen, J. Sandström, and S. Clegg. 2011. "On the Dark Side of Codes: Domination Not Enlightenment." *Scandinavian Journal of Management 27*(1), 24–33. doi: 10.1016/j. scaman.2010.12.001.

Hirschman, A. O. 1991. *The Rhetoric of Reaction.* Cambridge, MA: Harvard University Press.

Huberts, L. 2014. *The Integrity of Governance: What It Is, What We Know, What Is Done and Where to Go.* Houndmills: Palgrave Macmillan.

Maesschalck, J. 2004. "Approaches to Ethics Management in the Public Sector. A Proposed Extension of the Compliance-Integrity Continuum." *Public Integrity 7*(1), 21–41. doi: 10.1080/10999922.2004.11051267.

Maesschalck, J. 2010. "Nut en Noodzaak van Integriteit als Apart Beleidsdomein," in S. Verheij and E. Karssing, eds., *Jaarboek Integriteit 2011.* Den Haag: Bureau Integriteitsbevordering Openbare Sector, 44–53.

Maesschalck, J., and J. Bertok. 2009. *Towards a Sound Integrity Framework: Instruments, Processes, Structures and Conditions for Implementation*. Paris: Organisation for Economic Co-operation and Development.

Margretts, H., P. 6, and C. Hood, eds. 2010. *Paradoxes of Modernization. Unintended Consequences of Public Policy Reform*. Oxford: Oxford University Press.

Mouffe, C. 2002. "Which Public Sphere for a Democratic Society?" *Theoria* 49(99), 55–65. doi: 10.3167/004058102782485448.

Paine, L. S. 1994. "Managing for Organizational Integrity." *Harvard Business Review* 72(2), 106–17.

Sims, R. R. 2004. "Business Ethics Teaching: Using Conversational Learning to Build an Effective Classroom Learning Environment." *Journal of Business Ethics* 49(2), 201–11. doi: 10.1023/B:BUSI.0000015782.99051.d4.

Stansbury, J., and Barry, B. 2007. "Ethics Programs and the Paradox of Control." *Business Ethics Quarterly* 17(2), 239–61. doi: 10.5840/beq200717229.

Treviño, L. K., and G. R. Weaver. 2003. *Managing Ethics in Business Organizations: Social Scientific Perspective*. Stanford: Stanford Business Books.

Waples, E. P., A. L. Antes, S. T. Murphy, S. Connelly, and M. D. Mumford 2009. "A Meta-Analytic Investigation of Business Ethics Instruction." *Journal of Business Ethics* 87(1), 133–51. doi: 10.1007/s10551-008-9875-0.

19

Organizational Evil

Yahong Zhang and Cheon Lee

What Is Organizational Evil?

Evil refers to negative behaviors with culpable intention and destructive consequence. It manifests not only at the individual level, but also at the organizational level through organizational culture, which develops a set of morals and values that define the organization as separate from others. Organizational culture serves as a boundary-defining function by telling employees what is acceptable and expected of them at work (Jurkiewicz and Grossman 2015). An ethical organization would possess a positive culture that values social justice, equity, transparency, and so forth. On the contrary, an evil culture would praise evil actions that bring harm to other individuals, organizations, or the public as a whole.

According to Jurkiewicz and Grossman, organizational evil is "the institutionalization of a set of principles whose purpose is knowingly to harm individuals, with disregard for consequences beyond those that would cause immediate repercussions to the evil-doer" (2015, 3). Organizational evil appears when the evil culture prevails and dominates over the ethical culture in an organization; when top-level managers implement evil policies and practices; and when individual unethical behaviors are diffused among individuals in an organization. An organization is categorized as evil "when the majority of the policies, practices, programs, and reward systems that comprise its organizational culture intentionally cause harm to others, internal or external to the organization, as a means of obtaining a short-term organizational advantage" (Jurkiewicz and Grossman 2015, 4).

Organizational Evil in the Private Sector

Unlike in the public sector, private organizations confront the pressures of market competition and the threats of business failure. In order to generate profits and to survive in market competition, some companies—often with the approval from top-level management—make unethical decisions that have a negative impact on others. Examples of evil acts are deliberately forging financial statements, fabricating important test results, and neglecting required safety measures in order to cut down their operating costs. Campbell and Göritz (2014) explain that people accept organizational evil under three assumptions: "the end justifying the means," the value of "security," and the fact that employees are punished for deviant behavior. When an organization's leaders perceive themselves as fighting in a tough competition within the market, they may degrade positive values such as fairness and sustainability. Unethical behaviors thus become an attractive behavioral alternative under the name of the necessity for survival. In order to justify corrupt unethical behaviors, the organization may present "a win-win situation" to its employees—employees cooperate with the tenets of organizational evil, and thus attain benefits for their organization, which in turn ensures their job security. The "win-win" relationship between the organization and employees may further enhance the perception that all employees in the organization constitute a community sharing the same fate, and that the members who fail to collaborate will harm this community and thus should be punished. Influenced by the fear of punishment, employees will be more likely to collude, and organizational evil is thus reinforced.

Organizational evil in private organizations brings about negative consequences in many areas. First, it places their stockholders at risk. When organizational evil is exposed and then creates huge scandals, the stockholders will inevitably lose their monetary investment in the company. For instance, the bankruptcy of Lehman Brothers in 2008 led to more than $46 billion of its market value being immediately wiped out (Lioudis 2017). In such cases, top-level management of the organization should take the responsibility, because they have failed to fulfill their duties as agents of the stockholders. Second, organizational evil places customers at risk as well. Evil organizations may produce harmful products in order to maximize profit at the expense of customers' physical health, or even their lives. A recent scandal in China reveals that Changsheng Biotechnology—the nation's second-largest producer of rabies vaccines—forged the production and inspection data of rabies vaccines. This case is quite similar to the China milk scandal in 2008 in which melamine-laced powdered milk produced by several companies killed six babies and caused 54,000 others to be admitted to medical facilities after suffering kidney damage (Murphy 2018). Organizational evil in these cases has caused fatal damage to infants, as well as to other children who will suffer from the damages for their entire lives. In addition, organizational evil in the private sector destroys fair competition in a free market and undermines the fundamental principles of capitalism.

Organizational Evil in the Public Sector

Organizations in the public sector do not face market competition or threats to their survival. However, organizational evil does exist in public organizations as well. Oftentimes, public organizations institutionalize organizational evil in the name of the public interest. National governments can be vile and evil to their citizens and to other nations. For example, declarations of war and other military provocations against other countries may put many lives in danger in the name of the national interest. When organizational evil at the national level causes harm to others, the result can be catastrophic. Nazi Germany started the Second World War by invading Poland in 1939, causing fifty million or more deaths when including deaths caused by war-related famine and disease. The Holocaust resulted in the murder of approximately six million European Jews. Countries such as North Korea and Iraq have been ruled by dictators who massacred and oppressed their own citizens by evil principles that cannot be easily overthrown by individual citizens. The North Korean government forced its citizens to spy on each other and to report any anti-government opinions to the authorities. People who were reported were either sent to political prisoner camps or met their untimely end at public executions.

Organizational evil in the public sector especially in the central government causes greater harms to greater numbers of victims than private organizational evil. Private organizations can put poisonous products on the market, for example, but the harms can be caught well before they reach the level of public organizational evil. Public organizational evil, on the contrary, may legalize poisonous products for the interest of a small ruling group. Moreover, it may distort taxation regulations or financial policies, legalize unlawful incarcerations, deprive human rights at the will of political leaders, and even trigger wars between countries and sacrifice numerous lives.

Public organizational evil can also be found at lower levels of the government as well. For example, in order to acquire more resources, pass favorable policies and legislations, or to avoid auditing, government agencies may collude with members of committees in the congress or council. In exchange, these government agencies may allocate resources to localized projects in particular legislators' districts. Officials in local government may also collude and fabricate documents in order to apply for funding from a higher level of government for the use of the local government, or even for the government officials themselves. A more frequently ignored fact is that government units may have incentives to purposefully expand their power by enlarging the size of government and increasing project spending, even though they do not have the pressure of market competition or threats for survival. They may create more positions within the organization, provide more opportunities for promotion, increase salaries for employees, and advocate for many unnecessary projects. In such cases, government units may pursue their organizational-level interest at the expense of taxpayers, deliberately harming the public interest.

How Is Organizational Evil Developed and Retained?

Interwoven with organizational culture, organizational evil is usually developed within an organization over time and is retained for a long time after. We propose three models for understanding the development of organizational evil: the evil founder model; the top-down development model; and the diffusion model. In the evil founder model, the founders establish the basis of an organizational culture with evil principles from the start, and then hire employees who share the same values and norms, or who can adapt themselves in order to meet the expectations of the organization (Jurkiewicz and Grossman 2015). The employees who are opposed to performing evil actions in the evil organization will either leave the organization voluntarily or will be removed. Those who are socialized toward embracing organizational evil will remain and strengthen the presence and development of organizational evil. Extreme examples of such organizations would be those devoted to child pornography; sexual slavery; drug trafficking; gangs; mafia activities; and genocidal regimes, which are all illegal and evil organizations.

Organizational evil may also occur in the course of organizational development when a group of an organization's leaders seek to better their own interests or the collective interest of the organization, and thus undertake collectively unethical behaviors (Pinto et al. 2008). This follows the top-down model. Higher-positioned members of an organization can expedite the institutionalization of organizational evil because they possess greater authority and power, and thus they can easily implement evil practices through policy making and leadership influence. They may also reinforce organizational evil through hiring, training, rewards systems, and internal policies, making it so that culpable actions can be normalized and accepted in the organization and then become the prevalent culture. The subordinates may or may not recognize the development of organizational evil, but they are likely to follow instructions from the top in order to maintain job security.

In the diffusion model, organizational evil spreads from a few corrupt individuals and then becomes prevalent within an organization. A small number of individuals begin to take part in evil practices for their personal interests and receive no punishment for doing so. Such practices diffuse within the organization as others adopt them for their own personal benefit. Loopholes in regulations and a lack of punishment for unethical behaviors can expedite the diffusion of organizational evil among the members of an organization. When more people follow them, the evil practices become institutionalized, thus turning into organizational evil. As they become routinized and formalized, they are not considered as abnormal but rather as legitimate behaviors that can benefit the organization and its members. People in the organization may perceive such behaviors as unethical but ultimately necessary for the interests of themselves and their organization.

Organizational evil persists when organizations and their members try to protect it. Organizations become less transparent, hiding evil practices and making them more discreet. For outsiders, it is difficult to detect the presence of organizational evil, especially in organizations that are less open to the public, such as military organizations. Due to the difficulty of monitoring practices from outside, organizational evil in such organizations is usually revealed by whistleblowers from the inside. These whistleblowers must risk their current jobs and future careers in order to disclose the presence of organizational evil, as organizations and members regard such actions as acts of betrayal. Organizations can impose harsh punishments on whistleblowers in order to protect organizational evil, including cutting their salaries, reassigning them to unimportant positions, or laying them off. The "forsaken" whistleblowers will usually then choose to leave their organizations when they cannot withstand such humiliation or hardship.

Organizational Evil and Administrative Evil

The term "administrative evil" differs from "organizational evil" in two aspects. First, administrative evil refers to behaviors that cause harms but the actors do not realize they are causing harms, instead believing that "what they are doing is not only procedurally correct but, in fact, good" (Adams and Balfour 2015, 17). On the contrary, organizational evil is a rational choice of action—leaders of the organization have the option to act ethically or unethically, to cease the development of organizational evil or to facilitate it. Second, administrative evil focuses on the behaviors at the personal or micro level, while organizational evil features the practices at the organizational or collective level.

Adams (2011) points out that ordinary people may engage in administrative evil while performing their normal professional and administrative roles in an organization. They may not know they are doing anything wrong because they are just doing what those around them would agree that they should be doing. He exemplifies that during the Holocaust, ordinary German citizens fulfilled everyday roles that had been successfully packaged as socially normal and appropriate, although the roles carried out extraordinary destruction. Arendt (1963) labeled this normalization of evil as a "moral inversion," a phenomenon in which something evil or destructive is repackaged as positive and worthwhile. Under conditions of moral inversion, one can engage in evil acts while thinking of them as constructive or positive (Adams 2011).

In our modern society, the normalization of evil behaviors is not becoming more difficult but rather tends to be easier and easier to occur. A key reason is that modern organizations are "characterized by the diffusion of information and the fragmentation of responsibility" (Adams 2011, 282). With information scattered and diffused, employees may not have a complete enough picture with which to adequately comprehend the destructive activities of the organization, not to mention whether or not they can reverse the course of the damage. Those who have access to more information within the organization might note a problem, or a part of a problem, but they may assume that it is the responsibility of higher management to handle. In such cases, ordinary employees, in order to maintain their job security, will hesitate to bring negative news to superiors, thus choosing to employ "strategic ignorance" (Adams 2011, 283).

A prominent case of administrative evil in an American version is the torture and abuse of detainees at the Abu Ghraib prison, run by the US military in Iraq. The unmasked case shows that the prison guards frequently violated morality and human decency with tacit permission from their superiors, although the professional standards forbidding the abuse of prisoners were paid lip service in the facility. The case also reveals that the perpetrators did not believe they were doing anything wrong, but they explained that they had used the morally questionable interrogation techniques because they were expected to extract usable intelligence from the detainees in order to find weapons of mass destruction, to help their comrades suppress a growing insurgency, and to prevent acts of terrorism (Adams, Balfour, and Reed 2006). A similar dynamic took place in the Guantanamo Bay detention facility, a US military prison where officers used torture and ill-treatment as interrogation techniques that violate international law. Interrogators justified the use of torture for national security purposes, since many inmates were accused of crimes related to terrorist attacks.

As Adams and Balfour (2015) indicate, a turning point of administrative evil will be reached when the destructive behaviors are revealed by outsiders or people in the organization realize or discover that their behaviors are actually harmful to others. When the painful truth is unmasked, personal guilt and shame are immediately present. In turn, people may have two different reactions. The positive one is to bring the administrative evil to an end, while the negative reaction is to purposefully deny and cover up the evil. If such reaction stems from organizational leaders, the denial is likely to be read by their subordinates as guidance to collude in a cover-up or lie. Then a fundamental shift will take place from engaging in harmful activities unknowingly to doing so knowingly, and administrative evil will evolve to organizational evil.

Organizational Evil and Corruption

Corruption is evil, unethical, and illegal behaviors. Organizational corruption is a facet of organizational evil. Transparency International defines corruption as the abuse of entrusted power for private gain, which has gained great popularity in the literature. In the meantime, scholars view corruption as multifaceted, and do not share a conceptually monolithic view of corruption (Navot and Beeri 2018; Rose 2018). Rose (2018) discusses the biases of multiple existing definitions of corruption and proposes his definition as, "public officials intentionally misusing their privileged access to information for private gain" (231).

Corruption occurs on different scales, ranging from small favors between a small number of people (petty corruption) to corruption that involves a big group of actors and affects the public on a large scale (grand corruption). Corruption may spread from the individual level to the organizational level and become embedded with organizational culture. For instance, public employees at the street level have chances to interact with citizens while they provide public services. With a certain degree of autonomy and discretion in service delivery, they may accept bribes or even ask citizens for bribes in exchange for extra public services or for expedited delivery of public services. If such corrupt behaviors happen incidentally and only among a small number of public employees (who are bad apples), corruption is limited to the individual level. When such corrupt practices spread among a large number of street-level bureaucrats and eventually change the systemic pattern of public service delivery, corruption becomes prevalent and normalized in an organization, then organizational corruption is developed. As Ashforth et al. (2008, 671) indicate,

> The concept of corruption reflects not just the corrupt behavior of any single individual… but also the dangerous, virus like "infection" of a group, organization, or industry. If corrupt individual acts are left unchecked, they can spread to other individuals and magnify in scope and audacity, in ways that can eventually transcend individuals and groups and become embedded in the very culture of an organization and industry.

In reality, corruption takes place in various forms, including bribery, embezzlement, wire fraud, conflict of interest, patronage, nepotism, and state capture, with state capture being the largest-scaled and most disastrous organizational corruption. Different from individual-level corruption in which corrupt individuals pursue private gain through changing the implementation of existing rules (Bagashka 2014), state capture occurs when corrupt political actors directly formulate or change the rules, laws, and regulations of the state in favor of their interests and the interests of their political alliance and supporters, while the majority of the citizens have to sacrifice. With state capture, institutions are not operationalized to serve the general public, but instead become the tools for preserving corrupt interests (Zhang 2017). According to Zhang,

> State capture is the most fundamental and influential corruption because it makes the trespass of public good for the people in power legalized by changing game rules in the society. When a country is in a position of state capture, it is no longer a real or consolidated democracy. (148)

Corruption is a facet of evil. However, an evil action is not necessarily a corrupt action. First, in corruption, public interest is damaged. If an official abuses his subordinates, it is not corruption, although it is evil and criminal. Second, there are evident beneficiaries in corruption—public officials or their associates receive the benefits. In the case of Guantanamo Bay, the questionable interrogations are clearly unethical and violate the international law. But they are not corruption because interrogators or other people do not benefit from such practices; personal gain can hardly be seen as motivator for the practices. As another case, the Schutzstaffel (SS) was responsible for the genocidal killing of an estimated 5.5 to 6 million Jews and millions of other victims in the Holocaust during the Second World War. Ironically, the SS was very concerned about possible corruption in its ranks and mandated that officers and guards had to carry out their duties within a framework of ethics and responsibility that was consistent with the norms of professionalism and technical rationality (Sofsky 1997). On the contrary, if public officials in a government agency purposefully expand their power by creating more positions within the organization, providing more opportunities for promotion, or increasing salaries for employees, corruption takes place because the public interest is damaged and personal gain is observed—the personal gain goes to a small group of government officials who are hired, promoted, or provided with higher salaries. Lastly, the term organizational evil focuses more on ethical status than organizational corruption, while organizational corruption often indicates an illegal nature. However, state capture, as the most fundamental and influential organizational corruption, is an exception because under state capture, political leaders purposefully legalize their corrupt behaviors.

Conclusion

Organizational evil refers to the institutionalization of negative behaviors with culpable intention and destructive consequence. It appears when the evil culture prevails over the good culture in an organization, and when employees see corrupt behaviors as acceptable ones. Organizational evil focuses on the collective level, and thus it is differs from administrative evil. However, administrative evil may evolve to organizational evil if negative reaction prevails at the turning point and people in the organization purposefully collude in a cover up or lie about destructive actions.

Corruption is a facet of organizational evil. State capture, as the most fundamental and influential organizational corruption, can legalize trespass of the public good for political leaders by changing game rules in the society. When a country is in a position of state capture, the principles of democracy will be fundamentally undermined. With evil and corruption, organizations will in turn become less transparent in order to hide evil practices, and thus make the detection of organizational evil and corruption more difficult. On the other hand, if organizational evil is not remedied in a timely manner, it will fundamentally undermine the moral fiber of society and yield long-term disorder, which ultimately cause harm to ordinary citizens.

References

Adam, Guy B. 2011. "The Problem of Administrative Evil in a Culture of Technical Rationality." *Public Integrity* 13(3), 275–86.

Adams, Guy B., and Danny L. Balfour. 2015. "The Dynamics of Administrative Evil in Organization," in Carole L. Jurkiewicz, ed., *The Foundations of Organizational Evil* . New York: Routledge, 16–30.

Adams, Guy B., Danny L. Balfour, and George E. Reed. 2006. "Abu Ghraib, Administrative Evil, and Moral Inversion: The Value of 'Putting Cruelty First.'" *Public Administration Review* 66(5), 680–93.

Arendt, Hannah. 1963. *Eichmann in Jerusalem: A Report on the Banality of Evil.* New York: Viking Press.

Ashforth, Blake E., Dennis A. Gioia, Sandra L. Robinson, and Linda K. Trevino. 2008. "Re-viewing Organizational Corruption," *Academy of Management Review 33*(3), 670–84.

Bagashka, Tanya. 2014. "Unpacking Corruption: The Effect of Veto Players on State Capture and Bureaucratic Corruption." *Political Research Quarterly 67*(1), 165–80.

Campbell, Jamie-Lee, and Anja S. Göritz. 2014. "Culture Corrupts! A Qualitative Study of Organizational Culture in Corrupt Organizations." *Journal of Business Ethics 120*(3), 291–311.

Heidenheimer, Arnold J. 2002. "Perspectives on the Perception of Corruption." *Political Corruption: Concepts and Contexts 3*(January), 141–54.

Jurkiewicz, Carole L., and Dave Grossman. 2015. "Evil at Work," in Carole L. Jurkiewicz, ed., *The Foundations of Organizational Evil.* New York: Routledge, 3–15.

Lioudis, Nick K, "The Collapse of Lehman Brothers: A Case Study." Accessed October 8, 2018, https://www.investopedia.com/articles/economics/09/lehman-brothers-collapse.asp.

Murphy, Flynn. 2018. "China Vaccine Scandal: Investigations Begin into Faulty Rabies and DTaP Shots." Accessed September 20, 2018, https://www.bmj.com/content/362/bmj.k3244.

Navot, Doron, and Itai Beeri. 2018. "The Public's Conception of Political Corruption: A New Measurement Tool and Preliminary Findings." *European Political Science 17*(1), 93–110.

Pinto, Jonathan, Carrie R. Leana, and Frits K. Pil. 2008. "Corrupt Organizations or Organizations of Corrupt Individuals? Two Types of Organization-Level Corruption." *Academy of Management Review 33*(3), 685–709.

Rose, Jonathan. 2018. "The Meaning of Corruption: Testing the Coherence and Adequacy of Corruption Definitions." *Public Integrity 20*(3), 220–33.

Sofsky, Wolfgang. 1997. *The Order of Terror: The Concentration Camp.* Princeton, NJ: Princeton University Press.

Zhang, Yahong. 2017. "Corruption," in Fathali Moghaddam, ed., *The SAGE Encyclopedia of Political Behavior.* Thousand Oaks, CA: SAGE Publications, 147–51. doi: 10.4135/9781483391144.n70.

20

Travails of Studying Corruption

Krishna K. Tummala

orruption is ubiquitous. Transparency International (TI) expressed the sobering thought that of the 176 nations it studied "no country gets close to a perfect score."[1] Buttressing the 2016 observation, its 2017 report observed, "This year's Corruption Perceptions Index highlights that the majority of countries are making little or no progress in ending corruption, while further analysis shows journalists and activists in corrupt countries risking their lives every day in an effort to speak out."[2]

Corruption is also endemic; it is culturally conditioned. What is a corrupt practice in one culture might not be seen as such in another. Consequently, and more importantly, attempts to prescribe measures that succeeded in one nation to curb corruption may not work in others, and need not. Ecological constraints and contexts are crucial, as popularized by modern-day writers such Fred W. Riggs.[3]

Definition of Corruption

Two caveats are relevant, up front. One, this chapter is not iconoclastic but is intended only to show that the common expression "corruption" does not always make much sense. Two, neither is the purpose of this chapter to come up with a precise, universally acceptable and applicable definition of corruption. It only attempts to show the pitfalls in the study of corruption, while also examining the more recently suggested remedies out of the conference organized by David Cameron, former prime minister of the United Kingdom.

It would be useful to briefly dwell upon some important sampling from over the millennia on the subject of corruption. The most ancient text in this regard is that of Kautilya in India (321–296 BCE), who identified forty different ways of "embezzlement," instead of using the expression "corruption."[4] (At the US Constitutional Convention in Philadelphia, James Madison called it "peculation.") Arnold J. Heidenheimer identified three definitions of corruption: public-office-centered, market-centered, and public-interest-centered, although the first variety gets pre-eminence.[5] In 1997, the World Bank gave the simplest definition, that it is the "use of public office for private gain." Most recently, TI suggested that corruption generally speaking is "the abuse of entrusted power for private gain."[6] Mathew C. Stephenson came up with a 348-page bibliography on corruption, but has only two references to shell companies hiding money, often called "black money."[7]

Difficulties in Defining "Corruption"

(1) The most often used statistic is the "Corruption Perception Index" (CPI), developed by TI, which works with several partners in government, business, and civil societies. It surveys business executives, financial journalists, and risk analysts. Thus, TI's indices reflect their *perceptions*. The public in general, who suffer from corruption, are not part of the sample. For another, it measures "perception," and not "fact." Also, the measure does not cover the business sector and the nonprofit nongovernmental agencies. Thus, the indices produced annually are subjective, and of limited import. TI readily admits those methodological issues.

(2) If corruption were to mean the use of public office for private gain, two recent cases challenge that definition. One, the president of Brazil, Dilma Rousseff, was impeached on charges of corruption in 2016. But nowhere was it claimed that she ever took a penny from public exchequer to benefit her own coffers. All she did was misrepresent the fiscal health of the nation to make her budget look good. This is no different than what David Stockman, the director of the Office of Management and Budget (OMB), did during the presidency of Ronald Reagan in the United States. Stockman, while stating that "none of us really understands what's going on with all these numbers," readily admitted in an interview[8] that he could not reconcile the budget figures reflecting the promises made by President Reagan to cut taxes, increase defense spending, and yet balance the budget—an arithmetically impossible proposition. But as a good soldier, he went into the White House basement and fudged the numbers to make the president look good.

Second, Yingluck Shinawatra, former prime minister of Thailand, was accused of paying heavy subsidies to rice farmers, which was alleged to have cost the exchequer at least $8 billion. She lost her office in 2014, fled the country, and was sentenced *in absentia* to a five-year jail term. The Thailand Supreme Court considered it negligence of duty. Others argued that "the verdict sets an awkward precedent, criminalizing a prime minister for a public policy, which was a central part of her election manifesto."[9]

Were these two leaders punished under the rubric of corruption for having tried to preserve and defend the public office to which they were elected, and for trying to make good on their election promises? Does the fact that not a word had been said of President Reagan, who accepted the cooked-up statistics provided by his OMB director, mean the application of a double standard?

(3) At times the definition of corruption may be so liberally interpreted that many an otherwise possible felon might actually go scot-free. Robert McDonnell, former governor of Virginia, was convicted for taking expensive bribes while steering some contracts to friends in return. But on appeal, the US Supreme Court in its 2016 unanimous decision in *McDonnell v. United States* affirmed the right of elected officials to peddle influence, so long as they do not make a contract to do so. It also opined that just talking to other officials in and of itself does not fit the definition of an "official act."[10] "The decision," wrote Robert Roberts, "constituted a major blow to efforts by federal prosecutors to nationalize public corruption standards."[11]

This decision has had its own repercussions. Sheldon Silver, who served long as Speaker of New York State Assembly, was convicted in 2015 for extortion (of nearly $4 million in illicit payments in return for taking a series of official actions that benefited others), and also money-laundering. But a federal Appeals Court overturned that conviction in 2017 citing the McDonnell decision. (On appeal, the Manhattan jury convicted Sheldon on May 11, 2018.)[12]

(4) Considering the expansive interpretation of corruption, one also notices that all sorts of omissions and commissions are thrown in. For example, often non-performance or administrative inefficiency (however it is defined in the public sector) among civil servants invites the opprobrium that they are all corrupt. Similarly, in cases of ethical lapses at best, or moral turpitude at worst, one hears that a politician is corrupt. The impeachment of President Bill Clinton (not convicted) for his affair with Monica Lewinski was one such. President Zuma of South Africa was even found to be innocent when he was charged with raping his house guest, even as he admitted to the act. He survived a few no-confidence motions in his country's parliament. (He is out of office on other serious corruption charges.) Several similar cases are dragging on in courts in India, but the politicians involved are going on their merry ways, elected and re-elected.

(5) Some influential academicians even argued that all corruption is not bad; it is even useful. "Speed money," or "*bakshish*," make administrative wheels turn that otherwise

come to a screeching halt.[13] Indeed, even when a citizen is entitled for a service, and all the criteria are met and all papers duly filed, the "file" does not move and tends to languish among other piles of files. The easiest way to get these moving, and get things done, is to grease the palms of the "clerk" concerned. A righteously indignant client may indeed make a lot of noise, which might only make things worse, when a small sum of money exchanged would have accomplished the task easily, and even quickly. Moreover, there is no guarantee that a clean and uncorrupt bureaucracy is any more efficient than the other scoundrels. It may be argued, perverse as it might sound, that the clerk who receives a small sum and gets things done, is more efficient. While this is no great argument for bribing, it simply is a fact.

(6) Often missed is the crucial role the ecological constraints and contexts play in particular nations. Fred Riggs, mentioned earlier, argued that "culture" and context" are important to understand administrative behavior, and to propose successful measures to reform the same.[14] The oriental tradition of carrying some gift, however inconsequential it might be, while visiting someone higher up the ladder, or even senior in age, is a good example. It would be rude to go empty-handed. These are simply conventions that cannot be counted as bribes or corruption. John Githongo, providing an African perspective on corruption, makes a rather very interesting point. The very word "corruption" does not exist in many indigenous African languages in that "(T)he idea of stealing communal goods was literally taboo.... People understand the terms of 'theft' and 'thief,' but corruption is a modern and ambiguous concept to many Africans."[15]

(7) William Riordin makes a very intriguing distinction between "honest and dishonest graft." He defines "honest graft" as "I seen my opportunities and I took 'em," whereas "dishonest graft" implies such as "blackmailing gamblers, saloonkeepers, disorderly people, etc."[16] Even if that sounds humorous, or a little sarcastic, it is real politic in that there are opportunities that many take advantage of. Consider the debate between the Democratic nominee, Hillary Clinton, and the Republican nominee, Donald Trump, during the 2016 US presidential election. The former accused the latter of cheating for not paying taxes by taking advantage of loopholes in law. And Trump simply deadpanned that he was "smart" enough to use existing law. And he went on to win the White House.

(That he did not release his tax returns even after his election is another matter.) We also know that most laws are written in collaboration between legislators and the lobbyists, who finance the election campaigns of the legislators.

(8) In the above context the US Supreme Court's 2010 decision in *Citizens United v. FEC* is of interest where the status of "person" is conferred on the corporate sector.[17] By that definition, prohibiting political contributions by corporations would invoke the First Amendment Right of Free Speech, and thus would violate the Constitution. By upholding a constitutional principle, the Court also gave its imprimatur to a long-established political practice that, in fact, can be interpreted as corrupting the system to the detriment of the public interest. A discerning reader cannot fail to notice the heavy influence on national politics carried by major corporate houses.

The practice is not confined to the United States! The Guptas in South Africa were so close to former president Jacob Zuma that he allowed the use of an air force base to bring planeloads of guests to attend the wedding of a member of the Gupta family. Various scandals with involvement of this family are working through the courts. The Adanis were wooed by former prime minister Malcolm Turnbull in Australia to start a coal-mining venture worth US$16.5 billion in Queensland in the face of considerable opposition from environmental groups. Indian prime minister Narendra Modi, who made fighting corruption a major election plank, was accused of pushing through several ordinances early into his regime in 2014 (later abandoned) to make it easy to procure land for prominent industrialists, including the Ambanis. (Ironically, all these three are of Indian origin, or are

Indian nationals.) Another case is working through the Indian courts concerning the purchase of Rafale fighter aircraft from France, charged as involving "crony capitalism."

Besides political corruption there is an equally incendiary "electoral corruption." This may take several forms such as manipulation of voter lists, facilitating stuffing ballot boxes, individuals voting more than once, buying votes, providing munificent funds under the slogan of "development" just prior to elections, and undertaking massive and very visible public projects such as infrastructure development. Perhaps the most sinister of all is what is well known in the United States as "gerrymandering," where the majority party in the state legislature redraws boundaries of electoral districts in such way that it guarantees the election of its own candidates. The Supreme Court in June 2019 in fact refused to outlaw the practice. The issue now is in the hands of state legislatures and courts. In this context, the clear case of a state like California, which successfully removed the process from the legislative sphere and placed it in the hands of a non-partisan statutory entity is illustrative. In any case, these practices are rarely studied under the rubric of corruption, as commonly understood.

(9) There is yet another crucial question. What actually is the correct criterion for purposes of definition of corruption? For example, if one were to use where "black money" is stashed away, a rather startling picture emerges in that the most developed countries top the list! Nicholas Shaxson showed that taking into account where "black money" was parked, the United States and United Kingdom take the top positions.[18] But looking at the 2011 CPI index of TI (the year Shaxson studied), one would notice of the 183 countries surveyed the United Kingdom was ranked 16, and the United States 24 among the least corrupt nations. That is a great reversal of rankings depending upon the criterion followed. Joseph Lawler, citing a report of an investigation conducted by the Financial Crimes Enforcement Network (commonly known as FinCen, created by President George H. W. Bush in 1990), reported that as many as 30 percent of cash purchases of high-end real estate in 6 major cities involved a suspicious buyer. "In other words," he said that "money laundering plays a significant role in shaping US cities."[19]

(10) There is a difference between corruption as "extortion," when money is demanded for services rendered or to be rendered, and a benevolent payment made by the client seeking favors. Hence, the trouble in finding out which is the cause and which is the effect between bribe-giving and bribe-taking.

(11) Discussion on corruption mainly revolves around practices of the Less Developed Countries (LDCs), whereas the vanguard nations are no exception (except the scale and frequency might differ).

(12) Corruption studies largely pertain to the public sector, and not the private and nongovernmental sectors. What with major contracts awarded to the latter to provide services that formerly were the domain of the public sector, the distinction between these sectors is often so blurred that it demands the inclusion of all sectors for study of corruption.

(13) There is the naughty research question as to how to study and measure corruption. In other words, what should be the unit of analysis? Saying one nation is more corrupt than the other does not provide much meaningful analysis unless we know what exactly the unit and method of measurement are.

(14) The very national pride at times prevents some leaders from acknowledging the fact that there is corruption in their countries, certainly not during their regime. At least they tend to project a lesser degree of the extent of corruption nationally or their own, or find scapegoats. Zuma of South Africa famously put it thus: "Being black and successful is being made synonymous to being corrupt."[20]

(15) Consequently, one cannot fail to notice that rhetoric regarding curbing corruption, and legislation that ensues, most often outpace reality, thus revealing a certain dissonance between law and practice.

The Anti-Corruption Summit, 2016

Of the latest major effort in the fight against corruption was the conference organized in the United Kingdom by Prime Minister David Cameron,[21] which would allow for culling some lessons from other cited sources as well.

In his "Foreword," Cameron wrote, "[W]hile corruption is such a huge problem, the national and global efforts to deal with it are often weak. No country has a perfect record on these issues."[22] The then New Zealand prime minister, John Key, argued for the promotion of "a culture which makes it close to impossible for the corrupt to prosper or escape detection."[23] He does not, however, clearly state how to go about this.

Francis Fukuyama, an academic, dwelt on the evils of corruption thus:

> Corruption incentivises the best and the brightest to spend their time gaming the system, rather than innovating or creating new wealth. … (C)orruption undermines the legitimacy of political systems by giving elites alternative ways of holding onto power other than genuine democratic choice. It hurts the prospects of democracy when people perceive authoritarian governments to be performing better than corrupt democratic ones and undermines the reality of democratic choice.[24]

Paul Collier, identified as an award-winning development expert, makes the rather strange observation: "Corruption does not happen everywhere, it is concentrated in pockets: in particular industries, in particular societies and in particular times." Admitting that the British system was very corrupt at one time, he extolls that the British cleaned up without any international help. Then he commends: "Countries such as Britain can contribute to encouraging both internal and international initiatives." Needless to say, he ignores that Britain has been a very safe haven for parking "black money" (as mentioned above), and remained so till the Cameron initiatives to make ownership of property and tax payments transparent. Collier provides an interesting, if unrealistic, prescription to change the culture of corruption:

> One way to create the common knowledge that yesterday's behavior is unlikely to persist tomorrow is to close an entire organization and rehire those staff judged to have *reasonable integrity* into a new one under different management and higher standards[25] (emphasis supplied).

While Collier does provide a few examples from government reforms, the suggestion ignores that shutting up an entire governmental entity is of course impossible. Moreover, all the merit-system protections accorded to public bureaucracies would make it entirely difficult (if not impossible) to kick out all civil servants. And, more importantly, the prescription talks of "reasonable integrity," which is an implicit admission that people of total integrity may not be found, after all.

Christine Lagarde, the then head of the International Monetary Fund, recognizes that there are multiple definitions of corruption and makes several important points. One: while many of the direct economic costs of corruption are well-known, there are many indirect costs that are more debilitating, leading to low growth and higher economic inequality, and that undermine trust in government while, at the same time, eroding ethical standards of citizens. Two: she disagrees that it is a "cultural" problem. And, three, the approaches to combat must be "holistic, and multi-faceted." Ironically, later, while dealing with the strategies for addressing corruption, Lagarde contradicts her second point when she states that "anti-corruption strategy must be tailored to the circumstances of the particular country." Although she dealt with the issues within the public sector, she makes a telling point in terms of the private sector's role in corruption:

> When people complain about corruption, they sometimes forget—perhaps conveniently—that for every bribe taken by a public official, one is given by a member of the private

sector. Clearly then, addressing the behaviour of the private sector needs to be a key component of any effective anti-corruption strategy.

Lagarde further makes a very astute observation:

> When dealing with corruption, a robust framework of incentives and a well-calibrated economic liberalization cannot be substitutes for strong values and effective institutions. … Of course, developing values at a personal and institutional level may seem beyond the control of any government. It is clearly not something that can be legislated. Yet unless public officials take pride in their work—and their independence from both political and private influence—all other efforts will fail.

She makes two other important points. One, anti-corruption measures must not be so intimidating that they might lead to a paralysis on the part of public officials and resulting in non performance. Two, political leadership is imperative in the fights against corruption, but it shall be very guarded.

> Although active and sustained political leadership is critical to the success of any anti-corruption campaign, it is important that reforms in this area are not hijacked to implement a political agenda. One way of assessing whether anti-corruption efforts are credible is to note whether enforcement is limited to the persecution of political rivals, or instead also extends to the government's political support.[26]

Although this conference did not seem to have had much academic traction, it appears that several government entities took it seriously. TI had a screaming headline: "43 countries, 600 commitments: Was the London Anti-Corruption Summit a success?" The answer was: "Overall Transparency International judged the Summit a success in promoting new and ambitious anti-corruption pledges on a comprehensive set of key issues in a wide range of countries." But they continued to caution that "the real verdict will only come when governments follow through and adopt the reforms that prevent corruption and prosecute corruption when it happens."[27]

So far, no government has adopted any formal mechanism to implement the Summit commitments. It was hoped that this would be taken up by the UN General Assembly in September 2017. Yet, none is noted (by this writer). In other words, rhetoric may not always match performance.

Lessons Learned

What are the lessons I have learned from various sources cited here? Certainly, several myths are exploded.

(1) No country is an exception. All are corrupt; only the scale and frequency differ.
(2) Many studies deal with corruption in the public sector. This is quite legitimate as that is where taxpayers' money is involved and misused. But this is inadequate insofar as many functions of the state are now farmed out to the private sector, several nongovernmental and not-for-profit sectors. That requires a more comprehensive analysis.
(3) Remedies suggested often miss the cultural nuances prevailing in each country. One size does not fit all.
(4) A squeaky-clean bureaucracy does not necessarily produce efficient outcomes. In fact, a little "speed money" at times miraculously produces quick responses and delivery of services, although it is no argument to institutionalize such a practice.
(5) Corruption is no more a matter of simply money changing hands. Non-monetary corruption includes land grabs in the name of developing special economic zones (SEZs). Even stealing sand by private entrepreneurs (for construction) is well documented!

(6) Notwithstanding the current ultranationalist politics, the world remains very much interdependent. Thus, individual nations' attempts to curb corruption at home would have limited success. It must be a concerted international effort.

(7) Political rhetoric tends to outstrip real attempts at combating corruption. Institutions created to fight corruption are often directed to neutralize opposition political leaders, and for political advantage of the incumbent regime.

(8) Jeremey Pope laid out a six-part framework necessary for a successful anti-corruption agency:[28] Committed political backing at the highest level of government; adequate resources to undertake its mission; political and operational independence (of institutions created to curb corruption) to investigate even the highest levels of government; adequate powers to access documentation and for questioning witnesses; user-friendly laws, including criminalization of "illicit enrichment;" and leadership to be seen as of highest integrity. Using this criteria, most nations, in particular the poor, vast, and diverse LDCs fall far short.

(9) Finally, even at the expense of being called a cliché, "actions speak louder than words," as TI itself admonishes.

Notes

[1] Transparency International (TI)—Annual Report (2016). http://www.transparency_org/news/features/corruption_percpetion_index_2017.

[2] Transparency International (TI)—Annual Report (2017). http://www.transparency_org/news/features/corruption_perception_index_2018—"Global Corruption Barometer: Citizens Voices from Around the World," http://www.transparency.org/news/fatures/global_corruption_barometer_citizens_voices_around_the_world.

[3] Fred Riggs, *The Ecology of Public Administration* (Bombay: Asia Publishing House, 1961)—*Administration in Developing Countries* (Boston: Houghton Mifflin, 1964)—*Prismatic Society Revisited* (Morristown, NJ: General Learning Press, 1973)—*The Triumph of Politics: Why the Reagan Revolution Failed* (New York: Harper & Row, 1986)—With Daya Krishna, *Development Debate* (Jaipur: Printwell Publishers, 1987).

[4] Kautilya, *Kautilya's Arthsastra*, 8th ed., Shama Sastry, trans. (Mysore: Mysore Publishing House, 1967).

[5] Arnold Heidenheimer, ed., *Political Corruption: Readings in Comparative Analysis* (New Brunswick, NJ: Transaction Books, 1970), 4–6.

[6] TI, "Global Corruption Barometer: Citizens Voices from Around the World," http://www.transparency.org/news/fatures/global_corruption_barometer_citizens_voices_around_the_world, November 28, 2017.

[7] Mathew C. Stephenson, *Bibliography on Corruption and Anti-corruption* http://www.law.harvard.edu/faculty/mstephenson/2016PDFs/Stephenson%20Corruption%20Bibilography%20March%2016.pdf, 2016.

[8] William Greider, "The Education of David Stockman," *Atlantic Monthly*, December 1981, 27–54.

[9] Jonathan Head, *Commentary*, British Broadcasting Corporation (BBC), September 27, 2017.

[10] *McDonnell v. United States* (2016). 136 S. Ct. 2355.

[11] Robert Roberts, "The Search for Accountability: *McDonnellv. United States* and the Fundamental Right to Honest Government," *Public Integrity* 20(1), 2018, 14.

[12] Silver trial, along with those of former New York State Senate majority leader, Dean G. Skelos, and his son, Adam, were together appealed. Lawyers on both cases cited the McDonnell ruling. See, Benjamin Weiser, "Sheldon Silver's 2015 Corruption Conviction Is Overturned," *New York Times* (online, July 13, 2017). That Sheldon was convicted on re-trial by a Manhattan jury might come as comfort to prosecutors to go after corrupt elected public officials.

[13] Samuel Huntington, *Political Order in Changing Societies* (New Haven, CT: Yale University Press, 1968).

[14] Krishna K. Tummala, "Guest Editorial: An Ode to Fred," *PAR* (*Public Administration Review*) 68, No. 6, November–December 2008, 973–80.

[15] John Githongo, "An African Perspective on Corruption," *Policy Paper, Anti-Corruption Summit, London, May 12, 2016: A Collection of Essays,* https://www.gov.uk/government/publications/against-corruption-a-collection-of-essays, 20.

[16] William Riordin, *Plunkitt of Tammany Hall: A Series of Very Plain Talks on Very Practical Politics* (New York: Signet Classic, 1995), 3.

[17] *Citizens United v. FEC* (2010) 558 US 310. The decision was heavily criticized consequently to the point where some of the justices who participated in that decision seem to be having second thoughts, hoping they might have an occasion to revisit with that decision. Associate justices Steven Breyer, Ruth Bader Ginsburg, and Elena Kagan had expressed their reservations at various occasions. The very dissent of Justice Johan

Paul Stevens in the judgement, and his subsequent writings about how wrong that decision was, are very instructive.

[18] Nicholas Shaxson, *Treasure Islands: Tax Havens and the Men Who Stole the World*. London: Vintage Books, 2012. As many as 36,342 properties in London, covering 2.2 square miles, are held by offshore havens, per Transparency International: "UK's property market 'a safe haven for corrupt funds,'" https://www.ibitimes.co.uk/uks-property-market-safe-haven-corrupt-funds-1490445 March 4, 2015. BBC, December 16, 2017.

[19] Joseph Lawler, "Money Laundering Is Shaping US cities," *Washington Examiner,* March 27, 2017.

[20] BBC, December 16, 2017.

[21] *Policy Paper, Anti-Corruption Summit, London, May 12, 2016: A Collection of Essays.*

[22] David Cameron, "Foreword," *in Policy Paper, Anti-Corruption Summit,* 2.

[23] John Key, "New Zealand: A Culture of Fair Play," in *Policy Paper, Anti-Corruption Summit,* 68.

[24] Francis Fukuyama, "What Is Corruption?" in *Policy Paper, Anti-Corruption Summit,* 10.

[25] Paul Collier, "How to Change Cultures of Corruption," in *Policy Paper, Anti-Corruption Summit,* 14, 15, 18.

[26] Christen Lagarde, "Addressing Corruption—Openly," in *Policy Paper, Anti-Corruption Summit,* 81, 83, 85, 86, 87.

[27] TI, "Advocacy" (19 September 2017). "3 Things We've Learned Since the Anti-corruption Summit in London, 2016." The other two are: "Governments were most likely to have acted on ambitious commitments," and "It pays to collaborate," https://www.transparency.org/_view/feature/7952.

[28] Jeremy Pope, *TI Source Book, 2000.*

Summary of Critical Knowledge Indicators for Part II

- In what way does the capacity for individual integrity both help and hinder organizational corruption?

- How does the intent to act with integrity serve to promote corruption?

- What role does groupthink, cultural blindness, and confirmation bias play in facilitating corruptive behavior?

- Provide three examples of instruments used by organizations to combat corruption.

- What is meant when an ethics management system is characterized by both pluralism and dynamism?

- What determines which elements of an ethics program an organization should adopt?

- What values underscore the foundations of social equity?

- By what methods does the street-level bureaucrat dispense justice and equity of behalf of the state?

- Why is a representative bureaucracy essential for social equity?

- What are the consequences of institutional mistrust for citizenry across the globe?

- Why is trust not an inherently positive value?

- What does the prototype of cognitive and affective trust offer in terms of building trustworthiness?

- Is noble cause corruption ever justifiable?

- How can one identify corruption separate from misconduct or incompetence?

- Where is corruption most likely to be found within the criminal justice system, and which has the potential to be most damaging to societies?

- What is the impetus to develop global ethical standards?

- Can individuals be trained to be ethical?

- How does cognitive bias affect ethical behavior?

- What role does rational choice theory play in predicting corruptive behavior?

- Are humans inherently corrupt?

- In a cost-benefit analysis of corruption, what factors can influence the calculation?

- What characterizes the stages along the Corruption Continuum?

- What are the negative unintended consequences of ethics management?

- What causes ethical management systems to fail?

- How can a balance between rules-based and values-based approaches be achieved in ethical management systems?

- How is organizational evil defined separate from corruptive behavior?

- In what ways does organizational evil evince itself in public vs. private organizations?

- How does organizational evil develop in organizations?

- How do the challenges in studying corruption affect the ability of institutions to effect anti-corruption measures?

- Is corruption more likely to be associated with certain types of institutions?

- What role do global organizations such as Transparency International play in corruption and ethics management?

by Carole L. Jurkiewicz

PART III

Best Practices in Corruption Prevention and Ethics Management

21

Integrity of Governance
Toward a System Approach
Leo Huberts and André van Montfort

Integrity of Governance

Integrity has become an important issue (and value) in governance, in the public but also in the private sector (Boatright 2011). With many interpretations of what "integrity" is about, everybody applauds acting with integrity, but the views on its basics vary (Huberts 2018). In this chapter, integrity is defined as "acting in accordance with the relevant moral values and norms and rules" (Huberts 2014, 44–45). The focus will be on the public sector. Politicians and public servants show integrity if they fulfill their duties and functions in accordance with what is morally justified, measured against the moral norms, values, and corresponding rules that are relevant at that time and in that context.

The opposite of integrity are integrity violations, behavior that violates the relevant moral values and norms. Although the international research on what goes wrong in governance often focuses on "corruption" (Graycar and Smith 2011; Heywood 2015; Anechiarico 2017), there is also broader research, highlighting different types of unethical behavior or integrity violation in public administration (de Graaf, Strüwer, and Huberts 2018; Hardi, Heywood, and Torsello 2015; Lewis and Gilman 2012; Menzel 2016; Svara 2015). Consider, for instance, the (validated) typology of integrity violations based on research on police corruption and integrity, integrity of governance, and organizational misconduct (Lasthuizen, Huberts, and Heres 2011), distinguishing nine types of violations, including corruption (bribing and favoritism); conflicts of interest; fraud and theft; abuse of resources; misuse of power and information; indecency (intimidation, discrimination); and private-time misconduct (Huberts 2014).

What helps to promote integrity and curb integrity violations? In the literature, many methods, instruments, and strategies are distinguished, with a lot of discussion on their effectiveness and how they interrelate. A brief overview of what is known in the literature about the effectiveness of the most important instruments, methods, and strategies, leads to the conclusion that promoting integrity and curbing violations is served by an "integrity system perspective" (Huberts et al. 2014; Six and Lawton 2010; van Montfort, Ogric, and Huberts 2018), which will be clarified in this chapter. The thereby given sketch of the basic elements of a complete integrity system offers an evaluation framework with starting points for future research.

Separate Instruments and Strategies

Most studies on organization integrity focus on individual tools and methods utilized within a public organization to promote integrity and curb integrity violations. Among the many "integrity instruments," a number are commonly used within organizations and extensively researched: codes of conduct (Kaptein and Schwartz 2008; Menzel 2016), ethics training (Karssing 2007; van Montfort, Beck, and Twijnstra 2013; van Tankeren 2010), and investigations and sanctions (de Graaf 2010; Treviño and Weaver 2003).

Ethical leadership is generally considered one of the most important factors in shaping the ethical culture of organizations, as well as the ethics and integrity of employees (Heres and Lasthuizen 2012; Jurkiewicz and Giacalone 2017; Treviño, Weaver, and Reynolds 2006). Studies on leadership theories have indicated that conceptions of leadership are context dependent (Jurkiewicz and Giacolone 2017). What helps differs depending on characteristics of the organization and the "followers" of the leaders (Heres 2014).

The main conclusion that can be drawn from research on the use of such instruments as codes of conduct, investigations, employee training, and on leadership is that the picture is limited and inconclusive; even where the quality of those instruments is good, their effectiveness varies. Effectiveness is context dependent and related to the type of integrity violation (Huberts et al. 2014).

In the literature on individual instruments, much attention has been paid to discussing the pros and cons of two overarching strategies that guide the choice of separate tools and methods. On the one hand, there is values-based (integrity-based or incentive-giving) strategy that is supposed to advance employees' intrinsic motivation to integrity, thereby yielding more lasting effects. On the other hand, there is a compliance-based (rule-following and sanctioning) strategy that is designed to generate fear of sanctions and, thus, extrinsic motivation (Maesschalck 2004; Treviño and Weaver 2003).

Research on the effects of both strategies offer nuance on their effectiveness. For example, research on the presence and estimated effectiveness of integrity instruments in local government in the Netherlands showed that the presence of clear rules (including on accepting gifts, outside employment) and ethical codes with clarity on values is considered very effective (van den Heuvel et al. 2010).

The existing evidence on strategies clearly suggests that a balance of compliance-based and values-based approaches may work best. The limitations of the often-dominant focus on rules and compliance are clear (Heywood and Rose 2016), but the credibility and effectiveness of a value-based strategy is undermined when integrity violations are not addressed adequately through compliance (van Tankeren 2010). The interaction and combination of policies appears crucial (Treviño et al. 1999).

External Watchdog Organizations

In addition to the insights about the effectiveness of individual instruments and strategies, the literature also presents insights into types of external institutions and organizations that might help to promote integrity and curb violations, including corruption. First, national bodies to fight corruption come to mind. One institution that often has been presented as a successful example is the Hong Kong Independent Commission against Corruption (ICAC) (Scott 2011). The commission became famous for its "three-pronged strategy" of law enforcement, corruption prevention, and community education to tackle rampant corruption in Hong Kong, as well as for its major investment of resources (ICAC 2017).

Many other national or subnational anti-corruption institutions have been established elsewhere, several of which have been evaluated in research (Huberts et al. 2008; De Sousa 2010). This has led to some (supposed) success stories, as well as many partial and total failures. As De Sousa (2010, 19) concluded more eloquently,

> If there is one lesson to be learnt from the history of anticorruption activity, it is that there are no individual solutions but a cocktail of measures, no silver bullets but a mixture of successes and failures and no quick fixes but a long and hard learning process. ACAs are an innovative institutional response to corruption, but they are not the panacea.

A special agency can help, but its success is very dependent on its characteristics and—again—the context. It is, therefore, understandable that in recent years, increasing attention has been paid to the broader integrity system of the instruments and institutions that are collectively trying to establish integrity.

Shift to Integrity Systems

Many recent studies do not mainly pay attention to integrity instruments and external watchdog organizations as separate elements, but they focus primarily on the entire configuration of these elements. Such a system approach takes into account an extensive set of elements and conditions that are expected to be important to the integrity of the organization (Six and Lawton 2010). It focuses "on the connection between various components within and outside the organization, how the components are interconnected and how they are jointly responsible for the integrity performance of an organization" (van Montfort, Ogric, and Huberts 2018, 73).

An integrity system consists of *internal* elements such as codes of conduct, integrity training programs, institutions for reporting and investigation, and ethical leadership, and *external* elements such as audit institutions, the police, the media and other external watchdog organizations (Slingerland, Six, and Huberts 2012). An integrity system should be organized in such a way at the *internal level* that there is no need for *external watchdog organizations* to intervene. This applies to both national and local integrity systems.

National Integrity Systems

The famous *national integrity system* perspective was developed by Transparency International and Jeremy Pope (2000) as a model for describing and evaluating what measures countries can and do take to fight corruption and safeguard integrity. The model is built on *foundations* that comprise public awareness and society's values and are important for the effectiveness of the *pillars*, a number of crucial institutions, sectors, or activities for stopping corruption.

These pillars are rather diverse and include political involvement, an active legislature on good governance and fighting corruption, an auditor general as watchdog, an attorney general as guardian of the public interest, an ombudsman, independent anti-corruption agencies, adequate procedures for public procurement, a private sector operating within the laws and public awareness, media, civil society, and international organizations supportive of ethics and integrity. All pillars are interrelated, interdependent, and form the building blocks for a "holistic approach" (Pope 2000). Numerous national integrity systems have been assessed, often contributing to the discussion of what is missing and what might help (see https://www.transparency.ie/resources/NIS).

The national integrity system approach has similarities with, for example, OECD's (2000) policies on appropriate "ethics infrastructures," which identify similar actors at the national level (e.g., legislature, executive, judiciary, auditor-general, ombudsman, watchdog agencies, and civil society). The Australian National Integrity Assessment Approach (NISA), in contrast, replaces TI's Greek temple with a bird's nest metaphor for a more interdependent network representation (Sampford, Smith, and Brown 2005).

Organizational Integrity Systems

Building upon the work done on national integrity systems, an international comparative study on "organizational" integrity systems was initiated, with a focus on the policies, practices, and actors at the local-government level who aim to fight corruption and safeguard integrity (Huberts, Anechiarico, and Six 2008). Seven large cities or metropolitan areas were involved: Sydney/New South Wales, New York, Hong Kong, London, Hamburg, Amsterdam, and Antwerp. Among the "lessons learned" were the importance of the position and role of the core integrity agency. Several actors appeared to be active as guardians of integrity in a local integrity system: a core local integrity agency (with varying independence, roles, resources), the local auditor or comptroller, the local ombudsman, police and justice, and the media. Other "lessons" concerned "determine scope: defining integrity," "balance compliance-based and value-based approaches," "balance internal and external checks and balances," and "gain and maintain political and public support" (Huberts et al. 2008, 275–85).

Although that research is related to municipal integrity systems, its findings are also relevant for private-sector organizations. All organizations are confronted with integrity dilemmas and problems. A Dutch study on four large Dutch banks (Six et al. 2012) revealed that for each integrity risk to be contained, checks and balances need to be in place within and across various organizational levels. The overall conclusion of this study was that, conceptually, bank integrity systems are very similar to municipal and national integrity systems, even though the organization at the heart of the system is a commercial business, albeit with clear public tasks and responsibilities.

Recent Research on Local Integrity Systems

The presented state of the art in research on the effectiveness of integrity systems served as a starting point for a number of research projects in the Netherlands on the content and effectiveness of local integrity systems. These concerned in-depth analysis and evaluation of integrity systems in a number of municipalities in 2014 and 2016 (Heres et al. 2015; van den Heuvel, Huberts, and van Montfort 2017), followed in 2018 by studies and research on local integrity systems (qualitative case studies on Amsterdam and two small municipalities), a survey among all municipalities in the Netherlands on their integrity systems (Ogric, van Montfort, and Huberts 2018; van Montfort, Ogric, and Huberts 2018), and two studies on integrity systems in the financial sector, including a big bank.

These recent studies on local integrity systems addressed the state of the art of the literature on integrity systems and incorporated insights resulting from the ideas and formats on integrity systems of public agencies (BIOS 2018) and universities (Jeurissen, De Jong, and Odijk 2014). When looking specifically at the survey conducted among all Dutch municipalities in the spring of 2018, some notable conclusions can be drawn about the evaluation framework used and the integrity systems studied.

First of all, it is worth mentioning that although most previous studies do not pay attention to integrity systems as a whole, they are useful for making an overview of the important elements that should be present in a complete integrity system. For the purpose of the survey among Dutch municipalities, an overview of key internal elements of a complete municipal integrity system for civil servants was constructed. This comprehensive evaluation framework comprised forty internal elements divided into the following categories: attention to and clarity about integrity; clear regulations concerning integrity; ethical leadership; integrity in personnel policy; integrity-training programs; procedures for advice, reporting, and investigation; periodic registration and reporting; risk analyses or vulnerability studies; integrity unit or functionary; and a combination of value-based and compliance strategy. The category "integrity unit or functionary" consisted, for example, of elements concerning the importance of a specific institution or actor with integrity and anti-corruption as the primary task and responsibility. The complete evaluation model has been extensively described by van Montfort et al. (2018).

The survey data showed that the tools and methods discussed in the first part of this chapter (i.e., codes of conduct, ethics training, investigations and sanctions, and ethical leadership) and incorporated in the evaluation model are applied in almost all local civil-service organizations (van Montfort, Ogric, and Huberts 2018). As evidenced by unpublished survey data, these four ingredients of a local integrity system are considered indispensable by municipal officials for promoting integrity within their organizations.

According to the survey data, a small majority (54.7 percent) of the investigated municipalities had a complete or a very complete integrity system (van Montfort, Ogric, and Huberts 2018). Many Dutch municipalities appeared to have a very incomplete or an incomplete integrity system.

Finally, it should be noted that organizations can utilize the evaluation framework developed by us and the data obtained by the survey among Dutch municipalities for benchmarking the completeness of their own integrity systems. Such a benchmark will undoubtedly reveal a number of points for improvement. This applies to both public-sector and private-sector organizations, because "[t]here is little reason to assume that the requirements and actual situation regarding local integrity systems in the public sector differ significantly from the requirements and actual situation in the private sector" (van Montfort, Ogric, and Huberts 2018, 86).

Conclusion

The foregoing presented a sketch of shifts to a system approach in both the practice of public administration and the research into the integrity of governance. It provided also some findings of recent new research that seem relevant to progress on our knowledge on the basic elements of an integrity system of a public-sector (or private-sector) organization.

Knowledge development in this area is work in progress in research, but with direct relevance for practice. The conclusions on what an (organizational) integrity system should consist of offer an evaluation framework with food for thought for future research as well as for organizations to reflect on the presence (or absence) of the mentioned elements. In research it is often acknowledged that more attention has to be paid to "what works" (Demmke and Moilanen 2011; Huberts, Maesschalck, and Jurkiewicz 2008; Menzel 2005). The evaluation framework offers a challenging agenda for researchers to do that—to investigate (test) whether the elements are relevant (and under what circumstances).

This also points at reflection from scholars who question the Western, or cultural, bias in many perceptions of integrity, corruption, and policies (Mungiu-Pippidi 2006; Sissener 2001; Rothstein and Torsello 2013). The presented interpretation of integrity and corruption and the proposed elements for an integrity system seem indeed relevant for primarily "Western" societies. The relevance of those elements for "non-Western" integrity systems is something to reflect upon, also in research.

References

Anechiarico, F., ed. 2017. *Legal but Corrupt. A New Perspective on Public Ethics.* Lanham, MD: Lexington Books.

BIOS. 2018. *Model integriteitinfrastructuur[Model Integrity Infrastructure].* The Hague: CAOP. Available at http://www.integriteitoverheid.nl/dossiers/model-integriteitinfrastructuur/.

Boatright, J. 2011. "Trust and Integrity in Banking." *Ethical Perspectives 18*(4), 473–89.

de Graaf, G. 2010. "A Report on Reporting: Why Peers Report Integrity and Law Violations in Public Organizations." *Public Administration Review 70*(5), 767–79.

de Graaf, G., T. Strüwer, and L. Huberts 2018. "Integrity Violations and Corruption in Western Public Governance. Empirical Evidence and Reflection from the Netherlands." *Public Integrity 20*(2), 131–49.

De Sousa, L. 2010. "Anti-Corruption Agencies: Between Empowerment and Irrelevance." *Crime, Law and Social Change 53*(1), 5–22.

Demmke, C., and T. Moilanen. 2011. *Effectiveness of Good Governance and Ethics. Evaluating Reform Outcomes in the Context of the Financial Crisis.* Maastricht: European Institute of Public Administration.

Graycar, A., and R. G. Smith, eds. 2011. *Handbook of Global Research and Practice in Corruption.* Cheltenham: Edward Elgar.

Hardi, P., P. Heywood, and D. Torsello, eds. 2015. *Debates of Corruption and Integrity. Perspectives from Europe and the US.* Basingstoke: Palgrave Macmillan.

Heres, L. 2014. *One Style Fits All? The Content, Origins, and Effect of Follower Expectations of Ethical Leadership.* Enschede: Ipskamp.

Heres, L., and K. M. Lasthuizen. 2012. "What's the Difference? Ethical Leadership in Public, Hybrid, and Private Sector Organisations." *Journal of Change Management* 12(4), 441–66.

Heres, L., L. Huberts, A. Montfortvan, K. Peters, and D. Ranzijn. 2014. *Evaluatie Integriteitssysteem Gemeente Eindhoven [Evaluation Integrity System Municipality of Eindhoven].* Eindhoven: Municipality of Eindhoven.

Heywood, P. M., ed. 2015. *Routledge Handbook of Political Corruption.* Abingdon-on-Thames: Routledge.

Heywood, P. M., and J. Rose. 2016." The Limits of Rule Governance," in A. Lawton, Z. van der Wal, and L. Huberts, eds., *Ethics in Public Policy and Management: A Global Research Companion.* London: Routledge, 102–119.

Huberts, L. 2014. *The Integrity of Governance: What It Is, What We Know, What Is Done, and Where to Go.* New York: Palgrave Macmillan.

Huberts, L. W. J. C. 2018. "Integrity: What It Is and Why It Is Important." *Public Integrity* 20(1), 18–32. doi: 10.1080/10999922.2018.1477404.

Huberts, L., F. Anechiarico, and F. Six. eds. 2008. *Local Integrity Systems: World Cities Fighting Corruption and Safeguarding Integrity.* The Hague: BJu Publishers.

Huberts, L., F. Anechiarico, F. Six, and J. van der Veer. 2008. "Local Integrity Systems Analysis and Assessment," in L. Huberts, F. Anechiarico, and F. Six, eds., *Local Integrity Systems: World Cities Fighting Corruption and Safeguarding Integrity.* The Hague: BJu Publishers, 270–95.

Huberts, L.W.J.C., J. Maesschalck, and C. L. Jurkiewicz, eds. 2008. *Ethics and Integrity of Governance: Perspectives across Frontiers.* Cheltenham: Edward Elgar.

Huberts, L., F., Six, M. van Tankeren, A. van Montfort, and H. Paanakker. 2014. "What is Done to Protect Integrity: Policies, Institutions and Systems," in L. Huberts, ed., *The Integrity of Governance: What It Is, What We Know, What Is Done and Where to Go.* New York: Palgrave Macmillan, 167–97.

ICAC (Independent Commission Against Corruption). 2017. *Annual Report Independent Commission Against Corruption Hong Kong Special Administrative Region.* Available at: https://www.icac.org.hk/en/about/report/annual/index.html

Jeurissen, R., M. de Jong, and B. Odijk. 2014. *Het Stimuleringskader Integere Organisatie. Een ontwikkelmodel voor organisatie-integriteit [The Integrity Management Accountability Framework: A Framework for Organizational Integrity].* 2nd ed. De Lier: SIO.

Jurkiewicz, C. J. and R. A. Giacalone, eds. 2017. *Radical Thoughts on Ethical Leadership.* Charlotte, NC: Information Age Publishing (Ethics in Practice Series).

Kaptein, M., and M. S. Schwartz. 2008. "The Effectiveness of Business Codes: A Critical Examination of Existing Studies and the Development of an Integrated Research Model." *Journal of Business Ethics* 77(2), 111–27.

Karssing, E. D. 2007. *Morele competentie in organisaties* [Moral Competence in Organizations]. Assen: Van Gorcum.

Lasthuizen, K., L. Huberts, and L. Heres. 2011. "How to Measure Integrity Violations. Towards a Validated Typology of Unethical Behavior." *Public Management Review* 13(3), 383–408.

Lewis, C. W., and S. C. Gilman. 2012. *The Ethics Challenge in Public Service. A Problem-Solving Guide.* 3rd ed. San Francisco: Jossey Bass.

Maesschalck, J. 2004. "Towards a Public Administration Theory on Public Sector Ethics. A Comparative Study." PhD thesis. Leuven: Faculteit Sociale Wetenschappen KU Leuven.

Menzel, D. C. 2005. "Research on Ethics and Integrity in Governance. A Review and Assessment." *Public Integrity* 7(2), 147–68.

Menzel, D. C. 2016. *Ethics Management for Public and Nonprofit Managers: Leading and Building Organizations of Integrity.* 4th ed. New York: Routledge.

Mungiu-Pippidi, A. 2006. "Corruption: Diagnosis and Treatment." *Journal of Democracy* 17(3), 86–99.

Ogric, B., A. van Montfort, and L. Huberts. 2018. *Integriteitssysteem in Nederlandse gemeenten, Een bestuurskundig onderzoek naar de volledigheid van gemeentelijke integriteitssystemen voor ambtenaren in Nederland [Integrity System in Dutch Municipalities, A Govenance Study into the Completeness of Municipal Integrity Systems for Civil Servants in the Netherlands].* Amsterdam: Vrije Universiteit Amsterdam.

Pope, J. 2000. *Confronting Corruption: The Elements of a National Integrity System (TI Source book 2000)*. Berlin: Transparency International.

Rothstein, B., and D. Torsello. 2013. *Is Corruption Understood Differently in Different Cultures? Anthropology Meets Political Science*. QOG Working Paper Series. Götenburg: QOG. https:// qog.pol.gu.se/digitalAssets/1443/1443545_2013_5_rothstein_torsello.pdf.

Sampford, C., R. Smith, and A. J. Brown. 2005. "From Greek Temple to Bird's Nest: Towards a Theory of Coherence and Mutual Accountability for National Integrity Systems." *Australian Journal of Public Administration 64*(2), 96–108.

Scott, I. 2011. "The Hong Kong ICAC's Approach to Corruption Control," in A. Graycar and R. G. Smith, eds., *Handbook of Global Research and Practice in Corruption*. Cheltenham: Edward Elgar, 401–415.

Sissener, T. 2001. *Anthropological Perspectives on Corruption, Working Paper/Development Studies and Human Rights*. Bergen: Chr. Michelsen Institute (CMI).

Six, F., and A. Lawton, 2010. *Towards a Theory of Integrity Systems: A Configurational Approach*. Amsterdam: Vrije Universiteit.

Slingerland, W., F. Six, and L. Huberts. 2012. "Integriteitssystemen en hun werking [Integrity Systems and their Functioning]," in J. van den Heuvel, L. Huberts, and E. Muller, eds., *Integriteit: integriteit en integriteitsbeleid in Nederland [Integrity: Integrity and Integrity Policy in the Netherlands]*. Deventer: Kluwer, 219–38.

Svara, J. 2015. *The Ethics Primer for Public Administrators in Government and Nonprofit Organizations*. 2nd ed. Burlington: Jones and Bartlett.

Treviño, L. K., G. R. Weaver, D. G. Gibson, B. L. Toffler. 1999. "Managing Ethics and Legal Compliance: What Works and What Hurts." *California Management Review 41*(2), 131–51.

Treviño, L. K., and G. R. Weaver. 2003. *Managing Ethics in Business Organisations: Social Scientific Perspectives*. Stanford: Stanford University Press.

Treviño, L. K., G. R. Weaver, and S. J. Reynolds. 2006. "Behavioral Ethics in Organizations: A Review." *Journal of Management 32*(6), 951–90.

van den Heuvel, H., L. Huberts, and A. van Montfort. 2017. *Evaluatie integriteitssysteem gemeente Stichtse Vecht: Onderdeel college van B&W en ambtelijke dienst [Evaluation of the Integrity System of the Municipality of Stichtse Vecht: Part Concerning the College of Mayor and Aldermen and the Civil Service]*. Amsterdam: Vrije Universiteit Amsterdam.

van den Heuvel, J., L. Huberts, Z. van der Wal, and K. Steenbergen. 2010. *Integriteit van het lokaal bestuur [Integrity of Local Government]*. The Hague: Boom Lemma.

van Montfort, A. J. G. M., L. Beck, and A. A. H. Twijnstra. 2013. "Can Integrity Be Taught in Public Organizations? The Effectiveness of Integrity-Training Programs for Municipal Officials." *Public Integrity 15*(2), 117–32.

van Montfort, A., B. Ogric, and L. Huberts. 2018. "The (In)completeness of Local Integrity Systems: A Cross-Sectional Study on Municipal Integrity Systems for Civil Servants in the Netherlands." *Archives of Business Research 6*(9), 70–90. doi: 10.14738/abr.69.5199.

van Tankeren, M. 2010. *Het integriteitsbeleid van de Nederlandse politie: Wat er is en wat ertoe doet [The Integrity Policy of the Dutch Police: What There Is and What Matters]*. Apeldoorn: Politie en Wetenschap.

22

Approaches to Combating Corruption
Global Best Practices
Adam Graycar and Catherine Cochrane

Some countries, governments, organizations, and workplaces are more corrupt than others. Understanding how to best intervene to prevent, detect, and remedy corruption in these diverse settings requires a careful dissection of occurrences and an appreciation of the political or managerial capacity to deal with them. Best practices cannot be reduced to a simple checklist; there are no magic bullet solutions. Instead, there is a range of approaches to match appropriate interventions to context-specific problems resulting from, in broad terms, "the abuse of entrusted power for private gain" (Transparency International 2018b). As Graycar (2015) outlines, one way to do this is with the TASP (Types, Activities, Sectors and Places) framework that examines types, activities, sectors, and places to diagnose corruption problems and develop interventions. Differences like those between high-level political bribery and low-level favoritism are illuminated, and potential interventions, such as an anti-corruption agency (ACA) or an integrity-building strategy, are identified.

This chapter examines best practices in three parts: big-picture successes, national and subnational interventions, and integrity-building strategies. Big-picture successes may result from a country's historical development of corruption resistance, incremental but significant changes over a few decades, or "big-bang" approaches introducing immediate dramatic reforms. National and subnational interventions include legislation and institutions, particularly ACAs, that have been established in various forms. Another strategy is to build integrity within organizations by fostering strong ethics and values. Depending on the problems and their context, efforts to combat corruption may require either a top-down or a bottom-up approach, or both.

Big-Picture Successes

There are many examples of big-picture successes in combating corruption, each with unique characteristics as well as some similar themes, including democratic, bureaucratic, judicial, citizenship, and property reforms. Mungiu-Pippidi (2015) asks whether the performance of countries such as those in Scandinavia—which rank high on the Transparency International Corruption Perceptions Index (CPI) (Transparency International 2018a)—is because of what they do now or because of how they have developed over time. She identifies three key phases in their development and highlights factors contributing to success in each. The first phase involves the control of corruption by authoritarian monarchs through selective repression. In the second phase corruption is controlled by republicanism where elites are the trustees of the public interest and prevent special interests from appropriating the state. Third is a phase of representative democracy where the state is entrusted to bureaucrats to manage in the public interest, acknowledging that politicians are not necessarily good trustees for controlling corruption. Additionally, in each phase corruption is tempered by an impartial judiciary. No two countries have followed the same historical path or can expect to reach an exact prescribed point in their development, but all best-practice approaches should pay attention to how corruption resistance can be embedded in the long term.

Writing about South Korea after the Second World War, You (2015, 2017) outlines several reforms that contributed to a change in governance norms and a reduction in corruption. He documents how the sweeping land reforms of 1948 and 1950 that dissolved the landed aristocracy and produced a relatively equal distribution of wealth, as well as a rapid expansion of education, laid the structural foundations for the growth of ethical universalism. Gradual expansion of civil-service examinations (1950s to the 1990s), democratization (1960 and 1987), good-governance reforms (1988–), and post-financial crisis economic reforms (1998–99) also helped build corruption resistance. He explores how these incremental reforms were carried out, who the main actors were, what made such choices possible, and what impact they made (You 2015).

Estonia is deemed the least corrupt former Soviet republic after adopting a series of radical reforms (Kalniņš 2017). In the late 1980s the Soviet *glasnost* (openness) and *perestroika* (restructuring) policies were embraced with great zeal in Estonia. The country's elites were systematically replaced and a "virtuous circle" established (Kalniņš 2017). Civic and student activism increased, reformist political groups proliferated, and many skilled and liberal Estonians came home from abroad. Citizenship was redefined and conferred only on those (and their descendants) who had it before Soviet occupation. Competitive politics led to conditions for universalistic governance, and in the first election in 1990 there was high voter turnout. Merit-based recruitment was introduced to the civil service. All judges in the three-tier court system had to reapply for positions and fewer than 40 of the 154 judges appointed had held judicial posts under the Soviets. A new supreme court was established and none of the positions went to Soviet-era judges (Kalniņš 2017). These "big-bang" reforms produced monumental cultural change.

Nevertheless, "big-bang" reforms may not produce lasting change if anti-corruption endeavors are not maintained. Georgia was regarded as a failed state in 2003. It ranked 124/133 on the CPI. Kupatadze (2017) describes it as having a particularistic governance regime captured by private interests with a distribution of resources that benefited privileged individuals. The "Rose Revolution" that occurred in November 2003 set Georgia on course toward ethical universalism with impartial governance based on fairness and equality. The major problem addressed was bribery, particularly in sectors where citizens interact with the state most frequently, such as policing, registering property, licensing businesses, and tax administration. Civil-service numbers were halved, with new recruits replacing existing staff, and salaries were increased fifteen-fold. Other reforms included cutting red tape and deregulation, tax reform, and improvements to public services. After these "big-bang" reforms Georgia ranked 52/174 countries in the CPI. However, there are doubts that this transformation has been sustained. New elites have developed vested interests while patrimonialism and clientelism have replaced the bribery of the past (Kupatadze 2018). The types of activities and their context have changed, but corruption remains.

Not all countries have the benefit of historical development conducive to greater corruption resistance or are able to introduce "big-bang" reforms. Expectations that specific criteria can direct prescribed solutions are counterproductive and likely to lead anti-corruption endeavors astray (Mungiu-Pippidi and Johnston 2017, 252–53). Countries need to adapt the experiences of other jurisdictions to their contexts using a range of immediate dramatic reforms and mid-term incremental changes alongside a commitment to long-term development and vigilance that embeds corruption resistance over time. In addition, there are global initiatives that can assist this process, including international treaties and intercountry cooperation. Some prominent examples include the United Nations Convention Against Corruption, the OECD Convention on Combating Bribery of Foreign Public Officials in International Business, the Council of Europe's Criminal Law

Convention on Corruption, and the G20 Anti-Corruption Working Groups. These, in themselves, are not best practices, but by providing direction some of the outcomes appear promising, despite difficulties in reliably measuring changes in corruption levels.

National and Subnational Interventions

These examples of big-picture success provide hope and direction. Likewise, there are examples of national and subnational interventions, including legislation and institutions that demonstrate best practices. The United Kingdom *Bribery Act 2010* and the United States *Foreign Corrupt Practices Act* of 1977 have been credited with making companies more circumspect in their dealings. Numerous countries and subnational jurisdictions have established ACAs, and these exhibit various approaches to combating corruption (UNODC 2014). They are the most prominent institutional intervention but can also become part of the problem (Quah 2017).

Often the conditions that are most conducive to effective interventions occur in the aftermath of a crisis, as it facilitates public support and a sense of urgency, thereby lowering the barriers to reform (Jochim and May 2010, 316–17). Some may still resist, but that crisis-driven momentum can shift power balances, providing a unique opportunity for change. Such an opportunity was seized in Queensland, Australia, where between the 1950s and late 1980s the police force was diabolically corrupt (Fitzgerald Report 1989). The conservative state government, to whom it was responsible, would hear no criticism of police and allowed senior members to behave with impunity. In unusual circumstances, and against the wishes of the premier (state governor), a Commission of Inquiry was established in response to a series of scandalous media reports. The evidence exposed in the inquiry precipitated a crisis for both the police and government and led to the jailing of a police commissioner and several government ministers. The inquiry's recommendations for reform were endorsed by a new government in 1989 and formed a blueprint for the reform of the police force. Judicial review, criminal penalties, oversight from a newly established ACA, new leadership, a commitment to better education and training, and other integrity building efforts led to the transformation of the police force into a much cleaner organization (cf. Prasser, Wear, and Nethercote 1990).

Anti-corruption Agencies (ACAs)

ACAs are a departure from conventional law-enforcement approaches in combating corruption. Although loosely defined, they are typically specialized agencies with permanent operations focused on reducing corruption (Meagher 2005, 70). This is not to suggest they operate as the only entities tackling corruption, but rather that they can be distinguished by their "lead" role in fulfilling this purpose. In this way they can drive the anti-corruption mission, provide coordination among other agencies, and improve the quality of information and intelligence (72). There are diverse approaches to establishing ACAs that can be adapted to context-specific needs; questions of suitability center on appropriate design and effective implementation for particular jurisdictions.

The significant consequences of corruption for society and its unique characteristics as a type of crime—particularly its secretive nature, often without identified, direct, and complaining victims (Douglas and Head 2014, 167)—underpin demands for ACAs to tackle the problem. Additionally, the insidious power of corrupt networks often leaves even well-resourced and honest law enforcement agencies unable to proactively engage with the problem amid their much broader reactive policing responsibilities, including responding to the directly affected victims of more visible crimes. Indeed, former Hong Kong Independent Commission Against Corruption (ICAC) commissioner Peter Williams suggests that these networks almost constitute "the setting-up of an alternative illicit form of government" (Klitgaard 1988, 116), which, as Heidenheimer (2009, 141–42) notes, causes a blurring of the lines of what is recognized and reported as corruption. Additionally, Meagher (2005, 70) argues that there has been an increasing recognition that corruption is not a sequence of separate scandals each to be addressed by temporary interventions, but an ongoing phenomenon requiring a permanent response (see also Donaghue 2001, 5).

ACAs provide a policy response instrument through which corruption can be investigated, exposed, and punished—to increase risks and consequences—and prevented through reforms to systems, processes, and practices—to reduce opportunities and incentives. These reforms alter the risk-versus-reward equation at the core of the decision-making process that underpins corrupt activities and, thereby, act as a deterrent. The assumption that a permanent ACA can produce this deterrence and reduce corruption in the public sector (Douglas and Head 2014, 185–86) is reinforced by a number of other perceived advantages. First, insofar as there is often an absence of direct victims of corruption who seek justice, ACAs can be understood as proxies serving the public interest as a representation of a community of victims (McKillop 1994, 33). Second, an ACA independent of the police and courts provides some assurance against corruption that interferes with conventional law-enforcement processes (Douglas and Head 2014, 168). Combating police corruption was a central reason for the establishment of ACAs in Singapore, Hong Kong and, as mentioned above, Queensland.

Third, given ACAs are often established in response to a crisis, they offer a means by which to restore public confidence, legitimacy, and stability to systems of governance (Meagher 2005, 72). More deceptively, ACAs offer a means by which politicians, acting for political self-interest, can demonstrate a commitment to values of honesty and impartiality, regardless of whether the agency actually achieves results (see Smilov 2010, 68). Finally, in countries with adversarial judicial procedures focused on individual guilt or innocence, such as in common-law jurisdictions such as Australia, an ACA that utilizes inquisitorial hearings provides an alternative method that prioritizes seeking the truth and understanding lessons for systemic reforms to prevent any reoccurrence of activities.

Singapore's Corrupt Practices Investigation Bureau (CPIB)—established by British colonialists in 1952 but not particularly potent until the reforms enacted by the first Singaporean self-government in 1960—is an example of an ACA operating at the national level. Quah (2013; 2017, 29–30) identifies four key factors underpinning the CPIB's effectiveness. First, it has operational autonomy and popular legitimacy because political leaders have resisted interfering and demonstrated significant political will. Second, the bureau has pursued full enforcement via consistent processes irrespective of the rank or status of the accused person or of the dimension of the alleged offence. Third, it has invested in education and skills development for its staff both locally and through international cooperation. Fourth, the bureau has remained politically impartial and has conducted investigations into ruling-party politicians (Quah 2017, 29–30). When present, these factors contribute to best practices, but they are often limited by power structures and political conditions.

At the regional level the Hong Kong ICAC established in the British colony in 1974 is widely seen as one of the most successful ACAs (de Speville 1997, 10). Its success is an important factor in influencing the wider adoption of ACAs across the globe (Meagher 2005, 69). Since reunification with China, the Hong Kong ICAC's reputation has diminished amid allegations of interference from both the local administration and the central government (Iyengar 2016). Nevertheless, its earlier influence as a model for ACAs pursuing the multipronged approach of prevention, investigation, and education to combat corruption endures. Since the late 1980s the six Australian states have each established standing anti-corruption commissions that, despite variations in organization and functions, closely follow this multipronged approach.

The prevention function is one aspect of this multipronged approach that clearly distinguishes it from conventional law enforcement. The Independent Broad-based Anti-corruption Commission (IBAC) established by parliament in Victoria, Australia, provides insight into how the preventative function can harness the information uncovered in an investigation to affect substantial longer-term change. During 2015–2016 the IBAC investigated allegations against senior education department officials of subverting a tender process and misappropriating resources using false invoices and improper expense claims (Department of Education and Training 2016, 2017). In addition to pursuing criminal charges (still before the courts at the time of writing), the IBAC made recommendations for departmental reforms and required the provision of progress reports on their implementation. This scrutiny of the department's practices, processes, and culture is a step beyond what conventional law enforcement can achieve through its focus on individuals. The subsequent Integrity Reform Program undertaken by the department, particularly the implementation of a "three lines of defense" strategy for managing risk, demonstrates the capacity of an ACA to cooperatively build a more corruption-resistant public sector. Here, the focus is not on enforcement but on the benefits of public scrutiny and accountability to motivate change.

The New York City Department of Investigation (DOI) is an example of a local ACA. Like the ACAs discussed above, the DOI takes the multipronged approach of training, investigations, and prevention to "deliver a definitive and influential message of deterrence" (Gill Hearn 2011, 463). The DOI's preemptive strategy is also supported by a statutory reporting obligation, which addresses the problem of witnesses looking the other way, and protection against retribution is provided for whistleblowers. These are good examples of the range of complimentary measures that bolster the effectiveness of ACAs.

The widespread establishment of ACAs reflects a significant level of confidence in an institutional solution to corruption, particularly in the West (Mungiu-Pippidi 2015, 98–99). However, despite examples of ACAs producing significant results, Mungiu-Pippidi (2015, 113) warns against an overreliance on institutions (Heilbrunn 2004; Meagher 2005; Quah 2013, 2017). Likewise, in their significant and enduring contribution to this debate, Anechiarico and Jacobs (1996, xi–xii) raise concerns about the "anticorruption project" being used for "political cover," leaving public administration "absorbed in self-regulation" without evidence that it actually reduces corruption. Mungiu-Pippidi (2015, 100–101) argues that the recent failures of ACAs in some of the most corrupt countries in the world, such as Bulgaria, Romania, and Macedonia, have undermined the drive for institutional responses and demonstrated the gap between "the 'legal' country and the 'real' country"; that is, between the legal arrangements and actual practice. Meagher (2005, 69) concurs, arguing that "minimum political, legal, and socio-economic conditions" are required in a country before it is possible to establish an effective ACA. As such, Mungiu-Pippidi (2015, 113, 117, 129) argues that there needs to be "a better alignment of tools to contexts," understanding that combating corruption requires a "complex balancing act" that is specific to the opportunities and constraints in a given jurisdiction. Thus, although ACAs offer possibilities, they may not be a good fit in all settings.

Success Factors in ACAs

It is possible to identify some general characteristics that have contributed to the success of effective ACAs and that can be prioritized in the design and implementation of similar bodies in other jurisdictions. First, autonomy is essential, particularly in allowing an ACA to make independent decisions about investigations without political interference. This ensures consistency and impartiality regardless of the status of the accused. Second, resources must be sufficient and stable. Budget reductions are an easy way for political powers to weaken an ACA's capacity, thereby avoiding proper scrutiny of their activities. A mechanism that protects resources from fluctuations in the political will address this.

Third, the multipronged approach of prevention, investigation, and education, as demonstrated above in the IBAC example, allows for a comprehensive effort to reduce corrupt conduct while also building integrity. As noted, reliably measuring the impact on corruption levels is notoriously difficult, but this approach offers comparatively greater assurance than other ad hoc measures. In particular, appropriate powers of investigation are essential to exposing corrupt activities, acting as a key deterrent. Although there has been considerable debate about the merits of designing ACAs to maximize successful prosecutions versus the possibilities for preventative systemic reform—and the extent to which pursuing the latter may undermine the former—the multipronged approach offers case-by-case flexibility to pursue matters according to strategies that are likely to produce the best overall results. Finally, appropriate accountability mechanisms need to ensure that the necessarily strong investigative powers are used legally, ethically, and responsibly. Any accountability failures risk undermining the credibility and legitimacy of ACAs and hampering efforts to combat corruption.

Integrity-Building Strategies

Another approach to combating corruption is to proactively build integrity. Ethics and values cover standards of right and wrong and the personal qualities that support a person's ability to act upon ethical norms. Arguing that ethics are fundamental to an organization's well-being, Dobel (2018) documents how to build an ethical organization. This process starts with developing shared values and commitments and identifying how to strengthen an organization's ability to achieve its purposes against daily stresses and external pressures. He proposes a connection of mission, person, and task within organizations that are built on trust, respect, and communication, while also developing widespread knowledge of laws, rules, and processes. Likewise, van der Wal (2017, 237) suggests a mixture of hard formal and soft informal measures to build integrity alongside oversight measures, evaluations, and expectations management. There also needs to be strong communication about values statements and codes.

Good leaders are ethical leaders (Dobel 2018). Leaders need to be attuned to the positive and negative attributes of their organizations and have the ability to intervene quickly and thoughtfully, particularly in a volatile, uncertain, complex, and ambiguous world. A good leader builds a values base that includes integrity, responsibility, fidelity, courage, competence, respect, honesty, accountability, transparency, inclusiveness, and stewardship. However, these are ideals, and there may be slippages resulting from an acceptance of poor culture, incompetence, willful disregard or subversion of due process, or temptation. A careful diagnosis of any slippages can provide the basis for a targeted intervention and the reinforcement of the relevant value/s.

Conclusion

"Best practices" in this discussion of effective approaches to combating corruption is deliberately plural. The spectrum of corruption problems occurring in diverse settings with a range of capacities to confront them underlines the complexity of developing solutions. Thought must to be given to the strategies implemented at each level—be it global, national, or local—as well as the timeframe for implementation. Big-picture successes can result from long historical development, targeted midterm incremental changes, "big-bang" reforms, or, most likely, a combination of these in order to embed and reinforce corruption resistance. ACAs have worked well in some jurisdictions, particularly by including prevention in a multipronged approach that takes the response beyond what is offered by conventional law enforcement. In others, establishing new institutions has been ineffective or, at worst, has exacerbated problems. An ongoing focus on ethics and values can help preemptively build integrity, although leaders must be alert for slippages. In conclusion, there are no magic-bullet solutions to combat corruption. Instead, a carefully considered and context-specific combination of the best practices discussed here offers a sound path forward.

References

Anechiarico, Frank, and James B. Jacobs. 1996. *The Pursuit of Absolute Integrity: How Corruption Control Makes Government Ineffective.* Chicago, IL: University of Chicago Press.

De Speville, Bertrand. 1997. *Hong Kong: Policy Initiatives Against Corruption.* Paris: Development Centre of the Organisation for Economic Co-operation and Development.

Department of Education and Training. 2016. *Building Confidence in Our Systems and Culture: Integrity Reform in the Department of Education and Training.* December. Melbourne: State of Victoria. www.ibac.vic.gov.au/investigating-corruption/public-examinations/operation-ord.

Department of Education and Training. 2017. *Working with Integrity: The Department of Education and Training's Second Report to the Independent Broad-based Anti-corruption Commission.* September. Melbourne: State of Victoria. www.ibac.vic.gov.au/investigating-corruption/public-examinations/operation-ord.

Dobel, J. Patrick. 2018. *Public Leadership Ethics: A Management Approach.* New York: Routledge.

Donaghue, Stephen. 2001. *Royal Commissions and Permanent Commissions of Inquiry.* Chatswood: Butterworths.

Douglas, Roger, and Michael Head. 2014. *Douglas and Jones's Administrative Law.* 7th ed. Sydney: The Federation Press.

Fitzgerald Report (Commission of Inquiry into Possible Illegal Activities and Associated Police Misconduct). 1989. *Report of a Commission of Inquiry Pursuant to Orders in Council.* Brisbane: Queensland Government. http://www.ccc.qld.gov.au/about-the-ccc/the-fitzgerald-inquiry.

Gill Hearn, Rose. 2011. "The Role of Education in Changing Corrupt Practices," in Adam Graycar and Russel G. Smith, eds., *Handbook of Global Research and Practice in Corruption.* Cheltenham: Edward Elgar, 463–82.

Graycar, Adam. 2015. "Corruption: Classification and Analysis." *Policy and Society 34*(2), 87–96. doi: 10.1016/j.polsoc.2015.04.001.

Graycar, Adam, and Tim Prenzler. 2013. *Understanding and Preventing Corruption.* Basingstoke: Palgrave Macmillan.

Heidenheimer, Arnold J. 2009. "Perspectives on the Perception of Corruption," in Arnold J. Heidenheimer and Michael Johnston, eds., *Political Corruption: Concepts and Contexts.* 3rd ed. New Brunswick: Transaction Publishers, 141–54.

Heilbrunn, John R. 2004. *Anti-Corruption Commissions: Panacea or Real Medicine to Fight Corruption?* Washington, DC: World Bank Institute. http://siteresources.worldbank.org/WBI/Resources/wbi37234Heilbrunn.pdf.

Iyengar, Rishi. 2016. "Hong Kong's Anti-Graft Agency Is in Turmoil, Prompting Fears for the City's Transparency." *Time*, July 14. http://time.com/4405736/hong-kong-icac-corruption-china-transparency/.

Jochim, Ashley E. and Peter J. May. 2010. "Beyond Subsystems: Policy Regimes and Governance." *Policy Studies Journal 38*(2): 303–27. doi: 10.1111/j.1541-0072.2010.00363.x.

Kalniņš, Valts. 2017. "The World's Smallest Virtuous Circle," in Alina Mungiu-Pippidi and Michael Johnston, eds., *Transitions to Good Governance: Creating Virtuous Circles of Anti-Corruption.* Cheltenham: Edward Elgar, 102–27.

Klitgaard, Robert. 1988. *Controlling Corruption.* Berkeley: University of California Press.

Kupatadze, Alexander. 2017. "Georgia: Breaking Out of a Vicious Circle," in Alina Mungiu-Pippidi and Michael Johnston, eds., *Transitions to Good Governance: Creating Virtuous Circles of Anti-Corruption.* Cheltenham: Edward Elgar, 80–101.

McKillop, Bron. 1994. *Inquisitorial Systems of Criminal Justice and the ICAC: A Comparison.* Revised by New South Wales Independent Commission Against Corruption. Sydney: NSW ICAC.

Meagher, Patrick. 2005. "Anti-Corruption Agencies: Rhetoric versus Reality." *The Journal of Policy Reform 8*(1), 69–103. doi: 10.1080/1384128042000328950.

Mungiu-Pippidi, Alina. 2015. *The Quest for Good Governance: How Societies Develop Control of Corruption.* Cambridge: Cambridge University Press.

Mungiu-Pippidi, Alina, and Michael Johnston. 2017. "Conclusions and Lessons Learned," in Alina Mungiu-Pippidi and Michael Johnston, eds., *Transitions to Good Governance: Creating Virtuous Circles of Anti-Corruption.* Cheltenham: Edward Elgar, 234–66.

Prasser, Scott, Rae Wear, and J. R Nethercote, eds. 1990. *Corruption and Reform: The Fitzgerald Vision.* St. Lucia: University of Queensland Press.

Quah, Jon S. T. 2013. "Different Paths to Curbing Corruption: A Comparative Analysis," in Jon S. T. Quah, ed., *Different Paths to Curbing Corruption: Lessons from Denmark, Finland, Hong Kong, New Zealand, and Singapore.* Bingley: Emerald Group, 219–55.

Quah, Jon S. T. 2017. "Combating Asian Corruption: Enhancing the Effectiveness of Anti-Corruption Agencies." *Maryland Series in Contemporary Asian Studies,* No. 2, 229.

Smilov, Daniel. 2010. "Anticorruption Agencies: Expressive, Constructivist and Strategic Uses." *Crime, Law and Social Change 53*(1), 67–77. doi: 10.1007/s10611-009-9215-z.

Transparency International. 2018a. "Corruption Perceptions Index 2017." https://www.transparency .org/cpi.

Transparency International. 2018b. "How Do You Define Corruption?" https://www.transparency. org/what-is-corruption#define.

UNODC (United Nations Office on Drugs and Crime). 2014. "National and International Authorities/Bodies against Corruption." On Track against Corruption: An Online Resource Center to Fight Corruption. https://www.track.unodc.org/ACAuthorities/Pages/home.aspx.

Van der Wal, Zeger. 2017. *The 21st Century Public Manager: Challenges, People and Strategies.* London: Palgrave Macmillan.

You, Jong-sung. 2015. *Democracy, Inequality and Corruption: Korea, Taiwan and the Philippines Compared.* Cambridge: Cambridge University Press.

You, Jong-sung. 2017. "South Korea: The Odyssey to Corruption Control," in Alina Mungiu-Pippidi and Michael Johnston, eds., *Transitions to Good Governance: Creating Virtuous Circles of Anti-Corruption.* Cheltenham: Edward Elgar, 128–58.

23

Preventing Corruption in a Changing Military Culture

The Imperative of Ethical Leadership

Manfred F. Meine and Thomas P. Dunn

The Unique Nature of Military Leadership

If there is a singular essence within the US military, it is the unrelenting imperative of effective leadership. From the first day of entry in the military services, the importance of leadership and preparing military personnel for ever-increasing leadership responsibilities is central to the military culture. Although leadership and its development are important in any formal organization, the successful leadership of military personnel is paramount in the military environment, most especially during wartime.

Because of leadership's criticality to a successful military, extensive resources are expended to develop professional leaders, including the military academies, college, and high school ROTC programs and officer candidate schools, as well as a comprehensive in-service education process culminating in the various war colleges as officers move upward to the most senior leadership ranks. For enlisted soldiers there is a similarly extensive professional development structure as they move up in the non-commissioned officer ranks and assume ever more responsibility.

This extensive education and professional-development process throughout the services has long been reinforced by an up-or-out promotion process, based to a great degree on an annual evaluation process, especially for officers, to ensure military leaders are successful in meeting professional goals in leadership roles. Although this is a well-developed and long-standing process, it is important to consider just what role the question of ethics plays along the military career path. In addition, the military services are served by a unique tool with which to enforce ethical standards, the Uniform Code of Military Justice (UCMJ). Of primary importance is the provision that provides military leaders prosecutorial power over subordinates.

As a precursor to the current gender-integration initiatives, it is important to note that the power of the UCMJ may be one of the reasons that racial integration in the military after the Second World War is arguably one of the military's social-equity successes, and that power may well ensure some level of success for contemporary social equity questions. However, despite extensive leadership training programs and the power of extensive disciplinary possibilities, the military has not been immune from corrupt or unethical leadership.

The Uniqueness of Military Ethics

The Military Culture: Organizational versus Individual Ethical Behavior

The behavior of human beings ultimately reflects the actions of individual actors, since even the most complex of social organizations are, in essence, a collectivity of individuals, as noted by Jurkiewicz and Grossman (2012). Collective behaviors of individuals can easily move an organization to the extreme, with the resulting evil being so pervasive as to warrant its being meaningfully conceptualized as organizational evil. More specifically, beyond the unfortunate, but inevitable, instances of idiosyncratic evil, it seems clear that political agendas and socioeconomic factors may also contribute significantly to the phenomenon of organizational evil; with such evil being manifested in (1) organizations taking little or no action when unethical behaviors emerge, (2) the tacit acceptance of unethical actions, that is, "looking the other way," and, in the extreme, (3) the overt routinization of systemic unethical behaviors within the organization.

To understand the differing foci of military ethics considerations, it is useful to define individual ethics as behaviors involved in individual interactions. As such, sexual harassment or assault by one individual on another would belong in this category, as would lying, cheating, or stealing for personal benefit. Organizational ethics, on the other hand, focus on the impact of organizational cultures or climates that allow, support, or even encourage ethical or unethical behaviors. It would seem legitimate to assume that a significant number of "individual behaviors" are a derivative of the prevailing organizational ethics. In the area of organizational ethics, it is further useful to separate unethical behaviors for some form of personal or organizational gain such as passing inspections or reporting readiness, which could include directing, encouraging, or allowing falsification of records or reports to present a more positive picture to superiors or the public, from other types of unethical behaviors that further operational goals or support claims of successes, like the corrupt use of the "body count" focus during the Vietnam conflict to falsify claims of success in meeting imposed goals.

Furthermore, there is considerable debate about the appropriateness of applying traditional ethics concepts like utilitarianism or deontological ethics to the military setting, especially in their applicability to the conduct of war (McMasters 2010; Olsthoorn 2011). The Vietnam War continues to be an example of what the loss of the proper ethical culture can lead to in wartime and during the typical drawdown after protracted conflict potentially leading to a need to rebuild the military, similar to what the contemporary military is facing after the never-ending Afghanistan and Middle East conflicts or operations. Once again, the terms "hollow force" and "overstretched" military are in the national policy discussions.

Ethics and Wartime: The Never-Ending Debate?

Societal concern regarding military ethics predates modern history, but despite numerous changes in focus throughout the centuries, any discussion of military ethics has always been, by its very nature, an inevitably complex and frequently contradictory process, in large part as a result of the typical actions not only expected but routinely and universally required of a professional military. In essence, military forces are to defeat an enemy primarily by taking lives and inflicting destruction which, in itself, could be considered an unethical undertaking despite often being arguably justified by "just war" or "national security," or more provocatively—as von Clausewitz suggests in his treatise *On War*—for political ends, as demonstrated by US administrations during the Vietnam War.

While war has proven to be unavoidable at times, armed conflict is, arguably, inherently evil—to include its having been demonstrated to create a compatible environment for deviance and corrupt leadership, especially in light of the unrelenting strategy of demonizing the enemy as a means of motivating the troops to accomplish their missions, not infrequently, at "all costs." While the demonization strategy may have been and may continue to be an effective tool in achieving military goals, its use with troops trained in the skills of killing the enemy requires strong leadership to control those skills by also providing a contextual focus on the ethical imperatives surrounding the conduct of war. That focus can best be implemented by strengthening and enforcing value-based ethics on the part of military forces in general, and on military leaders specifically to help guide appropriate behavior.

The Evolution of Military Ethics

Internationally, the impetus for change in the modern era was the carnage of two world wars that led to the modern Geneva Conventions and the Laws of War seeking to regulate even the types of weapons and ammunition that may or may not be used in an effort to reach a more humane approach to warfare—if, indeed, "humane" is ever appropriate for use in the same sentence as "war." Unfortunately, despite such laudatory humanitarian efforts, there has typically been no shortage of so called war crimes on all sides of military conflicts worldwide. As such, it is understandable that there should be a strong and unrelenting focus on ensuring the most ethical organizational approach to military operations as well as to the behaviors of individual military personnel generally, and specifically in time of war.

An examination of selected events occurring during the Vietnam and other conflicts can serve to illustrate the ethical implications of the concept of organizational evil vis-à-vis the evil behavior of individuals in the military and the potential for corrupt leadership. Some of the Vietnam War's most disturbing organizational and individual deviant and unethical behaviors (exacerbated by coverups and politics) are still debated today and are combined with contemporary concerns regarding more recently alleged organizational transgressions leading to renewed focus on strengthening a culture of ethics in the US military.

Historically military ethics training in the United States centered on moral issues, but the Vietnam conflict in general, and events surrounding the My Lai massacre and other reports of indiscriminate killing followed by ensuing coverup efforts, sent shock waves through the system and were clearly the primary catalyst for a significant focus-change initiative to include elevated expectations for and scrutiny of ethics to prevent corrupt leadership.

The more contemporary wars in Iraq and Afghanistan have not been immune from some strikingly similar incidents; for example, the deaths of thousands of civilians attributed to regrettable but unavoidable collateral damage. Since similarly innocent deaths occurred both in Vietnam and in contemporary conflicts, the primary difference, according to Crawford (2013), being the moral and ethical accountability for such deaths and the resulting importance of identifying salient lessons that can be drawn to create a legacy for improving the professionalism of the US military in general and, more particularly, ethical behavior per se, in current and future conflicts.

Mission versus Career Focus

Military organizations are known for and expected to have a very strong mission focus; however, there is an inherent danger in allowing even such a crucial focus to become excessive since doing so can lead to leadership corruption and unethical actions, such as indiscriminate killing of both combatants and noncombatants to present a positive picture of mission accomplishment or success, for which a misuse of the body-count mission focus during the Vietnam conflict is a prime and disconcerting example.

While the mission question focuses on organizations, the individual career focus deals with individuals seeking to act in their own best interest. Here, too, there is the danger of an excessive focus on individual success sometimes encouraged by the "zero defects mentality" related to career progression, even resulting in officers cheating on exams related to nuclear-missile operational proficiency (Everstein 2014). Career focus can also influence the mission area since corrupt leaders can influence organizations to take actions or avoid actions simply to protect their own career goals. When inappropriate self-serving career focus actions take place in combat, they can have dramatic negative results.

Following any lengthy conflict, military drawdowns are common, therefore, not surprisingly, the hollow-force discussion resurfaced as the military was faced with post-Iraq and Afghanistan drawdowns (Kitfield 2013), at least until the arrival of the Trump administration. Despite much contemporary discussion about avoiding a zero-tolerance or risk-aversion mindset among military leaders, the insecurity generated by such force-reduction environments can easily lead to an unwillingness to take chances (DeGrandpre 2013; Ghallager 2014; Thornton 2000).

Since drawdowns and zero tolerance relate to performance, it is important to consider how performance expectations, evaluation standards, and organizational goals interface with ethical behavior. With military-related examples such as the Veterans Administrations falsification of patient waiting times to meet goals (Department of Veterans Affairs 2014), and Air Force Nuclear Missile Officers cheating on proficiency exams to avoid the consequences of no tolerance for failure (Everstein 2014), the answer is undeniably clear. Unethical and corrupt behavior committed by members of complex organizations who are under great pressure to achieve goals or meet standards, especially when those accomplishments are tied directly to sanctions or rewards, may explain Doty and Hoffman's (2014) claims that lying on the part of military personnel, including leaders, is a form of corruption that has actually become part of the military culture.

Adding to the complexity of any discussion on military ethics is the contemporary focus on the military's role in supporting and expanding the acceptance of cultural diversity and greater gender equity. As national military policy struggles and legal challenges have suggested, it may well be that the contemporary social equity–focused environment for military service may be even more of a challenging shift for military leaders as they work to build appropriate personnel policies.

Additional areas of concern that have not changed significantly since Vietnam are the questions of trust in military leaders and the unrelenting emphasis on loyalty in military organizations. Ironically, during Vietnam, trust issues undoubtedly led to disciplinary problems, and potentially even contributed to the large number of "fraggings." Previous Army studies have shown effective leadership to be a key component of soldier retention, but contemporary military issues such as sexual harassment and other forms of misconduct, even on the part of senior leaders, can quickly erode trust and can lead to an ineffective ethics culture in an organization (Glonek 2013; Imiola 2013).

Ironically, loyalty to the military, to the unit, to comrades-in-arms, and to strong leaders can easily contribute to overlooking unethical behaviors on the part of fellow service members and leaders. Such loyalty likely contributed to organizational deviance in Vietnam, potentially allowed the Abu Ghraib situation in Iraq to persist for an extended period of time, and could cause similar problems in the future. Within the context of the current discussion, it should come as no surprise that extreme loyalty has even been called a great threat to the Army profession (Johnson 2013).

Social Equity and Gender Integration in the Military
Women in the Military

Throughout much of human history the warrior role was exclusively male and, therefore, it could have been expected that the integration of women into military service would be a more challenging gender question even in the contemporary environment, but such has not been the case. Not unlike the initial social equity milestone involving race, gender integration may well turn out to be a second landmark in equity achievement by the military, although many of the specifics of that potential achievement have yet to be determined. It should also be acknowledged that, throughout that same history, military personnel who would now be identified as members of the LGBT community also served successfully, albeit having had to remain silent about their orientation or gender preferences.

Having begun in earnest with the integration of women from the previously separate women's organizations in the services, to full inclusion of women into all military occupations, even into the elite combat units, the military continues to march toward the unlimited integration of women. However, such contentious and high-profile concerns as those surrounding physical standards and combat readiness will continue to raise policy questions and operational issues moving forward. Regardless of the remaining challenges, there are a number of positive factors for women in the military, such as being paid the same as men for the same work and being generally afforded identical advancement opportunities as men, despite some lingering barriers resulting from the long history of women having being excluded from certain fields.

The integration of women culminated in the 2015 Defense Department announcement that all fields of the armed services of the United States would be opened to women (Rosenberg and Phillips 2015). While there are doubters that women can be successful in all areas, especially the physically demanding ones, it was nevertheless clear that the military was well on its way to achieving a long-awaited milestone, as well as having set a significant example in the achievement of gender equity for American society as a whole (Meine and Dunn 2016). Despite such a positive conclusion, the expanded role of women is still an evolving issue, albeit one moving forward slowly considering that the first female Marine Infantry student did not enter training until March 2018 (Werner 2018), and the past five graduating classes of the United States Military Academy have had just sixteen female officers entering the primary combat arms branches of Armor and Infantry out of 2,753 total graduates (Caslen 2018). There may be diminishing resistance to direct combat roles for women, but questions about their combat readiness continue, with Secretary of Defense James Mattis reportedly highlighting the low number of women in specific combat roles despite opportunities, and reporting that any definitive conclusions about their combat effectiveness are premature (Baldor 2018). All the while, the appropriate physical standards for women will continue to be debated publicly and, undoubtedly, behind a wide variety of closed doors, especially as the US Army moves toward a new fitness test with single-event standards regardless of gender or age (Myers 2018).

Sexual Assault and Misconduct Issues

Significant strides in gender integration have not been without unintended consequences as the number of sexual harassment claims and even sexual assaults, primarily against female military members, has not only escalated, but has become a frequent focus of media reporting as well. The fact that even senior military leaders have been involved in such incidents suggests this is an area where exposing and eliminating corrupt leadership is critical.

Although eliminating, or at least minimizing, sexual encounters between superiors and subordinates has become a human relations imperative within virtually all social organizations in both the private and public sectors, doing so among military personnel, regardless of their sexual orientation, is of heightened importance due to the unique level of coercive pressure routinely available to superiors over subordinates and the undeniable necessity of embracing and preserving the traditional authoritarian structure for its crucial role in accomplishing the seemingly endless variety of missions assigned to a modern, professional military. Strengthening the enforcement of anti-fraternization policies and vigorous investigation and disciplinary actions for violations may help, but also establishing a culture of respect between service members, and especially superior–subordinate relationships, is critical, especially if the military has any expectation of continuing to be successful in circumventing congressional efforts to enter a far-reaching slippery slope by taking prosecutorial and disciplinary actions away from commanders in cases of rape or sexual assault.

Alternative Lifestyles in the Military

Unquestionably, the most controversial and highly publicized gender-equity questions relate to alternative lifestyle issues confronting the US military. The service of gays and lesbians has been a lengthy struggle and debate, with a long history of homosexuality typically resulting in the elimination of gays and lesbians from the military, and homosexual physical relations being criminal violations of the Uniform Code of Military Justice, with extensive prison sentences possible. During the Clinton administration, efforts to live up to campaign promises led to the infamous and ambiguous "don't ask, don't tell" approach. This blatantly hypocritical approach of allowing gays and lesbians to serve as long as they did not reveal their sexual orientation, nor permitting any relevant inquiries, still meant that military personnel would be discharged from the service if they acted upon their orientation, or if the information revealing that orientation came to light. Despite the end of such policies, the criminality of certain acts associated with homosexual relations has remained in Article 25 of the UCMJ, no matter how unlikely to be applied to consensual acts (Title 10, United States Code, Ch. 47, 2010).

During the Obama administration, it appeared the issue may well have been resolved, with the military having formally recognized same-sex relationships, including marriages, and providing benefits to same-sex partners. Although time will tell what the long-term effects of this policy might be, the change in the military of allowing gays and lesbians to serve openly seems to have been accepted, with little or no overt resistance throughout the armed forces, and with few if any problems being reported publicly. But, despite the two long-standing gender issues having seemingly been resolved, they were followed by a new and even more volatile gender issue: namely, the status of military service for currently serving LGBT personnel, as well as potentially even more problematic issues involving future recruitment from among those in the LGBT community.

It is a given that there have been transgender service members in the past who served honorably and successfully, with some estimates being as high as 150,000 having served (Gates and Herman 2014) and with more than six thousand recently on active duty (Schaefer et al. 2016). But, like their gay and lesbian predecessors, they have had to serve in secret, and the idea that a male or female soldier could choose to alter their gender identity, even by employing complicated and expensive surgical procedures, would have previously been unthinkable, just as integrated units, women in combat and same-sex marriages were once unthinkable.

The Obama Administration Opens the Door

On June 30, 2016, the US secretary of defense announced that military service would be opened to transgender personnel, and that not only could they serve openly, but they could openly follow their personal gender identification. In addition, and even more profoundly significant, the military would not only provide gender-identity counseling but, if deemed "necessary," perform sex-change surgery at taxpayer expense (Mondale 2016).

Unfortunately for the LGBT community, that seemingly wide-open door to equitable access to military service soon began to close.

The Trump Transition

Although there was no shortage of scholarly and pragmatic reactions to the Obama initiative, of particular interest to this chapter was the seemingly positive statement by President

Trump's secretary of defense, James Mattis, who testified that he had little interest in the bedroom behavior of consenting adults (Mattis 2017).

Social Engineering and the Trump Administration

Even the most diligent attempt to determine the origin of the pejorative, but intellectually appealing, concept of "social engineering" would, at best be speculative, but the relevance of that controversial process to the US military appears to have become firmly established in the national narrative, with the philosophical, ethical, and pragmatic implications of utilizing America's armed forces as de facto agents of social change continuing to surface periodically in political discourse.

Soon after taking office, President Trump was accused of surprising his Defense Department with one of his "tweets" indicating that transgender personnel would not be permitted to serve in the military. He soon directed the department to study and develop a policy for implementation but, not surprisingly, lawsuits were soon initiated by both transgender military personnel currently serving and those preparing to serve and their supporters. With the ambiguity of policies and pronouncements within the Trump administration in regard to military service by transgender personnel, such as the on-again, off-again "bans" and "holds" on allowing open military service and the recruitment/enlistment of transgender personnel—based in part on claims of inconclusive science, the creation of an investigative panel, disruptive legal challenges, and the prospect of congressional involvement—left the question of the eventual outcome of what might be viewed as reverse social engineering unanswered until federal appeals courts upheld lower-court rulings to require the military to accept transgender recruits effective January 1, 2018. The Justice Department declined to challenge those rulings since a Defense Department study on the impact of transgender service was to be released in early 2018, but the issue has remained unsettled as some federal courts continued blocking implementing a ban on transgender service, while others, including the US Supreme Court, allowed it to move forward during continuing litigation.

Despite the temporary victory, transgender recruits confront strict physical and mental conditions making their entry into the military more challenging than for traditional recruits. According to a Pentagon spokesman, enlisting transgender recruits was to begin on January 1, 2018, while the Defense Department studied the issue. Early enlistment numbers are not yet available to show what level of interest there is in such service, raising the question: Has the debate to date really been "much ado about nothing?" On March 24, 2018, the *Associated Press* reported that President Trump had accepted the recommended Defense Department policy submitted by Secretary of Defense Mattis, which generally prohibits service by transgender persons with very limited exceptions (Thomas 2018). However, the federal courts have ruled that, effective January 1, 2018, the Defense Department must rely on the existing policy from the previous administration to allow LGBT persons to enlist in the military. With court challenges continuing, despite the first transgender enlistment contract having taken place as of February 23, 2018 (McLaughlin 2018; Ali 2018), it is too early to conclude the final outcome of the issue, which has been driven from the front pages of media focus and replaced by newer and arguably even more tumultuous political debates of the day.

While the future of these sociopolitical issues remains in question, the initial legal challenges proliferated and have continued to delay any final settlement of the question; with legal scholars predicting that if there is to be an ultimate resolution, it will be rendered by the nation's top court, where the key questions will be whether military service is an inherent right, and what if any reasonable limitations the military can set on that service, with the key focus being "reasonable." Despite the unfinished status of the LGBT military-service issue, the intellectual and pragmatic challenges should not be dismissed.

Ethical Leadership Challenges in a Rapidly Changing Gender Culture

Was the financial argument against transgender military service as significant as it was initially portrayed to be?

In order to consider this question, it is useful to once again refer to the women in the military issue. Looking back at a time when pregnancy resulted in mandatory release from active military service, to today's world of full financial support and benefits for pregnant soldiers, including maternity leave for both mother and father, one could reasonably conclude that the medical-cost argument for transgender service is a hollow one.

Since the cost of addressing ergonomic issues related to some of the physical and privacy questions related to service by women—such as refitting submarines to better accommodate female crew members and to improve privacy, and costly adjustments such as lowering valves and/or making valves easier to turn—has not deterred the military from moving forward, the comparatively negligible cost of accommodating transgender personnel also seems to offer no legitimate barrier to their integration.

What if any impact will the expanded service opportunities for both women and the LGBT community have on the military's challenges in dealing with sexual harassment and assault?

Despite significant strides in gender integration, that initiative has not been without problems, such as the noted increase in the number of sexual-harassment claims and even sexual assaults, primarily against female military members. Such incidents have become the frequent focus of media reporting as well (as evidenced in the dismissal of two drill sergeants at Fort Benning, Georgia, for sexual harassment [Myers 2017]). Even more disturbing is the fact that even high-ranking military leaders have been involved in such incidents, as exemplified by senior officers pressuring or coercing subordinates into inappropriate sexual situations, including one of the most senior and highly respected military leaders engaging in adulterous behaviors (Brook 2016). Regardless of the specific nature of attempts to deter sexual encounters and assaults between superiors and subordinates, such as establishing and enforcing an aggressive zero-tolerance posture for such violations, the key to the effectiveness of any such attempts will be establishing in the US military an overriding ethical culture that unequivocally emphasizes respect between service members and, especially, superior–subordinate relationships—a culture that is genuinely endorsed and actively promoted by senior leadership, both military and civilian.

What if any impact will the expanded gender integration have on morale, unit cohesion, and ultimately on combat effectiveness?

For much of American military history, and despite significant progress in expanding the role of women in the military services, women were still prohibited from serving in direct combat roles and restricted from certain elite organizations, but in today's combat environments, women in the "support units" have been routinely exposed to life-threatening combat encounters, to include close-quarters combat, as demonstrated during the Iraq and Afghanistan conflicts—a reality that has exposed these restrictions as outdated, virtually meaningless, and blatantly hypocritical. The unrelenting illumination of that hypocrisy by the advocates of a total gender integration of women in the military likely was a significant factor in the services being ordered to open all fields, including direct combat roles, to anyone who meets the standards, and even into previously unthinkable fields, such as the submarine service in the Navy, the Infantry and Ranger units in the Army and Marine Corps, and special operations positions in all services.

Despite the highly publicized successes to date, what remains to be seen includes (1) how many of the women who can meet the existing standards will seek such positions (or will be assigned to them), as well as (2) how many women who do seek or are assigned to direct combat roles will be unable to meet some of the more physically challenging standards currently in place, especially in some special-operations areas. It is interesting to note that in addition to the two women having successfully completed Army Ranger Training in 2016, it was not until September 2017 that the first female Marine officer successfully completed the arduous Marine Infantry Officer Training Course (Kheel 2017). While these are positive indicators moving forward, critics are likely to point to the large number of women who have been unsuccessful in both of these difficult and physically challenging courses.

At this point, one can only wonder if, as happened in fields like firefighting and police service, standards are likely to be reexamined and potentially altered or treated separately for the genders, a debate that has often been one of the most inflammatory and will likely be complicated by as yet unresolved issues of how to deal with transgender questions when military personnel transition from one gender to another.

What ethical and leadership challenges will be presented in dealing with and controlling or overcoming the inevitable social and cultural biases raised by the LGBT integration?

Considering that a significant portion of military recruits come from reportedly conservative southern states and communities, there is no doubt that building and maintaining a proper professional ethics culture executed by members grounded in clear and strong, ethics-based values and led by leaders whose ethics are reinforced by reliable support structures and potential sanctions for intentional ethical failings is essential in successfully navigating the many challenges ahead. It is critical therefore to focus on maintaining or, wherever possible, improving ethical leadership and enforcing methods and policies designed toward that end. To the extent that is an accurate assessment, the military is not alone, but is sharing yet another of the emerging challenges confronting any contemporary, complex organization, albeit within the daunting context of the uniquely dire consequences of armed conflict.

What if any leadership challenges will be raised by the semantics of the transgender integration question, and will these contribute to or ameliorate firmly entrenched, ideological biases?

In establishing policies related to transgender service, much of the focus has been on providing medical and psychological support for those dealing with gender dysphoria. While the intent of this focus is well intentioned, it also raises the troublesome possibility that the overt recognition of the potential need for "support" will result in a stigma of "there is something wrong with the person" and an ensuing reluctance to seek help, as has reportedly been the case with many service personnel as with the question of PTSD. Turning back to the frequently cited problems of the post-Vietnam conflict military, are we doomed to repeat the "zero defects" view of leadership, making speaking up about issues a career-threatening undertaking? Considering that a single inappropriate word uttered can be career-ending, especially for senior military leaders (Myers 2018), the impact of a "zero-defects" mentality is not an unlikely concern for engaged leadership moving forward.

Will there be sufficient political will to research these issues fully and in an unbiased way?

As the struggle to arrive at final policy decisions and provide the critical operational clarity for military leaders continues, one can only speculate when and if unbiased and much-needed research, involving both the natural and social sciences, will be authorized, conducted, and the results taken into account by military and civilian policy makers alike or if the politically charged and socially divisive questions will continue to make clear an ethical policy pathways difficult to develop, implement, and enforce.

A Final Thought

While the ethical dilemmas confronting the leaders of any high-profile complex organization are considerable, the potentially catastrophic consequences for the civilian/military leadership making those decisions are even more problematic. The seminal question then becomes how best to combat corrupt leadership in the changing military culture of the future and to enforce appropriate and acceptable standards of individual and organizational ethics while ensuring the commensurate ethical behavior on the part of individuals in general, and leaders in particular, in the continuously and rapidly evolving environment surrounding the strategic and tactical conduct of military operations and, ultimately, war.

References

Ali, Idress. 2018. "Pentagon Makes Recommendations to White House on Transgender Individuals." *Reuters*, February 23. https://www.reuters.com/article/us-usa-military-transgender/pentagon-makes-recommendations-to-white-house-on-transgender-individuals-idUSKCN1G722L Accessed February 27, 2018.

Baldor, Lolita C. 2018. "Mattis: Jury Is Out on Women Succeeding in Combat Jobs." *Military Times*, September 25. https://www.militarytimes.com/news/your-military/2018/09/25/mattis-jury-is-out-on-women-succeeding-in-combat-jobs/. Accessed October 1, 2018.

Brook, T. 2016. "Extramarital Affair, Misuse of Resources Cost Army General His Post." *USA TODAY*, July 27.

Caslen, Robert Jr. 2018. "From the Superintendent." *West Point*, Spring, 4.

Crawford, Neta C. 2013. *Accountability for Killing: Moral Responsibility for Collateral Damage in America's Post-9/11 Wars*. New York: Oxford University Press.

DeGrandpre, Andrew. 2013. "Commandant: Accountability Does Not Mean Zero Defects." *Military Times*, June 3. http://militarytimes.com/article/201130603/CAREERS03/306030005/Commandant-Accountability-Does-Not-Mean-Zero Defects. Accessed August 8, 2014.

Doty, Joe, and Pete Hoffman. 2014. "Front and Center: Admit It—Lying Is a Problem in the Military." *Army*, July, 19–21.

Everstein, Brian. 2014. 'Malmstrom Commander Resigns, 9 COs Removed in Cheating Scandal." *Air Force Times*, March 27. http://www.airforcetimes.com/article/20140327/NEWS05/303270055/Malmstrom-commander-resigns-9-COs-removed-cheating-scandal. Accessed August 14, 2014.

Gates, Gary J., and Jody L. Herman. 2014. "Transgender Military Service in the United States." *The Williams Institute, UCLA School of Law*, May. https://williamsinstitute.law.ucla.edu/research/military-related/us-transgender-military-service/. Accessed April 26, 2018.

Ghallager, Brendan. 2014. "Managing Risk in Today's Army." *Military Review*, January–February, 90–96.

Glonek, Jashua. 2013. "The Trust Lapse: How Our Profession's Bedrock is Being Undermined." *Military Review*, September–October, 40–47.

Imiola, Brian. 2013. "The Imaginary Army Ethic: A Call for Articulating a Real Foundation for Our Profession." *Military Review*, May–June, 2–5.

Johnson, Dan. 2013. "The Greatest Threat Facing the Army Profession." *Military Review*, September–October, 69–72.

Jurkiewicz, Carol, and Dave Grossman. 2012. "Evil at Work." *The Foundations of Organizational Evil*. Armonk, NY: M. E. Sharpe.

Kheel, R. 2017. "Marines Congratulate First Female Infantry Officer Graduate." *The Hill*, September 25.

Kitfield, James. 2013. "A Hollow Military Again—Special report, House Armed Services Committee." National Journal.Com, June 12. http://www.nationaljournal.com/congress/a-hollow-military-again-20130612. Accessed August 8, 2014.

Mattis, James. 2017. "CNN Public Broadcast of the Nomination Hearing for the Position of Secretary of Defense." January 12. http://www.cnn.com/2017/01/12/politics/james-mattis-defense-confirmation/index.html. Accessed May 3, 2018.

McLaughlin, Elizabeth. 2018. "First Transgender Recruit Joins US Military as Trump Debates Policy." *ABC News*, February 26. http://abcnews.go.com/Politics/transgender-recruit-joins-us-military-trump-debates-policy/story?id=53368719. Accessed February 27, 2018.

McMasters, Herbert R. 2010. "Remaining True to Our Values—Reflections on Military Ethics in Trying Times." *Journal of Military Ethics 9*(March), 183–94.

Meine, M. F., and T. P. Dunn. 2016. "Using the Military for Social Engineering: Ethical, Moral and Practical Issues." Presented at the 9th Annual SPMA International Conference, Pretoria, Gauteng, South Africa. October 27.

Mondale, A. 2016. "Military Leaders, Officials Say Clarity, Education—Not Just Policy—Key to LGBT Equality in the Mil." US Army Website. https://www.army.mil/article/171147/military_leaders_officialssay_clarity_education_not_just_policy_key_to_lgbt_equality_in_the_mil. Accessed September 28, 2017.

Myers, M. 2017. "Infantry Drill Sergeants Suspended after Sexual Assault Allegations from Female Recruits." *Army Times*, August 23.

Myers, M. 2018, "Here's an Early Draft of the Army's New Fitness Test Standards." *Army Times* August 1.

Olsthoorn, Peter. 2011. "Intentions and Consequences in Military Ethics." *Journal of Military Ethics* 10(February), 81–93.

Rosenberg, M. and D. Phillips. 2015. "All Combat Roles Now Open to Women, Defense Secretary Says." *New York Times*, December 3.

Schaefer, Agnes G., et al. 2016. *Assessing the Implications of Allowing Transgender Personnel to Serve Openly*. Santa Monica, CA: RAND Corporation.

Thomas, K. 2018. "AP Explains: Trump's Policy on Transgender Troops." Associated Press, March 24. http://www.indexjournal.com/news/national/ap-explains-trump-s-policy-on-transgender-troops/article_c066a9cf-7e0d-59db-baa9-996027173de0.html. Accessed March 25, 2018.

Thornton, Rod. 2000. "Cultural Barriers to Organizational Unlearning: The US Army, the Zero-Defects Culture and Operations in the Post-Cold War World." *Small Wars and Insurgencies* 11(3), 139–59.

Uniformed Code of Military Justice. 2010. Title 10, United States Code, Chapter 47. https://www.gpo.gov/fdsys/pkg/USCODE-2010-title10/html/USCODE-2010-title10-subtitleA-partII-chap47.htm. Accessed January 18, 2018.

United States Department of Veterans Affairs. 2014. "VA Access Audit and Wait Times Fact Sheet: System-Wide Overview." June 9. http://www.va.gov/health/docs/vaaccessauditsystem-widefactsheet060914.pdf. Accessed August 14, 2014.

Werner, Ben. 2018. "Military Branches Are Doing More to Recruit Women into Active Duty." *The U.S. Naval Institute*, April 13. https://news.usni.org/2018/04/13/service-branches-want-more-women. Accessed April 19, 2018.

Von Clausewitz, Carl. 1883. *On War*, trans. by James J. Graham. Altenmuenster, Germany: Jazzybee Verlag Juergen Beck.

24

Whistleblowing

Encouraging Responsible Reporting and Developing Effective Whistleblower Protections

Kathryn G. Denhardt

Whistleblowing is an act of disclosing information about wrongdoing to some higher authority or to the public (e.g., corruption, fraud, mismanagement, or threats to public health and safety, financial integrity, human rights, the environment, or the rule of law) (Transparency International 2018a). Though whistleblowing has been with us for as long as there have been people willing to challenge wrongdoing by institutions, the advent of digital technologies has made possible exponential changes in the scale of data releases and notoriety of the whistleblower. Troves of confidential or classified information can be made public by people who have legitimate access to the data (but are under obligation to keep the information secret) or by hackers (who successfully breach the firewalls of classified data).

Julian Assange founded WikiLeaks in 2006 to offer some level of safety and anonymity for whistleblowers to release those troves of data about allegedly illegal or immoral behavior of governments and businesses. He believed that the technology revolution provided "conspirators with the means to achieve ... 'higher total conspiratorial power' " while also "making them more vulnerable to sabotage" (Rutenberg 2017). The first major test of the impact of WikiLeaks came in 2010, when US Army intelligence analyst, Bradley Manning, released a large cache of classified national-security data, including videos of airstrikes in Iraq and Afghanistan in which civilians were killed, dossiers on detainees at Guantanamo Bay, Cuba, as well as hundreds of thousands of Army reports and US diplomatic cables. Manning acknowledged responsibility for the leaks, saying the motive was to spark a debate about the true nature of twenty-first-century asymmetrical warfare.

> Private Manning's actions lifted a veil on American military and diplomatic activities around the world, and engendered a broad debate over what information should become public, how the government treats leakers, and what happens to those who see themselves as whistle-blowers (*sic*). (Savage 2013)

Both Manning and Assange bore significant costs for their whistleblowing activities. Manning was found guilty of several espionage charges but was found *not guilty* of the more serious charge of aiding the enemy. Manning was sentenced to thirty-five years' imprisonment, much longer than others convicted of leaking secret government information. In January 2017, just before leaving office, President Obama commuted all but four months of the remaining prison sentence, releasing Manning (by now known as Chelsea Manning) after seven years in prison. Assange was granted asylum by Ecuador in 2012—initially to avoid rape charges in Sweden but later to avoid extradition to the United States to face charges related to release of the data. He lived in the Ecuadorean embassy in London for seven years but was arrested by British police in April 2019 after Ecuador withdrew his asylum. As of August 2019, he is in a maximum-security British prison and is scheduled for a US extradition hearing in February 2020.

In 2013, Edward Snowden, an employee of a contractor working for the US National Security Agency (NSA), stole a trove of highly classified documents showing the vast scope of information the NSA collected and the methods used to access that information. As those documents were released, we learned that with authorization from a secret court, the NSA had collected billions of phone records of unsuspecting Americans through bulk surveillance sweeps of data supplied by the phone service providers, had spied on foreign allies (including German chancellor Angela Merkel), and had developed various technologies for cracking encryption and accessing Internet data (Franceschi-Bicchierai 2014). To some, Snowden is a hero for revealing the scope of the government's secret surveillance activities, which threaten the privacy of its citizens as well as unsuspecting innocent people across the world. To others—including the US government—Snowden is a traitor. As of this writing, he remains in exile in Russia, where he sought asylum after being charged with espionage-related felonies by the US government. The released documents caused public outrage about violations of privacy and led the NSA's own internal auditor to find that the agency "broke federal privacy laws, or exceeded its authority, thousands of times per year" (*New York Times* 2014).

The vulnerability inherent in digital communications was again made vivid during the 2016 US presidential election, when Russian intelligence hackers sought to influence the election by stealing a trove of documents from the Democratic National Committee (DNC) and from Democratic presidential candidate Hillary Clinton's campaign chairman, then turning them over to WikiLeaks. It is open to debate whether Assange's release of the documents was legitimate whistleblowing or simply a desire to influence the election by damaging Clinton. The contents of the documents dominated the media for months of the campaign, keeping Clinton constantly on the defensive and providing fodder to her opponent. This made Assange "a reviled figure among supporters of the Democratic nominee and a hero to backers of Donald J. Trump" (Eder 2016).

Assange's warning that technology provided "conspirators with the means to achieve … an even 'higher total conspiratorial power'" (Rutenberg 2017) seems borne out in what we know about Russian efforts to influence the US election. In addition to the DNC emails, social networking sites also proved vulnerable to a form of sabotage. During the year leading up to the 2016 election, Russian sources bought digital ads on Facebook and Instagram, and using stolen identities to pose as Americans, they sought to "sow discord among the electorate by creating Facebook groups, distributing divisive ads and posting inflammatory images" (Frenkel and Benner 2018). The Justice Department has brought charges against at least thirteen Russians "for executing a scheme to subvert the 2016 election and support Donald J. Trump's campaign" (Frenkel and Benner 2018). Facebook has been called to task for not catching the Russian activity earlier and doing something to stop it (Frenkel et al. 2018). While foreign powers (including the United States) have a long tradition of trying to influence the elections of other countries, the ability to gain access to huge troves of secret information ramps up the game.

Though Trump's campaign appeared to benefit from the WikiLeaks and Facebook activities initially, perhaps helping him get elected, his presidency has been dogged by questions about whether his campaign colluded with the Russians and violated election laws in the process. In 2017 Robert Mueller was appointed as special counsel to oversee the investigation into Russian interference with the 2016 election, and the possibility that members of Trump's campaign had colluded with the Russians. The Mueller investigation's final report concluded,

> Although the investigation established that the Russian government perceived it would benefit from a Trump presidency and worked to secure that outcome, and that the Campaign expected it would benefit electorally from information stolen and released through Russian efforts, the investigation did not establish that members of the Trump Campaign conspired or coordinated with the Russian government in its election interference activities. (2019, 13)

The Mueller Report, however, does not lay to rest the question of whether Trump obstructed Mueller's investigation (214).

> [I]f we had confidence after a thorough investigation of the facts that the President clearly did not commit obstruction of justice, we would so state. Based on the facts and applicable legal standards, however, we are unable to reach that judgment. The evidence we obtained about the President's actions and intent presents difficult issues that prevent us from conclusively determining that no criminal conduct occurred. Accordingly, while this report does not conclude that the President committed a crime, it also does not exonerate him.

The Complicated Ethics of Whistleblowing

One might argue that whistleblowing has served a valuable purpose because of the fact all this information is being laid bare in view of the public rather than remaining secret—civilian casualties in remote bombings, the unvarnished discussions of diplomats, the dossiers of prisoners detained in Guantanamo, foreign efforts to influence elections. That none of the parties involved seems to have clean hands suggests that whistleblowing will almost always be a legally and morally complicated act. It can be seen as "heroic action that serves the public interest" (Svara 2015, 143) or a form of "political vigilantism" (Delmas 2015, 77). Or anything in between.

Delmas defines government whistleblowing as "the unauthorized acquisition and disclosure of classified information about the state or government[,] ... which involves transgressing the boundaries around state secrets, for the purpose of challenging the allocation or use of power" (2015, 77). The actions of Assange, Manning, and Snowden fall within this definition. Sorell might refer to their actions as *hacktivism*, a "form of political activism in which computer hacking skills are heavily employed against powerful commercial institutions and governments, among other targets" (Sorell 2015, 391). Sorell's concern is that the release of data can be anonymous and "operate with a kind of impunity that its technology seems to afford" (2015). It is this anonymity that leads Sorell to suggest that hacktivism can lack any of the accountability that typically accompanies democratic activism and the more common types of whistleblowing.

But Delmas points out that even the release of state secrets "may nonetheless be justified when it is suitably constrained and exposes some information that the public ought to know and deliberate about" (2015, 77). Though characterizing both the Snowden and Manning data releases as "political vigilantism," Delmas observes that media and public opinion about the justifiability of their actions are mixed:

> Public opinion appears ambivalent, both skeptical that Manning and Snowden are traitors and reluctant to call them heroes. Many news articles' headlines reflect this hesitation: "Traitor or Hero?" Ambivalence seems warranted: on the one hand, there are good reasons for condemning those who seize unlawfully and seek to disseminate national security information; on the other hand, leaks often play an important role in exposing serious government wrongdoing and informing the public debate, as the Pentagon Papers did in their times. (77–78)

Motives matter in the public's perceptions of whistleblower activity. One study utilized both public opinion poll data and a laboratory experiment to understand what determined respondents' "support for an employee's protest actions and their classification of the employee as a whistleblower" (Heumann et al. 2016, 6). The major finding of the study is that "self-interest taints the purity of the employee's motivation making it less likely for respondents to classify the employee as a whistleblower" (6). The study randomly manipulated other variables—employee's gender, the type of action protested, and whether the employee worked in the public or private sector—finding that none of these made a significant difference in the respondent's support for or classification of whistleblowing. It was self-interest that mattered.

But in outlining best practices in whistleblower legislation, Transparency International (2018a) takes the stance that the whistleblower's motives should be irrelevant. In critiquing several international whistleblower protection documents, Transparency International recommends there be "no good faith or motivation test (rather, adopt the 'reasonable belief that the information is true' approach)" (3). Transparency International recognizes the understandable concerns that some whistleblowers have a personal agenda or vendetta,

> but a good faith requirement can have the negative effect of shifting the focus from assessing the merits of the information provided to investigating the whistleblower's motives, exposing him or her to personal attacks. This can pose a serious deterrent to potential whistleblowers. (15)

Other best-practice considerations for whistleblower-protection laws will be discussed in the next section.

Whistleblower Protection Laws

Whistleblower protection regulations are now seen as an essential element of any organizational ethics program. After a host of corporate scandals such as Enron, Worldcom, Arthur Andersen, and Parmalat, the US Congress responded in 2002 by enacting the Sarbanes-Oxley Act (SOX). SOX addressed many ethics issues related to corporate governance and regulation (Green 2004), one of which was to require whistleblower protection policies be instated for all public companies as well as nonprofits (National Council of Nonprofits 2018).

Whistleblower protections vary greatly across organizations, sectors, and countries. In an effort to harmonize the fragmentation and variability of these laws across the European Union, where six member countries have no whistleblower protections, the European Commission proposed an EU-wide Whistleblowing Directive in April 2018 (European Commission 2018). While pointing out the strong foundation the proposed EU directive provides for whistleblower protection, Transparency International also identified needed improvements, such as that public-sector entities should be obliged to establish internal reporting mechanisms that include procedures to protect whistleblowers; employees should be able to report breaches of law directly to competent authorities; and when retaliation occurs, whistleblowers should be entitled to full reparation through financial and nonfinancial remedies (Transparency International 2018b).

It is probably not surprising that in 2019 we still find ourselves grappling with how to shape and codify protections for whistleblowers—and asking whether the protections make any difference. As the #MeToo movement exploded in the United States over the past year, it was made abundantly clear that sexual harassment and sexual assault are all too common across workplaces, and that internal mechanisms for reporting the wrongdoing are absent, useless or worse: actually contributing to retaliation against the whistleblower. The whistleblower literature is replete with examples of whistleblowers in both the public and private sectors experiencing devastating retaliation after seeking to report wrongdoing using official internal channels. For example, see Westervelt's "For VA Whistleblowers, A Culture of Fear and Retaliation" (2018). Dickerson's (2018) article on the US Federal Bureau of Prisons details horrific patterns of assault and terror against female prison guards, while male prison guards engage in sexual harassment themselves or even facilitate the harassment of female guards by male inmates. Those who report the harassment often face retaliation, and their careers suffer while careers flourish for those who retaliated against the whistleblower.

If a whistleblower chooses to report outside the organization, the retaliation can grow exponentially worse as the organization closes ranks. Whistleblower retaliation might occur in order to avoid serious ramifications for the organization or the culpable participants. It also might occur simply to avoid the embarrassment of publicity. Regardless of the rationale, the individual whistleblower is no match for the retaliatory power of the organization. It is for this reason that whistleblower protection policies are mandated, and the reason it is necessary to keep filling the loopholes of those policies with yet more whistleblower protections.

In an effort to improve whistleblower protection policies, Transparency International's *Best Practice Guide for Whistleblowing Legislation* (2018a) argues that policies should cover a wide range of wrongdoing categories, apply to both the public and private sectors, provide multiple avenues for making a disclosure (including anonymously), incorporate wide-ranging protections from retaliation, and outline sanctions when retaliation occurs. Importantly, in an age when contractors perform many vital functions in all sectors, Transparency International also advocates for a broad definition of whistleblower that includes "individuals who are outside the traditional employee–employer relationship, such as consultants, contractors, trainees/interns, volunteers, student workers, temporary workers and former employees" (Transparency International 2018a, 11).

Encouraging Internal Reporting: What Works?

We must surmise that, currently, internal reporting of wrongdoing does not work effectively in many—perhaps most—workplaces. But as whistleblowers finally get public and official attention—as may be occurring in our current environment—there will be many leaders and workplaces that want to change their cultures and practices for the better. What works?

Research indicates that it is possible to encourage internal reporting—an approach that avoids not only the high cost of speaking up, but also the even higher cost of wrongdoing going unreported or being covered up by the organization. The Ethics and Compliance Initiative's (ECI) *Ethical Leadership Around the World and Why It Matters* (2017), a research report from ECI's Global Business Ethics Survey, offers evidence that the "quality of the relationship between supervisors and [their direct] reports goes a long way in determining whether employees report workplace integrity issues to management" (i).

Ethical Systems is an organization focused on "Business Integrity Through Research." The website's "Research" tab includes a section on "Internal Reporting," where they report that "when organizations punish or discourage internal reporting, bad practices typically get worse" (Ethical Systems 2018). Drawing on Vadera, Aguilera, and Caza (2009), they state that among the most important factors that influence reporting intentions and behavior are *leadership, perceived support, organizational justice,* and *organizational culture* (Ethical Systems 2018). Concern that nothing will be done, as well as fear of reprisal are factors that inhibit speaking up. To overcome these problems and to create an ethical culture, organizations should "implement structures and policies that visibly protect and incentivize internal reporting" (Ethical Systems 2018). Research indicates that employees who feel supported are more likely to report internally. Research also shows that the stronger the perceived ethical climate, the more likely that problems will be reported internally rather than reported outside the organization.

Those who address the government sector offer similar diagnoses. The OECD (2016), whose members are made up largely of wealthier nations, states,

Past cases demonstrate that corruption, fraud, and wrongdoing, as well as health and safety violations, are much more likely to occur in organisations that are closed and secretive. In many cases, employees will be aware of the wrongdoing, but feel unable to say anything for fear of reprisals, concern about acting against the organisation's culture, or lack of confidence that the matter will be taken seriously. (1)

The United Nations Convention against Corruption (UNCAC) (2015) prefaces its *Resource Guide on Good Practices in the Protection of Reporting Persons* by stating,

corruption is a crime with far-reaching consequences, and yet most incidents of corruption go unreported and undetected. A primary reason for people's reluctance to report is the impression that authorities will not take their report seriously and that nothing will be done. (iii)

Because research suggests that less than 10 percent of corruption incidents are reported, the UNCAC (2015) argues that governments "are urgently required to address those obstacles, to strengthen the effective response to reports of corruption and to protect those persons who come forward" (iii). The OECD report describes whistleblower protection as "the ultimate line of defence for safeguarding the public interest. Protecting whistleblowers promotes a culture of accountability and integrity in both public and private institutions, and encourages the reporting of misconduct, fraud and corruption" (OECD 2016, 2).

The solutions offered by OECD and UNCAC are similar to those suggested by Ethical Systems: put in place dedicated whistleblower protection laws or legal provisions relating to "protected reporting or prevention of retaliation against whistleblowers" (OECD 2016, 2) and "competent authorities with balanced and clear mandates and the appropriate powers and resources to handle information properly and to proactively protect reporting persons" (UNCAC 2015, 85).

While whistleblower policies and structures are important, no policy will itself be enough. The organizational culture must also change. "Simply implementing new governance processes means nothing if there is not a culture of transparency and openness and a willingness to take action against those whose actions breach the moral and ethical boundaries expected of them, regardless of their position or power" (Green 2004, 50).

Chaleff (2004) argues that simply providing "better internal mechanisms for surfacing and investigating questionable practices" may be insufficient

if the unwritten rules of the culture place higher value on something other than open communication and self-correction. In public companies, it is the imperative for-profit growth and shareholder value. In a government agency, it may be keeping key powerful constituencies satisfied. (1)

Further, Chaleff suggests there will be less need for whistleblowing if courageous followers (as described in his book *The Courageous Follower: Standing Up to and for Our Leaders* (2009)) "stand up to the culture" (2004, 1). "Executives need to cultivate a culture in which whistleblowing is unnecessary" and also need to "establish safe channels of communication and make them as free as possible of the cultural pressures" (1).

Ethical Systems described such environments in *Speak Up Culture: Designing Organizational Cultures that Encourage Employee Voice* (2017). "All organizations understand the value of feedback—but only some encourage opinions both positive and negative and lend an ear to self-styled 'devil's advocates'" (1). Here is what leaders can do to help develop a speak-up culture:

Solicit Feedback. Be Proactive about engaging employees. Ask them to consistently voice their concerns and show you are open to receiving feedback ... Set an Example. Talk openly about ethical issues and highlight both positive and negative examples ... Never Tolerate Retaliation (1).

Even if the organization has a "speak-up culture," individual employees must find their own way to give voice to their concerns. Gentile's book *Giving Voice to Values: How to Speak Your Mind When You Know What's Right* (2010) offers strategies for individuals to learn how to voice and act on their values and do so effectively. The book acknowledges that individuals might rationalize unethical actions as consistent with their values (when in fact they are not), might abandon attempts to follow their values out of a belief that they will not be able to change the offending situation, or might fail to act because they believe the price they would pay would be too great. Nevertheless, it argues that some people do give voice to their values successfully, and by understanding how they do so, we can develop our own capacities in this regard.

Conclusion

Encouraging people to speak up when they see wrongdoing, and enabling them to do so, is beneficial to organizations across the sectors and to society at large. Even with the new reality that technology can allow individuals to anonymously release troves of secret or classified materials, the value of people reporting wrongdoing when they see it is, on balance, beneficial to organizations and nation-states. Research has shown us that certain strategies can be successful, both in helping individuals learn to give voice to their values, and in developing cultures in public and private organizations that adhere more closely to the values they espouse. The challenge now rests with leaders to place the greater public good ahead of their own self-interests and ahead of the short-term loss their organizations might experience when sensitive information is shown in the light of day.

References

Chaleff, Ira. 2004. "No Need for Whistleblowing: Stand Up to the Culture." *Executive Excellence.* February. http://www.courageousfollower.net/wp-content/uploads/No-Need-for-Whistleblowing .pdf.

Chaleff, Ira. 2009. *The Courageous Follower: Standing Up to and for Our Leaders.* 3rd ed. San Francisco: Berrett-Koehler Publishers.

Delmas. Candice. 2015. "The Ethics of Government Whistleblowing." *Social Theory and Practice* 41(1), 77–105. https://philarchive.org/archive/DELTEO-20v1.

Dickerson, Caitlin. 2018. "Hazing, Humiliation and Terror: Working While Female in Federal Prison." *New York Times,* November 18. https://www.nytimes.com/2018/11/17/us/prison-sexual-harassment-women.html.

Eder, Steve. 2016. "Julian Assange Releases More Emails and Defends WikiLeaks' Mission." *New York Times,* November 8. https://www.nytimes.com/2016/11/09/us/politics/julian-assange-wikileaks-emails.html.

Ethical Systems. 2017. *Speak Up Culture: Designing Organizational Cultures that Encourage Employee Voice.* https://www.ethicalsystems.org/sites/default/files/files/Speak%20Up%20Culture_Final. pdf.

Ethical Systems. 2018. *Internal Reporting.* Accessed September 25, 2018. https://www.ethicalsystems.org/content/internalreporting.

Ethics & Compliance Initiative. 2016. *Increasing Employee Reporting Free from Retaliation: A Research Report from the National Business Ethics Survey.* https://www.ethics.org/knowledge-center/increasing-employee-reporting-free-from-retaliation/

Ethics & Compliance Initiative. 2017. *Ethical Leadership Around the World and Why It Matters, Executive Summary.* Arlington, VA: Ethics & Compliance Initiative. https://higherlogicdownload

.s3.amazonaws.com/THEECOA/11f760b1-56e0-43c6-85da-03df2ce2b5ac/UploadedImages/research/EthicalLeadership-ExecutiveSummary.pdf.

European Commission. 2018. *Proposal for a Directive of the European Parliament and of the Council on the Protection of Persons Reporting on Breaches of Union Law.* Accessed November 17. https://eur-lex.europa.eu/legal-content/EN/TXT/?uri=celex%3A52018PC0218.

Franceschi-Bicchierai, Lorenzo. 2014. "The 10 Biggest Revelations from Edward Snowden's Leaks." *Mashable,* June 5. https://mashable.com/2014/06/05/edward-snowden-revelations/#oKHz5R62NPqk.

Frenkel, Sheera, and Katie Benner. 2018. "To Stir Discord in 2016, Russians Turned Most Often to Facebook." *New York Times,* February 17. https://www.nytimes.com/2018/02/17/technology/indictment-russian-tech-facebook.html.

Frenkel, Sheera, Nicholas Confessore, Cecilia Kang, Matthew Rosenberg, and Jack Nicas. 2018. "Delay, Deny and Deflect: How Facebook's Leaders Fought through the Crisis." *New York Times,* November 14. https://www.nytimes.com/2018/11/14/technology/facebook-data-russia-election-racism.html.

Gentile, Mary C. 2010. *Giving Voice to Values: How to Speak Your Mind When You Know What's Right.* New Haven, CT: Yale University Press.

Green, Scott. 2004. "A Look at the Causes, Impact and Future of the Sarbanes-Oxley Act." *Journal of International Business and Law* 3(1), 33–52. http://scholarlycommons.law.hofstra.edu/jibl/vol3/iss1/2.

Heumann, Milton, Al Friedes, David Redlawsk, Lance Cassak, and Aniket Kesari. 2016. "Public Perceptions of Whistleblowing." *Public Integrity* 18(1): 6–24. doi: 10.1080/10999922.2015.1093397.

Mazzetti, Mark, and Katie Benner. 2018. "12 Russian Agents Indicted in Mueller Investigation." *New York Times,* July 13. https://www.nytimes.com/2018/07/13/us/politics/mueller-indictment-russian-intelligence-hacking.html.

Mueller, Robert, III. 2019. Report on the Investigation into Russian Interference in the 2016 Presidential Election March. https://www.documentcloud.org/documents/5955118-The-Mueller-Report.html.

National Council of Nonprofits. 2018. *Whistleblower Protections for Nonprofits.* Accessed November 20. https://www.councilofnonprofits.org/tools-resources/whistleblower-protections-nonprofits.

New York Times Editorial Board. 2014. "Edward Snowden, Whistle-blower." *New York Times,* January 1. https://www.nytimes.com/2014/01/02/opinion/edward-snowden-whistle-blower.html.

OECD. 2016. *Committing to Effective Whistleblower Protection: Highlights.* Paris: Organisation for Economic Co-operation and Development. http://www.oecd.org/corruption/anti-bribery/Committing-to-Effective-Whistleblower-Protection-Highlights.pdf.

Rutenberg, Jim. 2017. "In Election Hacking, Julian Assange's Years-Old Vision Becomes Reality." *New York Times,* January 8. https://www.nytimes.com/2017/01/08/business/media/assange-wikileaks-dnc-hacks.html.

Savage, Charlie. 2013. "Manning is Acquitted of Aiding the Enemy." *New York Times,* July 30. https://www.nytimes.com/2013/07/31/us/bradley-manning-verdict.html.

Sorell, Tom. 2015. "Human Rights and Hacktivism: The Cases of Wikileaks and Anonymous." *Journal of Human Rights Practice* 7(1), 391–410. https://academic.oup.com/jhrp/article/7/3/391/2412155.

Svara, James. 2015. *The Ethics Primer for Public Administrators in Government and Nonprofit Organizations.* 2nd ed. Burlington, MA: Jones & Bartlett Learning.

Transparency International. 2018a. *A Best Practice Guide for Whistleblowing Legislation.* Accessed November 17. https://www.transparency.org/whatwedo/publication/best_practice_guide_for_whistleblowing_legislation.

Transparency International. 2018b. *Whistleblower Protection in the European Union Analysis of and Recommendations on the Proposed EU Directive.* Accessed November 17. https://www.transparency.org/whatwedo/publication/whistleblower_protection_in_the_eu_analysis_of_and_recommendations.

United Nations Convention Against Corruption. 2015. *Resource Guide on Good Practices in the Protection of Reporting Persons*. Vienna: United Nations Office on Drugs and Crime. https://www.unodc.org/documents/corruption/Publications/2015/15-04741_Person_Guide_eBook.pdf.

Vadera, Abhijeet K., Ruth V. Aguilera, and Brianna B. Caza. 2009. "Making Sense of Whistle-blowing's Antecedents: Learning from Research on Identity and Ethics Programs." *Business Ethics Quarterly 19*(4), 553–86.

Westervelt, Eric. 2018. "For VA Whistleblowers, a Culture of Fear and Retaliation." *WBUR News,* June 21. http://www.wbur.org/npr/601127245/for-va-whistleblowers-a-culture-of-fear-and-retaliation.

25

Transparency as a Tool to Combat Corruption in Italy

Anna Simonati

The Idea(s) of Transparency and the Rights of Access: The Normative Evolution

The concentrated synthesis in this chapter prevents examining the principle of administrative transparency from a global perspective and focuses thus upon Italy. Indeed, the Italian legal system is an interesting starting point, because various legislative reforms have recently influenced the acceptance of transparency more widely.

According to a common view, transparency compels administrative action to be comprehensible during the procedures and checkable in the final results (Arena 2001; Chardon 1908, vi; Chieppa 1994, 613; Contaldo 1993, i, 235; Piraino 1991, 263; Turati 1908, 22962). Consequently, transparency and publicity are not synonymous, as the former is not completely satisfied by publication of documents and information. Moreover, according to the principle of transparency itself—which is strictly connected with administrative efficiency—not everything should be transparent, because it is incompatible with preserving some specific general interests or the right of privacy of individuals.

This notion has been tacitly accepted (even though not clearly expressed) by the Italian legislator, especially in the general act on administrative procedure (Law 7.8.1990, No. 241). Various legal tools are expressions of the principle (for instance, the right of participation by private parties in the procedure and the duty to give reasons for administrative final measures). However, the instrument widely considered as the symbol of "traditional" transparency—and constantly implemented in the administrative and judicial practice—is the right of access to administrative documents, provided for in the 1990 law. It allows private parties to read or take copies of documents in order to defend their own legal positions; as a consequence of the aim at self-protection, the demand must give reasons and, when the documents contain secret information or confidential data of third subjects, the reason given in the application is the basis for the competent authority to make a comparison between the counter-interests, whose defense may justify a denial by the administration.

But other meanings of the principle have recently arisen in hard law. According to Legislative Decree 14.3.2013, No. 33 (amended by Legislative Decree 25.5.2016, No. 97), transparency is intended as total accessibility of information about organization and action of public authorities (and of private subjects involved in the fulfillment of public interest). The main aim is to encourage widespread control of the pursuit of institutional duties and on the use of public resources; besides, transparency is explicitly considered as a legal tool for the protection of the rights of individuals and the promotion of participation by private parties in the administrative procedures (Bombardelli 2013, 657; Canaparo 2013, 2; Carloni 2009, 3, and 2011, 13; Contieri 2014, 563; Esposito et al. 2013, 1; Gardini 2014, 875; Lentini 2017; Matarazzo 2013, 50; Mattarella 2013, 128; Patroni Griffi 2013, 10; Ponti 2016; Savino 2013, 797; Spasiano 2017, 118). In the original landscape of the 2013 reform, the "new" principle of transparency essentially worked through publication on institutional websites of specific groups of documents, information, and data. Everyone had—and still has—a right to directly and immediately access the websites, without any authentication and identification. If the duty of compulsory publication is not respected, anyone may obtain the so-called civic access to elements that are legally compulsorily to be published.

Such innovation was, at least partially, the consequence of the inputs coming from the supranational legal systems. In particular, transparency was described as a form of contrast to corruption in the Council of Europe Convention on Access to Official Documents (2009), which followed the 2002 Recommendation of the Council of Europe Committee of Ministers on access to official documents. Moreover, as expressed by the Italian legislator in the presenting report of Decree No. 33, the normative model was the US Freedom of Information Act of 1966 (FOIA). However, the doctrine immediately observed how the Italian rules were, in comparison with the American ones, limited and disappointing (Mancosu 2014, 1). As clearly indicated by the most careful scholars (Contieri 2014, 563; Esposito et al. 2013, 1; Gardini 2014, 875), in fact, according to the US FOIA system, free access to documents and data held by administration corresponds to a general principle that is always binding, even if it is not provided for in a legislative source; exceptions are the objects of specific rules (aiming at protecting basic public interests or the stronger expressions of the individual right of privacy), which must be strictly interpreted.

Therefore, a strong movement arising from civil society—and especially from a group of distinguished legal scholars—started an interesting debate and campaign in order to improve the content of the statute, toward a real FOIA model (see www.foia.it). Also as a consequence of these solicitations, in 2016 a new kind of civic access was introduced. It is the so-called "generalized" civic access, which allows private parties to obtain disclosure of documents and data beyond the borders of compulsory publication, with the exception of those containing secrets to be kept in the public interest and of those containing private data that is strongly confidential.

The co-existence of the three categories of access is not simple. As numerous sides are not made clear in the legislative rules in force, the national Data Protection Authority and the National Anticorruption Authority have in the latest years issued some guidelines whose aim is basically to suggest (not binding) best practices and concrete solutions (see mainly: Data Protection Authority, Act. No. 88, 2.3.2011 [with the highlights in English available at http://www.garanteprivacy.it/web/guest/home/docweb/-/docweb-display/docweb/18037072011]; Data Protection Authority, Act No. 243, 15.5.2014; Anticorruption Authority and Data Protection Authority, Act No. 1309, 28.12.2016.). Without examining details, one may infer that the implementation of disclosure of documents, data, and information should be managed by each administration in light of the principle of proportionality. Moreover, in accordance with the (public) interest to economy of administrative action, the solution for each case must be chosen in light of its characteristics in order to implement, as widely as possible, the principle of transparency. The guidelines represent the starting point for other interpretative acts that show the global effort by the Italian administrative system to solve the problems arising from the coexistence of the various kinds of access. In particular, a circular was issued in 2017 by the Department of Public Service (see Ministero per la semplificazione e la pubblica amministrazione, Accesso civico generalizzato [FOIA]. Circolare applicativa, 30.5.2017, No. 2, in http://www.funzionepubblica.gov.it/articolo/dipartimento/01-06-2017/circolare-n-2-2017-attuazione-delle-norme-sull%E2%80%99accesso-civico), in order to help the single authorities in their practical action. In the circular, the principle of reasonableness seems to be key concept, and the existence of a general right of information of citizens is recognized; therefore, administration is required to reduce the exercise of the power of denial.

At present, many legal scholars and a relevant part of the civil society is not yet satisfied because numerous (and quite strong) limits to the right of knowledge by the citizens survive, and there is still incertitude in concrete implementation.

The Polysemy of Transparency in the Italian Rules in Force

The Italian system is very interesting food for thought, because the "new" concept of transparency (introduced with the 2013 and the 2016 reforms) has not replaced the ancient one. This is evident not only in light of the mentioned survival of important limits to publicity and to access (in art. 24 of Law No. 241/1990 and in art. 5 bis of Legislative Decree No. 33/2013) but also—and more consistently—in light of the reference, in art. 6 of Legislative Decree No. 33/2013, to the necessary quality (especially for comprehensibility by the citizens) of administrative information to be published in the institutional websites.

Nowadays, the polysemy of the notion of transparency is something any Italian scholar and practitioner has to deal with. In the process of progressive enrichment of the notion of transparency—currently intended not only as a legal tool for good administration (Bauhr and Grimes 2012; Etzioni 2010, 389; Lathrop and Ruma 2010; Meijer 2013a, 2013b, 1, and 2013c, 398) but also as an instrument to contrast corruption and maladministration—Italy is not alone. In fact, in many national systems, transparency is at present more and more often perceived as a benchmark for the expression of public power(s) as a whole. This idea partially arises in Italy from Decree No. 33, which contains rules on publication of documents and data in many fields of public action in the broad sense (for instance, management of goods, service providing, health system, etc.). But it has been even more deeply accepted by other European legislators, such as the French and Spanish. In France, the *Loi* (Law) and the *Loi organique* (Organic Law) 11.10.2013, No. 2013–907 and No. 2013–906 (*relative*[s]*à la transparence de la vie publique*: on transparency of public life) contain various rules, whose primary aim is at contrasting conflicts of interest among public entities (Mancosu 2014, 2; Serrand 2016, 115). Quite similarly, in Spain the *Ley de transparencia, acceso a la información pública y buen gobierno* (Law of transparency, access to public information and good governance) of 9.12.2013, No. 19 is focused on transparency intended as openness of the action carried out by the public authorities in a broad sense (Dabbagh Rollán 2016, 83; Guichot 2014; Piñar Mañas 2014, 1; Wences et al. 2014).

The polysemy of the idea of transparency is also in line with the distinction between decision making (and especially of individual administrative measures), policy making in general, and administrative implementation and action (Cucciniello et al. 2016, 32; Cucciniello and Nasi 2014, 911; Grimmelikhuijsen and Welch 2012, 562; Heald, 2006, 25).

In this complex scenario, it is interesting to underscore that sometimes the scholars distinguish as a particular field for transparency the area of financial data (Benito and Bastida 2009, 403; Pina, Lourdes, and Sonia 2010, 350). On this side of the issue, one may note a sort of paradox: in fact, notwithstanding that the need for transparency was born in the field of the markets, at present in this field the degree of comprehensibility by people in Italy is particularly low, and transparency often is considered fulfilled with just publication of groups of data (Berti de Marinis 2016, 992; Pittaluga 2016, 7). As has already been pointed out, transparency of public (and especially administrative) powers instead currently requires a higher level of attention in order to make the published information not just physically accessible, but at least a trend toward being comprehensible.

Administrative Transparency as a Teleologically Multifaceted Principle

As has been pointed out, in Italy transparency is traditionally intended as the source of the duty for administrations to build a fair relationship with the citizens, but in the recent reforms its purpose explicitly mainly consists of contrast of corruption and maladministration (Canaparo 2016; D'Urgolo 2017; Fanti 2016). The link between the two ideas of transparency is clear in the legislator's mind, as is shown by the rules on the necessity, inside each administrative entity, of an officer responsible for the prevention of corruption, one who normally also works as responsible officer for transparency. His/her duties have primarily to do with the correct implementation of the compulsory publication of documents and data and of the management of the requests for civic and generalized access (see Legislative Decree No. 33/2013, art. 43).

Therefore, transparency has become a "teleologically fragmentary" principle. As has been indicated, its evolution is (at least partially) the effect of the solicitation expressed by public opinion and doctrine. However, the need for contrasting corruption has been translated almost solely into rules compelling the publication in the institutional websites of documents, data, and information, with some timid proactive effort at the introduction of generalized access. Such an approach may be indeed considered a little disappointing, especially because the rules about generalized access are not exhaustive, and many problems in implementation (for instance, with reference to the balance between the need for knowledge and the need to protect the secrets in the public interest and the individual right of privacy) remain open.

To solve these problems, strong cooperation between different groups of scientists and with the practitioners would be priceless, because transparency can properly work only if a virtuous circle is created by connecting different know-hows. And, indeed, multidisciplinarity is at present necessary, at least because of the numerous rules that require the use of informatic technologies in order to disclose documents and data. In fact, (easy) accessibility of the institutional websites by the citizens is an important weapon against corruption and may facilitate the widespread control on administrative action that is desired in the rules in force. But the Italian authors writing on this topic are almost always legal scholars. This means, of course, that the standpoint is quite narrow. Meanwhile, great space is dedicated to comparative research (Galetta 2016, 1019), which has allowed distancing from idealization of the different legal systems and learning from other experiences.

Moreover, many Italian scholars look with interest to the efforts made by the foreign doctrine, in order to focus on the practical implementation of transparency (Ball 2009, 293; Cucciniello et al. 2016, 37; de Graaf and van der Wal 2017, 196). It is necessary to underscore that in Italy empirical research is still rather weak. The reason probably lies in Italy's short history of transparency as an anti-corruption legal tool, while in other contexts quantitative indicators have reached a higher degree of legal and practical ripeness. The lack of empirical data is also frequently felt by public opinion as a weak side of the Italian system because, of course, a focus on implementation offers an overview of transparency "in action" (Etzioni 2014, 687). For instance, some foreign doctrinal contributions state that the focus by legislators on transparency as a tool against corruption and maladministration is sometimes excessive, because encouragement for deep social control of public action may reduce the capacity of policy makers to make decisions, particularly if they are presumed to be unpopular (De Fine Licht 2011, 183; De Fine Licht et al. 2014, 111; Grimmelikhuijsen et al. 2013, 575; Grimmelikhuijsen and Meijer 2014, 137; Kosack and Fung 2014, 84; Porumbescu 2017; Roberts 2010; Welch et al. 2005, 371; Worthy 2010, 561).

However, analyzing administrative transparency by using only the empirical method could produce the strong danger of confusing goals and means. In fact, if the purpose of transparency is only identified in the contrast to corruption and maladministration, the results are much more simply "calculated" upon quantitative indicators that are based on the number of documents and data published in the institutional websites and available to the public. Consequently, transparency and online publication overlap, at least in tendency. But actual transparency, as a corollary of the principle of good administration in a broad sense, also requires comprehensibility of administrative action, which is essentially a qualitative parameter. Very properly, Italian doctrine (which, as has been pointed out, is frequently able to influence the rule-makers and public opinion), even after the latest normative reforms, still accepts the idea of transparency as a corollary of the principle of fairness in administrative action (Bombardelli 2013, 657). Within this principle, the anti-corruption function may and must be traced back accordingly with the fundamental parameter of proportionality of administrative action (Bombardelli 2013, 661; Simonati 2013, 757).

Conclusion

The relationship between good administration and transparency has become in recent years in Italy increasingly complicated. This is partially a consequence of the progressive expansion of administrative action and of the growing intervention of formally private subjects in pursuit of the public interest. Besides, the modern sensitivity for the contrast of corruption and maladministration has led the legislator to issue plenty of rules about access by citizens to information and data, especially by publication on institutional websites.

In this complex scenario, different interlocutors are deeply involved. First, the national legislator is necessarily influenced by supranational and foreign law, because the different legal systems nowadays continuously dialogue with each other. Second, more and more often, public opinion can call for reforms, which has partially happened for the introduction of new kinds of documental and data disclosure as tools against corruption. However, the role of the doctrine is still fundamental: not only for the solution of technical problems in implementation, but also to steer public opinion itself in its perception of the quality of the reforms, as the so-called "FOIA movement" shows. Moreover, but not least, new legal sources in a broad sense (such as guidelines by independent authorities) and circulars from the ministries are issued to contribute in the difficult implementation of administrative transparency.

One might say there is a different level of ripeness in the legal rules about the "traditional" concept of transparency (intended as a corollary of the macro-principle of good administration) and the "modern" concept of transparency as a weapon to contrast corruption through disclosure. While the former rules have been in force since 1990 and are widely implemented, the latter concept still produces doubts among scholars and practitioners. Nonetheless, all of them should be considered as sides of the same coin. The disclosure of documents, data, and information is the first step to make administrative action transparent, notwithstanding that further efforts—especially toward real comprehensibility—are required to make transparency effective for widespread control against corruption. However, such an aim should not superficially prevail over other basic needs in a democratic legal system, such as the protection of fundamental public-law secrets and the individual's confidential data.

Fragmentation is probably a nonerasable ontological element of transparency, and it is also a permanent source of the flexibility and vitality of the principle. This is, as well, why reasoning about the systemic position of transparency in the comprehensive context of good administration as a whole—without reducing it to the simple sum of the concrete measures against corruption and maladministration—may still be fruitful, notwithstanding the latest legislative tendencies that, at first sight, seem to go in another direction.

References

Arena, Gregorio, ed. 2001. *La funzione di comunicazione nelle pubbliche amministrazioni.* Rimini: Maggioli.

Ball, Carolyn. 2009. "What is Transparency?" *Public Integrity 11*(4), 293–308.

Bauhr, Monica, and Marcia Grimes. 2012. *What is Government Transparency? New Measures and Relevance for Quality of Government.* Working Paper Series, n. 16, University of Gothenburg. QoG Gotheborg: Quality of Government Institute.

Benito, Bernardino, and Francisco Bastida. 2009. "Budget Transparency, Fiscal Performance, and Political Turnout: An International Approach." *Public Administration Review 69*(3), 403–17.

Berti de Marinis, Giovanni. 2016. "Regolamentazione del mercato finanziario e principio di trasparenza." *Responsabilità civile previdenza 3*, 992–1013.

Bombardelli, Marco, 2013. "Fra sospetto e partecipazione: la duplice declinazione del principio di trasparenza." *Istituz. Fed. 3–4*, 657–87.

Canaparo, Paolo. 2013. "Il decreto legislativo 14 marzo 2013, n. 33: i nuovi confini della trasparenza pubblica e il diritto alla conoscibilità dell'azione amministrativa." *GiustAmm.it 4*, 1–27.

Canaparo, Paolo. 2016. "L'anticorruzione e la trasparenza: le questioni aperte e la delega sulla riorganizzazione delle pubbliche amministrazioni." *federalismi.it 1*, 1–56.

Carloni, Enrico. 2009. "La "casa di vetro" e le riforme. Modelli e paradossi della trasparenza amministrativa." *Diritto pubblico 3*, 779–812.

Carloni, Enrico. 2011. "La trasparenza 'totale' delle amministrazioni pubbliche: caratteri, finalità, potenzialità." *Rassegna Astrid 22*, 1–15.

Chardon, Henri. *L'administration de la France. Les fonctionnaires.* Paris: Perrin, 1908.

Chieppa, Roberto. 1994. "La trasparenza come regola della pubblica amministrazione." *Diritto economia 3*, 613–25.

Contaldo, Alfonso. 1993. "Breve contributo per una definizione del principio di trasparenza." *Nuovo diritto 4*, 235–38.

Contieri, Alfredo. 2014. "Trasparenza e accesso civico (Transparency and civic access)." *Nuove autonomie 23*(3), 563–76.

Cucciniello, Maria.,and Greta Nasi. 2014. "Transparency for Trust in Government: How Effective Is Formal Transparency?" *International Journal of Public Administration 37*, 911–21.

Cucciniello, Maria, Gregory A. Porumbescu, and Stephan Grimmelikhuijsen. 2016. "25 Years of Transparency Research: Evidence and Future Directions." *Public Administration Review 77*, 32–44.

D'Urgolo, Giandomenico. 2017. "Trasparenza e prevenzione della corruzione nella P.A.: la recente introduzione del 'Freedom of Information Act' (FOIA) nell'ordinamento italiano." *GiustAmm. it, 3*, 1–14.

Dabbagh Rollán, Victor Omar. 2016. "La Ley de Transparencia y la corrupción. Aspectos generale y percepciones de la ciudadanía española." *Revista de Ciencias Sociales 68*, 83–106.

de Fine Licht, Jenny. 2011. "Do We Really Want to Know? The Potentially Negative Effect of Transparency in Decision Making on Perceived Legitimacy." *Scandinavian Political Studies 34*, 183–201.

de Fine Licht, Jenny, Daniel Naurin, Peter Esaiasson, and Mikael Gilljam. 2014. "When Does Transparency Generate Legitimacy? Experimenting on a Context-Bound Relationship." *Governance 27*, 111–34.

de Graaf, Gjalt, and Zeger van der Wal. 2017. "Without Blinders: Public Values Scolarship in Political Science, economics, and Law—Content and Contribution to Public Administration." *Public Integrity 19*(3), 196–218.

Esposito, Vincenza, Francesca Del Grasso, and Gennaro Passananti. 2013. "Il diritto sociale alla trasparenza tra il diritto di accesso ed il diritto civico." *FiLOdiritto* (October 7), 1–6.

Etzioni, Amitai. 2010. "Is Transparency the Best Disinfectant?" *Journal of Political Philosophy 18*, 389–404.

Etzioni, Amitai. 2014. "The Limits of Transparency." *Public Administration Review 74*, 687–88.

Fanti, Vera. 2016. "La pubblicità e la trasparenza amministrativa in funzione del contrasto alla corruzione: una breve riflessioni in attesa del legislatore delegato." *GiustAmm.it 3*, 1–16.

Galetta, Dina Urania. 2016. "La trasparenza per un nuovo rapporto tra cittadino e pubblica amministrazione: un'analisi storico-evolutiva in una prospettiva di diritto comparato ed europeo." *Rivista italiana diritto pubblico comunitario 5*, 1019–65.

Gardini, Gianluca. 2014. "Il codice della trasparenza: un primo passo verso il diritto all'informazione amministrativa?." *Giornale diritto amministrativo 8–9*, 875–91.

Grimmelikhuijsen, Stephan G., and Albert J. Meijer. 2014. "Effects of Transparency on the Perceived Trustworthiness of a Government Organization: Evidence from an Online Experiment." *Journal of Public Administration Research and Theory 24*, 137–57.

Grimmelikhuijsen, Stephan G., Gregory A. Porumbescu, Boram Hong, and Tobin Im. 2013. "The Effect of Transparency on Trust in Government: A Cross-National Comparative Experiment." *Public Administration Review 73*, 575–86.

Grimmelikhuijsen, Stephan G., and Eric W. Welch. 2012. "Developing and Testing a Theoretical Framework for Computer-Mediated Transparency of Local Governments." *Public Administration Review 72*, 562–71.

Guichot, Emilio, ed. 2014. *Trasparencia, Acceso a la Información Pública y Buen Gobierno. Estudio de la Ley 19/2013, de 9 de diciembre.* Madrid: Tecnos.

Heald, David. 2006. "Varieties of Transparency," in Cristopher Hood and David Heald, eds., *Transparency: The Key to Better Governance?* Oxford: Oxford University Press, 25–43.

Kosack, Stephen, and Archon Fung. 2014. "Does Transparency Improve Governance?" *Annual Review of Political Science 17*, 65–87.

Lathrop, Daniel, and Laurel Ruma. 2010. *Open Government. Collaboration, Transparency and Participation in Practice.* Sebastopol, CA: O'Reilly Media.

Lentini, Giuliano. 2017. "Il segreto e la trasparenza: dall'amministrazione chiusa all'amministrazione aperta. Le tappe dell'evoluzione dei rapporti tra i pubblici poteri ed i cittadini." *Amministrativamente 1–2*, 1–36.

Lindstedt, Catharina, and Daniel Naurin. 2010. "Transparency Is Not Enough: Making Transparency Effective in Reducing Corruption." *International Political Science Review 31*, 301–22.

Mancosu, Giorgio. 2014. "La transparence publique par l'ouverture des données personnelles? Focus sur les systèmes juridiques italien et français." *federalismi.it 3*, 1–20.

Matarazzo, Alfonso Ermanno. 2013. "Il nuovo codice della trasparenza." *Lo stato civile italiano 5*, 50–53.

Mattarella, Bernardo Giorgio. 2013. "La prevenzione della corruzione in Italia." *Giornale diritto amministrativo 2*, 123–33.

Meijer, Albert J. 2013a. "Transparency," in Mark Bovens, Robert E. Goodin, and Thomas Schillemans, eds., *Oxford Handbook of Public Accountability.* Oxford: Oxford University Press, 507–24.

Meijer, Albert J. 2013b. "Understanding the Complex Dynamics of Transparency." *Public Administration Review 3*, 1–8.

Meijer, Albert J. 2013c. "Local Meanings of Targeted Transparency. Understanding the Fuzzy Effects of Disclosure systems." *Administrative Theory and Praxis 35*, 398–423.

Patroni Griffi, Filippo. 2013. "La trasparenza della Pubblica Amministrazione tra accessibilità totale e riservatezza." *federalismi.it 8*, 1–12.

Pina Vicente, Torres Lourdes and Royo Sonia, 2010, "Is E-Government Promoting Convergence towards More Accountable Local Governments?" *International Public Management Journal 4*, 350–80.

Piñar Mañas, José Luis. 2014. "Transparencia y derecho de acceso a la información pública. Algunas reflexiones en torno al derecho de acceso en la Ley 19/2013, de transparencia, acceso a la información y buen gobierno." *Revista catalana de dret públic 49*, 1–19.

Piraino, Salvatore. 1991. "La trasparenza dell'azione amministrativa: diafanità di un concetto." *Nuova rassegna 3–4*, 263–65.

Pittaluga, Giovanni Battista. 2016. "Quale tutela del consumatore finanziario." *Economia diritto terziario 1*, 7–16.

Ponti, Benedetto, ed. 2016. *Nuova trasparenza amministrativa e libertà di accesso alle informazioni.* Rimini: Maggioli.

Gregory A., Porumbescu. 2017. "Linking Transparency to Trust in Government and Voice." *American Review of Public Administration* (December 10). doi: 10.1177/0275074017734642.

Roberts, Alasdair. 2010. *Blacked Out: Government Secrecy in the Information Age.* New York: Cambridge University Press.

Savino, Mario. 2013. "La nuova disciplina della trasparenza amministrativa." *Giornale diritto amministrativo 8–9,* 795–805.

Serrand, Pierre. 2016. "La transparence administrative et le code des rélations entre le public et l'administration." *Giornale storia costituzionale 31,* 115–24.

Simonati, Anna. 2013. "La trasparenza amministrativa e il legislatore: un caso di entropia normativa?." *Diritto Amministrativo 4,* 749–88.

Spasiano, Mario R. 2017. "I principi di pubblicità, trasparenza e imparzialità," in Maria Alessandra Sandulli, ed., *Codice dell'azione amministrativa.* Milano: Giuffré, 117–37.

Turati, Filippo. 1908. "Sess. 1904–1908, 17.6.1908." In *Atti del Parlamento italiano - Camera dei Deputati,* 22962.

Welch, Eric W., Charles C. Hinnant, and M. Jae Moon. 2005. "Linking Citizen Satisfaction with E-Government and Trust in Government." *Journal of Public Administration Research and Theory 15,* 371–84.

Wences, Isabel, Mario Kölling, and Sabrina Ragone, eds. 2014. *La Ley de Trasparencia, Acceso a la Información Pública y Buen Gobierno. Una perspectiva académica.* Madrid: Centro de Estudios Políticos y Constitucionales.

Worthy, Ben. 2010. "More Open but Not More Trusted? The Effect of the Freedom of Information Act 2000 on the United Kingdom Central Government." *Governance 23,* 561–82.

26

Auditability
Key to Accountability and Ethics
Juanita M. Rendon

All organizations, such as federal government entities as well as state and local government organizations, spend millions of taxpayer dollars each year on goods and services to meet their missions. As increased amounts of public dollars are spent, more scrutiny is warranted to ensure public trust in the management of public funds. The Association of Certified Fraud Examiners (ACFE) states that organizations lose an estimated 5 percent of their annual revenue to occupational fraud.[1] The ACFE indicates that corruption continues to be a major fraud risk for organizations across industries. The ACFE also contends that "occupational fraud remains an enormous threat to the global economy."[2]

Accountability and ethical behavior are some of the hallmarks of an ethical organization. Some of the ways that organizations promote accountability and ethical behavior include establishing codes of conduct and ethics training; however, these measures taken by organizations are not always effective. Instances of unethical behavior and fraudulent behavior continue to plague organizations and still occur across the government and industry. Asset misappropriation, financial statement fraud, and corruption are the three types of occupational fraud often occurring against an organization from people within the organization such as employees and management.[3] Unfortunately, fraud, waste, and abuse occur throughout all levels of the government, as well as in industry and throughout the world. For example, recent fraudulent activities within US Navy procurement reflect the lack of accountability and lack of ethical behavior.[4] When fraud, waste, and abuse occur in a government organization, public trust is undermined.

If codes of conduct and ethics training are not working, this author contends that what is missing is the lack of focus on auditability as related to people, processes, and internal controls within organizations as an approach to ensuring accountability and ethical behavior. This chapter shows how organizations can apply auditability theory to help ensure accountability and ethical behavior in their organizations.

The chapter provides an overview of the auditability theory as related to accountability and ethics in public organizations. First, auditability theory is discussed, including the auditability triangle. Next, the three components of the auditability triangle—competent people, capable processes, and effective internal controls—are discussed. Finally, a summary and conclusions are presented.

Auditability Theory

When addressing auditability in an organization, it is important to understand that an independent audit of an organization is different than an organization being auditable. For example, an independent financial audit of a company's financial statements involves auditors examining all appropriate and relevant documentation and evidence about the company in order to provide an audit opinion stating that, within reasonable assurance, the company's financial statements are free of material misstatements and fairly represent the financial condition of the company.[5] In other words, the relationship between financial reporting by a company and the audit of the financial reports of that company is that "auditing is fundamentally a derived activity, which adds credibility to financial statements."[6]

The theory of auditability focuses on whether a company is auditable. Power contends that auditability is much broader than an audit.[7] He discusses the concept of "making things auditable" and refers to achieving auditability via continuous "auditable measures of performance, systems of control, and reliance on other experts."[8] The concept of "making risk management auditable" requires organizations to manage risk by establishing processes and procedures within their organizations to be able to provide transparency regarding operating within the established guidelines.[9] Organizational oversight and accountability are part of risk management.[10] In order to be auditable, an organization needs to incorporate competent personnel, capable processes, and effective internal controls in their organization. These are the three components of the Auditability Triangle, which is discussed next.

Auditability Triangle

Auditability theory can be illustrated with the Auditability Triangle as shown in figure 26.1.[11] The Auditability Triangle includes three components of governance, which are integrated within an organization. The three components include competent personnel, capable processes, and effective internal controls.[12]

Auditability theory and the Auditability Triangle can be applied to any public or private organization, especially in the procurement arena. Organizations such as federal government entities, as well as state and local government organizations, spend millions of taxpayer dollars each year on goods and services to meet their missions. As increased amounts of public dollars are spent, more scrutiny is warranted to ensure public trust in the management of public funds and to ensure transparency, integrity, and accountability. The following sections elaborate on each of the components of the Auditability Triangle.

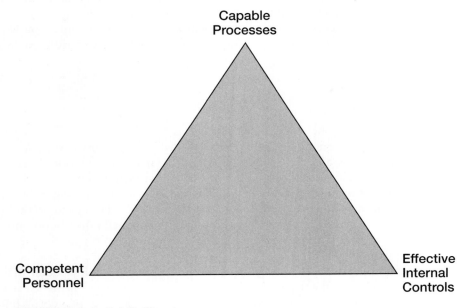

FIGURE 26.1 Auditability Triangle

Competent Personnel

The first component of the Auditability Triangle is Competent Personnel.[13] In order to be auditable, an organization's personnel should be properly educated, sufficiently trained, and adequately experienced.[14] Organizations generally have minimum education and experience requirements when hiring and retaining their personnel. Similarly, the federal government has minimum requirements for education and experience for its personnel, as well as certification requirements such as in the Department of Defense (DOD) acquisition workforce.[15]

While there are education and experience requirements in place for the DOD acquisition workforce, deficiencies in workforce competency exist, which could make the DOD vulnerable to fraud. For example, the Government Accountability Office (GAO) has issued reports on the critical need for improvement of the acquisition workforce competency, especially regarding procurement fraud, to help reduce fraud vulnerabilities within the DOD.[16] In addition, previous research found deficiencies in the DOD's contracting workforce's knowledge to detect procurement fraud.[17] Army, Navy, and Air Force contracting professionals self-assessed themselves as high when it comes to procurement fraud knowledge to do their job; however, they scored low (scored approximately 60 percent) on the procurement fraud knowledge assessments regarding procurement fraud schemes and internal controls.[18]

In addition, the results of the research studies showed that these contracting professionals across the different military departments perceived that their organizations were not vulnerable to procurement fraud.[19] The possible implication of the results of these research studies is that perhaps the DOD contracting workforce does not have enough procurement fraud knowledge to identify fraud in its organizations. The GAO found that the DOD acquisition professionals need to possess the appropriate skills and have sufficient procurement fraud knowledge to help deter and detect fraud.[20]

Kramer contended that organizations should have fraud awareness training to help deter and detect fraud and highlights the importance of effective internal controls to deter fraud. Even though there are many different types of fraud that are committed by fraudsters across industries and in the government, there are usually common threads that can be found across fraudulent incidents.[21] Furthermore, Okubena (2016) found that organizations need to have procurement personnel who have the appropriate qualifications and suitable training to reduce corruption and fraudulent activity in South Africa's public sector.[22] In addition to competent personnel, organizations need to also have capable processes to be auditable.

Capable Processes

The second component of the Auditability Triangle is Capable Processes.[23] In order to be auditable, an organization should have processes that are appropriately institutionalized, adequately measured, and consistently improved.[24] Garrett and Rendon developed a contracting framework that includes six phases as well as contracting activities within each phase.[25] The six phases include "procurement planning, solicitation planning, solicitation, source selection, contract administration, and contract closeout."[26] Hong and Kwon found that effective processes related to procurement sourcing, buying, and distribution need to be in place within an organization in order for that organization to obtain the maximum value regarding procurement.[27]

When applying the Contract Management Maturity Model, Rendon found that the US Navy's contract management process level of capability was lower in the solicitation phase, the contract administration phase, and the contract closeout phase.[28] Whiteley, Foster, and Johnson found that the majority of the procurement failures that occurred in the "Fat Leonard" Navy procurement alleged acts of fraud were found in the contract administration phase, the procurement planning phase, and the solicitation planning phase of the contract management process phases. Almost 92 percent of the Fat Leonard alleged acts of fraud involved collusion.[29]

In addition, Hidaka and Owen found that the DOD had the most deficiencies in the procurement planning, solicitation planning, and contract administration phases of contract management.[30] Basheka conducted research on public procurement corruption and the effect it had on service delivery.[31] Stevulak and Campbell addressed corporate corruption from the supply side, as well as corporate accountability indices, which include corruption indices and social-responsibility indices.[32] Furthermore, Transparency International (TI) has created international anti-corruption conventions, as well as instituted "integrity pacts" for preventing corruption in public contracting.[33]

Deficiencies in DOD contract management result from a lack of trained personnel, a lack of capable contracting processes, and weak internal controls.[34] In addition to needing competent personnel and capable processes, organizations also need effective internal controls to be auditable.

Effective Internal Controls

The third component of the Auditability Triangle is Effective Internal Controls.[35] In order to be auditable, an organization's internal control system should be effective in that it should be adequately enforced, sufficiently monitored, and properly reported.[36]

Internal controls that are properly designed and implemented help organizations, both public and private, protect assets from fraud, waste, and abuse. Accountability, integrity, and transparency should be fundamental goals of an organization. The Committee of Sponsoring Organizations (COSO) provides guidance for developing an internal control system.[37] The five components of the COSO Integrated Internal Control Framework include the control environment, risk-assessment, information, and communication, control activities, and monitoring activities.[38] The control environment component addresses setting the tone at the top and encompasses the ethical environment of the organization. The risk-assessment component addresses the potential risks and ways to mitigate risk, including fraud risk. The information and communication component addresses the organization's accounting system as well as the external and internal communication within the organization. The control activities component addresses the specific controls or procedures that have been established by an organization, including segregation of duties. The monitoring activities component addresses the importance of needing ongoing scrutiny of organizational internal controls. In 2014, the GAO published *Standards for Internal Control in the Federal Government*—known as the Green Book—which provides guidance to federal organizations and is based on the COSO integrated internal control framework.[39]

The majority of the internal control deficiencies that were identified in the "Fat Leonard" Navy procurement alleged acts of fraud were found in the control environment and in the information and communication components of the integrated internal control framework.[40] When analyzing the ethical failures in the federal government reports, Tan found that the majority of the organizations were deficient in the control environment, control activities, and monitoring activities components of the integrated internal control framework.[41] In addition, Hidaka and Owen found that the DOD had the most weaknesses in the control environment, control activities, and risk-assessment components of the integrated internal control framework.[42]

Tan found that the growth of globalization and increased outsourcing of goods and services, as well as an increased pressure to reduce costs, make government organizations increasingly vulnerable to procurement fraud. Effective internal controls that are implemented and monitored, as well as appropriate fraud deterrence approaches, are crucial in the fight against procurement fraud.[43] In addition, Okubena contended that internal control principles, which include separation of powers, need to be enforced and applied to deter corruption and fraud in South Africa.[44]

Collusion, conflicts of interest, and fraudulent purchases are just a few of the possible procurement fraud categories that could occur in an organization. Rendon and Rendon discussed the procurement fraud matrix, which includes the five components of the integrated internal control framework, the six contract management phases, and the six categories of procurement fraud schemes.[45] The internal control components and the contract management phases have been previously addressed. The six categories of procurement fraud schemes include collusion; conflicts of interest; bid-rigging; billing schemes; fraudulent purchase schemes; and fraudulent representation type schemes.[46]

Internal control failures happen when an organization has weak internal controls or when an organization does not implement its established internal controls. Ineffective internal controls lead to opportunities for employees within the organization to commit fraud. The following section presents a summary and conclusions.

Conclusion

Corruption continues to be a major fraud risk for organizations in industry, in the government, and internationally. Lack of accountability, lack of transparency, lack of ethics, lack of competent personnel, lack of effective internal controls, and lack of capable processes undermine public trust and public integrity. As previously noted, DOD contract management deficiencies resulted from lack of trained personnel, lack of capable contracting processes, and weak internal controls.[47]

This chapter addressed the issues of accountability and ethics and focused on auditability and the Auditability Triangle as a tool to ensure accountability and ethical behavior within organizations. While the examples provided were related to procurement fraud, auditability theory can be applied to any areas within an organization. For organizations to be auditable, it is vitally important for them to incorporate the three components of the Auditability Triangle—competent personnel, capable processes, and effective internal controls. The use of the Auditability Triangle theory as well as the procurement fraud matrix provide organizations with some conceptual frameworks to help in establishing auditability in their agencies to help deter fraud, detect fraud, and fight corruption. As organizations continue to strive for accountability and ethical behavior in their operations, auditability will continue to rise in importance.

Notes

[1] Association of Certified Fraud Examiners (ACFE), *Report to the Nations: 2018 Global Study on Occupational Fraud and Abuse* (Austin, TX: ACFE, 2018), https://s3-us-west-2.amazonaws.com/acfepublic/2018-report-to-the-nations.pdf.

[2] ACFE, Report to the Nations, 7.

[3] ACFE, Report to the Nations.

[4] David Larter, "Navy Rebukes 3 Admirals for Accepting Dinners, Gifts." *Navy Times,* July 18, 2015, http://www.navytimes.com; Jacob T. Whiteley, Jimmy A. Foster, and Kyle A. Johnson, "Contracting for Navy Husbanding Services: An Analysis of the Fat Leonard Case" (master's thesis, Naval Postgraduate School, 2017), http://hdl.handle.net/10945/56838.

[5] O. Ray Whittington and Kurt Pany, *Principles of Auditing and Other Assurance Services.* 19th ed. (New York: McGraw-Hill/Irwin, 2014).

[6] Michael Power, *Organized Uncertainty* (Oxford, England: Oxford University Press, 2007), 290.

[7] Power, *Organized Uncertainty.*

[8] Michael Power, "Making Things Auditable," *Accounting, Organizations, and Society 21* (2) (1996), 289.

[9] Power, *Organized Uncertainty.*

[10] Power, *Organized Uncertainty.*

[11] Juanita M. Rendon and Rene G. Rendon, *Defense Procurement: An Analysis of Contract Management Internal Controls* (NPS-CM-15-003) (Monterey, CA: Acquisition Research Program, Naval Postgraduate School), 10.

[12] Rendon and Rendon, *Defense Procurement*.

[13] Rene G. Rendon and Juanita M. Rendon, "Auditability in Public Procurement: An Analysis of Internal Controls and Fraud Vulnerability," *International Journal of Procurement Management* 8(6) (2015), 710–30.

[14] Rendon and Rendon, "Auditability in Public Procurement"; Juanita M. Rendon and Rene G. Rendon, "Procurement Fraud in the U.S. Department of Defense: Implications for Contracting Processes and Internal Controls," *Managerial Auditing Journal* 31(7) (2016), 748–67, doi: 10.1108/MAJ-11-2015-1267.

[15] Keith F. Snider, "DAWIA and the Price of Professionalism," *Acquisition Review Quarterly* 3(2) (1996), 97–108.

[16] Government Accountability Office (GAO), *Contract Management: DOD Vulnerabilities to Contracting Fraud, Waste, and Abuse* (GAO-06-838R) (Washington, DC: GAO, 2006), http://www.gao.gov/new.items/d06838r.pdf; GAO, *Defense Acquisition Workforce: Better Identification, Development, and Oversight Needed for Personnel Involved in Acquiring Services* (GAO-11-892) (Washington, DC: GAO, 2011), https://www.gao.gov/assets/590/585429.pdf.

[17] Peter W. Chang, "Analysis of Contracting Processes, Internal Controls, and Procurement Fraud Schemes" (master's thesis, Naval Postgraduate School, 2013), https://calhoun.nps.edu/handle/10945/34642; Joe C. Castillo and Erin M. Flanigan, "Procurement Fraud: A Knowledge-Level Analysis of Contracting Personnel" (master's thesis, Naval Postgraduate School, 2014), https://calhoun.nps.edu/handle/10945/44533; Jeremy A. Grennan and Michael A. McCrory, "Auditability in the U.S. Navy: Knowledge Assessment of the Contracting Workforce" (master's thesis, Naval Postgraduate School, 2016), https://calhoun.nps.edu/handle/10945/5170; Rendon and Rendon, "Procurement Fraud in the U.S. Department of Defense."

[18] Chang, "Analysis of Contracting Processes," 38 Castillo and Flanigan, "Procurement Fraud," 55; Grennan and McCrory, "Auditability in the U.S. Navy"; Rendon and Rendon, "Procurement Fraud in the U.S. Department of Defense."

[19] Chang, "Analysis of Contracting Processes," 51–52; Castillo and Flanigan, "Procurement Fraud," 65; Grennan and McCrory, "Auditability in the U.S. Navy"; Rendon and Rendon, "Procurement Fraud in the U.S. Department of Defense."

[20] GAO, Contract Management.

[21] Bonita K. P. Kramer, "Rooting Out Fraud in Your Organization," *Management Accounting Quarterly* 10(4) (2009), 1–16.

[22] Olumuyiwa Okubena, "Accountability and Transparency: Procurement Issues in Selected Municipalities in South Africa," *Journal of Finance, Accounting, and Management* 7(2) (2016), 39–52.

[23] Rendon and Rendon, "Auditability in Public Procurement."

[24] Rendon and Rendon, "Auditability in Public Procurement"; Rendon and Rendon, "Procurement Fraud in the U.S. Department of Defense."

[25] Gregg A. Garrett and Rene G. Rendon, *Contract Management Organizational Assessment Tools* (McLean, VA: National Contract Management Association, 2005).

[26] Garrett and Rendon, *Contract Management Organizational Assessment Tools*, 21. See also R. G. Rendon, "Contract Management," in R. G. Rendon and K. F. Snider, eds., *Management of Defense Acquisitions* (Monterey, CA: American Institute of Aeronautics and Astronautics, 2008).

[27] Paul Hong and He-Boong Kwon, "Emerging Issues of Procurement Management: A Review and Prospects," *International Journal of Procurement Management* 5(4) (2012), 452–69.

[28] Rene G. Rendon, "Benchmarking Contract Management Process Maturity: A Case Study of the U.S. Navy," *Benchmarking: An International Journal* 22(7) (2015), 1481–508.

[29] Whiteley, Foster, and Johnson, "Contracting for Navy Husbanding Services."

[30] Didaka Hidaka and Jared L. Owen, "An Analysis of Internal Controls for DOD Contracting Management" (master's thesis, Naval Postgraduate School, 2015), http://hdl.handle.net/10945/47961.

[31] Bennon C. Basheka, "Public Procurement Corruption and Its Implications on Effective Service Delivery in Uganda: An Empirical Study," *International Journal of Procurement Management* 2(4) (2009), 415–32.

[32] Cathy Stevulak and Jeffery Campbell, "Supply-Side Corruption: Perspectives on a Trillion-Dollar Problem," *Journal of Corporate Citizenship* 29 (2008), 33–48.

[33] Transparency International, "Transparency International."

[34] Department of Defense Inspector General (DODIG), Summary of DOD Office of Inspector General Audits of Acquisition and Contract Management (DODIG Report No. D-2009–071), (Washington, DC: DOD, 2009); GAO, Contract Management; GAO, Defense Acquisition Workforce.

[35] Rendon and Rendon, "Auditability in Public Procurement."

[36] Rendon and Rendon, "Auditability in Public Procurement"; Rendon and Rendon, "Procurement Fraud in the U.S. Department of Defense."

[37] Committee of Sponsoring Organizations of the Treadway Commission (COSO), *Internal Control—Integrated Framework, Executive Summary* (2013), https://na.theiia.org/standards-guidance/topics/documents/executive_summary.pdf.

[38] COSO, *Internal Control*; J. Stephen McNally, "The 2013 COSO Framework and SOX Compliance," *Strategic Finance* (June 2013): 45–52.

[39] GAO, *Standards for Internal Control in the Federal Government* (GAO-14-704G), (Washington, DC: GAO, 2014), http://www.gao.gov/assets/670/665712.pdf.

[40] Whiteley, Foster, and Johnson, "Contracting for Navy Husbanding Services," 67.

[41] Li H. J. Tan, "An Analysis of Internal Controls and Procurement Fraud Deterrence" (master's thesis, Naval Postgraduate School, 2013), http://hdl.handle.net/10945/39022.

[42] Hidaka and Owen, "An Analysis of Internal Controls for DOD Contracting Management," 48.

[43] Tan, "An Analysis of Internal Controls," 98.

[44] Okubena, "Accountability and Transparency."

[45] Rendon and Rendon, *Defense Procurement*, 725.

[46] Rendon and Rendon, "Auditability in Public Procurement," 9.

[47] DODIG, *Summary of DOD Office of Inspector General Audits*; GAO, *Contract Management*; GAO, Defense Acquisition Workforce.

References

Association of Certified Fraud Examiners (ACFE). 2018. *Report to the Nations: 2018 Global Study on Occupational Fraud and Abuse.* Austin: ACFE. https://s3-us-west-2.amazonaws.com/acfepublic/2018-report-to-the-nations.pdf.

Basheka, Benon C. 2009. "Public Procurement Corruption and Its Implications on Effective Service Delivery in Uganda: An Empirical Study." *International Journal of Procurement Management* 2(4), 415–32.

Committee of Sponsoring Organizations of the Treadway Commission (COSO). 2013. *"Internal Control—Integrated Framework, Executive Summary."* https://na.theiia.org/standards-guidance/topics/documents/executive_summary.pdf.

Chang, Peter W. 2013. "Analysis of Contracting Processes, Internal Controls, and Procurement Fraud Schemes." Master's thesis, Naval Postgraduate School. https://calhoun.nps.edu/handle/10945/34642.

Castillo, Joe C., and Erin M. Flanigan. 2014. "Procurement Fraud: A Knowledge-Level Analysis of Contracting Personnel." Master's thesis, Naval Postgraduate School. https://calhoun.nps.edu/handle/10945/44533.

Department of Defense Inspector General (DODIG). 2009. *Summary of DOD Office of Inspector General Audits of Acquisition and Contract Management.* DODIG Report No. D-2009–071. Washington, DC: DOD.

Garrett, Gregg A., and Rene G. Rendon. 2005. *Contract Management Organizational Assessment Tools.* McLean, VA: National Contract Management Association.

Government Accountability Office (GAO). 2006. *Contract Management: DOD Vulnerabilities to Contracting Fraud, Waste, and Abuse.* GAO-06-838R. Washington, DC: GAO. http://www.gao.gov/new.items/d06838r.pdf.

Government Accountability Office (GAO). 2011. *Defense Acquisition Workforce: Better Identification, Development, and Oversight Needed for Personnel Involved in Acquiring Services.* GAO-11–892. Washington, DC: GAO, https://www.gao.gov/assets/590/585429.pdf.

Government Accountability Office (GAO). 2014. *Standards for Internal Control in the Federal Government.* GAO-14-704G. Washington, DC: GAO. http://www.gao.gov/assets/670/665712.pdf.

Grennan, Jeremy A., and Michael A. McCrory. 2016. "Auditability in the U.S. Navy: A Knowledge Assessment of the Contracting Workforce." Master's thesis, Naval Postgraduate School. https://calhoun.nps.edu/handle/10945/5170.

Hidaka, Daisuke, and Jared L. Owen. 2015. "An Analysis of Internal Controls for DOD Contracting Management." Master's thesis, Naval Postgraduate School, http://hdl.handle.net/10945/47961.

Hong, Paul, and He-Boong Kwon. 2012. "Emerging Issues of Procurement Management: A Review and Prospects." *International Journal of Procurement Management* 5(4), 452–69.

Kramer, Bonita K. P. 2009. "Rooting Out Fraud in Your Organization." *Management Accounting Quarterly 10*(4), 1–16.

Larter, David B. 2015. "Navy Rebukes 3 Admirals for Accepting Dinners, Gifts." *Navy Times*. July 18, http://www.navytimes.com.

McNally, J. Stephen. 2013. "The 2013 COSO Framework and SOX Compliance." *Strategic Finance*. June, 45–52.

Okubena, Olumuyiwa. 2016. "Accountability and Transparency: Procurement Issues in Selected Municipalities in South Africa." *Journal of Finance, Accounting, and Management 7*(2), 39–52.

Power, Michael. 1996. "Making Things Auditable." *Accounting, Organizations, and Society 21*(2), 289–315.

Power, Michael. 2007. *Organized Uncertainty*. Oxford: Oxford University Press.

Rendon, Juanita M., and Rene G. Rendon. 2015. *Defense Procurement: An Analysis of Contract Management Internal Controls*. NPS-CM-15-003. Monterey: Acquisition Research Program, Naval Postgraduate School.

Rendon, Juanita M., and Rene G. Rendon. 2016. "Procurement Fraud in the U.S. Department of Defense: Implications for Contracting Processes and Internal Controls." *Managerial Auditing Journal 31*(7), 748–67. doi: 10.1108/MAJ-11-2015-1267.

Rendon, Rene G. 2008. "Contract Management," in Rene G. Rendon and Keith F. Snider, eds., *Management of Defense Acquisitions*. Monterey: American Institute of Aeronautics and Astronautics, 159–88.

Rendon, Rene G. 2015. "Benchmarking Contract Management Process Maturity: A Case Study of the U.S. Navy." *Benchmarking: An International Journal 22*(7), 1481–508.

Rendon, Rene G., and Juanita M. Rendon. 2015. "Auditability in Public Procurement: An Analysis of Internal Controls and Fraud Vulnerability." *International Journal of Procurement Management 8*(6), 710–30.

Snider, Keith F. 1996. "DAWIA and the Price of Professionalism." *Acquisition Review Quarterly 3*(2), 97–108.

Stevulak, Cathy, and Jeffrey Campbell. 2008 "Supply-Side Corruption: Perspectives on a Trillion-Dollar Problem." *Journal of Corporate Citizenship 29*, 33–48.

Tan, Li H. J. 2013. "An Analysis of Internal Controls and Procurement Fraud Deterrence." Master's thesis, Naval Postgraduate School. http://hdl.handle.net/10945/39022.

Transparency International. 2018. "Transparency International." http://www.transparency.org/about.

Whittington, O. Ray, and Kurt Pany. 2014. *Principles of Auditing and Other Assurance Services*. 19th ed. New York: McGraw-Hill/Irwin.

Whiteley, Jacob T., Jimmy A. Foster, and Kyle A. Johnson. 2017. "Contracting for Navy Husbanding Services: An Analysis of the Fat Leonard Case." Master's thesis, Naval Postgraduate School. http://hdl.handle.net/10945/56838.

27

Accountability Institutions, Corruption Control, and Democratic Malaise

Institutional Development and the Challenge of the Public Administration for Brazil's Political System

Fernando Filgueiras

The objective of this chapter is to analyze the development of accountability institutions in Brazil. The focus of the analysis is the process of institutional change, in order to explain the catalysts of change and its impact on the organization of public integrity and the fight against corruption.

In the first section is a theoretical approach to the problem of the relationship between accountability and democracy. The second section deals with the Brazilian case. In the analysis of this case the process of institutional development in Brazil will be approached, identifying the factors of change. In this way, it will be possible to analyze the complex arrangement of organizations responsible for promoting accountability in Brazil. In the third and final section of the chapter, the consequences of this organizational arrangement of accountability institutions are analyzed, focusing on their impact on the democratic regime in Brazil.

The chapter considers that this complex arrangement of accountability institutions produces a procedural ecology. Understanding this procedural ecology makes it possible to analyze the problems of coordination and institutional performance, as well as the processes of change and management of public integrity.

Accountability Demands and Institutional Change

The literature on the issue of accountability develops around the perspective of the principal–agent theory (Filgueiras 2016). The premise of this perspective on accountability is conceived as the set of agents responsible for monitoring and controlling bureaucratic organizations, achieving compliance, and implementing the principal's preferences. Within democratic political regimes, the agents are organizations that exercise control, delegated by principals, which are citizenship and constituted powers. The question of accountability is that of exercising authority according to legitimate bases of state action in society (Ferejohn 1999).

The problem with the principal–agent theory is that supposes an endogenous process of delegation, often disregarding political contexts and exogenous processes (Olsen 2017b). Empirical studies show that principals and agents do not always fulfill their institutional roles (Schillemans and Busuioc 2015).

The fact is that an institutional approach to accountability institutions must account not only for endogenous factors but also for exogenous factors in the political context and demands for more accountability within democracies (Olsen 2017a). Democracies have been grappling with increasing demands for accountability. In societies where there are high levels of trust and satisfaction, a popular passivity is likely to occur that leads to low accountability demands.

Accountability institutions act in the context of this procedural ecology. Procedural ecology is the interdependent relationship of the system of institutions, in which the actions performed by an institution depend on the actions of other institutions. This interdependence is fixed in formal and informal rules and procedures involving a set of institutions to achieve an end. The process, therefore, fixes this ecology so that the result depends on the joint, coordinated, and cooperative action of the institutions.

The challenge of institutional coordination requires a multilevel governance system, with decision making and coordination bodies that, in view of the involvement of various institutions, can define a coordinated and negotiated pattern of public action. This perspective on coordination of institutional action involves a nonhierarchical structure for interchange between institutions in different levels (Smith 1997; Hix 1998; Peters and Pierre 2001).

Accountability Institutions in Brazil

In the case of Brazil, what was seen at the beginning of the process of democratization was the absence of accountability institutions and a structure of ethical management and corruption control (O'Donnell 1996, 25). Brazilian democratization meant the return of basic conditions of polyarchy, considering a transition process that would come in response to a crisis of the authoritarian regime implanted in 1964 (Santos 1998; Abranches 1988; Limongi 2006). Political competition, the presence of opposition parties, and clearer institutional rules promoted the development of accountability institutions motivated by the fight against corruption and the expansion of check-and-balance mechanisms (Melo, Pereira, and Figueiredo 2009).

The institutions of the accountability system must be autonomous and recognized by their operators as bearers of a public authority for the supervision, control, correction, and punishment of illegal acts, in order to preserve the public interest (Mainwaring 2003). In the case of Brazil, the extension of this ecology of institutions is quite broad, passing through the three republican powers and the media. Nevertheless, the core of this ecology is composed of four institutions: the Federal Audit Office, the Public Prosecutor's Office, the Federal Police, and the Federal Comptroller's Office. These organizations are responsible for supervising, controlling, correcting, and judicially prosecuting actions against public managers and politicians in cases of corruption, illegitimate acts, and misuse or misconduct of the public interest (Aranha 2017).

The Federal Audit Office is an advisory body of the National Congress and was founded in 1891. The Federal Audit Office, through the Federal Constitution of 1988, exercises the external control of the public administration, through audit actions, and informs the National Congress of the correct exercise of the powers delegated to public agents. Over time, the Federal Audit Office has left its strictly legalistic competencies to assume performance auditing and public management-control competencies (Speck 2000; Loureiro, Teixeira, and Cacique 2009).

In the case of the Public Prosecutor Office, the establishment of its powers by the 1988 Constitution also represented a critical situation. In its text, the Federal Constitution ensures functional and administrative autonomy, making the office immune to political interests and more empowered to act in the public scene. Also, it is up to the public prosecutor to defend the democratic regime in order to assure public and social patrimony. The Public Prosecutor's Office has an essential accountability function. They have typical powers of supervision and promotion of legal proceedings against public managers and elected politicians (Arantes 2011a).

The same happens with the Federal Police. Having the function of judicial police of the Union, which is responsible for the criminal investigation of criminal offenses against the public and social order, to the detriment of goods, services, and interests of the Union or its municipal entities and public companies, as well as other infractions whose practice has an interstate or international repercussion and requires uniform suppression. The internal socialization of agents and delegates of the Federal Police has a strong component of reinforcing suppressive action against organized crime and corruption, associated with a strengthening of democracy (Arantes 2011b).

Finally, the creation of the Federal Comptroller's Office in 2003 underlay a process of long incrementalism in the internal audit and control of the Brazilian public administration. Prior to the creation of the Federal Comptroller's Office, the internal audit system was decentralized to the various public organizations and coordinated by the Ministry of Finance (Olivieri 2010). Law 10683/2003 established the Federal Comptroller's Office, which assumed and centralized all internal audit activities of the federal government as well as initiatives to prevent and combat corruption with functional autonomy. The Federal Comptroller's Office represents, in the case of Brazil, a process of functional conversion dictated by the critical junctures of corruption scandals in the passage from the Fernando Henrique Cardoso government to the Lula government (Filgueiras and Araújo 2014; Balbe 2013).

Exogenous Factors of Institutional Change

Political change in Brazil has implied a process of incremental development of accountability institutions (Taylor and Praça 2014). Institutional development occurred incrementally, as new rules and routines were gradually added for the functioning of accountability institutions, in addition to the new resources. In the case of accountability institutions, this incrementalism has been occurring in the context of exogenous factors, through critical junctures in which new rules that imply changes in institutional practices are being added to the competences of the institutions of the accountability system. In addition, these incremental changes in the institutions of the accountability system in Brazil meant a greater ability to unveil and make public various corruption scandals, which allowed for junctures of changes in the rules that strengthened the role played by these institutions in society (2014).

In relation to exogenous factors, the Constitution of 1988 meant a first critical juncture, because it established competences to a set of institutions that compose a complex frame of control and audit between the powers of the republic. This framework of competences of the institutions refers to a theoretical understanding that it is incumbent upon all the republican powers to exercise internal control of their activities and to the legislative branch the external control, through the Federal Audit Office. Associated with this, the constitution also delegated powers to the Public Prosecutor's Office to control public administration, as well as proposing judicial and extrajudicial remedies.

The Constitution of 1988 initiated an incremental process of change, creating a powerful system of institutions capable of fighting and punishing the deviations and misconduct of public servants. On the one hand, the form of agreement with which the process of democratization was fundamental for the development of accountability institutions is notorious. In the context of society's strong demand for accountability, it is possible that the performance of accountability institutions sets up the politicization of the accountability process, or ends up challenging and confronting the existing political order, promoting order changes.

The problem of distrust and dissatisfaction with political institutions has proved to be a contemporary problem of democracy, in view of a context of systemic changes and the emergence of new modes of mobilization and social participation (Dalton 1999; Hardin 1999; Levi 1998; Norris 1999; Offe 1999; Putnam 1993).

In this context, demands for accountability have grown. The question is to what extent these demands for accountability constitute administrative routines or are politicized in the context of political order. Since the impeachment process of President Dilma Roussef initiated by the Federal Audit Office complaint about the problems with the fiscal regime, even in the actions of the Public Prosecutor's Office and the Federal Police in the criminal prosecution of the Lava Jato (Car Wash) case, accountability institutions in Brazil have assumed a central position in society. This has resulted in a profound political instability and deep crisis that makes the scenario uncertain.

Endogenous Factors of Institutional Change

In the endogenous factors of the change, the structuring of careers fulfilled a very important factor in this process, as well as the budgetary question. The accountability institutions have undergone organizational changes since 1988, which implied a new behavior of agents within these institutions (Olivieri, Teixeira, Loureiro, and Abrucio 2013). The creation of the office of Inspection and Control Analysts (AFC), the organizational and career changes of the federal police, the strengthening and autonomy of the public prosecutor, and the internal changes in the Federal Audit Office have strengthened the capacity of accountability institutions.

The agents of these institutions, endowed with greater autonomy and legitimized by public opinion, began to constitute activities of control and interpretation of the norms that positioned them as fundamental political agents of Brazilian democracy. Institutional change, in this case, was also the result of changes in the everyday life of institutions in which agents participate in the process of creating rules and procedures. They influenced the implementation of these rules, mobilized resources for their application, controlled relevant public-sector information, and selected the mode by which institutional choices would be made.

Regarding the organization of the careers of accountability institutions, the agents' linkage to the strategic nucleus of the state made possible not only a set of internal revisions to the organizations, but growing autonomy in relation to private interests and a process of gradual institutional capacity building. Careers in the Federal Comptroller Office, the Federal Police, the Federal Public Prosecutor's Office, and the Federal Audit Office are attractive to individuals with better education who are heavily involved in admissions. The average and medium remuneration of these careers are the highest of the federal bureaucracy. Comparing, in figure 27.1 below, the average of the gross remuneration of the employees of these institutions with the remunerations of the other organizations of the executive branch, one perceives a gap that separates bureaucracies of accountability institutions in relation to the bureaucracies responsible for the process of implementation and management of public policies.

The same can be said in relation to the budget of accountability institutions. The actors of these organizations struggle for resources in order to empower themselves in the areas of government. The growing accumulation of endogenous skills and conditions conducive to stability and management of public servants extends the capabilities and autonomy of the accountability institutions. These endogenous conditions mean a steadily increasing incremental budget of these organizations in order to provide better conditions for the control and punishment of corruption.

The accountability institutions are endowed with a greater capacity of action ahead of the bureaucracies responsible for the implementation of public policies. Accountability, in this sense, is autonomous in the policy cycle, so that organizations could constitute

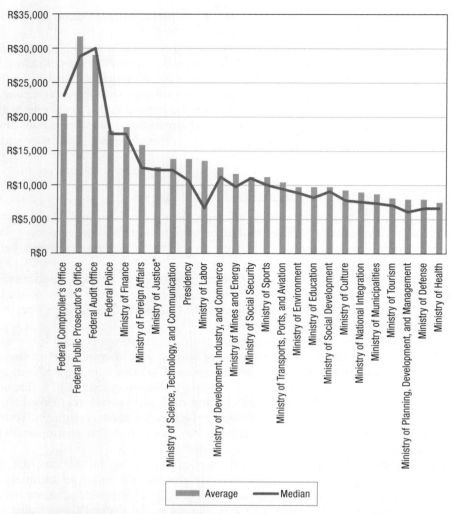

FIGURE 27.1 Average and Median Remuneration of Accountability Institutions and the Federal Executive Branch

Source: Public Prosecutor Office; Federal Audit Office, March 2017; SIAPE—Personnel Administration System, Federal Government of Brazil.

institutional learning, greater resources, and perspectives to act in public management and the political system. The centrality of these institutions to the control of public administration establishes political resources for accountability institutions, so that they can increase their budgetary, personnel, and institutional resources as well as their political resources in the public sphere. The agents of accountability institutions interpret norms, set regulations, manage practices, and directly become involved with the results achieved by policies. In the role of norm interpretation, the agents of accountability institutions act politically because they act directly in the decision-making and implementation process.

Systemic Factors of Institutional Change

The interaction of accountability institutions is marked by the interdependence. The increased interaction between the accountability institutions system has not resulted in a cooperative or coordinated process of joint action, as organizations fight rationally for recognition of public opinion and have strong political interests. The information the institutions of accountability came to retain serves them as a strategic resource, ensuring the fulfillment of their interests and their position in the struggle for public opinion. These institutions began to retain information and to control actions that respond to the exogenous and endogenous factors of institutional change.

On the one hand, to the exogenous factors of change, information serves to confront the critical junctures of the corruption scandals, where institutions begin to fight for public opinion. On the other hand, information is a strategic resource that serves the interests of the agents of control bureaucracies, in consideration of political and corporate interests. The information acquired by bureaucratic organizations is made available instrumentally. Agents decide how information will be used and passed on, relative to their political interests (Gailmard and Patty 2007).

Bureaucracies are not politically neutral (Simon 1957). In addition, accountability routines can be powerful political tools. The control of the Brazilian public administration is done in the context of administrative and criminal procedures that aim not only to correct the application of public resources, but also to correct the principles of public administration included in article 37 of the Federal Constitution.

Coordination problems arise from a mutual reinforcement between systemic factors and exogenous and endogenous factors to organizations. Endogenous factors have created broad capacities for all accountability organizations. The result of this process is an institutional conflict within the system of accountability, so that organizations struggle for power and resources, reducing the margin of cooperation.

The change in the system of accountability institutions in Brazil was not accompanied by an ecological change in which the interaction between these institutions is not capable of producing coordinated and cooperative actions, not ensuring a rational sequencing of activities aimed at improving accountability. Each organization of the accountability institutions composes an autonomous "island of excellence" endowed with high capacity.

The control of the information retained by the agents of the accountability institutions presents itself as a fundamental strategic resource. The logic of the dispute between the institutions of the Brazilian accountability system can be seen not only around procedures but also around public opinion. Given the context in which institutional capacities to unveil corruption have widened, the institutions of the accountability system began to challenge public opinion in order to consolidate their interests in the political arena.

Institutional Changes and Unintended Democratic Malaise

In the context of a divided and politically unstable society, the accountability institutions assume a leading role and may challenge the prevailing political order (Olsen 2017b). In the case of Brazil, this challenge occurs in a conflictive institutional context, in two dimensions: (1) in the systemic dimension of accountability institutions, that is, in the political conflict between the different accountability institutions; (2) in the exogenous dimension of accountability institutions, involving mainly the conflict between the institutions of government bureaucracy and the institutions of the political system.

The interaction between institutional changes of political representation and political culture ensures that accountability institutions are empowered as representative political institutions, subject to processes of displacement of legitimacy. It is not, therefore, a question of thinking about this process that is alien to the changes in values and attitudes that circumscribe political culture in democracies, since public opinion is an important variable in shaping the legitimacy of the performance of accountability institutions. This is a process that has its origin in the very strengthening of democracy, a process in which the critical position of citizens reflects the empowerment of counter-majoritarian institutions (Rosanvallon 2006).

The fact is that the displacement of democratic legitimacy and the empowerment of accountability institutions make the accountability institutions fundamental political actors with a representative capacity to challenge the political order and promote institutional changes in the sphere of democracy. The impact of the accountability institutions operates in two dimensions: (1) in the dimension of public management, reducing the discretion of managers in the decision-making process and the implementation of policies; (2) in the dimension of the political system, reducing the margin of the majority in the democratic system.

Regarding the unintended impact of accountability institutions, there is a profound reduction in the discretion of public managers in the decision-making process and in the implementation of policies. The result of this process is to increase the costs of administrative machines, create obstacles to innovation in public service, processes, and resources, and create constraints on economic investment (Anechiarico 2010).

The accountability institutions challenge the political order in order to trigger changes through political reforms or the constitution of an agenda based on the issue of fighting corruption and management failures. In the context in which corruption within the political system is gradually unveiled in public, the expansion of demands for accountability promotes political instability and triggers a process of changing the establishment of the political system.

The accountability institutions are fundamental to the democratic regime. However, they must act in the context of fixed institutional procedures, within a scope that prevents the extrapolation of their routines, hierarchies, and processes. The accountability institutions, as they act in political dynamics, will necessarily fall into the old dilemma: Who controls the controller?

References

Abranches, S. H. H. 1988. "Presidencialismo de Coalizão: o Dilema Institucional Brasileiro [Coalition Presidentialism: The Brazilian Institutional Dilemma]". *Dados—Revista de Ciências Sociais 31*(1), 5–34.

Anechiarico, F. 2010. "La Corrupción y el Control de la Corrupción como Impedimentos para la Competitividad Económica [Corruption and the Control of Corruption as Impediments to Economic Competitiveness]". *Gestión y Política Pública 19*(2), 239–61.

Aranha, A. L. 2017. "Accountability, Corruption, and Local Government. Mapping the Control Steps." *Brazilian Political Science Review 11*(2), 1–31.

Cyert, R. M., and March, J. G. 1963. *A Behavioral Theory of the Firm.* Englewood Cliffs, NJ: Prentice Hall.

Dalton, R. 1999. "Political Support in Advanced Industrial Democracies," in P. Norris, ed. *Critical Citizens.* Global Support for Democratic Government. Cambridge: Oxford University Press.

Ferejohn, J. 1999. "Accountability and Authority," in A. Przeworski, S. Stokes, and B. Manin (Orgs.). *Democracy, Accountability, and Representation.* Cambridge: Cambridge University Press, 31–53.

Filgueiras, F. 2016. "Transparency and Accountability: Principles and Rules for the Construction of Publicity." *Journal of Public Affairs 16*(2), 192–202.

Gailmard, S. and J. Patty. 2007. "Slackers and Zealots: Civil Service, Policy Discretion, and Bureaucratic Expertise." *American Journal of Political Science 51*(4), 873–89.

Hardin, R. 1999. "Do We Want Trust in Government?," in Mark Warren, ed. *Democracy and Trust.* Cambridge: Cambridge University Press, 22–41.

Hix, S. 1998. "The Study of the European Union II: A New Institutionalist Approach." *Journal of Public Policy 13*, 351–80.

Levi, M. 1998. "A State of Trust," in V. Braithwaite and M. Levi, eds. *Trust and Governance.* New York: Russell Sage Foundation.

Limongi, F. 2006. "A Democracia no Brasil. Presidencialismo, Coalizão Partidária e Processo Decisório [The Democracy in Brazil. Presidentialism, Party Coalition, and Decision Process]." *Novos Estudos 76*, 17–41.

Loureiro, M. R., C. Olivieri, and A. C. Braga. 2011. "Bureaucrats, Parties, and Interest Groups," in M. Font and L. Randall, eds., *Brazilian State: Debate and Agenda*. Lanham, MD: Lexington Books, 111–30.

Loureiro, M. R., M. A. C. Teixeira, and T. Cacique. 2009. "Democratização e Reforma do Estado: o Desenvolvimento Institucional no Tribunais de Contas no Brasil Recente [Democratization and State Reform: Institutional Development in the Courts of Accounts in Recent Brazil]." *Revista de Administração Pública* 43(4), 739–72.

Lupia, A. 2001. "Delegation Power: Agency Theory," in N. Smelser and P. Baltes, eds., *International Encyclopedia of the Social and Behavioral Sciences*. Oxford: Elsevier, 3375–77.

Mainwaring, S. 2003. "Introduction: Democratic Accountability in Latin America," in S. Mainwaring and C. Welna, *Democratic Accountability in Latin America*. Oxford: Oxford University Press, 3–33.

McCubbins, M., R. Noll, and B. Weingast. 1987. "Structure and Process, Politics and Policy: Administrative Arrangements and Political Control of Agencies." *Virginia Law Review 75*, 431–82.

Melo, M. A., C. Pereira, and C. M. Figueiredo. 2009. "Political and Institutional Checks on Corruption: Explaining the Performance of Brazilian Audit Institutions." *Comparative Political Studies 42*(9), 1217–44.

Moisés, J. A. 2010. "Os Significados da Democracia Segundo os Brasileiros [The Meanings of Democracy According to Brazilians]." *Opinião Pública 16*(2), 269–309.

Norris, P. 1999. *Critical citizens*. "Global Support for Democratic Government." Oxford: Oxford University Press.

Norris, P. 2011. *Democratic Deficit: Critical Citizens Revisited*. New York: Cambridge University Press.

O'Donnell, G. 1996. "Uma Outra Institucionalização: América Latina e Alhures [Another Institutionalization: Latin America and the Elsewhere]." *Lua Nova 37*, 5–31.

O'Donnell, G. 1998. "Horizontal Accountability in New Democracies." *Journal of Democracy 9*(3), 112–26.

Offe, C. 1999. "How Can We Trust our Fellow Citizens?," in M. Warren, ed., *Democracy and Trust*. Cambridge: Cambridge University Press.

Olivieri, C., M. A. C. Teixeira, M. R. Loureiro, and F. Abrucio. 2013. "Organizational Learning of Controllers and Controlled Agencies: Innovations and Challenges in Promoting Accountability in the Recent Brazilian Democracy." *American Journal of Industrial and Business Management 3*(6), 43–51.

Olsen, J. P. 2017a. *Democratic Accountability, Political Order, and Change. Exploring Accountability Processes in an Era of European Transformation*. Oxford: Oxford University Press.

Olsen, J. P. 2017b. "Accountability Democrática e Mudança da Ordem Política Europeia [Democratic Accountability and Change of the European Political Order]." *Revista do Serviço Público 68*(4), 745–84.

Peters, B. G., and J. Pierre. 2001. "Developments in Intergovernmental Relations: Towards Multi-Level Governance." Policy & Politics *29*(2), 131–35.

Putnam. R. D. 1993. *Making Democracy Work*. Civic Traditions in Modern Italy. Princeton, NJ: Princeton University Press.

Santos, W. G. (1998). *Décadas de Espanto e uma Apologia Democrática*. Rio de Janeiro: Rocco.

Schillemans, T., and M. Busuioc. 2015. "Predicting Public Sector Accountability: From Agency Drift to Forum Drift." *Journal of Public Administration Research and Theory 25*(1), 191–215.

Simon, H. A. 1957. *Administrative Behavior*. New York: Free Press.

Smith, M. 1997. "Studying Multi-Level Governance: Examples from French Translations of the Structural Funds." *Public Administration 75*(4), 711–29.

Speck, B. W. 2000. *Inovação e Rotina no Tribunal de Contas da União:* O Papel da *Instituição Superior de Controle Financeiro no Sistema Político-Administrativo Brasileiro* [Innovation and Routine in the Federal Audit Office: The Role of the Superior Institution of Financial Control in the Brazilian Political-Administrative System]. São Paulo: Fundação Konrad-Adenauer Stiftung.

Taylor, M., and S. Praça, 2014. "Inching Toward Accountability." *Latin American Politics and Society 56*(2), 27–48.

Taylor, M., and V. Buranelli. 2007. "Ending Up in Pizza. Accountability as a Problem of an Institutional Arrangement in Brazil." *Latin American Politics and Society 49*(1), 59–87.

28

Keeping up Ethical Standards When Fighting Organized Crime
A Case Study in Law Enforcement
Emile Kolthoff and Hans Nelen

This chapter provides an account of a research into serious integrity violations within four Dutch law-enforcement organizations—the Police, Customs, the Royal Netherlands Marechaussee (KMar), and the Fiscal Information and Investigation Service (FIOD)—that could be linked to organized crime (Nelen and Kolthoff 2017). Following a number of notorious cases involving the provision of confidential police information to criminals by a police officer, and the involvement of customs officers in drug trafficking and corruption, the question was raised in the Dutch parliament in 2016 whether these cases were isolated incidents or reflected structural problems within law-enforcement agencies. The research that was conducted to answer this question also covered various issues in relation to the prevention and repression of serious integrity violations within law enforcement. In this chapter, an overview will be provided of the main research results. We also delve into possible causes of the integrity violations we found, and reflect on some possible remedies to prevent them.

Goal of the Research and Methods

The aim of the research was to identify and describe the nature, extent, and seriousness of integrity violations within the four law-enforcement organizations named above in relation to organized crime. The research also considered how law-enforcement agencies had tried to guard themselves against such violations and strengthen the resilience of their employees. The study was based on a range of methods. Quantitative data were collected through a systematic inventory of reports of integrity violations in relation to organized crime, submitted in the period 2012–2016 to the National Police Internal Investigations Department (Rijksrecherche), the thirteen National Police Security, Integrity and Complaints offices (VIK), the FIOD Integrity and Security Bureau (BIV), and the KMar Internal Investigation Section (SIO). In addition, a survey was conducted during a seminar open only to officials working in the areas of investigation, enforcement, and prosecution. The participants were asked about their own experiences with integrity violations (in relation to organized crime), observations of such violations in their own organizations, and the measures put in place to prevent and combat serious integrity violations. The qualitative research material consists of data from fifty-five interviews and the report drawn up by the investigators from the in-depth discussion that formed the second part of the seminar. In addition, an in-depth analysis was performed on five criminal investigation cases of the Rijksrecherche.

Organized Crime in the Netherlands

There is sufficient empirical evidence to demonstrate the hypothesis that organized crime as it appears in the greatest part of Europe, does not—or only in exceptional cases—meet the image of a classical mafia family with sustainable, pyramidal organizations and a strict hierarchy, a clear division of responsibilities, a code of conduct, and an internal sanction system (Siegel and Nelen 2008). The way criminal groups are organized can better be described as "criminal networking" (Spapens 2010). So-called "facilitators" frequently operate at the periphery of these criminal partnerships. They sometimes provide their services to multiple criminal groups. Document forgers, transport providers, company brokers, legal counselors, money changers and financial advisors may play facilitating roles, but corrupt officials also can be important facilitators. Given that organized crime in Netherlands is characterized as "transit crime," abusing the existing legal infrastructure and legal flows of merchandise, a corrupt officer can play an important role in passing checkpoints at international air and sea ports and at border crossings. Corrupt officials can also be useful for more general purposes, for example, the leaking of information on current criminal-investigation activities.

For the purposes of this report, the definition of "organized crime" was adopted as suggested by the Fijnaut research group (1996): "Organized crime occurs when groups whose primary focus is on illegal gains systematically commit crimes with serious consequences for society and are relatively effective at covering up these offences." In terms of serious integrity violations, in addition to bribery, the research expressly looked at violations of professional secrecy (leaking information), undesirable contacts (in the family environment, circle of acquaintances, and so forth), undesirable side activities, and facilitating the activities of organized crime (doing favors for criminal networks).

Number and Types of Cases

The research revealed that during the last couple of years, more policy attention has been paid within the four law-enforcement organizations to integrity violations in relation to organized crime than in the years before. However, due to a lack of proper prior measurement and an absence of reliable, uniform recording of integrity-violation data, it was not possible to draw any reliable and valid conclusion on the extent of the problem of serious integrity violations within law enforcement. In other words, we do not know exactly how many law-enforcement officials were bribed in the period 2012–2016. No indications were found, though, that suggest a significant rise or fall in the number of cases over time.

In total, the data over a five-year period revealed 256 reports of serious integrity violations in relation to organized crime. Most reports were related to the work of police officers. This fact can be largely explained by the aforementioned different sizes of the four organizations (roughly sixty thousand persons are employed within the police force versus twenty thousand employees for the three other organizations in total). A second explanation is related to the nature of police work, and the fact that police officers spend more time working on the street and in close proximity to criminals. These circumstances increase the likelihood that criminals might just try to manipulate them for their own ends.

Figure 28.1 provides an overview of the conclusions of all 256 cases on which in the presented research information was collected. In eighty cases (31 percent), the research led to the conclusion that they involved both an integrity violation and a relationship with organized crime. For the police and the KMar, these violations mainly involved leaking of confidential information or establishing undesirable contacts with criminals (or both). The investigations at the FIOD and Customs mainly focused on other sorts of integrity violations, such as facilitating organized crime (in particular in the form of favors such as circumventing customs checks).

In one out of eight cases (13 percent), there was evidence of an integrity violation, but no link with organized crime could be identified. The category of cases in which there is a suspected relationship with organized crime but no clear evidence of improper conduct by an individual official, makes up almost a third of the total (30 percent). These research results confirm the difficulty in integrity investigations of conclusively establishing the facts of a case or the involvement of a law-enforcement officer. Examples of this category are situations in which it is clear that criminals were informed of an upcoming police action (the suspected building was cleared just before the police raid), or that they were overheard on a telephone tap about information they received, but no evidence could be found pointing to a specific police officer.

In 8 percent of the 256 cases, the agent under investigation was fully exonerated of any involvement in an integrity violation related to organized crime. Examples of this category were situations in which criminals deliberately mentioned the name of a police officer in a telephone conversation, knowing their phone was tapped, with the goal being to spread rumors and frustrate criminal investigations against themselves. The remainder (18 percent) of the cases was formed by the cases in which the investigations had not been completed.

Once a serious integrity violation in relation to organized crime is established, the penalties are generally severe: most violators convicted in a criminal-law case were dismissed in disgrace.

Integrity violations come in many varieties. In the research by Kolthoff and colleagues (2007) into police integrity, ten categories were distinguished. Most of these categories are not relevant for the research discussed here, because they refer to the behavior of individual employees without any influence thereupon by externals. Examples are theft or embezzlement during employment. Because of the explicit link with organized crime in this study, the emphasis is on a number of specific integrity violations. The categorization we used stems from the secondary analysis on the data from the Dutch organized crime monitor (Kruisbergen et al. 2012). The seven integrity violations that resulted from that analysis are bribery, the incorrect handling of (confidential) information ("leaking"), unwanted contacts with criminals (in the family atmosphere, acquaintances, etc.), not acting against activities of organized crime, facilitating organized crime, advising members of criminal groups, and unwanted side activities.

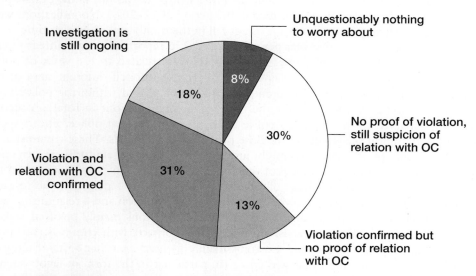

FIGURE 28.1 Outcome of Investigations into Serious Integrity Violations in Relation to Organized Crime in the Period 2012–2016 (n=256)

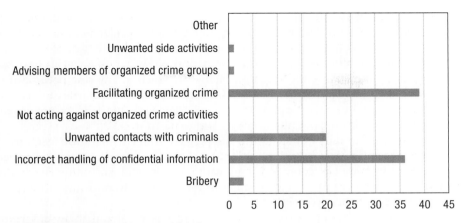

FIGURE 28.2 Types of Integrity Violations

In figure 28.2, the types of integrity violations are shown in the eighty cases in which both an integrity violation and a relationship with organized crime were established. The figure shows that two types of integrity violations predominate, namely facilitating activities of organized crime and incorrect dealing with confidential information. However, one should realize that in many cases there was an overlap of various types of integrity violations. The categories "unwanted contacts with criminals" and "incorrect handling of information," for example, were often found in combination in one case. Because the researchers identified only one answer category during their inventory, the image presented is somewhat distorted. If we look at the different types of integrity violations in figure 28.2, for example, bribery seems not to be a big problem. However, this finding is partly an artifact of the method of registration by the investigative agencies. It should be kept in mind that proving bribery as a rule is far more difficult than determining unwanted contacts or leaking of confidential information. Quite often, the classification of an integrity violation in one of the latter categories had already taken place before the bribery element could be demonstrated.

Possible Causes of Integrity Violations

From the literature, survey, and interviews, indications have emerged suggesting that the pressure being put by organized crime on law-enforcement and public-administration officials is increasing. When criminal subjects weigh up whether it would be worthwhile to approach representatives of law-enforcement organizations and manipulate them for their own ends, their line of thinking seems to have changed. Rather than avoiding them, they tend to get closer to governmental and administrative institutions—in this case, law-enforcement agencies—and cozy up to them. This development also explains the research finding that, unlike in the past, when CID officers were targeted, primarily the members of local police units are involved in integrity violations in relation to organized crime. These officers are supposed to maintain intensive contact with the local population, but at the same time must keep their distance from people who are heavily involved in criminal activities. That is a balancing act, which not everyone in the police force is able to perform well, as this research shows.

Another important development in the opportunity structure is the digitization of society. This development is reflected in almost all forms of organized crime; nearly every criminal partnership uses digital tools. Conversely, the logistical processes of law-enforcement organizations are almost entirely automated, and investigation agencies have access to technological tools enabling the available databases, which in any case have been massively expanded, to be consulted anywhere, and at any time. Once criminals can exploit the vulnerabilities of digital communication traffic—whether with the help of employees of law-enforcement organizations or not—they're not going to stop.

The case studies and interviews confirm the picture from the literature (Simpson and Piquero 2002) that officials involved in integrity violations can be characterized as people with little self-control, are not good at dealing with adversity and frustration (both professional and private), and are motivated by a desire for a more adventurous, more riveting, and (sometimes) a more luxurious life.

In line with the results of previous studies, this research revealed that law-enforcement officials with a migrant background are overrepresented—compared to their proportion of the overall workforce—in the group of integrity violators. This finding is related to their extended social networks of family and acquaintances. Considering the relatively high involvement of some ethnic groups in crime (including organized crime), the likelihood that the networks of officials with a migrant background would include someone from the criminal world is statistically higher than for native-born Dutch officials. Moreover, it is well known from the literature that trust is pivotal to prolonged corruption relationships. It is no coincidence that family and friendship ties sometimes lead to the building of bridges between criminal networks and the world of surveillance and investigation. The officials involved are then confronted with the issue of dual loyalties: the strong family and friendship ties with their local neighborhoods cannot be denied, but at the same time, the officials are necessary role models for law-enforcement organizations that want to introduce more diversity into their ranks (Nelen and Nieuwendijk 2002).

Organizational Culture

Organizational culture has a strong influence on the behavior of employees. This also seems to be the case within law-enforcement organizations. The organizational culture can be a (partial) source for the occurrence of integrity violations. This section explores this phenomenon in more detail based on scientific literature.

Organizational culture arises from the customs and manners that employees have taught themselves in dealing with problems in the performance of their duty (Paoline 2003; Schein 1990; Trompenaars 1993). It is a social construct that is shaped and shared by the employees. It concerns having the same ideas about aspects such as efficiency, effectiveness, authority, and the interpretation of moral values and standards. Employees working long enough in the organization can identify with the culture and transfer the shared beliefs through a process of socialization of new hires (Bate 1984). Schein (1985, 9) summarizes this aptly in his definition of the concept of organizational culture:

> A pattern of basic assumptions—invented, discovered, or developed by a given group as it learns to cope with its problems of external adaptation and internal integration—that has worked well enough to be considered valid and, therefore, to be taught to new members as the correct way to perceive, think, and feel in relation to those problems.

A law-enforcement organization rarely will have one homogeneous culture. In general, subcultures can be distinguished with different views and customs (Paoline 2003; Punch 1985; Punch 2009; Waddington 1999). Some of these subcultures can include deviant characteristics and thereby differ from the prevailing moral values and standards in the organization or the external environment. Subcultures have a partially isolated position and mostly encourage the concealment of violations committed by group members (Ashforth and Anand 2003; Skolnick 2002).

With concern as to violations committed at the group level, such subcultures arise especially in departments and teams that are driven by performance agreements, with vague or broad guidelines as to how these results should be achieved, without much attention to integrity (Kolthoff 2007). The subcultures are characterized by a strong mutual dependency, but a less-strong dependency on external parties; rewards at group level, as opposed to rewarding individual employees; a close connection and stable structure; and employees working close to each other in spatial terms (Ashforth and Anand 2003). It is plausible that these characteristics also relate to the collective-integrity violations that relate to organized crime, within law-enforcement organizations. The most striking evidence for this conclusion is that in none of the eighty cases in which integrity violations in relation to organized crime were identified, an investigation started because of an internal report by a colleague or boss. Law-enforcement officials hardly blow the whistle on their colleagues or superiors. They may have a gut feeling that something is wrong but have no interest in taking action and just look the other way.

Most of the studies that focus on unethical behavior within organizations consider the socialization processes as an important factor (Anand, Ashforth, and Joshi 2004; Ashforth and Anand 2003; Baucus 1994; Brief, Buttram, and Dukerich 2001; Cooper 2012; Simpson and Piquero 2002). In the socialization process in which deviant behavior is learned, neutralization of stressful feelings seems to be the central focus. The self-image of the newcomer, being a person with integrity, is kept intact as much as possible. Slow habituation to rule-breaking and unethical behavior, euphemistic use of language, and rationalizing/justifying behavior are important mechanisms in the socialization process (Ashforth and Anand 2003; Bandura 1999).

Strongly linked to the latter are probably also prevailing frustration with the organization—for example, regarding pay, working conditions, and the career perspective; working at the margins of society in frequent contact with injustice and hypocrisy; or the functioning of the criminal justice system (Kleinig 1996; Kort et al. 2014). The implicit or explicit goal is that the newcomer does not see the committed violations as disagreeable (Ashforth and Anand 2003; Bandura 1999). It is a slow change of the self-image and of one's own value framework (Sherman 1982; Van Laere 1980). Collegiality or loyalty can be positioned as the dominant value (Skolnick 2002).

Vulnerabilities and Areas for Improvement

Through their service-issued phones, employees of law-enforcement organizations often have access to a variety of data and recording systems. Searches outside of work time are therefore considerably easier. In relation to flexible working opportunities, employees sometimes show a certain naivety around the handling of social media and sensitive information.

In our research, various recommendations have been made to reduce vulnerabilities around database searches. For instance, it was recommended to introduce an automated system that could enable the detection of abnormal patterns of search behavior by law-enforcement officials, police officers in particular. A case was also made for random checks of the types of subscription services consulted by officials using their service-issue phones. However, all of these proposed measures appear—at least within the police—to have met with resistance, since many police officers perceive them as being at odds with the principle of trusting each other and each other's integrity.

In conversations with police officers, inadequate operational supervision of employees by managers was a frequently recurring theme. It is clear that the span of control for team leaders of local units is too big. They increasingly have to manage large groups of employees and cannot stay in close contact with their individual staff members. As a result, the supervision and control of employees in local teams are insufficient, and the chances that individual officers abuse their autonomy have increased.

This research shows that many employees working within the four law-enforcement organizations studied—the police in particular—are convinced that there is a lot of room for improvement in the employee screening process. In short, the complaint is that, increasingly, fewer employees are subject to the more stringent forms of screening, that the background checks are less comprehensive than in the past, and that ongoing screening of employees is not carried out often enough. The group that featured most prominently in the integrity violations examined in this research—members of local units—is subject to the lowest form of screening through a Trustworthiness and Suitability Assessment.

In terms of learning from experience, it appears that Customs—particularly following a number of large-scale corruption cases at the Port of Rotterdam—has put a lot of effort into developing reviewing systems and processes for potential vulnerabilities. Major corruption cases are extensively discussed internally and, where possible, individual experiences are shared with employees, so that lessons can be drawn from them. The police appear to be less advanced in this regard. Cases are not yet systematically evaluated and discussed within the section where the violation occurred, let alone more widely.

The close-knit culture within law-enforcement organizations has both positive and negative effects. Collegiality and loyalty are important values of this culture; by necessity, officers have to be able to trust and rely on each other in difficult circumstances. The downside of these values is that officers sometimes defend each other uncritically. In addition, speaking up is far from being an integral part of the culture.

Speaking up is still not standard behavior for managers either. According to many respondents, there is still room for improvement in terms of managers leading by example. Focusing on integrity as a leadership or management issue implies that it may be buried under all the other priorities managers have to deal with. But it is an important matter that deserves attention, because it is precisely these direct managers who hold the key to reporting the dubious behavior of their staff and putting a stop to it. Furthermore, they must send an unequivocal message to their employees about what behavior is desirable and what is undesirable within the organization (Treviño, Hartman, and Brown 2000).

References

Anand, V., B. E. Ashforth, and M. Joshi. 2004. "Business as Usual: The Acceptance and Perpetuation of Corruption in Organizations."*Academy of Management Executive 18*(2), 39–53.

Ashforth, B. E., and V. Anand. 2003. "The Normalization of Corruption in Organizations." *Research in Organizational Behavior 25*, 1–52.

Bandura, A. 1999. "Moral Disengagement in the Perpetration of Inhumanities." *Personality and Social Psychology Review 3*(3), 193–209.

Bate, P. 1984. "The Impact of Organizational Culture on Approaches to Organizational Problem-solving." *Organization Studies 5*(1), 43–66.

Baucus, M. S. 1994. "Pressure, Opportunity and Predisposition: A Multivariate Model of Corporate Illegality." *Journal of Management 20*(4), 699–721.

Brief, A. P., R. T. Buttram, and J. M. Dukerich. 2001. "Collective Corruption in the Corporate World: Toward a Process Model," in M. E. Turner, ed., *Groups at Work: Theory and Research.* Mahwah, NJ: Erlbaum, 471–99.

Cooper, J. A. 2012. "Noble Cause Corruption as a Consequence of Role Conflict in the Police Organisation."*Policing and Society 22*(2), 169–84.

Fijnaut, C. J. C. F., F. Bovenkerk, G. J. N. Bruinsma, and H. G. van de Bunt. 1996. *Georganiseerde criminaliteit in Nederland: Eindrapport Enquêtecommissie Opsporingsmethoden* (Bijlage VII). Den Haag: SDU.

Inspectie Veiligheid en Justitie. 2016. *Maatregelen integriteit: Een onderzoek naar maatregelen die moeten voorkomen dat politieambtenaren onjuist gebruik maken van politie-informatie.* Den Haag: Ministerie van Veiligheid en Justitie.

Kleinig, J. 1996. *The Ethics of Policing.* Cambridge: Cambridge University.

Kolthoff, E. 2007. *Ethics and New Public Management: Empirical Research into the Effects of Businesslike Government on Ethics and Integrity.* The Hague: BJU Legal Publishers.

Kolthoff, E., L. Huberts and H. van den Heuvel. 2007. "The Ethics of New Public Management: Is Integrity at Stake?" *Public Administration Quarterly 30*(4), 399–439.

Kort, J., M. I. Fedorova, and J. B. Terpstra. 2014. *Politiemensen over het strafrecht.* Apeldoorn/ Nijmegen: Politie & Wetenschap/Radboud Universiteit Nijmegen.

Kruisbergen, E. W., H. G. Van de Bunt, E. R. Kleemans, R. F. Kouwenberg, K. Huisman, C. A. Meerts, and D. De Jong. 2012. *Monitor georganiseerde criminaliteit: Vierde ronde.* Den Haag: Boom Lemma.

Nelen, H., and A. Nieuwendijk. 2002. "Ambtelijke corruptie in Nederland; de verschijningsvormen verkend." *Tijdschrift voor de Politie 64*(10), 14–17.

Nelen, H., and E. Kolthoff. 2017. *Schaduwen over de rechtshandhaving. Georganiseerde criminaliteit en integriteitsschendingen van functionarissen in de rechtshandhaving. Onderzoeksrapport in opdracht van het WODC.* Den Haag: Boom Criminologie.

Paoline, E. A. 2003. "Taking Stock: Toward a Richer Understanding of Police Culture." *Journal of Criminal Justice 31*(3), 199–214.

Punch, M. 1985. *Conduct Unbecoming: The Social Construction of Police Deviance and Control.* London: Tavistock.

Punch , M. 2009. *Police Corruption: Deviance, Accountability and Reform in Policing.* Cullompton, UK: Willan.

Schein, E. H. 1985. *Organizational Culture and Leadership.* San Francisco: Jossey-Bass.

Schein, E. H. 1990. "Organizational Culture." *American Psychologist 45*(2), 109–19.

Sherman, L. 1982. "Learning Police Ethics." *Criminal Justice Ethics 1*(1), 10–19.

Siegel, D., and J. M. Nelen. 2008. *Organized Crime: Culture, Markets and Policies.* New York: Springer.

Simpson, S. S., and N. L. Piquero. 2002. "Low Self-control, Organizational Theory, and Corporate Crime." *Law & Society Review 36*(3), 509–48.

Skolnick, J. H. 2002. "Corruption and the Blue Code of Silence." *Police Practice and Research 3*(1), 7–19.

Spapens, T. 2010. Macro Networks, Collectives, and Business Processes: An Integrated Approach to Organized Crime. *European Journal of Crime, Criminal Law and Criminal Justice 18*(2), 185–215.

Treviño, L. K., L. P. Hartman, and M. Brown. 2000. "Moral Person and Moral Manager: How Executives Develop a Reputation for Ethical Leadership." *California Management Review 42*(4), 128–42.

Trompenaars, F. 1993. *Riding the Waves of Culture: Understanding Cultural Diversity in Business.* London: Nicholas Brealey.

Van Laere, E. M. P. 1980. *Oorzaken van normafwijkend gedrag binnen de politie-organisatie.* 's-Gravenhage: Ministerie van Binnenlandse Zaken, Directie Politie, Afdeling Onderzoek en Ontwikkeling.

Waddington, P. A. J. 1999. "Police (Canteen) Sub-culture: An Appreciation." *The British Journal of Criminology 39*(2), 287–309.

29

Post-Genocide Recovery and Governance

Haris Alibašić

This chapter offers a perspective on the post-genocide recovery and the respective role of governance, perception of justice from the survivors' perspective, prosecution of war criminals and genuine reconciliation, formulating missing links to transition to the long-term stability of post-conflict countries. The text begins with the working definition of genocide and reviews more recently recorded and prosecuted cases of genocide in Bosnia and Herzegovina, Cambodia, Kosovo, and Rwanda, and post-conflict recovery efforts in those countries. The circumstances of genocide denial and revision of history and the role of adequate prosecution of war crimes are also included in this chapter. The chapter concludes that the recovery and governance of countries after genocide can only be achieved through suitable acknowledgment of war crimes, prosecution of war criminals, and recognizing the uniqueness of economic, social, political, and governance factors in postwar recovery. At a minimum, post-genocide governance and democratization of post-conflict societies must allow for adequate memorialization of the events for post-event recovery. At a time when the world is witnessing genocidal events unraveling in Syria, Iraq, and parts of the Africa continent, the considerations over postwar and post-genocide reconstruction and governance are at a critical juncture.

Post-Genocide Recovery

Post-genocide countries are faced with disrupted administrative networks, destroyed infrastructure, interrupted economy, vulnerable legal, judicial, and political systems, dysfunctional institutions, and corruption at all levels of government. In most cases, the levels of destruction and devastation leave the consequences of genocide and atrocities unmitigated, with post-conflict recovery taking years and decades. The international bureaucracies, in their effort for a quick recovery and the establishment of democracy in a post-conflict situation, ignore the principles of memorialization and remembrance by survivors as a means to reconciliation and amnesty. In part, international bureaucrats, driven by the forces of technical rationality, apply the most rational path to recovery with adverse consequences to post-genocide governance.

As noted by Balfour and Alibašić (2016, 3),

> During the twentieth century, the Holocaust and other eruptions of evil and administrative evil (such as the genocides in Bosnia and Kosovo) showed that the assumptions and standards for ethical behavior in modern, technical-rational systems often failed to prevent or mitigate evil in either its subtle or its more obvious forms.

Post-conflict countries are fertile ground for the application of technical–rational structures, deprived of consideration of ethical and moral norms and behavior. The structures devoid of moral considerations exemplify the role the international community plays in perpetuating the notion of expedited democratization and short-term recovery. Kingston (2017) noted the issues of forced repatriation of refugees to their homes despite safety and human-rights concerns in Rwanda. Likewise, Cobban (2015) discussed the necessary practices for amnesty and reconciliation after the genocide. The unmitigated issues lead to further disruptions and destruction of communities. The motives for operative scrutiny of post-genocide recovery and managing countries after war crimes include factors of geopolitical, cultural, economic, governance, and conflict-avoidance importance.

Defining Genocide and Genocidal Events

The earliest definition of genocide was formulated by Lemkin (1944) during the Second World War, defining modern warfare with the intent of annihilation of the nation, ethnic, or minority group as

> a coordinated plan of different actions aiming at the destruction of essential foundations of the life of national groups, with the aim of annihilating the groups themselves. The objectives of such a plan would be the disintegration of the political and social institutions, of culture, language, national feelings, religion, and the economic existence of national groups, and the destruction of the personal security, liberty, health, dignity, and even the lives of the individuals belonging to such groups.

Moreover, under Article II of the 1948 United Nations Convention on the Prevention and Punishment of the Crime of Genocide, "genocide" signifies

> any of the following acts committed with intent to destroy, in whole or in part, a national, ethnical, racial, or religious groups, such as (a) Killing members of the group; (b) Causing serious bodily or mental harm to members of the group; (c) Deliberately inflicting on the group conditions of life calculated to bring about its physical destruction in whole or in part; (d) Imposing measures intended to prevent births within a group; and (e) Forcibly transferring children of the group to another group.

The notion and definition of genocide denote the established evidence of not only the intent of obliteration of one group of the population by the dominant group but also a physical decimation of the population, multiplied by impacts on social, economic, and cultural factors. The applicability of this definition of genocide is appropriate to events in Cambodia, Rwanda, Kosovo, and Bosnia and Herzegovina. Within the framework of defining the post-conflict recovery, the appropriate definition of genocide is paramount to addressing governance issues in post-genocide countries.

The prevalence of genocide in more recent history includes Cambodia and was as late as the early nineties epitomized with atrocities occurring in Rwanda, Bosnia, and Herzegovina, and to a lesser extent in Kosovo. Gaeta (2009) clarified that the intent to destroy a protected group is the defining element in defining genocide (105). The conflict and genocide in Cambodia and Rwanda are explained in depth by Barnett (1996), Kiernan (2008) and Schlund-Vials (2016). In Cambodia, as a result of Khmer Rouge purges and killings approximately two million of its residents died. In Kosovo, over a million people were displaced, and over ten thousand civilians were killed during the Serbian aggression (Independent International Commission on Kosovo 2000). In the early nineties, during Rwanda's genocide, an estimated 800,000 Tutsis were murdered by their neighbors and their fellow countrymen (Gourevitch 1998).

In Bosnia and Herzegovina, Serbian aggression directed at Bosniaks resulted in catastrophe and genocide, with over a hundred thousand Bosniaks killed, a million displaced, and fifty thousand women raped as reported by Donia (2015) and Sells (1996). Moreover, Becirevic (2014), Barnett (1996), Gutman (1993), Hoare (2014), Nettelfield and Wagner (2015), and Power (2013) reported extensively on war crimes and genocide that occurred in Bosnia and Herzegovina from 1992 to 1995. The failure to recognize genocide after the war and attempts at revision of historical facts by the Serbian political leadership in Bosnia and Herzegovina and Kosovo significantly undermined the efforts of reconciliation and recovery in the region.

Post-Genocide Realities

Post-conflict recovery is a queried issue with relevance to both the concerns over governance and ethical issues related to sustainable development and restoration of post-conflict states. As argued by Tyner, Sirik, and Henkin (2014) "the establishment of governance structures is also necessary for post-conflict reconstruction" (281). However, the aspects of post-genocide governance in the aftermath of atrocities is often ambiguous and leaves the issues of memorialization and justice unattended. With the genocide and its devastating and long-lasting effects, it is discernable that post-atrocity communities and societies fail to fully recover in all aspects of cultural, social, economic, and governance factors. Nonetheless, the evaluation of elements contributing to the sagacity of recovery and the sustained return of survivors is vital to offering the potential lessons to sustaining the international aid efforts in post-conflict situations.

The international community is balancing its admiration and opprobrium to the mechanism of a war crimes tribunal, powered by fierce opposition from leading global powers. In addition to the postwar economic efforts, the safety of the population, the measured responses to the issue of recognizing war crimes and prosecuting them are paramount. The return of refugees is critical, and the sooner the process of survivors' return to their homes is completed the more chances of success for a sustained recovery of the postwar societies. Žíla (2015) observed the notion of repatriation and the sense of belonging of survivors. The perception of return and sense of belonging are easily shattered in the absence of safety, economic opportunities, and space for remembrance. In such situations, the conditions are ripe for corruption and government fraud, leading to uncertainties and the prospect of Hegiras, exodus, and migration.

Tyner (2014) recognized the importance of identifying and marking the mass graves in Cambodia as tools for obtaining justice, and not merely to remember the violence, but to note the violence was administered (76). Correspondingly, post-genocide recovery requires more than recognizing and marking the mass graves, uncovering the truth, and prosecuting the perpetrators. The post-genocide governance requires clearly defined roles of bureaucracies in promoting the remembrance and memorialization on the path to reconciliation in an attempt to prevent future occurrence of violence against protected groups. In post-genocide situations, in a rush to institute and impose democratic processes, the international aid agencies and global post-conflict institutions neglect and deliberately ignore manners of memorialization, sidelining closure, and justice, In the attempt to expedite economic recovery, the international—and by extension local political and government factors—disqualify a vital aspect of post-genocide reconstruction, leading to rewriting of history, to genocide denial, negations, and ultimately to fertile soil for corruption. Alibašić (2015), Halilovich (2013), Longman (2017), Memisević (2017), and Tyner (2014) all note attempts at revising history and equalization of guilt in the post-genocide countries. Failure to address the root cause of genocide leads to further segregation and ethnic homogenization (Swee 2015). Moreover, the unaddressed and unmitigated past leads to distorted realities on the ground, weakened institutions and erosion of governance, corruption, and renewed conflicts.

Governance in Post-Conflict Countries

The definitional question of governance in the post-genocide situation is of substantive importance. In many instances, researchers have found the post-conflict governance structure to mimic the intervening countries' views of governance (Paris, 2015). Research has noted international aid governance as squandering opportunities for meaningful invest-ment in infrastructure and economic development (Hassan and Isakhan, 2016). Paris (2015) noted the failure to recognize the shortcoming of imposing governance made it "difficult for interveners to recognize the shortcomings of their state building strategies, or to change these strategies even when they were failing" (164). Furthermore, in some cases, the post-conflict governance in pursuit of stability led to the alignment of the interna-tional community with the political elite in countries eroding democratic institutions and consolidation (Beha and Selaci, 2018). Moreover, Beha and Selaci (2018, 111) claimed "political stability is maintained through constant support of this relationship within the patron–client hierarchy, and through the use of nationalist rhetoric that serves to legitimize the hierarchy."

The post-genocide governance is primarily concerned with rehabilitation, and recon-struction of social and economic factors of the societies. The patterns of developmental strategies are identified through donor countries' geopolitical ambitions, preceding the short-term gains in favor of a long-term geostrategic solution, cementing the political gains on the ground. For example, in their critical evaluation of Australian government involvement in post-conflict reconstruction, Hassan and Isakhan (2016) pointed out "the neo-liberal state-building approach to reconstructing a country following a pro-tracted conflict or the toppling of a regime can be characterized as a minimalist short-term approach that puts faith in the ability of governmental institutions and free markets to govern the complexities of reconstruction" (89). With the post-conflict international intervention misaligned with the local infrastructure deeply rooted in the political elite and the establishment controlling the economy, most citizens face constant threats of eco-nomic uncertainty, leading to bribery, fraud, and corruption at the top level of govern-ment and bureaucracies.

Reconciliation of the Past and Genocide Denial

The communities recover with survivors being able to return to homes safely, supported with meaningful employment. However, the parameters of safety include the guaranteed justice, protection, and, accordingly, memorialization of the past. Post-genocide recov-ery in Bosnia and Herzegovina and Cambodia, and to a certain extent in Kosovo and Rwanda, is stymied by perpetrators of war crimes and their proxies in blatant attempts to misplace and displace memories and revise and rewrite history. Halilovich (2013) observed the patterns of revisionism and suppression of memorialization in Bosnia and Herzegovina. Moreover, the expectation of reconciliation is often misplaced and misaligned with expe-dited democratization and restructure of post-genocide societies.

The environment for appropriate memorialization includes the adequate recogni-tion of the historical facts in post-genocide societies. Inopportunely, the notable trends in post-genocide countries are the absence of justice, the length of time between the war crimes and eventual prosecution, and genocide denial contributing to the sense of injus-tice. Mulaj (2017, 123) observed "the perpetrators and their community—frequently—deny genocide with the view to avoiding responsibility and reparations." In the case of Bosnia and Herzegovina, genocide denial and attempts at rewriting history have gone to yet another level. As noted by Memišević (2017):

> dealing with the past in Bosnia remains a key challenge. The courts of Republika Srpska [a smaller entity in Bosnia—author's note] have not conducted criminal proceedings for any genocide charges so far. The prime suspects are considered to be heroes in significant segments of the Serbian population in Republika Srpska, Serbia, and Montenegro. Many members of the formations that directly or indirectly participated in the genocide are even integrated into security structures." (381)

Similar concerns were expressed in other countries after the genocide occurred. In Cambodia, Tyner et al. (2014, 282–83) argued the government is still controlled by the former Khmer Rouge members stating that "rather than directly addressing the violent past, the new regime promoted, and continues to promote, national reconciliation" "through a selective remembrance of the past." The extent and politics of genocide are often obscured and obfuscated by the ruling party. Cambodian society failed to face the full scope and historical lessons of its genocide.

In some instances, during and after the war, foreign political influencers dictate the narrative on genocide. During the war and aggression in Bosnia and Herzegovina in the early nineties, despite evidence on the ground of mass killings and atrocities committed by Serbian led military, the Bush administration attempted to conceal facts and suppressed use of the word genocide to avoid creating a moral imperative for intervention (Power, 2013). Similarly, Simms (2002) described the British position under Prime Minister Harding that emboldened further Serbian aggression and genocide in Bosnia and Herzegovina. The tendency to equate and to blur distinctions between victims and aggressors is frequent, suggesting the same guilt among all sides in the conflict in order to circumvent the international aid and involvement.

Corruption Impeding Post-Genocide Human Development

The ideals of international post-conflict intervention are tested by the realities on the ground. Increased levels of corruption are not a modern phenomenon and not confined to a single country or culture. However, countries with post-genocide recovery are more susceptible to cases of fraud, stemming from dysfunctional institutions, political elitism, and limited economic opportunities. In Transparency International's (2017) *Corruption Perception Index* Cambodia was ranked 161 out 180 countries, while Bosnia and Herzegovina, Kosovo, and Rwanda were ranked 91st, 85th, and 48th respectively. With corruption being one of the major issues facing these post-genocide countries, foreign aid must be scrutinized to achieve more equitable recovery. All post-conflict countries suffer from corruption, high unemployment, limited opportunities for advancement, nepotism, and fraud. Freedom House (2018) ranks Cambodia and Rwanda as not free, both trending toward authoritarianism, rife with corruption, allegations of fraud and voter oppression. Bosnia and Herzegovina and Kosovo are ranked as partially free, facing significant challenges of corruption. The United Nations Development Program (UNDP) Human Development Report's "Global Human Development Indicators" for 2018 signify low human development in Rwanda and Cambodia, ranking them at 158 and 146, respectively, while Bosnia and Herzegovina was ranked 77, and Kosovo 85 in 2016. Table 29.1, entitled "Post-Genocide Recovery and Governance Rankings," details the rankings and estimated foreign aid per country, alongside the Freedom House, Transparency International and UNDP rankings. Despite foreign intervention and substantial foreign aid, corruption, governance, and political instability, and low human development remain significant causes of concern for post-genocide countries.

While corruption is a severe impediment to the sustainable economic development of post-genocide economies, growth, and strengthening of the society, it also undermines public trust and diminishes public value. The public value is a valuable assessment tool for the level of corruption. However, the public value proposition needs to be coupled with public trust to prevent corruption in democratically elected governments. Corruption in countries with no checks and balances in place is a potent trigger for violence, and with the democratic institutions weakened or undermined, it is more pronounced in countries affected by atrocities. Andersson's (2017) negative assessment is accurate: "a one-dimensional view of corruption" and, perhaps, furthers "syndromes of corruption, reflect the combinations of political participation and the strengths of institutions in a society" (60).

TABLE 29.1 Post-Genocide Recovery and Governance Rankings

Country	Genocidal Events Occurrence	Pre-Genocide Population	Genocide Casualties	Estimated Population in 2018	Post-Conflict Foreign Aid in US Dollars (estimated from various sources)	Freedom House "Freedom in the World" Ranking in 2018 (out of 100: 0=least free, 100=most free)	Transparency International Corruption Perception Index/ Rank in 2017	UNDP Human Development Indicators Index/Rank 2018
Bosnia and Herzegovina	1992–1995	4,163,000	100,000	3,347,000	$5 billion	55	38/91	0.768/77
Cambodia	1975–1979	7,100,000	1,870,000	15,800,000	$22 Billion**	30	21/161	0.582/146
Kosovo	1997	1,700,000	10,000	1,804,000	$4 Billion	52	39/85	0.739/85*
Rwanda	1994	7,000,000	1,000,000	11,900,000	$15 Billion	23	55/48	0.524/158

Source: Freedom House. 2018. Freedom in the world. Table of Country Score. Accessed on December 27, 2018, at https://freedomhouse.org/report/freedom-world-2018-table-country-scores.

Transparency International. 2018. Corruption Perceptions Index 2017. Accessed on December 28, 2018, at https://www.transparency.org/news/feature/corruption_perceptions_index_2017.

United Nations Development Programme (UNDP). 2018. Human Development Reports. Global Human Development Indicators. Access on December 28, 2018, at http://hdr.undp.org/en/countries.

*United Nations Development Programme (UNDP). 2016. Kosovo Human Development Report 2016. Accessed on December 28, 2018, at http://hdr.undp.org/en/countries.

** Includes $15 billion in assistance and concessionary loans over the past two decades from China. From Congressional Research Services. 2018. Cambodia: Background and U.S. Relations. Updated December 14, 2018. Accessed on December 28, 2018, at https://fas.org/sgp/crs/row/R44037.pdf.

Ignoring historical facts, realities and past atrocities trivializes the governance and leads to unrests and protests. In recent years, waves of anti-corruption protests swept countries around the world, followed by arrests of those protesting corruption and threats to, and killings of, journalists exposing corruption. Post-genocide countries lack institutional protections for protesters. The institutions intended to protect citizens' rights to protest and freely express their opinions have either never existed, or were weakened or undermined, such protests are often violently crushed.

At its very core, the concept of good governance puts aggregate value and benefits over individual relative action, illuminating the relative intrinsic dangers of not addressing underlying ethical tensions of understanding the individual needs. In post-genocide situations, the myopia of administrative duties is transformed and under pressure, with a particular administrative role. Neshkova and Rosenabum (2015) posited that "corruption has no one face, and it is not always straightforward and easy to detect," as corrupt acts may be hidden (97–98). A culture of conforming governance and technical rationality in post-genocide countries has significant ramifications for the survivors of the genocide and the prospects of long-term recovery. The appearance of progress is often masked behind the realities of corruption and further alienation of the already-affected population. Corrupt practices are often amplified through denials that atrocities even took place, making reconciliation and recovery improbable (Alibašić 2015).

Conclusion

The central role in understanding the governance of post-conflict countries after atrocities and genocide is the framing of issues, the evolving role of reconciliation, and the perception of justice in society. Moreover, bureaucratic roles in the aftermath of genocide are redefined through rational, technical approaches leading to ethical failures to fulfill the expected forms of technical–rational public policy and administrative practices. The pervasiveness of corruption in post-genocide countries confounds the public value, further erodes public trust, and undermines already-dysfunctional institutions. The constant interference of foreign powers in post-genocide countries leaves the society vulnerable to overreliance on foreign aid and outside influence, finding it increasingly difficult to hold elected and appointed officials to account, and opens doors to a waste of resources. Corruption, fraud, and the misuse of public resources are substantially more likely under such conditions, leading to endless failed campaigns to address them. The assessment of elements aiding the long-term recovery and governance of post-genocide countries is critical to improving the current methods and means of implementing international aid and relevant aid policies. Recognition and memorialization of atrocities and genocide and disavowing revisionism will lead to meaningful reconciliation and recovery of post-genocide countries. Finally, governance in post-genocide countries encompasses the essential alteration of society, requiring sustainable policies and resilient programs and institutions, all the while evaluating the place of international bureaucracies and aid in accomplishing sustained recovery.

References

Alibašić, Haris. 2015. "Reconciling the Past in Bosnia and Herzegovina: Genocide Denial and the Role of Moral Inversion." *Pregled 56*(3), 191–98.

Andersson, Staffan. 2017. "Beyond Unidimensional Measurement of Corruption." *Public Integrity 19*, 58–76.

Balfour, Danny L., and Haris Alibašić. 2016. "Administrative Evil," in Ali Farazmand, ed., *Global Encyclopedia of Public Administration, Public Policy and Governance*. Cham, Switzerland: Springer, 1–5.

Barnett, Michael N. 1996. "The Politics of Indifference at the United Nations and Genocide in Rwanda and Bosnia," in Thomas Cushman and Stjepan Mestrovic, eds., *This Time We Knew: Western Responses to Genocide in Bosnia*. New York: NYU Press.

Becirevic, Edina. 2014. *Genocide on the Drina River*. New Haven, CT: Yale University Press.

Beha, Adem, and Gëzim Selaci. 2018. "Statebuilding without Exit Strategy in Kosovo: Stability, Clientelism, and Corruption." *REGION: Regional Studies of Russia, Eastern Europe, and Central Asia* 7(2), 97–123.

Cobban, Helena. 2015. *Amnesty after Atrocity?: Healing Nations After Genocide and War Crimes*. New York: Routledge.

Donia, Robert J. 2015. *Radovan Karadžić: Architect of the Bosnian Genocide*. New York: Cambridge University Press.

Freedom House. 2018. *Freedom in The World 2018*. Accessed on December 22, 2018 at https://freedomhouse.org/report/freedom-world-2018-table-country-scores.

Gaeta, Paola. 2009. *The UN Genocide Convention: A Commentary*. Oxford: Oxford University Press.

Gourevitch, Philip. 1998. *We Wish to Inform You that Tomorrow We Will Be Killed with Our Families: Stories from Rwanda*. New York: Macmillan.

Gutman, Roy. 1993. *A Witness to Genocide: The First Inside Account of the Horrors of Ethnic Cleansing in Bosnia*. Shaftesbury: Element.

Halilovich, Hariz. 2013. *Places of Pain: Forced Displacement, Popular Memory and Trans-local Identities in Bosnian War-torn Communities*. New York: Berghahn.

Hassan, Ahmed, and Benjamin Isakhan. 2016. "The Failures of Neo-liberal State Building in Iraq: Assessing Australia's Post-conflict Reconstruction and Development Initiatives." *Australian Journal of Politics and History* 62(1), 87–99.

Hoare, Marko A. 2014. "Towards an Explanation for the Bosnian Genocide of 1992–1995." *Studies in Ethnicity and Nationalism* 14(3), 516–32.

Independent International Commission on Kosovo. 2000. *The Kosovo Report: Conflict, International Response, Lessons Learned*. New, York: Oxford University Press.

Kiernan, Ben. 2008. *The Pol Pot Regime: Race, Power, and Genocide in Cambodia Under the Khmer Rouge, 1975–1979*. 3rd ed. New Haven, CT: Yale University Press.

Lemkin, Raphael. 1944, 2005. *Axis Rule in Occupied Europe: Laws of Occupation, Analysis of Government, Proposals for Redress*. 2nd ed. Washington, DC: Foundations of the Laws of War. Carnegie Endowment for International Peace.

Kingston, Lindsey N. 2017. "Bringing Rwandan Refugees 'Home': The Cessation Clause, Statelessness, and Forced Repatriation." *International Journal of Refugee Law* 29(3), 417–37.

Longman, Timothy. 2017. *Memory and Justice in Post-genocide Rwanda*. Cambridge: Cambridge University Press.

Memišević, Ehlimana. 2015. "Battling the Eighth Stage: Incrimination of Genocide Denial in Bosnia and Herzegovina." *Journal of Muslim MinorityAffairs* 35(3), 380–400.

Mulaj, Klejda. 2017. "Genocide and the Ending of War: Meaning, Remembrance and Denial in Srebrenica, Bosnia." *Crime, Law and Social Change* 68(1–2), 123–43.

Neshkova, Milena I. and Allan Rosenbaum. 2015. "Advancing Good Government Through Fighting Corruption," in J. L. Perry and R. K. Christensen, eds., *Handbook of Public Administration*, 3rd ed. San Francisco: Jossey-Bass.

Nettelfield, Lara J., and Sarah Wagner. 2015. *Srebrenica in the Aftermath of Genocide*. New York: Cambridge University Press.

Paris, Roland. 2015. "States of Mind: The Role of Governance Schemas in Foreign Imposed Regime Change." *International Relations* 29(2), 139–76.

Power, Samantha. 2013. *A Problem from Hell: America and the Age of Genocide*. New York: Basic Books.

Sells, Michael A. 1996. *The Bridge Betrayed: Religion and Genocide in Bosnia*. Berkley and Los Angeles: University of California Press.

Simms, Bernard. 2002. *Unfinest Hour: Britain and the Destruction of Bosnia*. London: Penguin Books.

Schlund-Vials, Cathy J. 2016. "Evincing Cambodia's Genocide: Juridical Belatedness, Historical Indictment, and Rithy Panh's The Missing Picture." *Contemporary French and Francophone Studies* 20(20), 287–96.

Swee, Eik L. 2015. "Together or Separate? Post-conflict Partition, Ethnic Homogenization and the Provision of Public Schooling." *Journal of Public Economics 128*, 1–15.

Transparency International. 2017. Corruption Perception Index 2017. Accessed on December 25, 2018, https://www.transparency.org/news/feature/corruption_perceptions_index_2017.

Tyner, James A. 2014. "Dead Labor, Landscapes, and Mass Graves: Administrative Violence during the Cambodian Genocide." *Geoforum 52*, 70–77.

Tyner, James A., Savina Sirik, and Henkin, Samuel. 2014. "Violence and the Dialectics of Landscape in Cambodia: Memorialization in Cambodia." *Geographical Review 104*(3), 277–93.

United Nations. 1948. *Article II of the 1948 United Nations Convention on the Prevention and Punishment of the Crime of Genocide.*

United Nations Development Programme (UNDP). 2018. *Human Development Reports. Global Human Development Indicators.* Accessed on December 28, 2018, http://hdr.undp.org/en/countries.

Žíla, Ondřej. 2015. "The Myth of Return: Bosnian Refugees and the Perception of 'Home.'" Geographica Pannonica *19*(3), 130–45.

30

Strengthening the Fight against Corruption

Complementing the Use of Ethics Codes with a Culture-Based Model of Ethics Training

Hugo D. Asencio

Corruption—commonly defined as the abuse of public office for private gain—is present in all societies regardless of their circumstances and has many negative consequences for them. Scholars have found evidence to suggest that this social malaise not only decreases government effectiveness and efficiency (Rose-Ackerman and Palifka 2016) but also increases debt (Liu et al. 2017) and artificially elevates spending in the public sector (Liu and Mikesell 2014). Corruption has also been found to increase income inequality and poverty (Rose-Ackerman and Palifka 2016). Further, corruption has been found to decrease satisfaction with democracy and government performance, interpersonal and institutional trust, and increase acceptance of rule-breaking conduct (Villoria et al. 2013). Given the many negative outcomes of corruption, in the last couple of decades, many nations and transnational organizations have banded together in an attempt to address this social problem.

Today, many governments worldwide use codes of ethics—or codes of conduct—in combination with other administrative and legal controls to fight corruption. In fact, codes have been widely recognized in a number of international agreements, such as the Organization of American States, the Council of Europe, and the United Nation's conventions against corruption, to name a few. Codes are typically rules-based and are designed to articulate standards for acceptable and unacceptable behavior. The general view—particularly among policy makers—is that such an approach to codes can help deter public servants from engaging in wrongdoing (Menzel 2017).

While codes are helpful, they are not sufficient to address the problem of corruption. Adopting codes that emphasize legal compliance can deter some individuals from engaging in corruption. Nevertheless, without addressing the organizational dynamics from which corruption emerges and is sustained, this social malaise is likely to persist. In light of this, the present essay argues for the need to further strengthen the fight against corruption around the globe by complementing the use of codes with ethics training designed to develop public servants' capacity to develop and sustain organizational cultures where wrongdoing is not only less likely but also, and more important, where moral reasoning and integrity are both encouraged and possible.

The Use of Ethics Codes and Their Effectiveness

Codes of ethics gained prominence in the 1980s and 1990s after major corruption scandals in both government and private organizations around the world. Since then, both elected and appointed public officials have typically expressed positive attitudes toward them (Menzel 2017). The common view is that by specifying acceptable and unacceptable conduct (Svara 2014), codes are effective in deterring unethical behavior (Menzel 2017), particularly by individuals who want to do the right thing (Menzel 2010). Codes are also seen as symbolic tools motivating ethical conduct by providing public servants with a standard to strive for and articulating for them a unique sense of responsibility given their role in the community (Gilman 2005).

Today, codes have become popular anti-corruption tools used by many governments around the world. This is illustrated by the fact that to date the United Nations Public Administration Network makes available in its website the public administration codes of ethics—or codes of conduct—for over one hundred countries. Similarly, according to the Organization for Economic Cooperation and Development (OECD) website, most of the thirty-six OECD countries have developed codes for public officials and administrators.

Despite the popularity of ethics codes, empirical research on their effectiveness in promoting integrity and controlling wrongdoing in government agencies is limited. The few empirical studies that have been reported in recent years find that codes have no significant impact on corruption control in 154 countries (Garcia-Sanchez et al. 2011), as well as no significant impact on the ethical attitudes and behaviors of German public servants (Thaler and Helmig 2016).

Limitations of Ethics Codes

Just like any other anti-corruption measures, ethics codes, while helpful, are limited in addressing the problem of corruption. With some exceptions, codes are primarily used as part of what Ashforth et al. (2008) call a *check-off* approach to ethics, in which they are simply negotiated and put in place with no appreciation of underlying public service values. Thus, codes not only become decoupled from the day-to-day experiences of public organizations but are also seen by public servants as *window-dressing*. Even when codes are developed to *inspire* administrators to advance public service values, without training, implementation and enforcement mechanisms, they are limited in achieving their purpose and simply become words on a piece of paper. In most cases, codes are too narrow and mainly emphasize compliance and adherence to the law, which does little to build administrators' ethical competencies. While the law is the key standard in public agencies (Menzel 2017), its specificity does not address all the situations that may arise (Martinez 2009), which require that administrators analyze complex situations to decide what the right thing to do is.

Further, as currently designed in many public sectors worldwide, ethics codes are limited in curbing corruption because they only focus on the individual public official or administrator. As previously mentioned, codes outlining standards for appropriate and inappropriate conduct can deter some public servants from engaging in wrongdoing. Nevertheless, providing legal and even ethical standards for them to act upon, while important, is not enough. Once corruption has become standard operating procedure for getting things done within government agencies, such legal and ethical standards, while well intended, do not address the institutional context from which this social malaise manifests itself and is perpetuated.

As scholars point out, some organizational arrangements and dynamics can encourage wrongdoing or even discourage ethical action of otherwise morally competent individuals (Jurkiewicz and Grossman 2012; Cooper 2012; Lewis and Gilman 2012; Zimbardo 2007). The case of abuse and torture committed by US military police soldiers at the Abu Ghraib prison in Iraq illustrates that even individuals considered as *good apples* can engage in illegal and unethical actions—despite the presence of an institutional code of conduct—in large part, as a result of the group and organizational dynamics—for example, peer pressure and obedience to authority—that oftentimes influence individual behavior within institutions (Asencio et al. 2017).

Despite the aforementioned, as highlighted by the myriad of administrative and legal controls adopted by many governments around the world to address the problem of corruption, not sufficient emphasis is given to such group and institutional dynamics. With some exceptions, policy makers largely prefer an anti-corruption approach focusing on: reducing the number of transactions over which public servants have discretion; reducing the gains from corruption; increasing the likelihood of getting caught through strong controls; increasing the penalties for engaging in corrupt activities; and reducing information asymmetries between citizens and public servants so as to better allow citizens to *check* public servants' actions. Thus, as highlighted by Transparency International's yearly corruption rankings, this social problem not only persists worldwide but, in many country cases, even continues to grow; this, can be attributed, in large part, to the fact that such an anti-corruption approach, while helpful at some levels, does not address the patterns of relationships and shared values and beliefs—that is, the organizational culture—that have developed over time within government organizations; and these can produce a certain mindset among public servants, thereby encouraging them to act in ways—that is, engage in corruption—not necessarily consistent with their own preexisting ethical norms.

Complementing the Use of Ethics Codes with Ethics Training

To better control corruption and encourage integrity in governments worldwide, it is important to complement the use of codes with ethics training. To start, as often advocated but rarely implemented (Lewis and Gilman 2012), the current *compliance-based* model of ethics training needs to be complemented with an *integrity-based* model. While having ethics training programs that emphasize what the law says and what rules means (Menzel 2017) does not hurt in the fight against corruption, such programs do not equip administrators with the reasoning and decision-making skills they need to resolve complex ethical situations. Such programs only *teach* them how to stay out of trouble. It is necessary, therefore, for ethics training to emphasize: creating awareness of the public service values that ought to guide administrative and political decisions, as well as developing individuals' ethical reasoning and decision-making skills. Still, since neither approach by itself is sufficient to prevent corruption and ensure ethical action in public agencies, the best elements from the two training models need to be fused into a *fusion model* (see Lewis and Gilman 2012, for discussion).

While important, a fusion model of ethics training focusing on developing individuals' ethical competence still needs to be supplemented with what is called here a *culture-based* model. Given the crucial role that organizational dynamics play in influencing individual behavior, as already highlighted by Dennis Thompson in his authoritative book *Ethics in Congress*, greater attention to such dynamics when conducting ethics training may help reinforce individual ethical action by creating a more conducive environment within public organizations. Thus, a culture-based model needs to focus on developing individuals' capacity to create and sustain organizational cultures where ethical reasoning and action are encouraged and possible (Asencio et al. 2017).

A culture-based model needs to target both leaders and employees in government agencies. On one hand, ethics training designed for leaders needs to focus on developing their ethical leadership competencies, as these play an important role in developing and sustaining the environment which, as previously mentioned, may encourage otherwise morally competent individuals to engage in corruption. The significance of a culture-based model for leaders is highlighted by a recent empirical study by Asencio (2018). In it, he finds evidence to suggest that public leaders displaying ethical leadership may reduce corrupt behaviors—that is, bribing and favoritism—through: the social learning role they play;

social exchange processes; and their communication skills, which are all important in the development of an organizational culture where wrongdoing is not only less likely but, more important, where ethical reasoning and decision making are possible.

A culture-based ethics training model targeting public leaders also need to focus on having them understand the two pillars of ethical leadership advanced by Linda Treviño and her colleagues' research, which can be instrumental in developing an ethical culture in public agencies: (1) being a *moral person*—that is, having integrity; being honest and trust-worthy; showing concern for people and the broader society; being open, that is, being approachable and a good listener; behaving ethically in one's personal and professional life; holding ethical values and principles; making decisions based on ethical principles; and being objective and fair; and (2) being a *moral manager*—that is, role-modeling ethical behavior through visible action; communicating with employees about ethics and values; setting clear ethical standards for them; and holding them accountable for their (un)ethical conduct.

On the other hand, a culture-based model designed for public employees needs to focus on having them understand the importance of not depending on the ethical competencies of leaders alone. While having ethical leaders in public agencies helps (Asencio 2018), the reality is that the responsibility for creating and sustaining an environment in which ethical action is the norm, not the exception, cannot be assigned to leaders alone. Centralizing such responsibility may tell employees that they have no obligation to contribute to the ethical health of their agency or to act based on their sense of duty. Also, it may tell them that an ethical culture is simply a matter of having leaders manage the ethics program; that is, ensuring that an ethics code is in place, that an ethics officer exists, that people are trained on legal requirements, that an ethics hotline exists, and that accountability policies are in place, for example.

Another consequence of relying on leaders alone to create an ethical culture is that when corrupt actions are committed, particularly by leaders, the organization may be subject to collapse as the culture may lack the capacity to endure such actions. In the current administrative environment, no government agency is immune to leaders who may go rogue. Leaders—even those who are well educated, apparently qualified (Frederickson and Meek 2017), and who possess a track record of ethical action—can become isolated, overconfident, arrogant, and lose any sense of morality. Thus, a culture-based model of ethics training needs to help employees understand the dangers of depending on leaders alone for the ethical well-being of public organizations.

Further, such a culture-based model needs to focus on having employees understand the importance of caring for the quality of their relationships with their peers. After all, an ethical culture is not created nor sustained by simply having leaders manage the ethics program. Having such a program does not hurt, but an ethical culture develops over time as a result of the relationships among organizational members themselves. Thus, honesty as a value guiding administrative decisions is not simply inculcated or talked about by leaders. It is not just imitated because leaders tell the truth either. When leaders are honest, it helps, but honesty largely emerges as an ethical pillar within a culture because individuals themselves have been honest with each other over time. The same can be said about other values, such as incorruptibility, accountability, and transparency, for example, which cannot just be inculcated by a moral manager or outlined in a code of ethics; they need to emerge in an organization over time as a result of the patterns of relationships among its members.

Given the aforementioned, to better address the problem of corruption and encourage ethical behavior in public sectors worldwide, it is important to complement the use of ethics codes with ethics training. Surely, having codes that outline acceptable and unacceptable behavior may deter some wrongdoing. Nevertheless, in order for codes to truly have meaning and thus guide administrative and political actions, they need to embody the ethical values and principles that have emerged over time in a public agency. Thus, it is fundamental that all members—employees and leaders—be involved in their development, as creating codes without their input—and before most of them have become part of the organization —does very little to either *control* their behavior and, worse, to *inspire* them to make decisions based on ethical values and principles. If policy makers around the world simply continue to adopt codes and hand them down to administrators, even when such codes seek to inspire behavior, they will continue to be lifeless documents (Jurkiewicz 2013) hanging on the walls in government agencies.

Conclusion

The use of ethics codes spelling out standards for right and wrong administrative and political conduct, while useful, are insufficient to address the problem of corruption. Codes emphasizing legal compliance can deter some wrongdoing in government agencies, but, while well intended, they do not address the group and organizational dynamics that give birth to corruption and keep it alive. Thus, to further enhance the fight against this social problem worldwide, the use of ethics codes needs to be complemented with ethics training focusing on developing public leaders and employees' capacity to foster organizational environments where corruption is not only less probable but, above all, where ethical reasoning and practice are both stimulated and viable. A culture-based model of ethics training may be helpful in developing such capacity.

References

Asencio, Hugo D. 2018. "The Effect of Ethical Leadership on Bribing and Favoritism: A Field Research Study." *Public Integrity*. doi: 10.1080/10999922.2018.1468204.

Asencio, Hugo, Theodore Byrne, and Edin Mujkic. 2017. "Ethics Training for U.S. Military Leaders: Challenging the Conventional Approach." *Public Integrity* 19(5), 415–28. doi: 10.1080/10999922.2016.1272153.

Ashforth, Blake E., Dennis A. Gioia, Sandra L. Robinson, and Linda K. Treviño. 2008. "Introduction to Special Topic Forum: Re-Viewing Organizational Corruption." *Academy of Management Review 33*(3) (July), 670–84. doi: 10.5465/amr.2008.32465714.

Cooper, Terry L. 2012. *The Responsible Administrator: An Approach to Ethics for the Administrative Role*. 6th ed. Hoboken: Wiley.

Frederickson, George, and Jack Wayne Meek. 2017. "Searching for Virtue in the City: Bell and Her Sisters." *Public Integrity* 19(3), 234–49. doi: 10.1080/10999922.2016.1270698.

Garcia-Sanchez, Isabel Maria, Luis Rodriguez-Dominguez, and Isabel Gallego-Alvarez. 2011. "Effectiveness of Ethics Codes in the Public Sphere: Are They Useful in Controlling Corruption." *International Journal of Public Administration 34*(3), 190–95. doi: 10.1080/01900692.2010.532184.

Gilman, Stuart. 2005. *Ethics Codes and Codes of Conduct as Tools for Promotingan Ethical and Professional Public Service: Comparative Success and Lessons*. Washington, DC: World Bank.

Jurkiewicz, Carole L. 2013. "The Anatomy of Ethical Dysfunction," in H. George Frederickson and Richard K. Ghere, eds., *Ethics in Public Management*. 2nd ed. New York: M. E. Sharpe, 23–41.

Jurkiewicz, Carole L., and Dave Grossman. 2012. "Evil at Work," in Carole L. Jurkiewicz, ed., *The Foundations of Organizational Evil*. Armonk: M. E. Sharpe, 3–15.

Lewis, Carol W., and Stuart C. Gilman. 2012. *The Ethics Challenge in Public Service: A Problem Solving Guide*. 3rd ed. San Francisco: Jossey-Bass.

Liu, Cheol, and John L. Mikesell. 2014. "The Impact of Public Officials' Corruption on the Size and Allocation of U.S. State Spending." *Public Administration Review 74*(3) (May/June), 346–59. doi: 10.1111/puar.12212.

Liu, Cheol, Tima T. Moldogaziev, and John L. Mikesell. 2017. "Corruption and State and Local Government Expansion." *Public Administration Review 77*(5) (September/October), 681–90. doi: 10.1111/puar.12711.

Martinez, J. Michael. 2009. *Public Administration Ethics for the 21st Century.* Santa Barbara: ABC-CLIO.

Menzel, Donald C. 2010. *Ethics Moments in Government: Cases and Controversies.* Boca Raton, FL: CRC Press.

Menzel, Donald C. 2017. *Ethics Management for Public and Nonprofit Managers: Leading and Building Organizations of Integrity.* 3rd ed. New York: Routledge.

Rose-Ackerman, Susan, and Bonnie J. Palifka. 2016. *Corruption and Government: Causes, Consequences, and Reform.* 2nd ed. New York: Cambridge University Press.

Svara, James H. 2014. "Who Are the Keepers of the Code? Articulating and Upholding Ethical Standards in the Field of Public Administration." *Public Administration Review* 74(5) (September/October), 561–69. doi: 10.1111/puar.12230.

Thaler, Julia, and Bernd Helmig. 2016. "Do Codes of Conduct and Ethical Leadership Influence Public Employees' Attitudes and Behaviours? An Experimental Analysis." *Public Management Review* 18(9), 1365–99. doi: 10.1080/14719037.2015.1103890.

Villoria, Manuel, Gregg G. Van Ryzin, and Cecilia F. Lavena. 2013. "Social and Political Consequences of Administrative Corruption: A Study of Public Perceptions in Spain." *Public Administration Review* 73(1) (January/February), 85–94. doi: 10.1111/j.1540-6210.2012.02613.x.

Zimbardo, Philip. 2007. *The Lucifer Effect: Understanding How Good People Turn Evil.* New York: Random House.

Summary of Critical Knowledge Indicators for Part III

- What are the key variables that impact the effectiveness of integrity programs?

- Describe the evaluation framework integral to integrity programs.

- How does each of the three phases of corruption control build upon the other, according to Transparency International?

- What are the key functions of anti-corruption agencies (ACAs)?

- Define the uniqueness of military ethics as compared to ethics in other sectors.

- How have military ethics evolved over time?

- How can organizations encourage responsible reporting of ethical violations?

- Describe the most effective whistleblower protections.

- What are examples of data management prescribed by the Data Protection Authority of Italy?

- What role does transparency play in the anti-corruption function of Italian government?

- Define the three points of the Auditability Triangle.

- Provide three categories of procurement fraud that can occur in organizations.

- Describe procedural ecology in the Brazilian system of institutions.

- What are the three components of the Auditability Triangle?

- List the five components of the COSO Integrated Internal Control Framework.

- Compare the effects of exogenous vs. endogenous vs. systemic factors of accountability shifts in Brazil.

- How does political representation and culture ensure institutional accountability in Brazil?

- What types of integrity violations are most often found in relation to organized crime?

- What societal and organizational factors enhance the probability of integrity violations?

- What have been found as the most effective recovery methods for countries that have experienced genocide?

- What are the ideals of international post-conflict intervention, and why do they generally lead to further harms?

- How effective are codes of ethics in effecting anti-corruption efforts?

- What elements of ethics training are most effective in combatting corruption?

By Carole L. Jurkiewicz

Index